The Go

JOHN

Also by James Montgomery Boice

The Gospel of

JOHN

Volume 5
Triumph through Tragedy
John 18–21

JAMES
MONTGOMERY
BOICE

BakerBooks
Grand Rapids, Michigan

Published by Baker Books
a division of Baker Publishing Group
P.O. Box 6287, Grand Rapids, MI 49516-6287
www.bakerbooks.com

Paperback edition published 2005
ISBN 0-8010-6588-7

Previously published by Zondervan

Printed in the United States of America

The Library of Congress has cataloged the hardcover edition as follows:
Boice, James Montgomery, 1938–
        [Gospel of John]
        The Gospel of John / James Montgomery Boice.
            p.   cm.
        Includes bibliographical references and indexes.
        Contents: v. 5. Triumph through Tragedy, John 18–21.
        ISBN 0-8010-1183-3 (hardcover)
        1. Bible. N.T. John Commentaries.   I. Title.
BS2615.3.B55   1999
226.5′077—dc21   99-22764

To him who loved us
and washed us from our sins in his own blood

Contents

Preface

From a human viewpoint, the path of John's Gospel has been downhill. An initial appearance of Jesus of Nazareth as the light of this world and a time of popularity have been followed by progressively increasing indifference and rejection on the part of the masses and the intense hatred and open opposition of the religious leaders. Now the story reaches its very nadir as the indifference of the people and the hatred of the leaders combine to have Christ crucified. Yet the low point is also the peak; for in the wisdom and purpose of God the tragedy of the cross is a triumph since it is this that provides an atonement for sins and makes salvation possible. Moreover, it is followed by the resurrection.

This is the message of this fifth and last volume of expositional commentaries of John's Gospel. But it is not just the message of Christ's triumph. It is an indication of how we can triumph as well. In God's plan and in accordance with God's wisdom, even the worst of that which befalls Christians can be transformed into victory.

It has been my pattern in previous volumes to deviate at times from a strict verse-by-verse exposition in order to consider more thoroughly a subject introduced by the exposition. There have been extended discussions of witnessing, baptism, the Sunday-versus-Sabbath question, the Scriptures, Christ our Good Shepherd, death, heaven, the Holy Spirit, and the marks of the church. Two subjects have been treated this way in this volume. The first is the two-part trial of Jesus before the Jewish and Roman authorities. Four studies have been devoted to the Jewish trial (chapters 5–8), and the greater part of twelve studies have been devoted to the trial before Pilate and Herod (chapters 10–21). The second theme is the atonement. The nature, necessity, perfection, and scope of the atonement are considered in chapters 27–30.

For the benefit of those who have purchased the preceding volumes I can point out that the outline introduced earlier is now completed. Volume 1 deals with the coming of the light of the Lord Jesus Christ into the world (chapters 1–4). Volume 2 covers the growth of hostility toward Jesus on the part of the religious leaders (chapters 5–8). Volume 3 deals with the actions of Jesus in beginning to call out a people to himself from among Israel, beginning with the healing and call of the man who had been born blind (chapters 9–12). Volume 4 contains Christ's final discourses (chapters 13–17). The present volume, volume 5, concludes with the account of Christ's arrest, trial, crucifixion, and resurrection (chapters 18–21). It shows the story to be "Triumph through Tragedy."

Some of the material in this volume has already appeared in other forms. The messages on the resurrection have appeared in booklets published in connection with the *Bible Study Hour*. Material on the trials and the atonement is also being used in this way. All the messages have already been aired over the *Bible Study Hour* as radio sermons and have appeared in the monthly publication, *Bible Studies,* which is mailed regularly to the program's supporters.

Publication of this volume represents an end of a considerably lengthy project. My study of the Gospel of John began in reality during the years of graduate work in Basel, Switzerland, as a result of which a preliminary study of the Gospel appeared under the title *Witness and Revelation in the Gospel of John.* In December 1970, I began to preach on this Gospel for the Sunday morning services of Tenth Presbyterian Church, which I still serve as pastor. With the exception of various interruptions for special services and events, that series of expositions continued through July 1978. The series began on the radio in the late spring of 1971 and continued to December 1978. The series numbers 270 studies in all. During this time I have been blessed by the support and encouragement of the session and congregation of Tenth Church. I have been helped immeasurably by the editing and proofreading skills of Miss Caecilie M. Foelster, my secretary. Greatest of all has been the presence and encouragement of the Lord, who increasingly opened up the meaning of the Gospel to me and showed me levels of meaning and application that I had not dreamed of before.

May God himself bless this exposition to the hearts of all who read it, as he has blessed these years of study to me. May he be glorified. May he draw many to that One who "loved us, and washed us from our sins in his own blood." Amen and Amen.

James Montgomery Boice
Philadelphia, Pennsylvania

Triumph through Tragedy

222

The Final Days

John 18:1

When he had finished praying, Jesus left with his disciples and crossed the Kidron Valley. On the other side there was an olive grove, and he and his disciples went into it.

Years ago, when I was in college, there was a course in world literature that always contained on its final examination the question: <u>Is it possible to have a Christian tragedy?</u> It was a question designed to test the understanding as well as the knowledge of the student, as all good examination questions do, for basic to the question (to be answered from the literature studied) was the problem of whether a true experience of Christianity and true tragedy are compatible. The poorer students did not even know what the question meant. Better students analyzed works commonly categorized as tragedy—*Paradise Lost, Moby Dick, The Scarlet Letter*—but did not answer the question. Only perceptive students answered that in the final analysis a Christian tragedy is impossible, for <u>the essential Christian presuppositions of a sovereign but benevolent God ultimately override the tragic elements.</u>

This does not eliminate the marks of tragedy, of course. In fact, it may be argued that only Christianity of all the world's religions actually takes the tragedy of the human situation with full seriousness. This is the meaning of the fall, the cross, the bondage of the will, the final judgment. But even greater than these things stands the benevolent and wise purposes of the sovereign God in human history. Life may be dark. Tragedy may come. At times the whole world may seem to be crumbling into pieces. But this is not the end. Therefore, in spite of the tragedy, God still works all things together "for the good of those who love him, who have been called according to his purpose" (Rom. 8:28).

Dark Days

It would be possible to illustrate this thesis, not only theoretically but also by numerous examples from the lives of Christians. But among all these examples there is surely nothing more dramatically illustrative of the Christian principle of triumph through tragedy than the events of the closing days of the earthly life of Christianity's founder, Jesus of Nazareth. A detached observer might look upon these days as dismal in the extreme. He would see a young man, a brilliant and compassionate young man, unjustly arrested through the hostility of jealous older men whose authority he threatened. He is falsely convicted and executed. And even then, the execution is not by some "humane" form of execution but by the unbelievably cruel and agonizing death of crucifixion. What could be worse? Nothing! Yet the story, as told by those friends of his who had witnessed most if not all the events, is not the story of a tragic defeat but of a victory. Indeed, the outcome, far from being one of despair and desolation, is actually a gospel—that which is "Good News" to an otherwise tragedy-bound humanity.

One obvious, historical reason for this is that the crucifixion of Christ was followed by a resurrection, which was good news in itself. But this is not the whole of the testimony, or even its heart. The resurrection was good news; it showed that death was not the end of Christ's life, nor need it be the end of ours. But in addition to this, it is also the case, according to the testimony of these witnesses, that the crucifixion itself was good news. Christ's death was good. Thus, the true meaning of the phrase "triumph through tragedy" is not merely that tragedy is followed by triumph but, far more profoundly, that in the hands of God the tragedy actually becomes the triumph. The apparent defeat becomes victory.

We can say more! For not only does the tragedy in the hands of God become triumph, without the tragedy there really is no triumph. What would the great promises of the final discourses of John's Gospel be without these chapters? Just pipe dreams! What would the miracles be without these latter assurances that they are designed to present to us a sure way of salvation? Nothing! However, in actual fact, these chapters rightly culminate all that has gone before and show how and why the blessings spoken of earlier come to us.

One commentator has written, "Without these two chapters (18, 19) . . . none of the precious things which have thrilled the heart in the previous chapters could be possible; nay more, none of His own assertions as to what He would be and do, of giving eternal life, of having any of the world, of coming again for them, of sending the Holy Spirit, of preparing a place for them, of having them in the glory with Him, or of having that glory at all; there would be no assembly of God, or restoration of Israel, no gathering of the nations, no millennium, no new heavens and new earth, no adjustment in righteousness of the 'creation of God' of which He is the beginning, no display of grace, no salvation, no revelation of the Father—all these and much more were contingent on His death and resurrection. Without these all things in this book drop out and leave a blank, the blackness of darkness."[1]

So there are dark days, these final days in the earthly life of our Lord. But they are days that are at the same time days of light for those who are of the light. By contrast, the true darkness is for those who will not come to Christ. He and not another is this world's light, and that light is nowhere better seen than in his own cruel death and resurrection.

Days of Blessing

This is not just a later theological reflection on the crucifixion and resurrection narratives either. This is John's own emphasis from beginning to end. As we study these chapters together his unique emphasis will emerge fully. But even in this opening section it is apparent.

For example, John 18 begins with the departure of Jesus from Jerusalem to the Garden of Gethsemane. He was with the party that entered the Garden that night. He was with Jesus (so closely, in fact, that he was one of the three selected to go off with Jesus and accompany him while he prayed). He witnessed all that transpired in the Garden. Nevertheless, he omits many of the important features that the other Gospel writers contain and introduces others that they omit—all to stress the glory and power of the Son of Man, rather than his mere humanity or apparent weakness.

By consulting the other Gospels we are reminded of what else happened in the Garden. Each of the other Gospels tells us that, having selected Peter, James, and John to go with him, Jesus went off from the others and prayed three times that if it was the will of God, the cup of death might pass by him. Matthew and Luke record the fact that prior to this, Jesus began to be greatly agitated, depressed, and sorrowful; he declared, "My soul is overwhelmed with sorrow to the point of death" (Matt. 26:38; cf. Mark 14:34). Luke, who is particularly concerned with the humanity and sufferings of Christ, reports that in spite of the fact that angels appeared and ministered to him, Jesus nevertheless was "in anguish" and "prayed more earnestly, and his sweat was like drops of blood falling to the ground" (Luke 22:44).

John knew these facts as well as any of the other writers (cf. John 12:24–27). Yet he omits them in his account, noting only that Jesus "left with his disciples and crossed the Kidron Valley . . . [where] there was an olive grove" and was there arrested. Why does John do this? For emphasis. He wishes to stress, not the human weakness of Christ, but rather his mastery over this as well as all other situations.

It is not only in John's omissions that this particular emphasis is noticeable. It is noticeable also in what he includes, particularly in regard to Christ's statements. In the earlier Gospels the scene in the Garden is prefaced by Jesus' prophecy of his coming arrest and death. He speaks of the shepherd being killed and the sheep scattered (Matt. 26:31; Mark 14:27); he speaks of his being numbered with the transgressors in fulfillment of Isaiah 53 (Luke 22:37). But although John knew these sayings (cf. John 10), he has included as an introduction to this episode, not the prophecy of Jesus' death and suffering, but rather the great promises of Jesus recorded as part of the high priestly prayer of John 17. To be even more accurate, the real preface of this entire section of the Gospel is the verse that begins chapter 13: "It was just before the Passover Feast. Jesus knew that the time had come for him to leave this world and go to the Father. Having loved his own who were in the world, he now showed them the full extent of his love" (v. 1).

John emphasizes the fact that the arrest was under the control of Jesus. For one thing, Jesus initiates the actual confrontation, going forth to the soldiers, asking, "Who is it you want?" rather than waiting for the kiss of Judas, as the other Gospels seem to indicate. John includes that otherwise unmentioned episode in which the soldiers and officers fall to the ground as a result of Jesus introducing himself to them with the majestic name of God: Jehovah ("I am"). Finally, even at the moment of the arrest Jesus is dominant; he issues a command—"I told you that I am he. If you are looking for me, then let these men go" (18:8)—and it is followed.

These converging emphases are to show that it was no meaningless and unanticipated tragedy that overtook Jesus of Nazareth at the close of his otherwise promising ministry and so ended it. Rather, it was that ordering of events set forth by God, which events were thus not only to be inevitably fulfilled but also to be filled with great blessing, not only for Christ himself but also for his followers.

Christ's Days, Our Days

In a sense everything that we are to study in the remainder of John's Gospel has bearing on this great theme: that there is no tragedy for Christians. But because we will be looking at this in terms of Christ's life, it is especially necessary at the beginning that we also stop to see that it must have a profound bearing upon our lives too. For we shall have suffering. There is no doubt of that. We are called to it. There will be dark days. Will they be bitter days? Will we gripe and complain? Or will they be days of victory? Much of the answer depends upon how well we learn the lessons of these chapters.

Let me ask this question: How do Christians most often think of their suffering? Some consider it a breach of trust on the part of God, of course. They reproach him for it. Others simply endure suffering grimly, refusing to ask from whom it has come or even if God might have a purpose in it. But I am not thinking of these. I am thinking of more mature Christians who, because they believe in a sovereign God, readily accept the thought that their suffering, grief, or disappointment first of all passed through God's hand and is intended for them as good. I am asking how they regard suffering. How do they think of it?

From my experience I would say that mature Christians usually think of it in one of three ways, or a combination of them. First, some think of suffering as something to be endured so that in God's own time he might intervene to remove it and thus get glory to himself for removing it. An example of this would be sickness, particularly acute sickness that might lead to death. These Christians think that its purpose is that God might remove it so that they can then praise him for their healing. Another example would be an unpleasant line of work, which they could praise God for after the work has been changed for something new.

Second, there are those who look upon suffering as something for God to transform. Perhaps, if they were bolder, they might pray for its removal outright. But since they have no confidence that God will do this (or else sense, often rightly, that he has no intention of doing so), they pray that God might make things different. They expect him to change the suffering so that it is no longer the pain or discouragement that it might be for other people.

Third, there are Christians who simply look beyond the dark days of suffering to glory and therefore strive to ignore the suffering. They see no purpose in it, but they go through it for the joys that lie beyond.

Are these views right? Let me acknowledge first that there is an element of truth (and sometimes, in a particular case, the whole truth) in each of them. It is true that suffering is sometimes given so that God might remove it and thus be glorified. The affliction of the man who had been born blind, whose story is told in John 9, would be such an example. Sometimes, too, the suffering is deeply transformed. It is also true, whatever the case in the other areas may be, that there is a realm of joy beyond the sufferings. In Christ's case, there was a resurrection and ascension—beyond the cross. He looked forward to it. Similarly, we are encouraged by those scenes of the redeemed saints in glory recorded by John in Revelation. We rejoice to know that there will be no tears there, neither death, sorrow, crying, or pain (Rev. 21:4).

But is this the uniquely Christian approach to suffering, based upon these chapters from John and other passages? Is the Christian's answer only escape or transformation or sublimation? I think not. Rather the answer is the acceptance of suffering in its fullness for Christ's sake, thereby helping to make up the fullness of his sufferings (as Paul said he himself did) and bringing glory to his name, not by an escape from suffering but by the sheer force of the way in which we bear it.

Two Groups of People

Donald Grey Barnhouse, the founder of the *Bible Study Hour,* once preached a sermon entitled "Tragedy or Triumph." It was an analysis of this problem, and at one point he gave this illustration. He said that one morning early in his ministry a woman stopped him on the street to ask if he would come to see her son. Her son had tuberculosis and was dying. He said, "I'll go home with you now."

"Oh, no," she replied. "Don't come with me. He is very bitter. He might curse you, and I don't want him to know that I asked you. Just drop in later." This was all right with the young pastor. So about half an hour later he rang the bell on the front of one of Philadelphia's little row houses, noticing as he did that there was a front room in which the young man's bed had been placed and in which he was lying. He introduced himself as the pastor of the nearby church and then openly noticed the woman's sick son.

As he walked over to him the young man became angry and began to curse. "Why does God make me spit my lungs into this cup?" he demanded. "Oh, God is so cruel to me!" He cursed God for his suffering, and became so agitated that Barnhouse thought it would be best to leave. In about a week that young man died.

Several years later Barnhouse was holding a series of Sunday night services in a theater in West Philadelphia. As he finished preaching one night, someone asked, "Will you go to see a young man in this neighborhood who is dying of tuberculosis?" He immediately thought of the other incident, but he went to see the young man and was surprised to find the case completely different. Again, it was a little row house. The man was in the front room. But when Barnhouse began to talk to him the young man exclaimed, "Oh, life is so wonderful since Christ has saved me!" He told his story. He said that he had gotten so weak in the last few months that he had been able to spend only one hour out of twenty-four out of bed. But during that one hour each day he would get dressed and take a walk around the block.

One evening, while he was taking his walk, he noticed the lights on in the neighborhood theater and went in to rest. Barnhouse was preaching, and he listened while he spoke of the love of Christ. He received Jesus as his own personal Savior and Lord. During the months that followed, in that one hour out of bed each day, he visited families in his block and told them of what Christ had done to save them and of how much he loved them. Now, however, he was too weak to go out at all. "But," he said, "I have about fifty relatives in this city. I would like to invite them over next Sunday. And if I do, would you come and speak to them?" Barnhouse said he would, and when he arrived on the next Sunday evening he found a full house of people. They were everywhere—on the stairs, upstairs, in the kitchen, some even on the floor. The young man told of his conversion, and then he invited Barnhouse to tell the story he had told in the theater the night the young man was saved. Afterward he said, "That was the message spoken the night I believed in Jesus. This is how I came to trust in Christ. I know that the next time you are all together it will be for my funeral, but I wanted to witness to you about Christ before I died." A few days later he did die—triumphantly.

Do you think that testimony failed to have its effect on those relatives? Of course it did not. But it was effective, not because the second man had less pain or because his death was transmuted. Rather it was because he received it as being from God himself, which it truly was, and thereby glorified God in it.

Barnhouse's own comment is as follows: "As we review these two cases, almost identical in circumstances but so different in outlook, we realize anew that the world is divided into two groups—those who are born again, and those who are not. People are either the children of God or they are the children of wrath and of disobedience. In order to become a child of God you must believe on the Lord Jesus Christ. As a result of searching the Word of God, and of the experiences of my ministry, I believe that God permits whatever happens to an unbeliever, also to happen to a Christian. The unbeliever cries out against God; but the Christian says, 'Lord, do to me whatever you please.' No matter what your condition in life, if you are not a believer in Jesus Christ, God has a double of you somewhere who is believing in Jesus Christ. If you are in the Home for Incurables, and do not know Christ and think your lot is terrible, someone else in the Home for Incurables is praising God. The Devil has his doctors, and God has his doctors who love in simple faith and trust the Lord. The Devil has his lawyers who connive and cheat; God has his honorable, upright lawyers who seek to aid those in difficulty. God has his rich men and the Devil has his.

"Describe yourself to me. Tell me how old you are, what is your condition, what are your circumstances. I will duplicate them in the life of some Christian. To put it the other way around, whatever happens to a Christian, the same is happening to an unbeliever, and he is crying out, 'God, you can't do this to me!' But the Christian can say, 'O, God, you can do anything you wish to me. You redeemed me. You bought me with your blood. I am yours, and I know that all things will work together for good because I love you.'"[2]

A Privilege

Here is one last story. Dr. Helen Roseveare, a British medical doctor, served for more than twenty years in Africa, in the state of Zaire. For twelve and a half years she had a frantic but generally wonderful time serving as the only doctor in an area containing more than half a million people (today about one and a half million). But in 1964, revolution overwhelmed the country, and she and her coworkers were thrown into five and a half months of almost unbelievable brutality and torture. There were several cases of tremendous deliverance, sometimes involving circumstances so far-fetched that a non-Christian could hardly believe them. But there was still torture, beatings, the wretched misery of seeing others multilated and destroyed, and fear—a bone-crushing, overwhelming fear.

On one occasion, when she was on the verge of being executed, a seventeen-year-old student came to her defense and was savagely beaten as a result. He was kicked about like a football and left for dead. She was sick. For a moment she thought that God had forsaken her, even though she did not doubt his reality. But God stepped in and overwhelmed her with the sense of his own presence—in his triumphant bigness—and asked something like this: "Twenty years ago you asked me for the privilege of being a missionary, the privilege of being identified with me. This is it. Don't you want it? This is what it means. These are not your sufferings; they are my sufferings. All I ask of you is the loan of your body."

ill

As the force of that hit home, the doctor said that she was overcome with a great sense of privilege, for privilege it was. She rejoiced to be able to serve her Lord in this or whatever other circumstances he might order for her. "He didn't stop the sufferings. He didn't stop the wickedness, the cruelties, the humiliation or anything. It was all there. The pain was just as bad. The fear was just as bad. But it was now altogether different. It was in Jesus, for him, with him." That is her testimony.

A

I close by asking: Are you a believer in Jesus Christ? And are you aware of the privilege of being just where you are and who you are and in precisely the circumstances you find yourself to be in? Jesus has put you there, wherever it is. He has made you, whoever you are. He has created those circumstances, whatever they may be. It is for you to praise him right there and allow those circumstances, even the most tragic circumstances, to be the grounds of his triumph.

223

Gethsemane

John 18:1-2

When he had finished praying, Jesus left with his disciples and crossed the Kidron Valley. On the other side there was an olive grove, and he and his disciples went into it.

Now Judas, who betrayed him, knew the place, because Jesus had often met there with his disciples.

It is true, as pointed out in the last chapter, that the apostle John does not emphasize the sufferings of Christ in the Garden of Gethsemane, choosing rather to stress his mastery over this as over every other situation. But this does not mean that John was ignorant of what had taken place in the Garden or even that he does not have it in mind as he unfolds his version of the story. We know that he was personally aware of these events, for he was there and was even one of the inner three disciples who accompanied the Lord as he departed a stone's throw from the other eight disciples to pray. We know that John knew the nature of that prayer; for he has anticipated it in chapter 12, where he quotes Jesus as saying, "Now my heart is troubled, and what shall I say? 'Father, save me from this hour'? No it was for this very reason I came to this hour" (v. 27).

1365

John is not ignorant of the events that transpired in Gethsemane. But he is, as also noted in our last study, concerned to place his own perspective on them. What is it? We might answer that he wants to show Christ in his divine strength rather than in his human weakness, the triumph rather than the tragedy. But that is a general answer rather than an answer to the question of John's perception of Jesus' struggle in Gethsemane itself. Since we want to consider this account thoroughly, we therefore ask: Does John indicate a particular way in which the struggle in Gethsemane should be viewed? Is there anything in the text to focus our thinking?

I believe there is such an indication in the word "garden," which John uses in verse 1. To us this is hardly remarkable, for we are accustomed to speak always of the Garden of Gethsemane. But this was apparently not a common name in John's day. We notice, for example, that John does not use the word "Gethsemane." Again—this is even more significant—neither Matthew, Mark, nor Luke uses the word "garden." The full name by which we know this place, the Garden of Gethsemane, never occurs anywhere. What is more, it is never referred to as a garden except in John's Gospel.

Is this particular way of referring to Gethsemane only a peculiarity? Or is more involved?

West of Eden

I would say that it is possible, if not probable, that John is suggesting a contrast between the Garden of Gethsemane, in which Christ so clearly triumphed, and the Garden of Eden, in which the father of the human race fell so sorely. Moreover, let me point out that I am not the first to think this. This was a popular interpretation of John 18:1 by the church fathers and is one that occurs in the works of commentators and expositors from subsequent generations.

Arthur W. Pink draws the contrast out at some length: "The entrance of Christ into the Garden at once reminds us of Eden. The contrasts between them are indeed most striking. In Eden, all was delightful; in Gethsemane, all was terrible. In Eden, Adam and Eve parleyed with Satan; in Gethsemane, the last Adam sought the face of His Father. In Eden, Adam sinned; in Gethsemane, the Savior suffered. In Eden, Adam fell; in Gethsemane, the Redeemer conquered. The conflict in Eden took place by day; the conflict in Gethsemane was waged at night. In the one, Adam fell before Satan; in the other, the soldiers fell before Christ. In Eden the race was lost; in Gethsemane Christ announced, 'Of them whom thou gavest me have I lost none' (John 18:9). In Eden, Adam took the fruit from Eve's hand; in Gethsemane, Christ received the cup from His Father's hand. In Eden, Adam hid himself; in Gethsemane, Christ boldly showed Himself. In Eden, God sought Adam; in Gethsemane, the last Adam sought God! From Eden Adam was 'driven'; from Gethsemane Christ was 'led.' In Eden the 'sword' was drawn (Gen. 3:24); in Gethsemane the 'sword' was sheathed (John 18:11)."[1]

Good versus Evil

We may begin by contrasting the circumstances of Adam and Eve as they faced their trial in Eden with Jesus' circumstances in Gethsemane. It is a contrast between good and evil, or as Pink says, between that which was "delightful" and that which was "terrible."

We remember that Adam and Eve had entered Eden at the peak of God's creative activity. They had a world without sin or death and thus perfect in every way. God had made the man and woman vice-regents over this world, giving them explicit dominion over "the fish of the sea and the birds of the air, over the livestock, over all the earth, and over all the creatures that move along the ground" (Gen. 1:26). Adam and Eve had all this without any threat or even suggestion of a lessening of God's great favors. Yet, turning from this overwhelmingly delightful prospect, they sinned.

By contrast, Jesus faced what Adam and Eve could not even begin to imagine: first, physical death in what is probably the most prolonged and excruciating form known to man, and second, spiritual death, from which even his highly disciplined and divinely motivated soul shrank in deep horror. The full measure of what was before Christ is seen in his great agony, bloody sweat, and heart-breaking prayer ("My Father, if it be possible, may this cup be taken from me," Matt. 26:39; cf. Mark 14:36; Luke 22:42). Nevertheless, Jesus did not turn from this but embraced it willingly for our salvation.

God versus Satan

The second gripping contrast between Adam and Eve's conduct in Eden and Christ's conduct in Gethsemane is that our first parents spent their time talking to Satan while Jesus spent his time talking with God. The need for prayer seems to be something that was very much on Christ's mind, for all his actions are geared to meeting it. He leaves Jerusalem for this, a quiet place where he was accustomed often to go, presumably to pray (John 18:2). He separates himself from the larger number of his disciples. He admonishes them to pray (Luke 22:40). Then he prays earnestly himself, returning to pray twice more after interrupting himself to encourage the disciples in their own vigil. Clearly, Jesus felt the need for prayer. But Adam and Eve, though on the brink of that sin that would condemn the race, did not pray. Rather they seemed oblivious to the danger as they communed with Satan.

Why did Christ feel the need for such prayer? Clearly because he felt the force of temptation. We must not think, just because we have the story of the temptation of Christ by Satan at the very start of his ministry (Matt. 4:1–11; Mark 1:12–13; Luke 4:1–13), that Jesus was therefore never tempted again. On the contrary, on one occasion he identified a rebuke by Peter as one of Satan's disguised temptations (Matt. 16:23). And even on this occasion he seems to have temptation in mind, for he admonishes the disciples to pray lest they be drawn into it (Matt. 26:41; Mark 14:38; Luke 22:40, 46).

To what was he tempted? Here we can only speculate, and that carefully, for where Scripture is silent we must say little. Yet we can imagine that the central temptation would be to leave the work of the atonement undone or else seek the accomplishment of our salvation by some other means. The prayer itself seems to suggest the former—"If it be possible, may this cup be taken from me." The former temptation by Satan in the wilderness suggests the latter—"All this will I give you, if you will bow down and worship me" (Matt. 4:9).

Or again, maybe the temptation was to feel abandoned both by God and men. If this was the nature of Christ's temptation, it would explain the appearance of the angel to strengthen him, for the angel would signify that despite appearances he was not alone.

The lesson for us is not in the nature of his temptations, though ours are often quite similar: to avoid God's work, to attempt to do it in a way other than the way God has mandated, to feel abandoned. Rather, it is in Christ's dependence on prayer. Do we thus value prayer? Do we pray earnestly? Or do we dally with Satan, as Adam and Eve did, or sleep on, as the disciples did?

Two Fell, One Conquered

The third point of contrast between Adam and Eve, on the one hand, and the Lord Jesus Christ, on the other, is also obvious. They fell while he conquered. How soon did they fall? Almost instantly, it would appear. Satan presented his arguments, and they quickly ate the forbidden fruit. Jesus, on the other hand, wrestled in prayer and only prevailed at the end.

Matthew gives us the clearest statement of Christ's prevailing grace in prayer, for he shows progress in Christ's thought and attitude from one prayer to the next. Christ's first prayer, which Matthew records in 26:39 is that the cup that God had poured for him might be taken away, if that should be possible. The actual words are: "My Father, if it be possible, may this cup be taken from me. Yet not as I will, but as you will." The second prayer, offered after he had come back to find the disciples asleep and had admonished them to "watch and pray" with him, employed nearly the same words as the first but without the explicit request that the cup be removed: "My Father, if it is not possible for this cup to be taken away unless I drink it, may your will be done" (v. 42). The third prayer—which, however, is not recorded—must have been to the effect, "I know now that you have given me this cup and that it is your will that I drink it; therefore, I will drink it completely." We know that Jesus must have come to this point, for immediately after this he rose up and went forth to meet those who were coming to seize him.

How long did this take? Today we can read the entire account of this prayer, beginning with Matthew 26:39 and ending with Matthew 26:44, in less than one minute, reading slowly. But Jesus probably prayed at least one hour if not three. For when he came to awake Peter after his first period of prayer, he asked, "Could you men not keep watch with me for one hour?" (v. 40). This seems to suggest that he prayed for about one hour during this first period of prayer and possibly an equal amount during each of the other two. It was only after this that he apparently came to embrace the will of God fully in the matter of his death.

I have no doubt that this conflict, like all the other incidents in Scripture, was recorded for our benefit. And when I ask, "But what benefit are we to derive from it?" I realize that it is to show us how we too may prevail in prayer when we are cast down, distressed, and tempted. Often that phrase, to "prevail in prayer," is used as though it means that we are to keep at prayer until God at last does what we desire. But that is not how Christ prevailed. He kept at prayer until—I speak of Christ's humanity—his will was conformed to God's will, for that was the victory.

We too shall have troubles. Temptations will come; there will be crosses to bear. But we will have victory when, through a submission of our will to God in prayer, we embrace with willing hearts whatever God has for us. In that case, it will not be our will versus God's, as was the case with Adam. Rather it will be God's will and ours together, as was the case with the Son of God and the Father.

The Fruit of the Cup

One of the contrasts Pink makes is particularly suggestive, for he points out that "Adam took the fruit from Eve's hand" while "in Gethsemane, Christ received the cup from his Father's hand." This leads me to state as a great biblical principle that it is always better to have the cup of life from God's hand, no matter what it contains, than anything else, however desirable, from the hand of another.

Why is this? It is because of who God is. He is the wise, all-powerful, loving God of the universe, the one who truly wishes our good and in addition to that also knows what the good is and how to effect it. Others may wish us well, or they may not. But even if they do, what they choose or recommend for us is not necessarily what turns out to be beneficial in the long run. We think of Eve as she looked upon the fruit and "saw that the fruit of the tree was good for food and pleasing to the eye, and also desirable for gaining wisdom" and then took of the fruit and gave it to her husband also (Gen. 3:6). But the tree that seemed to be desirable from the human perspective actually brought death to the race. On the other hand, the cup presented to Christ—although it contained both physical and spiritual death and although it was, in the world's eyes, not a thing of wisdom, but rather of foolishness—this cup was actually life and wisdom for God's people.

Not One Lost

The final contrast of these many contrasts between Adam and Eve in Eden and Christ in Gethsemane is the most significant. It is simply that Adam and

Eve by their sin plunged the race into misery. They fell and carried their progeny over the cliff of sin into destruction. Christ, on the other hand, stood firm. He did not sin, nor did he shrink from his work. As a result, he saved all whom the Father had given him. In Adam all were lost. Christ could say, "Those you gave me I have kept. None of them is lost."

But why should *I* tell it? Let us permit the Apostle to the Gentiles to tell it, for this contrast forms the basis of that magnificent statement of the superiority of Christ to Adam, found in Romans 5:12–21. In those verses he writes,

> Therefore, just as sin entered the world through one man, and death through sin, and in this way death came to all men, because all sinned—for before the law was given, sin was in the world. But sin is not taken into account when there is no law. Nevertheless, death reigned from the time of Adam to the time of Moses, even over those who did not sin by breaking a command, as did Adam, who was a pattern of the one to come.
>
> But the gift is not like the trespass. For if the many died by the trespass of the one man, how much more did God's grace and the gift that came by the grace of the one man, Jesus Christ, overflow to the many! Again, the gift of God is not like the result of the one man's sin: The judgment followed one sin and brought condemnation, but the gift followed many trespasses and brought justification. For if, by the trespass of the one man, death reigned through that one man, how much more will those who receive God's abundant provision of grace and of the gift of righteousness reign in life through the one man, Jesus Christ.
>
> Consequently, just as the result of one trespass was condemnation for all men, so also the result of one act of righteousness was justification that brings life for all men. For just as through the disobedience of the one man the many were made sinners, so also through the obedience of the one man the many will be made righteous.
>
> The law was added so that the trespass might increase. But where sin increased, grace increased all the more, so that, just as sin reigned in death, so also grace might reign through righteousness to bring eternal life through Jesus Christ our Lord.

That is precisely it. That is the meaning of Gethsemane. One writer puts it this way, "Sin, death, and judgment flowed from the act of Adam. Righteousness, life, and kingship flow from the cross of Christ. The sin of Adam was a stone cast into a pool which sent ripples to every inlet. The cross of Christ was the rock of ages cast into the ocean of the love of God, and it is the destiny of all who are in Christ to be carried on the swell of this majestic love and life and power both now and forever."[2]

224

Judas, Who Betrayed Him

John 18:2

Now Judas, who betrayed him, knew the place, because Jesus had often met there with his disciples.

In our first two studies of the last segment of John's Gospel (chapters 18–21) we have dealt for the most part with theology. That is, we have discussed the meaning of Christ's suffering, viewing it as a triumph rather than a tragedy and contrasting it to the circumstances surrounding the fall of Adam and Eve in the Garden of Eden. This was necessary because this is the perspective with which John himself views the crucifixion, and we must begin here if we are to understand this last and most important section of his narrative.

But it is not only theology that enters into these last chapters. In fact, on the surface theology is not spoken about at all. Rather they are history. They tell what happened during these last hours and days of Jesus' earthly life. They tell who and what and why. Consequently, they are to be studied as history primarily, though in conjunction with that we must necessarily see what these events mean for Christianity.

This is of great importance. Sometimes in our Christian preaching and witnessing the events of these climactic days of Christ's life are allowed to pass almost imperceptibly into the realm of mere ideas with the result that the historical base and, therefore, truthfulness of Christianity evaporates. But these are not ideas only. They are facts. They are presented to us in Gospels, which are purportedly "good news" accounts of what actually transpired. Only by keeping the full importance of these events as history do we have something that may legitimately be proclaimed as good news to sinners.

Why Judas?

In a sense we were in the midst of the final events even before beginning our study of chapter 18. For as far back as chapter 12, Jesus has set these in motion by means of his dramatic entry into Jerusalem on what we have come to term Palm Sunday. Ever since then Jesus has been preparing his disciples for the end, and equally important, his enemies among the rulers of the people have been plotting to destroy him. With chapter 18, these events actually get underway, for the forces of antagonism now break forth to effect Christ's arrest, trial, condemnation, and crucifixion.

As John relates his version of the story he begins with Judas. Judas is the one who betrayed Jesus, as each of the Gospel writers knows, and it was his activity, first in confering with the chief priests and then in leading the arresting party to the Garden of Gethsemane, that actually made the arrest of Jesus possible. What about Judas? What precisely was his role in all this, beyond the mere fact of his betrayal? To put the matter in its baldest form, why was Judas and his betrayal necessary for the chief priests at all?

To this question two answers are usually given, either that Judas was necessary in order to lead the arresting party to Christ's hiding place during these last days or else that he was necessary in order to assure a secret arrest because of the leaders' fear of the people. But this is not as clear a matter as one might suppose. To begin with, as Frank Morison has pointed out in a very popular study of the historical forces leading to the crucifixion of Christ, "To regard Judas merely as a common informer, ready (for a consideration) to lead the authorities to the secret hiding place of his erstwhile Friend and Leader, is absurd."[1] For Jesus was not in hiding. In fact, he can hardly have been more open. Earlier he had removed himself from the dangerous vicinity of Jerusalem, knowing that his hour was not yet fully come (John 11:54). But from the moment he had arrived in Bethany from Jericho on the Friday preceding his crucifixion no attempt seems to have been made to conceal his movements at all. The resurrection of Lazarus, which took place on that day, was done openly. On the next day, Saturday, many came to see him and talk both to him and Lazarus. On Sunday Jesus entered Jerusalem with great display while those who were with him and those who came out from the city to greet him cried out, "Hosanna! Blessed is he who comes in the name of the Lord! Blessed is the King of Israel!" (John

12:13). On Monday, Tuesday, and Wednesday he had traveled back and forth openly.

Under these circumstances how could it be that the leaders of the people needed Judas, still less would have been willing to pay him money, to tell them where Jesus was? Obviously, if they had felt free to arrest Jesus, the leaders could have done so in Jerusalem at nearly any unguarded moment. Or they could easily have sent to Bethany and have arrested him there.

It is possible at this point to introduce the other common explanation of Judas's role: to effect the arrest of Christ in secret for fear of the people. But this is at best a half-truth, as Morison indicates. True, there was undoubtedly a real fear on the part of the chief priests and Pharisees of what the people might do. There was fear of a disturbance that might cause the intervention of the Roman armies with dire consequences for them. Even greater, there was fear that the vast multitudes in Jerusalem might actually believe on Jesus. Earlier the leaders had said, "What are we accomplishing? Here is this man performing many miraculous signs. If we let him go on like this, everyone will believe in him, and then the Romans will come and take away both our place and our nation" (John 11:47–48). Out of that council had come the decision to have Jesus killed. But surely there were other times at which these leaders might have taken Jesus secretly—in Bethany in the early morning or late evening, on the road between Bethany and Jerusalem, in a quiet corner of the capital, even in the upper room. That they did not do this but rather relied on Judas to bring them information necessary to achieve the arrest suggests that there were other and even more important factors.

Fear of Jesus

Here Morison makes a suggestion that is of great value in determining why events moved as they did. He says, "Personally, I am convinced that beneath the ostensible and acknowledged fear of the people, there was a deeper and more potent fear—a fear that explains all their singular hesitancies and vacillations, until a welcome message reached their astonished ears—the fear of Christ Himself."[2]

There are two senses in which this must have been true. In the first place, these shrewd leaders of the people could not have been unaware of Christ's unusual appeal to the masses. Like John the Baptist before him, Jesus had preached on occasion to great crowds of people, some of whom would travel considerable distances to hear him. On at least one and possibly more occasions in Galilee, those who heard him had been fed by him and wanted to make him a king, a political Messiah. He had turned them down then. But who could tell what would happen if for some reason Jesus should decide that he really would assume a messianic role? Moreover, suppose he should decide to make his bid in Jerusalem at this feast? It would not seem at all impossible to the Jewish leaders that Jesus might well whip the expectations of the city to a new peak of excitement and frenzy, particularly since he seemed already to have launched himself on such a course by entering the capital on a donkey the previous Sunday.

This would not be their only or worst fear, however. There was also the matter of Christ's undeniable, supernatural power. Early in his ministry they had, like true skeptics, denied the miracles or else, as in the case of the man born blind, attributed them to some unrelated intervention by God (John 9:24). But by this point they were openly acknowledging the miracles and were afraid of them.

Moreover, there had been the matter of their former unsuccessful attempts to arrest him. John reports several of these, though there may have been others. On one occasion a body of officers, who probably were temple guards, was dispatched by the chief priests to take him. But after a while they returned with the task undone. "Why didn't you bring him in?" they were asked.

Their reply was an incredible reply for soldiers. "No man ever spoke the way this man does" was their answer (cf. John 7:32, 45–49).

Later, at the end of chapter 8, another move was made against Christ, this time to stone him. "But Jesus," we are told, "hid himself, slipping away from the temple grounds" (v. 59). A third time we are told that "again they tried to seize him, but he escaped their grasp" (10:39).

What would the rulers have been thinking as a result of their abortive attempts to take Jesus? Probably they would not have voiced their most fundamental fear, even to themselves. But they must have been fearing—because of Christ's obvious power and their own earlier failures—that in the ultimate analysis he might perhaps be unarrestable? *Unarrestable!* If this were the case, it would explain their failure to do anything during the earlier part of this last Passover week, their final abrupt decision that very nearly failed, and their use of Judas.

The Time Element

The one thing that is immediately apparent to anyone who studies carefully the circumstances of Jesus' arrest and trial is that they were all greatly rushed. This is apparent from the fact that the first trial (or hearing) was held at night, which was illegal under Jewish law regarding capital cases. It is also apparent from the fact that in order to try Jesus' case, Pilate was prevailed upon to come out of his palace early on what would normally not have been a trial day. Even more significantly, it is evident from the case itself, which was obviously unprepared. Judicially, the case was a blunder, for it was obviously failing until Caiaphas hit upon the illegal but brilliant stroke of interrogating the witness himself. The result was that, when challenged in the name of Jehovah, Jesus declared his divinity and was convicted on a charge of blasphemy (Matt. 26:63–66; Mark 14:60–64; Luke 22:70–71).

Briefly put, the problem the leaders faced was that they were arresting Jesus so close to the Passover sabbath that it was a matter of real difficulty to hold the two trials (their own and the Roman) and have him condemned and executed before the Passover began at what I believe to be sundown on Thursday.[3] Their solution was to hold an initial hearing at night and the formal trial, followed by the Roman trial, at the earliest possible moment the next morning. But why did they wait that long? Or why, assuming that they compressed the events in order to get the whole thing out of the way as quickly as possible, were they not better prepared when they actually made their move against Jesus?

The only reasonable explanation is that they had not been planning on making an arrest before the Passover but that Judas had somehow brought them information that led them to think that, in spite of the difficulties, this was indeed the opportunity they had been waiting for. What might Judas have said? Here, of course, we are only speculating, for the Scriptures do not give us his exact words. But if we remember that Jesus had been talking about his forthcoming death in Judas's presence, and if we remember the leaders' fear of perhaps not being able to effect Christ's arrest, which they may well have shared with Judas earlier, it is entirely possible that Judas left the upper room with the message: "Jesus is thinking and talking about death. He has been suggesting this for some time, but he is now talking as if his death is imminent. I would say that the mood of surrender is upon him. If you move now, without delay, I think he would willingly go with you and your worst fears would be resolved. Moreover, he is going to go to Gethsemane at the foot of the Mount of Olives and will wait there until I come. Hurry and make your arrangements. I will lead you to him."

At this point the question would have been whether or not the necessary arrangements could be made in time. There had to be a preliminary hearing at which the accusation could be worked out. The Sanhedrin would have to be gathered. And then, most important of all, they would have to determine whether Pilate, the Roman governor, would consent to hear a capital case early the next morning on what would normally not have been a court day. Someone would have to go and ask him, probably Caiaphas himself. Meanwhile, the arresting party would have to be aroused and set in order. When we view the events in this light we can see why so much time elapsed between Judas's departure from the upper room and Christ's eventual arrest in the Garden at least three hours later.

During this time, Jesus was clearly waiting in the Garden for his arrest instead of going back over the Mount of Olives to Bethany as was his custom. He waited while Judas carried his message, the leaders made their arrangements, and the arresting party made its way out of the city to seize him.

Who Killed Jesus?

All this has bearing upon two very important matters. First, it indicates that Jesus was in control of these events from the beginning. They did not come upon him by accident, but rather he willed them in conformity to his knowledge of the will of his Father. We have seen this truth already. Clearly, when Jesus came up to Bethany from Jericho, as he did on the preceding Friday, and then raised Lazarus, he precipitated the final decision of the leaders to have him killed. He did so knowingly. When he rode into Jerusalem on Palm Sunday he carried the confrontation a step farther. When he cleansed the temple, as the synoptic Gospels record (Matt. 21:12–17; Mark 11:15–18; Luke 19:45–47; cf. John 2:13–16 for an earlier incident), he further intensified the leaders' ire. On this very night, he dispatched Judas on his errand of betrayal. At last, we find him waiting in the Garden for the arrest.

Historically, there has been a heated discussion as to who killed Jesus. Gentiles who have not known their Bible too well (or the evil of their own hearts) have tried to blame the Jews. Jews (and others) have blamed the Gentiles; for it was Gentiles in the person of Pilate, the Roman governor, who actually pronounced the death sentence. Sometimes these views have led to fierce anti-Semitism or an opposite anti-Christian feeling. But these are not the most important details. In fact, they are relatively insignificant. By contrast, the most important thing that can be said about the death of Christ is that God the Father willed it. It was God who ordained that he should be killed for our sin. The second important fact is that Jesus also willed his death out of love for us and in obedience to the revealed will of his Father.

Moreover, he ordered the events of this last Passover week to indicate the meaning of what he was doing. For just as he ordered his entry into Jerusalem to correspond to the exact time at which the Passover lambs were being led up to the city, so also did he time his death to coincide with the killing of those same lambs. He was the great Passover Lamb of which they were but shadows. It was his blood, rather than theirs, which was to take away the sins of the world.

Again, there is this final lesson. It concerns Judas, who was so close to Christ and yet was unsaved. Think how close he was. He had been with Jesus for at least three years. He had heard his teaching. He had even understood his teaching; for although he had not understood the meaning of Christ's death, he had at least understood Christ's warning that he was to die. Judas was that close to Jesus. He understood his thoughts. Yet he was unsaved. I put it to you: It is possible to be quite close to Christ, to sit in a Christian church listening to good sermons, to hear good Bible teaching by radio, even to understand what you hear, and yet fail to make that personal commitment to Christ that is the necessary human response to God's work of salvation.

How foolish it is to come that close and yet be lost. How much wiser, by contrast, to put your faith in that One who is altogether lovely and who willingly died for your salvation.

225

The Arrest!

John 18:3–11

So Judas came to the grove, guiding a detachment of soldiers and some officials from the chief priests and Pharisees. They were carrying torches, lanterns and weapons.

Jesus, knowing all that was going to happen to him, went out and asked them, "Who is it you want?"

"Jesus of Nazareth," they replied.

"I am he," Jesus said. (And Judas the traitor was standing there with them.) When Jesus said, "I am he," they drew back and fell to the ground.

Again he asked them, "Who is it you want?"

And they said, "Jesus of Nazareth."

"I told you that I am he," Jesus answered. "If you are looking for me, then let these men go." This happened so that the words he had spoken would be fulfilled: "I have not lost one of those you gave me."

Then Simon Peter, who had a sword, drew it and struck the high priest's servant, cutting off his right ear. (The servant's name was Malchus.)

Jesus commanded Peter, "Put your sword away! Shall I not drink the cup the Father has given me?"

I do not know how you might have described the arrest of Jesus of Nazareth in the Garden of Gethsemane on the night before his crucifixion had you been there to observe it, for I do not know the perspective you might have had. If you were Caiaphas, you would doubt-less have reported it as a triumph: "At last we have seized him!" If you were the captain of the band of soldiers who actually effected the arrest, you might have reported it quite factually: "Fourteenth of Nisan, eleven thirty p.m., arrested, one prisoner, Jesus of Nazareth." I do know, however, that if you had been John the evangelist and if you had been led in your writing by the Holy Spirit, as he was, you would have reported that, from beginning to end Jesus, and not his captors, was in complete charge of the situation. It was he who delayed in the Garden while the arresting party was coming. It was he who went forth to meet them, thereby surrendering himself voluntarily. Moreover, even at the very moment of the arrest, he showed his control over circumstances, for he demonstrated power toward the soldiers, grace toward his own disciples, and mercy to those who were (perhaps unwittingly in this case) his enemies.

It is a ludicrous situation, men with weapons coming forward to arrest the Son of God, and John does not allow us to miss the irony. We remember, for example, that it is John who has stressed more than any other Gospel writer that Jesus is the light of this world. He has done that in the opening chapter, where the word "light" in reference to Jesus occurs six times in just nine verses. Later he twice quotes Christ's own claim to be "the light of the world" (8:12; 9:5). Now those of the darkness come in the darkness with "lanterns and torches" to seek him out.

Moreover, they come with weapons. From his enemies' point of view, these were no doubt thought to be necessary. His enemies were afraid of Christ and were worried about what might happen if he should choose to resist them. They were right to be worried. If he chose to resist them, no weapons would have been sufficient. Jesus was arrested, so John clearly indicates, because he willingly chose to give himself up to die to save us.

Today also those who are the enemies of Christ depend on equally fool-ish lights and weapons. It is not literal lamps upon which our contempo-raries rely, of course. It is rather the light of "progress" or the light of "rea-son." But however valuable these lights may be in purely human terms, they are clearly foolish when arrayed against him who is himself the Light. His light cannot be extinguished by our lights, for ours owe their existence to him. He is the source of all light and reason. Thus, our thinking runs to fool-ishness when we fail to acknowledge him, as Paul indicates in Romans when he says that having refused to glorify God as God, men and women became vain in their imaginations, "and their foolish hearts were darkened. Although they claimed to be wise, they became fools and exchanged the glory of the immortal God for images made to look like motal man and birds and ani-mals and reptiles" (1:21–23). Similarly, human weapons, which the enemies of Christ frequently resort to when reason fails, are also useless.

God's Power

John is not especially interested in the weakness of men, however. What he is really interested in is the power of Jesus, which he conveys by a rather remarkable incident. It is an incident that none of the other Gospels relates. John writes that Jesus, having seen the approaching soldiers and knowing all that was in store for him, went forth to them and initiated the arrest by a question: "Who is it you want?"

It must have been dark in the Garden in spite of the full moon of Passover (or else a supernatural blindness had been placed upon Christ's enemies), for they did not fully recognize him. If they had, they would have replied, "You! We seek you." Instead they answered, "Jesus of Nazareth."

At this point, according to John, Jesus answered by saying "I am" ("he" is not in the Greek text), and immediately, so we are told, the arresting party "drew back and fell to the ground," where they remained until Jesus apparently released them by asking his question once again.

What produced this strange reaction? It may be, as some commentators have argued, that it is really not a miracle. There have been cases where the hand of an evil person has been stayed momentarily by the innocence or overbearing presence of the one to be victimized. Kings have sometimes had this effect on mere soldiers of the enemy. Executioners have sometimes been unable to strike an innocent person. Alexander Maclaren, who explores this line of thought in his commentary, writes, "There must have been many in that band who had heard him, though, in the uncertain light of quivering moonbeams and smoking torches, they failed to recognize him till he spoke. There must have been many more who had heard of him, and many who suspected that they were about to lay hands on a holy man, perhaps on a prophet. There must have been reluctant tools among the inferiors, and no doubt among the leaders whose consciences needed but a touch to be roused to action. To all, his calmness and dignity would appeal, and the manifest freedom from fear or desire to flee would tend to deepen the strange thoughts which began to stir in their hearts."[1] Thoughts like these may well have caused Christ's captors to fall back in dismay or consternation.

But this does not seem to be the whole of the picture, as Maclaren also recognizes, for John does not merely say that the officers and soldiers paused for a moment in their efforts to arrest Jesus. He says that they actually stepped backward and fell to the ground. Moreover, and this is of great importance, they did so in response not merely to Christ's presence but rather to the majestic words he uttered: "I am" or (as most of our translations have it) "I am he."

Is this significant? It is if we remember that the meaning of the great name of God, Jehovah, revealed to Moses at the burning bush at the time of God's commissioning him to lead the people of Israel out of Egypt, is "I am that I am." It is a form of the verb "to be." Thus, when Jesus replied to his enemies by saying, "I am," it may well have been that he used his own great name, Jehovah, the name above every name (Phil. 2:9–11), and that hearing this name uttered by the God-man threw the arresting party into utter confusion and rendered them helpless even to stand before him.

Maclaren says, "I am inclined to think that here, as there [he is thinking of the transfiguration], though under such widely different circumstances and to such various issues, there was for a moment a little rending of the veil of his flesh, and an emission of some flash of the brightness that always tabernacled within him; and that, therefore, just as Isaiah, when he saw the King in his glory, said, 'Woe is me, for I am undone!' and just as Moses could not look upon the Face, but could only see the back parts, so here the one stray beam of manifest divinity that shot through the crevice, as it were, for an instant, was enough to prostrate with a strange awe even those rude and insensitive men. When he said, 'I am He,' there was something that made them feel, 'This is One before whom violence cowers abashed, and in whose presence impurity has to hide its face.'"[2]

It is a great contrast, this revelation of the glory and power of Jesus at the very moment of his arrest in Gethsemane, but it is only one more example of the paradox of the incarnation found throughout the pages of the Word of God. We look to his birth and see a picture of human weakness, a baby lying in a manger. But we turn to the fields of Bethlehem and find that birth announced by angels. He is born poor, but a star leads eastern kings to present their gold, frankincense, and myrrh. At his baptism he identified himself with those who repent of their sins; but he had no sin, and a voice from heaven is heard declaring, "This is my Son, whom I love; with him I am well pleased" (Matt. 3:17). He is so exhausted that he falls asleep in the back of a boat that soon is pitching wildly in a storm on Galilee. The disciples, seasoned fishermen, are frightened. They wake him, and he immediately calms the waves. At the grave of Lazarus, Jesus weeps, but then he speaks the word in power and the dead man comes forth in resurrection. In the Garden he prays in agony that if it might be possible this cup should pass from him. But moments later he goes forth to confront his enemies and overpower them with the sheer force of his presence.

This strange blending of opposites is a clue to the first reason why Jesus did what he did on this occasion. It was to show at this important moment that he was more than man. Man? Yes, but also *God manifest in flesh.* He would have it known that it was as God as well as man that he was about to die for our salvation. He must be a man to die. But he must also be God if that death was to be adequate as a ransom price for our sin. This he declares at the moment of his capture.

Second, the incident of his display of power over his enemies shows that *his death is voluntary* and not coerced. If he had been unwilling to die, no amount of troops or weapons could ever have forced him. He could have walked away as he did on numerous former occasions.

Finally, Jesus acted as he did to make it clear that those who were arresting him and those who stood behind their action by commanding it were *without excuse.* Some in the arresting party may never have seen Christ before. But they will never be able to plead that they were without any indication as to who he was. They were not ignorant of his divine glory. Thus, if they continued on their way after he had released them from their bondage to his power, it was because they did not want to recognize or heed the truth and not because it was unknown to them. So also will it be in the day of Christ's second appearing. In that day too his deity will be made manifest and the guilt and sinful intransigence of man will be exposed. That will be a day of judgment and not of grace. Today is the time to turn from sin and acknowledge him both as Savior and Lord.

Grace for Christ's Disciples

There is also a second feature of the arrest of Christ that the other Gospel writers overlook. He commands the officers and soldiers that since it is he they had come to take, his disciples should be allowed to go their way (v. 8). This is a statement of grace toward his disciples—effective grace. Those whom he had protected were allowed to go their own way so that, as John says, "The words he had spoken would be fulfilled: 'I have not lost one of these you gave me'" (v. 9). The reference is to the statements of John 6:39 and 17:12.

When John calls attention to the statements of Christ given earlier he is, of course, broadening the protecting grace of Christ from this one incident in which only the eleven disciples were protected to that general exercise of God's grace in which all Christ's people are saved. It is true that Jesus did protect the eleven, for without a doubt these soldiers and officers had intended to arrest the disciples too. We know this because Mark tells us of their attempt to seize a certain young man who was wrapped in a linen cloth but who left it in their hands and fled away naked when they laid hands upon him (Mark 14:51–52). Nevertheless, as John quotes Jesus on this occasion he is also aware that this is but one small example of a greater protection by which Jesus constantly preserves those of all ages whom the Father has given him.

How does Jesus exercise this persevering grace toward those who had believed in him? Here are a number of verses that tell us what God is able to do and therefore will do for his people. Hebrews 7:25—"Therefore he is completely able to save those who come to God through him, because he always lives to intercede for them." Second Timothy 1:12—"He is able to guard what I have entrusted to him for that day." Hebrews 2:18—"Because he himself suffered when he was tempted, he is able to help those who are being tempted." Philippians 3:20–21—"The Lord Jesus Christ, who, by the power that enables him to bring everything under his control, will transform our lowly bodies so that they will be like his glorious body." Jude 24–25—"To him who is able to keep you from falling and to present you before his glorious presence without fault and with great joy—to the only God our Savior be glory, majesty, power, and authority through Jesus Christ our Lord, before all ages, now and forevermore! Amen."

When we put these verses together they tell us that Jesus shows his effective, persevering grace with us by lifting us from the darkness of this world into his own marvelous light, by interceding for us in heaven, by guarding our spiritual deposits, by seeing us through temptation, by saving even our bodies at the time of the last resurrection, and by bringing us at last and without blemish into the presence of his own and the Father's glory. He does this by placing himself between us and our enemies.

Mercy to All

There is one final incident in John's account of Christ's arrest that is, unlike the first two incidents, narrated by each of the other Gospel writers also. It concerns Peter who, when he saw that Jesus was about to be arrested, quickly drew the sword he was wearing and swung at the young man leading the column. No doubt Peter intended to strike off his head. But the young man ducked—his name was Malchus, a servant of the high priest, Caiaphas—and so lost only his ear. Luke tells us, in reporting the full account, that Jesus then touched his ear and healed him (Luke 22:51). John adds that he also rebuked Peter, saying, "Put your sword away! Shall I not drink the cup the Father gives me?" (18:11).

As we look at this incident we see many truths in it. One lesson is the folly of that fleshly activity that, insensitive to God's plan and purposes, seeks to strike out in God's defense. Peter's zeal for Christ was not conditioned by knowledge, which was the inevitable outcome of his failure in the preceding hours to observe Christ's command to him to "watch and pray" (Matt. 26:41). He was courageous but ignorant. Later he would not even be courageous, for he would deny Christ before a servant. Peter failed. And so shall we if our zeal is not nurtured upon the knowledge that Christ gives and is not strengthened by him.

This and other lessons aside, surely the greatest truth of this incident is that Jesus was here showing mercy even to his enemies, and this even at the time they came to thrust him toward his execution.

In this last verse Jesus speaks of "the cup the Father gives me." It is one of two cups spoken of often in Scripture. One is the cup of salvation. It is mentioned in Psalm 116:13 ("I will lift up the cup of salvation and call on the name of the LORD"). The other cup is the cup of God's wrath or tribulation, which is referred to here. Earlier Jesus had prayed that this cup might pass from him (Matt. 26:39). Two cups: the cup of salvation and the cup of God's wrath! Every person who has ever lived shall drink from one of them. But those who drink of the cup of salvation by God's grace will drink of it only because Jesus drank the cup of God's wrath in their place.

226

The Jewish Trial

John 18:12–14

Then the detachment of soldiers with its commander and the Jewish officials arrested Jesus. They bound him and brought him first to Annas, who was the father-in-law of Caiaphas, the high priest that year. Caiaphas was the one who had advised the Jews that it would be good if one man died for the people.

Something about trials, particularly great trials that set precedent and determine the flow of history, uniquely captures and enthralls people's minds. For example, in all of American history, probably no single event has created so much interest nor sustained it for so long a time as the inevitable outworking of justice following the break-in at the Democratic campaign headquarters in the Watergate complex in Washington, D.C., on the night of June 16, 1972, culminating in the resignation of President Richard M. Nixon, effective August 9, 1974, over two years later.

True, the chief defendant never came to trial, though scores of his staff and other underlings did. But the issue revolved about this president—his character, politics, and abuse of power. It was that issue that kept the American electorate enthralled for this long period. At times the press seemed to

1383

cover little else. When, at the peak of the investigations, the Ervin Committee began televised hearings in the Senate Caucus Room (on May 17, 1973), the nation almost stopped its regular work to follow the day-by-day revelations. Businessmen brought television sets to their offices. Bars tuned their sets to these historic deliberations. Even in the nation's capital, public hearings were suspended. In the evenings, the Public Broadcasting Service reran portions of the day's hearings for the nighttime television audience and as a result experienced the greatest response to any programming in its history—82,000 letters and over $1,250,000 in new memberships and contributions. The Ervin Committee itself received letters at a rate of between 1,000 and 9,000 per day, and by November the total topped 1,000,000. Besides what other investigative bodies spent, the Ervin Committee alone spent at least $1,500,000.

This unique interest in the outcome of some monumental trial is also observable in ancient history and in our own abiding interest in those ancient events. Several trials come to mind—Socrates before the leaders of Athens, Charles I facing a sober but liberty-minded English Parliament, Alfred Dreyfus in France, Aaron Burr, Mary Stuart, the defendants at Nuremberg.

These trials have engaged the minds and imaginations of millions. Yet, no trial has so challenged our race or so charged our emotions as the trial of Jesus by the Jewish and Roman authorities in Palestine.

Walter M. Chandler, a former member of the New York bar of lawyers and author of an excellent book on the trial of Jesus, has written, "These [other] trials, one and all, were tame and commonplace, compared with the trial and crucifixion of the Galilean peasant, Jesus of Nazareth. These were earthly trials, on earthly issues, before earthly courts. The trial of the Nazarene was before the high tribunals of both heaven and earth; before the Great Sanhedrin, whose judges were the master-spirits of a divinely commissioned race; before the court of the Roman Empire that controlled the legal and political rights of men throughout the known world, from Scotland to Judea and from Dacia to Abyssinia."[1]

It is of great importance that we study the trial of Jesus thoroughly. We study it because of its interest and its obvious implications. We ask: Was it rightly done? Was Jesus guilty as charged? Or was he innocent? What were the charges against the prisoner? Were proper procedures followed or were they violated? And—which is perhaps the most important question of all—what does this have to say to us about our own systems of law and our relationships to Jesus?

Two Trials

We must begin with a general overview of the events in which the trial (literally, trials) took place. These have four main features.

First, there was *the arrest,* which has already been discussed in the previous chapter. This took place on the evening before the Jewish Passover in the year A.D. 30, probably on Wednesday, April 5. This would have been late, at eleven or twelve o'clock at night. It occurred through the agency of a band of temple officers or Roman soldiers who were guided by Judas.

Second, there was *the Jewish trial*. This had three separate parts. First, there was a preliminary hearing by night before Annas. This is what John seems to be describing in his Gospel, though the issue is somewhat confused due to his use of the phrase "the high priest" for both Annas and Caiaphas, before whom the second part of the trial was conducted. The reason for this double use of the reference is that, according to Jewish law, the high priest held his high office for life but the Romans, under whose indulgence the Jewish system of government was allowed to function, albeit somewhat impoverished, had displaced high priests who were not to their liking and had put others in their place. Thus, at the time of Christ's arrest, there were: Caiaphas (the Roman appointee), Annas (the elder high priest, who would have been recognized as the true high priest by all Jews), and others (who had also been appointed by the Romans and afterward deposed). Apparently, John describes the appearance of Jesus before Annas, at which time Jesus refused to testify against himself and was therefore unjustly struck by a minor court officer (18:19–23).[2]

The second phase of the Jewish trial was before Caiaphas, to whom Annas had sent Jesus when he perceived that his own method of interrogation was fruitless. The trial before Caiaphas was the significant trial; therefore, it is the one described at length by the Synoptic writers (cf. Matt. 26:57–68; Mark 14:53–65; Luke 22:54). Various witnesses were brought forward who, however, could not agree on their testimony and were therefore dismissed. According to the Synoptic accounts, this trial was moving toward a swift motion of acquittal (and should have resulted in acquittal) when Caiaphas himself intervened illegally to demand of the prisoner: "I charge you under oath by the living God: Tell us if you are the Christ, the Son of God" (Matt. 26:63). When Jesus, who was not under obligation to testify against himself but who nevertheless would not refuse this official challenge in the name of Jehovah, replied, "Yes, it is as you say," he was immediately convicted of blasphemy by a unanimous vote.

The third phase of the Jewish trial took place the following morning at daybreak (Matt. 27:1; Mark 15:1; Luke 22:66–71). The pertinent questioning of the previous night was reiterated formally and a judgment secured. This phase of the trial involved the entire Sanhedrin, the highest court of Judaism.

The third feature of these final events was *the Roman trial*. This was necessary because, although the Jewish court could convict, it could not execute and therefore had to seek Roman concurrence in its verdict. This trial also had three parts. First, there was the prearranged appearance before Pilate (Matt. 27:2, 11–14; Mark 15:1–5; Luke 23:1–5; John 18:28–38). Here, for reasons yet to be studied, the anticipations of the Jewish leaders seemed to be frustrated; for rather than proceeding with a *pro forma* trial and judgment, which the leaders had been led to expect, Pilate suddenly balked and tried to free the prisoner. The second part of the trial is an appearance before Herod, for when Pilate heard that Jesus was a Galilean, he tried to escape responsibility by sending Jesus to one who might be thought to have better jurisdiction (Luke 23:6–12). Herod sent Jesus back, however. So the third part of the Roman trial, the part at which Jesus was actually given over to crucifixion (though he had not been convicted of anything and was, in fact, pronounced innocent), was before Pilate. This trial, the crucial one, is recorded by all the Gospel writers (Matt. 27:15–26; Mark 15:6–15; Luke 23:13–25; John 18:39–19:16).

The final feature of these events was *the crucifixion,* the execution of the sentence of the two courts.

Hebrew Law

It is evident from this brief survey of the features of Christ's arrest, trial, and execution, that the first major concern of the student with these events should be the Jewish trial. But it is impossible to understand this trial apart from at least a rudimentary knowledge of Hebrew law and legal practice.

Unfortunately, this is not such an easy subject to familiarize oneself with. To begin with, there is a double base for Hebrew law: the Mosaic law (or Pentateuch), and the Talmud, or oral (not written) law, built upon it. Again, the Talmudic law is of great volume and is very complex. It has two parts: the Mishnah, which is the basic law, and the Gemara, which is what we would call a commentary upon it. The relation between the Gemara and the Mishnah might be compared to the debate over a proposed law in the United States Congress, preserved in the *Congressional Record,* and the law that results. Only in the case of the Talmud, the law comes first and the Gemara follows. A further complication is that there are actually two Talmuds, the Babylonian Talmud and the Jerusalem Talmud. The Jerusalem Talmud was written down first (in the fourth century). The Babylonian Talmud was written down in the fifth century and is four times longer. Published in English translation and in contemporary format, the Babylonian Talmud might occupy as many as four hundred volumes. Moreover, as if the matter were not difficult enough, there is a puzzling question as to which laws eventually expressed in the Mishnah were actually followed in judicial proceedings at the time of Jesus.

On the other hand, in dealing with the trial of Jesus the matter is not really as difficult as these comments make it sound. For one thing, we need only deal with Hebrew law in the matter of a crime punishable by death, a capital offense, and not with the many hundreds of other matters dealt with in the Talmud. For another, many able scholars have already sifted through this material and summarized the relevant principles admirably. We may consider them under several categories:

1. *The court in capital cases.* The only court authorized to sit in capital cases in Israel was the Great Sanhedrin or Grand Council. It numbered seventy-

one members and convened at Jerusalem. Its name was derived from the Greek word *sunedrion*, which denoted a legislative body gathered together to debate in a deliberate or sitting posture, but it did not date merely from the impingement of Greek culture upon the Hebrew people. Tradition placed the founding of the Great Sanhedrin in the wilderness under Moses, for Numbers 11:16–17 records God's instruction to Moses to gather together "seventy of Israel's elders" to perform judicial functions. These seventy plus Moses would have been seventy-one. Whatever its history, the Sanhedrin certainly existed and was vested with the highest authority in religious and other national matters in Israel (except for the authority of Rome) at the time of Jesus.

The Sanhedrin was organized traditionally into three chambers—a chamber of 23 priests, a chamber of 23 scribes, and a chamber of 23 elders—though often this was not strictly followed. To these, two presiding officers were added, making a total of seventy-one. The three chambers represented the religious, legal, and democratic elements of Jewish life. This threefold division is referred to by Jesus in Matthew 16:21, which says, "From that time Jesus began to explain to his disciples that he must go to Jerusalem and suffer many things at the hand of the elders, chief priests and teachers of the law, and that he must be killed and on the third day be raised" (cf. Mark 14:53).

2. *Qualifications of judges.* Since members of the Great Sanhedrin alone were authorized to judge capital cases, the qualifications for membership in the Sanhedrin are therefore synonomous with qualifications for such judges. Some of these qualifications were obvious. The member of the Sanhedrin was to be a Hebrew of the Hebrews, that is, a full-blooded Jew born of two Jewish parents. He was to be learned in law and to have had prior legal experience. He had to be a linguist, for trials of those who did not speak Hebrew would take place and interpreters were not allowed in Jewish courts. He must be humble and of good repute. Most important, he was not to sit if he had any personal interest in the outcome of the trial. Thus, even a well-qualified member of the Sanhedrin would have to step aside temporarily if he was related to the defendant or stood to benefit from a verdict.

3. *Witnesses.* The qualifications of witnesses and their role in legal proceedings is perhaps the most interesting feature of Jewish law, for unlike the previous matters mentioned, in this Jewish law took a course strikingly different from Roman law and those derivative legal systems that we know today in the Western world.

First, the role of witnesses was considerably more important than in the trials we know. In our trials a witness is called upon to testify merely to what he knows, and the total case is made up of the collected testimony of whatever number of witnesses is necessary to establish the defendant's guilt or innocence. This was not true in Israel. In Hebrew law the testimony of the witness had to be complete. That is, it had to pertain to the whole of the crime of which the defendant was accused. One authority says of this system, "Even where there appeared a legal number of duly qualified witnesses, the testimony was insufficient to convict, unless they agreed not only with regard to the prisoner's offense, but also with regard to the mode of committing it. Rabbinic law does not subject a person to capital, nor even to corporal punishment, unless all witnesses charge him with one and the same criminal act, their statements fully agreeing in the main circumstances, and declaring that they saw one another, while seeing him engaged in the crime."[3]

The second qualification for witnesses is suggested in the foregoing, namely, that there must be two or more witnesses to convict (Num. 35:30; Deut. 17:6–7; 19:15). This maxim is an obvious one in any legal system, but in Judaism it was carried to a heightened degree in that the witnesses had to agree on each particular or else the prisoner was to be discharged immediately.

Here certain formulas were used. First, there was an examination of the witnesses (separately, of course) in matters relating to the time and place of the alleged crime. It was called the Hakiroth and consisted of seven set questions: (1) Was it during a year of Jubilee? (2) Was it in an ordinary year? (3) In what month? (4) On what day of the month? (5) At what hour? (6) In what place? (7) Do you identify this person? The second set of questions, termed the Bedikoth, embraced all matters not brought out in the first series of questions and constituted what we might call a cross-examination. This was taken with the utmost seriousness and rigor. Thus, if one witness's testimony varied from another's testimony in even the slightest of these particulars, the testimony was immediately declared invalid. An example of this is the way in which Susanna was acquitted of the false charge of adultery in the apocryphal book of that name, when the elders who had conspired against her were unable to agree on the type of tree under which the act was supposed to have been committed. If it was clear that the testimony had been falsely borne, the witnesses were then punished with the same fate that would have fallen upon the defendant had he or she been convicted. This is what happened to the false judges who had accused Susanna.

A third characteristic of witnesses under Jewish law was that they themselves must be the accusers. This means that there were no prosecutors in Hebrew courts, no lawyers for the state. Instead, those who had seen the crime were, first, to arrange for the arrest of the criminal and, second, present the accusation before the nation's judges.

Finally, it is particularly noteworthy that they were also to have explicitly warned the defendant of the potential legal consequence of his or her crime immediately before the crime was committed. This provision of the law was termed "antecedent warning." It seems to have had three purposes: (1) to protect the potential offender against his own ignorance and rashness and thus deter the crime if possible, (2) to aid in establishing criminal intent at the later trial, and (3) to assist the judges in assessing the proper penalty. So far as is known, this maxim has no counterpart in any judicial system of any nation either ancient or modern and is, in fact, so stringent that it is impossible to see how the death penalty could have been secured against anyone in Israel except under the most extreme and unusual circumstances. And indeed, that was precisely its intent, for so highly did the Jews regard the life of an Israelite that anything that could possibly head off an execution was rigorously employed. The Mishnah says, "The Sanhedrin, which so often as once in seven years, condemns a man to death, is a slaughterhouse" (Makhoth).

4. *Mode of trial.* The mode of trial in capital cases is something to be considered more completely in our subsequent study of Jesus' actual trial. But we may note here a few basic requirements. First, it was to be conducted between the offering of the morning sacrifice and the offering of the evening sacrifice, that is, in daylight and with a reminder that all that was done was to be done within the clear view of God and by those who stood in a proper relationship to him. Second, the judges were never to seek to condemn the accused but were by contrast to take his side and seek every means for his acquittal. Third, the accused could not be convicted by a bare majority; rather, a majority of two (that is 37 of the total of 71 judges) was necessary. Fourth, by strange contrast, a unanimous vote for condemnation was also invalid; for this was judged to be an emotional decision based on mob action. Fifth, the initial guilty vote and the sentence could not be pronounced on the same day. Thus, assuming that the trial had led to condemnation, the assembly was then adjourned while each man went home to consider if something had not been overlooked that could bring acquittal. Only after a night had passed and the court was reassembled and a new vote taken, could the sentence be passed and the execution follow.

Even then delays were sought. Chandler writes: "If a majority of at least two votes were registered against him, he stood convicted a second time. But the humane and indulgent spirit of Hebrew law continued to operate and deferred immediate sentence. The judges continued to deliberate. No one thought of quitting the judgment hall on the second day of the trial. No one ate anything, no one drank anything on this second day. . . . All the merciful tendencies of Talmudic interpretation were invoked and pleaded by the judges, the defenders of the accused. It was hoped that a few hours' time would discover facts favorable to the doomed man. New arguments, it was thought, might be offered and new witnesses might be forthcoming in his behalf."[4]

Even as the death march left the great hall of the Sanhedrin, the judges would continue to seek for new arguments. If one occurred, the procession was immediately recalled and the new evidence considered.

Deceitful Hearts

The point of this is that Jesus was not condemned under a primitive, barbaric, or even inadequate judicial system, but under the best. He, the righteous One—the One who on one occasion demanded which of his enemies was able to convict him of sin and left them speechless—was condemned to death by the most merciful and careful system of judicial processes known to our race. If we ask, as we must, "But how could that happen? How could the very Son of God be condemned?" the answer is simply that the problem, then as now, is not so much in the system itself as it is in the hearts of those who interpret and implement the system and its codes. The human heart is "deceitful above all things and beyond cure," as Jeremiah once wrote (Jer. 17:9). It is this that circumvents the law or (as in this case) actually uses the law to destroy the innocent.

Can anything cure this sickness? Nothing human certainly! But what is impossible for men is possible for God, and it was to accomplish precisely this that Christ came. He, the innocent One, was condemned for those who were guilty. Moreover, he was condemned that they, who were sinners, might be made righteous. We are such men and women. In their shoes we too would condemn the innocent. But Jesus died for us. He redeemed us in order that we might be delivered from sin and its consequences and henceforth live for him.

227

The Charge against the Prisoner

John 18:19–24

Meanwhile, the high priest questioned Jesus about his disciples and his teaching.

"I have spoken openly to the world," Jesus replied. "I always taught in synagogues or at the temple, where all the Jews come together. I said nothing in secret. Why question me? Ask those who heard me. Surely they know what I said."

When Jesus said this, one of the officials nearby struck him in the face. "Is this the way you answer the high priest?" he demanded.

"If I said something wrong," Jesus replied, "testify as to what is wrong. But if I spoke the truth, why did you strike me?" Then Annas sent him, still bound, to Caiaphas the high priest.

If their conduct were not so repre-hensible and their character so base, one could almost feel sorry for the leaders of the Sanhedrin as they assembled on the night of April 5, A.D. 30, to convict Jesus of Nazareth of crimes worthy of death. For one thing, they were obviously unprepared for the trial. If they had planned to arrest and try Jesus at this Passover, they would have done it earlier in the week when they would have had the necessary time required for such a trial under Jewish law. But

1391

instead they acted suddenly and at a relatively late hour. That they did so was due only to the message brought to them from the upper room by Judas; but this, as we have seen, found them unprepared.

Again, there was the matter of witnesses. Where, in Jerusalem in the middle of the night, were they to find witnesses to Jesus' alleged crimes? The judges could not be witnesses themselves. Jewish law prohibited this. Witnesses would have to be rounded up quickly from those who might have heard Christ say some incriminating thing, but this would have to be done with the knowledge that the best witnesses to Christ's speech and actions were probably scattered all over the country in those many towns and villages where Jesus had conducted his itinerant ministry. Moreover, even when these witnesses were found, they would still have to provide evidence according to the strict demands of Jewish law.

Perhaps in the sudden excitement of the moment the elders, priests, and scribes thought that Jesus, being shocked and overcome by the arrest, might possibly prove his own accuser. But their hopes along this line were quickly disabused, as John, the only Gospel writer who records the first segment of the Jewish trial, the segment before Annas, indicates. Annas conducted what we would call a preliminary hearing. He asked Jesus about his disciples and his doctrine. Jesus refused to answer this series of questions, thereby indicating that he knew Jewish law—that accusations must come from witnesses and not from the accused—and that he therefore intended to be tried properly (if at all) by the laws of Israel.

John reports him as saying, "I have spoken openly to the world, I always taught in synagogues or at the temple, where all the Jews come together. I said nothing in secret. Why question me? Ask those who heard me. Surely they know what I said" (18:20–21). This was not an evasive answer, though it may sound so to us. It was merely a demand to be tried properly.

It becomes clear at this point that the court was partial. For although Jesus had spoken correctly and according to his right under law, one of the court officers immediately turned and struck him for what he considered to be Christ's impudence. "Is that any way to answer the high priest?" he demanded. Instead of replying angrily Jesus merely repeated his previous position. If there had been any wrongdoing, it should be brought forward legally and established by witnesses. If not, even the blow he had received was improper.

Christ before Caiaphas

We do not know much about Annas, who conducted this preliminary hearing. But I suspect, as I read the accounts, that he was just a bit more upright than his unscrupulous son-in-law, Caiaphas. At any rate, having met with an obstinate refusal by Jesus to testify against himself, and recognizing that Jesus both knew the law and would obviously not be terrified into a foolish mistake by silly court brutality, Annas assumed that there was nothing more that he could do and so sent the prisoner to Caiaphas. John indicates this in verse 24.

At this point, although John does not record it, the serious part of the trial began. It is this segment that the synoptic Gospels give us (Matt. 26:57–68; Mark 14:53–65; Luke 22:54). Caiaphas presided.

There were many illegalities in Christ's trial, as we are going to show in our next study, but underneath the many illegalities ran a strong undercurrent of legality in the sense of formal adherence to certain points of law. One of these was the calling of witnesses. Mark says that many "testified falsely against him," adding, "their statements did not agree" (Mark 14:56). Matthew declares, "The chief priests and the whole Sanhedrin were looking for false evidence against Jesus so that they could put him to death. But they did not find any though many false witnesses came forward" (Matt. 26:59–60). Apparently, there was a search for testimony that might have condemned Jesus, but the priests could not procure it. Clearly, valuable time was wasted in these fruitless accusations.

In Three Days

There were three categories of testimony according to the Mishnah: a vain testimony, a standing testimony, and an adequate testimony. The first of these, a vain testimony, referred to accusations that were obviously irrelevant or worthless and were therefore eliminated at once. This would be the kind of testimony which in our courts is "stricken from the record" and which the jury is instructed to "disregard." The second class of testimony, a standing testimony, is testimony with substance and relevance. It is permitted to stand until confirmed or disproved. The last category refers to evidence in which the witnesses agree together. This alone is "adequate" to convict.

According to this division, it is clear that the first accusations (the accusations of many "false witnesses") were vain testimony and hence were not even admitted provisionally. But at last two men came forward with a very explicit piece of evidence which at once put the trial on a new and promising footing. Matthew says that two accused him of saying, "I am able to destroy the temple of God and rebuild it in three days" (26:60–61). Mark says that they gave this false testimony: "We heard him say, 'I will destroy this man-made temple and in three days will build another, not made by man'" (14:57–58). This accusation was obviously of great importance.

In the first place, it was apparently true. At least, there was an element of truth in it. The fact that there were two witnesses who testified to substantially the same thing is one indication of its truthfulness. But in addition to this, in one of those unintentional and therefore particularly striking corroborations of one or more Gospels by another, John actually gives the incident in which these words were spoken. He says that on the occasion of the first cleansing of the temple, Jesus, when asked for a sign, replied, "Destroy this temple, and I will raise it again in three days," to which John then remarks, "But the temple he had spoken of was his body" (John 2:19, 21). We notice that although John does not refer to this incident in his own account of the trial, as we might expect him to do, he nevertheless gives us a piece of narration that fits the situation in the other Gospels perfectly. For this was spoken in the courtyard of the temple in Jerusalem and thus before the very types of people who were likely even at this late date still to be hanging around the temple in the service of the scribes and priests.

The second reason why this particular accusation was important in the eyes of the priests is that it was also of a serious nature. It was the kind of accusation which if substantiated would result in the penalty of death. It might be construed as sorcery, for no one could tear the temple down and then rebuild it in three days without what we might call "black magic." Again, it could also be construed as sacrilege, for the temple was the holiest place in Israel. The penalty for both of these crimes was death.

As I reflect on this charge, however, I cannot help but feel that Frank Morison is right when he suggests that there was probably more to the issue. For one thing, in spite of the various wordings used to report this saying of Jesus, the highly unlikely phrase "in three days" occurs in them all. Moreover, this is a phrase that Jesus had used on other occasions in which it was perfectly clear that he was prophesying that his resurrection would occur three days after he would be put to death. Are we to think that these statements were unknown to the high priests? Are we to think that a man as shrewd as Caiaphas was not aware of what Jesus' enigmatic saying implied? I cannot doubt that they understood precisely what he was claiming, even though they may not have had it in a form sufficiently clear to condemn him legally. They knew that he had said in effect, "You will kill me, but I will prove my divine nature and authority by rising from the dead on the third day."

After his own careful development of this position, Morison says this, "I see no escape from the logic of that conclusion. We may hold that He was mistaken; that He was held by some strange mental obsession which periodically flashed out in His public utterance. But that He said this singular and almost unbelievable thing seems to me to be very nearly beyond the possibility of doubt."[1]

That the high priests thus understood Jesus should be demonstrated alone by their later concern to have the tomb guarded. Matthew tells us that this occurred after the crucifixion. "The next day, the one after Preparation Day, the chief priests and the Pharisees went to Pilate. 'Sir,' they said, 'we remember that while he was still alive that deceiver said, "After three days I will rise again." So give the order for the tomb to be made secure until the third day. Otherwise, his disciples may come and steal the body and tell the people that he has been raised from the dead. This last deception will be worse than the first'" (27:62–64).

So the essence of the accusation of the two witnesses was that Jesus had claimed to be God and that he was able to prove this by his own resurrection. It was a damaging accusation, a fatal one. And yet—and here is a striking fact—this testimony was legally overthrown.

Oath of the Testimony

We are not told why the testimony was overthrown. It may have been on the basis of the slight variations we have already noted ("I am able to destroy the temple" in Matthew, "I will destroy this . . . temple" in Mark, "Destroy this temple" in John). It may have been that the witnesses could not agree on the exact place where the words were spoken or when they were spoken. After all, they had been spoken three years earlier. There may have been other inconsistencies. What we do know is that in spite of its essential accuracy the testimony did not stand. And what we can infer on that basis is the seething anger and frustration of the presiding officer, Caiaphas.

Caiaphas was in a difficult position. He had taken a chance on arresting Jesus at a very late hour in Passover week and was therefore committed to conducting a quick trial during the course of this one night after which he would present the judgment of the Jewish court for ratification by Pilate in the morning. If he failed, it would be a disaster. Word of the trial would leak to the population, and Christ's prestige and authority would undoubtedly rise to the same degree that the prestige and authority of the Jewish court would tumble. Besides all this, Caiaphas really did have a case. Jesus had claimed to be God's Son in a unique way, thus making himself liable to the penalty of death for blasphemy. Jesus was guilty when judged on the presuppositions of the Jewish court. Yet—this was the real frustration—Caiaphas could not procure a legal condemnation. He was close. He was right. Yet the situation was slipping from his grasp.

At this point Caiaphas revealed that shrewdness of character and determination for which the Romans had undoubtedly made him the chief Jewish ruler. What he did was illegal, but it was a stroke of genius politically. Seeing that the case was dissolving before his eyes, he abruptly turned to interrogate the prisoner himself, demanding of him on the basis of the most solemn form of oath known to Israel, the famous Oath of the Testimony, "I charge you under oath by the living God: Tell us if you are the Christ, the Son of God" (Matt. 26:63).

It was a brilliant stroke for several reasons. For one thing, the oath was brilliant. Although Jesus was not compelled to give evidence against himself, being a pious Jew he would not refuse such a solemn challenge and therefore replied, "It is as you say. But I say to you: In the future you will see the Son of Man sitting at the right hand of the Mighty One and coming on the clouds of heaven" (v. 64). The substance of the charge was also brilliant. If Caiaphas had merely asked Jesus if he was the Christ or Messiah, he could have answered yes without jeopardy, for it was not a capital offense to make such a claim. Time would itself prove that the claim was either false or true. Or again, if Caiaphas had merely asked Jesus if he was the Son of God, Jesus could also have answered yes without danger. For, as he indicated on another occasion, all Jews had a right to be called sons of God (cf. John 10:33–36). However, by combining the two, Caiaphas interpreted the one term by the other, thereby asking in effect, not whether Jesus was a mere human messiah or else a son of God in the general Jewish sense, but whether he was a divine Messiah. When Jesus answered yes to that accusation, he was immediately convicted of blasphemy and sentenced to death.

Savior or Judge?

The Jewish trial exposes the true nature of the hearts of men and women. We tend to look upon our own natures as being essentially good. But this is not the way God views them, and a trial like this brings out our nature. Jeremiah says of man, "The heart is deceitful above all things and beyond cure" (17:9). This does not mean, according to biblical teaching, that we are all as evil as we could possibly be. Given enough time and opportunity we could all be much worse. But it does mean that the roots of even the most heinous crimes ever perpetrated in the history of the world are within us and that, being placed in a situation similar to that of others who did these things, we have nothing within to hinder us from doing likewise.

The trial of Jesus also reminds us of his claims and promises. True, Jesus was condemned illegally. We will look at some of the illegalities in more detail in our next study. But still, the issues themselves were the right issues, and the claims for which he was convicted were real claims. He had made three of them. He had claimed to be God. He had claimed that he would rise from the dead after three days. He had claimed that he would return again in judgment. Are these claims true? The resurrection was true. If it was true, Jesus was also obviously who he claimed to be, for God would not have vindicated his claim to be the unique Son of God if this was blasphemy. Indeed, the final judgment is proved by the resurrection. For as Paul said to the Greeks in Athens, "[God] has set a day when he will judge the world with justice by the man he has appointed. He has given proof of this to all men by raising him from the dead" (Acts 17:31).

So the question is not whether the claims of Jesus of Nazareth are true but rather how we ourselves will respond to them and therefore also how we will greet him when he comes. Will we greet him as those who, like the rulers of his day, attempted to banish his presence from their lives? Or will we greet him as those for whom he died and who trust him as the only wise God and our Savior?

228

Illegalities of Christ's Trial

John 18:19–24

Meanwhile, the high priest questioned Jesus about his disciples and his teaching.

"I have spoken openly to the world," Jesus replied. "I always taught in synagogues or at the temple, where all the Jews come together. I said nothing in secret. Why question me? Ask those who heard me. Surely they know what I said."

When Jesus said this, one of the officials nearby struck him in the face. "Is this the way you answer the high priest?" he demanded.

"If I said something wrong," Jesus replied, "testify as to what is wrong. But if I spoke the truth, why did you strike me?" Then Annas sent him, still bound, to Caiaphas the high priest.

I n *Jesus: The Man Who Lives,* England's great scourge of the establishment, Malcolm Muggeridge, said some cynical things about justice. He called it "another of the world's great fantasies." He wrote, "To call for justice in this world (which Jesus never once did; nor did He at any point give any indication of expecting justice, or, in any of His reported utterances, so much as mention the word) amounts in practice to calling for something which by its nature cannot be just—viz, law. To cry out for justice in human terms is as foolish as calling for iced water in the middle of the Sahara. From men we can look for mercy and pity, and, thanks to Jesus, from God for forgiveness; but Justice—never! . . . If we were capable of rendering or receiving justice we should need no laws to codify injustice; no parliamentarians to make laws, lawyers to argue them, police to enforce them, revolutionaries to reject them with a view to remaking them in due course, prisons and executioners to dispose of all who refuse to abide by them. 'I only care for justice,' is the cry of every counterfeiter, whether of the hopes, the fears, or just the cash wherewith we live. By comparison with asking for justice, the moon is a trifle, eternity a throwaway line, and happiness on ready sale at every supermarket."[1]

I do not know whether these cynical but witty remarks are justified—though Muggeridge has certainly had more opportunity to observe the workings of this world's justice than I have. But I do know that his remarks are amply justified in the case of the trial of Jesus, for the laws governing his case were broken so many times that it is difficult to see how the trial could have been more illegally run or the laws of Israel more thoroughly flouted.

The Arrest

The first area of illegality in the trial of Jesus is from the period immediately preceding the trial, that is, the arrest. Here three separate errors were committed: (1) the arrest was by night, (2) the arrest was achieved through the agency of a traitor and informer, and (3) the arrest was without the necessary basis of a specific and formal accusation of wrongdoing later to be presented to the court. These related errors should have resulted in an immediate acquittal of Jesus, even if no further errors had been made. The situation was similar to the way in which a case should be thrown out of an American court if, for example, the arresting officer had neglected to inform the suspect of his rights, a confession was coerced, evidence was gathered by illegal entry or seizure, or some other illegal act was done.

The matter of *trial by night* is quite clear, for it was an established and inflexible rule that proceedings in capital cases could not be conducted at night. Moreover, this restriction did not apply merely to the trial itself but also to the events leading up to it, particularly the arrest. We know that the arrest of Jesus was after dark, for in addition to the time elements of that night, which we have already carefully considered, there is the simple fact that the arresting party arrived in the Garden of Gethsemane with "torches, lanterns and weapons" (John 18:3).

The law bearing upon *the role of Judas* in the arrest is derived from Leviticus 19:16, which says, "Do not go about spreading slander among your people. Do not do anything that endangers your neighbor's life. I am the LORD." This meant that a witness had to be of good character and, moreover, could not bear witness against a close companion, friend, or relative. He was, of course, also forbidden to take a bribe. He could not be an accessory or accomplice. Judas was all these. So it was illegal for him to have been used in the way he was used in the arrest.

There is a contrast here with modern law, for in most Western law the use of accomplice testimony is allowed, though viewed with distrust. In England, according to Chandler, conviction for a crime may rest on the uncorroborated testimony of an accomplice after the jury has been warned that such testimony is to be closely scrutinized. In the United States the testimony of an accomplice is also admissible, but it must be corroborated at some points by other testimony if it is to stand. From the point of view of securing a conviction it is clear that the use of accomplice testimony is of great value, as the frequent practice of granting immunity to force the testimony of an accomplice indicates. Yet, in spite of the obvious value of such testimony, Hebrew law forbade it. As Chandler says, "The arrest of Jesus was ordered upon the supposition that he was a criminal; this same supposition would have made Judas, who had aided, encouraged, and abetted Jesus in the propagation of his faith, an accomplice. If Judas was not an accomplice, Jesus was innocent, and his arrest was an outrage, and therefore illegal."[2]

The third illegal aspect of the arrest was the lack of a formal accusation on the basis of which the later trial was to be conducted. Legally, Judas should have made that accusation to the authorities in advance of the arrest and then have appeared in court to sustain it. This was not done. Instead, the opening part of the trial was a nearly unsuccessful attempt to find precisely this accusation.

The Private Examination

The second area of illegality in the arrest and trial of Jesus was the private appearance before Annas. From the nature of the arrest we can well understand why this examination took place. There was no real case against Jesus, and this was an attempt to secure one from the prisoner's own testimony. Still it was illegal, and that for several reasons: (1) it was by night, which we have already seen to be forbidden; (2) it was by a single judge, which was also forbidden (The Pirke Aboth, a part of the Mishnah, says, "Be not a sole judge, for there is no sole judge but One"); and (3) the accused was never to be compelled to testify. Jesus was entirely within his rights when he refused to answer the interrogations (cf. John 18:19–23).

The Charge

The Sanhedrin knew that Jesus was claiming to be the unique Son of God. If this was not true, as they believed it was not, it was a form of blasphemy punishable by death. On the other hand, whether the charge was true or not, the difficulties growing out of the late hour and the conflicting testimony of the witnesses provoked the court into demonstrably illegal proceedings.

One illegality was that there was _no formal indictment_ against Jesus. This should have been the basis for the arrest. It should have been presented at the start of the trial by the two or more witnesses needed to establish guilt in Jewish legal proceedings. But there was no charge. Instead, much valuable time was wasted trying to find one. The first accusations were thrown out of court as being irrelevant, unsupported, or silly. The more serious charge that Jesus had claimed to be able to destroy the temple and build it up again in three days was also likewise disallowed. It was only after these attempts had failed that a condemnation was secured on the basis of Jesus' direct reply to a question placed to him under oath by Caiaphas.

Moreover, it was _not Caiaphas's place_ to do this. In fact, anything of this nature was expressly forbidden. The high priest was not allowed to express an opinion or interrogate either the witnesses or the accused. Rather, he was to keep perfectly silent. When the balloting was taken, he was to vote last, for his prestige was considered to be so great that any opinion expressed by him might be imagined to sway the other members of the Sanhedrin. Caiaphas violated all these restrictions when he intruded into the proceedings by asking Jesus, "I charge you under oath by the living God: Tell us if you are the Christ, the Son of God" (Matt. 26:63).

The Trial Itself

The trial itself was illegal on numerous grounds: (1) it was conducted at night, (2) it was conducted on the day before a Jewish Sabbath, (3) it was completed in one twenty-four-hour period, (4) it secured a conviction on the basis of the defendant's own confession, and (5) it concluded with a unanimous and therefore invalid verdict.

The basic rule for _trial by daylight_ rather than at night is from the tractate "Sanhedrin" of the Mishnah: "Let a capital offense be tried during the day, but suspend it at night" (Sanhedrin 4, 1). This was not done, as we have seen. Although there had been no plans to arrest and try Jesus at this particular Passover, this had been altered by the report of Judas that Jesus would be in the Garden until a late hour and would be (so we may suppose the report of Judas to have been) in an arrestable mood. There would have been much excitement among Caiaphas, Annas, and the other priests at this news. But how could they arrest Jesus, conduct a trial, and have him condemned before the beginning of Passover on the day following? Legally it could not be done. There was not enough time. But they decided that they could squeeze the necessary procedures in if they held the trial that night and simply confirmed the verdict formally at dawn.

Chandler writes, "It will be seen that this determination to arrest and try Jesus at night, in violation of law, became the parent of nearly every legal outrage that was committed against him. The selection of the midnight hour for such a purpose resulted not merely in a technical infraction of law, but rendered it impossible to do justice either formally or substantially under rules of Hebrew criminal procedure."[3]

It was another requirement of the Jewish law, particularly in capital cases, that no court could lawfully meet on a Sabbath or other feast day, nor *on a day preceding a Sabbath or a feast day*. According to Jewish law, no work could be done on a Sabbath. Yet a trial was work, and so was the execution that would inevitably follow if the accused were found guilty. In Western law a trial may be suspended. But a trial could not be suspended in Jewish law, except for the one night that was to intervene between the first and second of the required hearings in a capital case. Thus, a trial was not to be started if it could not finish before a Sabbath. In Jesus' case this was not done. Moreover, not only was Jesus tried on a day preceding a Sabbath; he also was tried on a feast day, for the Feast of Unleavened Bread had begun by the time he was arrested.

The trial was also illegal because it was concluded *within the space of one day*. We remember that according to Jewish law there were actually to be two trials. On the first day, the entire case was to be heard and the first of two votes taken. If the accused was found innocent, the trial ended at that point. If he was found guilty, the trial was suspended for the night while the judges reconsidered the evidence and tried to find some way by which the accused (and now condemned) man might be exonerated. Only after a night like this did they return to the judgment hall and retry the case. Every attempt was made to secure acquittal. It was only in the afternoon of this second day that a second vote was taken after which, if the vote was still for condemnation, execution followed.

It is true, according to the Gospel records, that there were two trials and thus a semblance of legality—one at night and one in the early morning. But they were not on separate days; in fact, they were within a few hours of each other. And, equally important, the reason for the day's delay—to allow the judges to have time to retire to their homes for discussion, prayer, and meditation—was frustrated. Nor did they carefully retry the case in the short space of time allotted by the morning hours.

Fourth, the trial was illegal because it secured a condemnation of Jesus on the basis of *his own confession* produced under oath.

Fifth, the condemnation of Jesus was illegal because *the vote of the Sanhedrin was unanimous*, which by Hebrew law should have resulted in an acquittal. Mark tells us, "They *all* condemned him as worthy of death" (14:64). This, of course, is a strange part of Jewish law, particularly to those in the English-speaking world who are accustomed to precisely the opposite; that is, the requirement for a unanimous vote to convict under trial by jury. But this strangeness does not mean that it is foolish or even unwise. Chandler presents the reasoning as follows, "In the first place . . . there were no lawyers or advocates, in the modern sense, among the ancient Hebrews. The judges were his defenders. Now if the verdict was unanimous in favor of condemnation, it was evident that the prisoner had had no friend or defender in court. To the Jewish mind this was almost equivalent to mob violence. It argued conspiracy at least. The element of mercy, which was required to enter into every Hebrew verdict, was absent in such a case."[4] Whether wise or unwise, this was the law in Israel, and it was violated on this occasion.

No Defense

One last area of illegality may be considered. It is in some ways the most obvious of all: there was no defense of the prisoner. That there should be a defense is such an obvious part of legal proceedings—it is a right under most enlightened systems of justice—that its absence in this case immediately calls the entire activity of the court in question and renders it more the outworking of the hate of the authorities against Jesus than a true trial.

Were there none in Israel, none in Jerusalem even at this late hour on the eve of Passover, who could have testified to Christ's character? Were there none who could have borne witness to his ability to perform miracles in fulfillment of the Jewish prophecies concerning the coming Messiah? Were there no judges to plead the Old Testament and Christ's fulfillment of it in his defense? As we said, there is no need to think that the priests would necessarily have been persuaded by this evidence. But regardless of this, their refusal to consider a defense was nothing less than a failure to do their duty. It was a surrender to manipulation and mob rule.

What the priests, scribes, and elders did on the occasion of Christ's trial is not so different from what men and women are doing even today. Christ is proclaimed as the unique Son of God, but millions reject this while refusing to hear his defense. There is a defense. It is presented regularly in countless Christian churches, on radio and television programs, in books, and other forms of communication. But they will not hear it. They will not go to church. They will not read Christian literature. They turn the radio and television off or watch an entertainment channel. What shall we say of such people? Are they honest? No more than Caiaphas! Are they wise? Hardly! For if Jesus is who he claimed to be, the fact is a matter of life and death to all people.

Have you heard the prisoner? Have you considered his defense? If you have not, I challenge you to do so. The next chapter will help get you started. If you have, why wait? Come to him now. Believe on him. Jesus was either a megalomaniac, a deceiver, or the Son of God. If he is the Son of God, he should be your Savior.

229

In the Prisoner's Defense

John 18:19–24

Meanwhile, the high priest questioned Jesus about his disciples and his teaching.

"I have spoken openly to the world," Jesus replied. "I always taught in synagogues or at the temple, where all the Jews come together. I said nothing in secret. Why question me? Ask those who heard me. Surely they know what I said."

When Jesus said this, one of the officials nearby struck him in the face. "Is this the way you answer the high priest?" he demanded.

"If I said something wrong," Jesus replied, "testify as to what is wrong. But if I spoke the truth, why did you strike me?" Then Annas sent him, still bound, to Caiaphas the high priest.

The standards that human beings have developed for the administration of justice have varied widely in the long history of the race and from place to place, but there is one standard without which no sane person would attempt to establish justice at all. It is the right of the accused to a defense. We may imagine a situation in which a mother comes into the house to find that her child has used his brand new set of paints to decorate the living-room walls with murals. We may imagine further that she had specifically told him just the day before that he was to paint on paper only. She cannot imagine any possible words or circumstances that could in any way justify the disaster. She may be determined to punish him. But still she does not proceed to a spanking until she has at least heard her son's defense. "Why have you painted on the walls?" she might ask. "Why did you disregard my warning that you were only to paint on paper?"

So obvious is the right of the accused to a defense that this is observed both formally and informally in virtually every system of law and justice known. If the defense is omitted, the judicial proceedings are not actually a trial but are rather a mob action, no matter what legal formalities may or may not be included.

A Question Not Asked

So we ask, "What was the defense of Jesus of Nazareth in his trial by the Jewish Sanhedrin in Judea nearly two thousand years ago?" The answer is that there was no defense at all. This basic right of the accused was omitted.

We have to say at the beginning that if the proper requirements of Jewish law had been followed, as they should have been, there would have been no need for a defense for the simple reason that the trial would never have proceeded this far. His arrest was illegal, as we have already seen. It was by night, which Jewish law forbade. It was through the agency of an accomplice and informer. There had been no formal charge upon which the warrant for arrest had been issued. Each of these illegalities should have resulted in an immediate end to the prosecution and release of the prisoner if proper procedures had been followed. Again, the conduct of the trial was illegal. It was by night. Those who should have been Christ's defenders became his accusers. The high priest intervened, which he had no right to do. Most important of all, there was no proven charge against the prisoner. He was convicted in the end only because he voluntarily answered a question put to him by the high priest in which he claimed to be the divine Son of God and the Messiah.

But assuming that everything had been legal up to this point, which it was not—assuming that the arrest had been properly executed upon proper warrant, that charges had been properly filed and established under cross-examination, that these charges had related to Christ's claim to be God's unique Son, the Messiah—what was the next legal step under Hebrew law? Assuming that a *prima facie* case of guilt had been made, what should the judges have done next after hearing the case against him? The answer is that they should have begun to inquire diligently into all matters pertaining to the truth or falsity of his claim. In other words, the greatest illegality of the trial of Jesus was the question not asked. For having heard Christ's statement that he was indeed "the Christ, the Son of God," the high priest should then have asked, "What sign do you have then, that we may see and believe you?" The absence of this question reveals the trial to be a judicial murder rather than a fair inquiry into Christ's innocence or guilt.

We must not suppose that even if they had heard a defense the judges of Israel would have been obliged to accept it. They might have ruled it inadequate or false. But they are to blame, not because of the verdict itself (save that they reached it before the trial even began), but because they denied Jesus all defense whatsoever.

Messianic Prophecies

What defense could be given? One might imagine that the very nature of Christ's claims would put them beyond the realm either of falsification or verification. But this is not the case. We remember that the accusation was twofold: Jesus had falsely claimed to be (1) the Messiah and (2) the unique Son of God. These are religious claims made against the background of the revealed law of Israel, the Old Testament, which both Jesus and his accusers recognized to be determinative. Did Jesus' claims fit in with what the Old Testament taught? On that matter the judges of Israel were not only competent but were obligated to make judgment.

How should this trial have gone if this proper line of defense had been followed? Clearly, there should have been a defense of Christ's claim to be the Messiah, followed by a defense of his claim to be the unique Son of God. The first part might have gone like this.

1. According to the Jewish Scriptures, *the Messiah was to be born in Bethlehem, and Jesus was born in Bethlehem.* The relevant passage for this point is Micah 5:2, "But you, Bethlehem Ephrathah, though you are small among the clans of Judah, out of you will come for me one who will be ruler over Israel, whose origins are from old, from ancient times." The proof of Jesus' having been born in Bethlehem could have been established even at this very late hour by numerous witnesses, including that of no less a person than his mother, who was in Jerusalem at the time of the trial. It was also in the official Roman records; for the trip to Bethlehem (in connection with which Jesus was born) was made at the demand of Rome in order to provide a census, and Jesus would have been registered at that time.

Luke was to tell about it later, saying, "In those days Caesar Augustus issued a decree that a census should be taken of the entire Roman world. (This was the first census that took place while Quirinius was governor of Syria.) And everyone went to his own town to register. So Joseph also went up from the town of Nazareth in Galilee to Judea, to Bethlehem the town of David, because he belonged to the house and line of David. He went there to register with Mary, who was pledged to be married to him and was expecting a child. While they were there, the time came for the baby to be born, and she gave birth to her firstborn, a son. She wrapped him in cloths and placed him in a manger, because there was no room for them in the inn" (Luke 2:1–7).

2. *The Messiah was to be born of a virgin, and Jesus was so born.* Isaiah was the one who recorded this prophecy. He wrote, "The virgin will be with child and will give birth to a son, and will call him Immanuel" (Isa. 7:14). No doubt,

the reality of a virgin birth would be a hard point to convince these leaders of, just as it is hard to convince many of it today. But Mary, even if no one else, would have testified to it had she been called as a witness. Presumably she at least told Luke, for Luke (as also Matthew) included it in his account of the days preceding the birth in Bethlehem (Luke 1:26–30; cf. Matt. 1:24–25).

3. *The Messiah was to be born of the house of David, and Jesus was so born.* All Jews understood this to be the nature of the promise made to David himself, recorded in 2 Samuel 7, "When your days are over and you rest with your fathers, I will raise up your offspring to succeed you, who will come from your own body, and I will establish his kingdom. . . . Your house and your kingdom will endure forever before me; your throne will be established forever" (vv. 12, 16). However, lest there be any doubt that it was indeed the Messiah who was in view in this prophecy, the later prophets made it most clear. Jeremiah wrote, "The days are coming . . . when I will raise up to David a righteous Branch, a king who will reign wisely and do what is just and right in the land. In his days Judah will be saved and Israel will live in safety. This is the name by which he will be called: The LORD Our Righteousness" (Jer. 23:5–6). Similarly, Isaiah had written, "A shoot will come up from the stump of Jesse; from his roots a Branch will bear fruit. The Spirit of the LORD will rest on him—the Spirit of wisdom and of understanding, the Spirit of counsel and of power, the Spirit of knowledge and of the fear of the LORD" (11:1–2).

Was Jesus of the house of David? A short inquiry would quickly have shown that this was so. Moreover, a careful inquiry would have shown that not only was he descended from David through his natural mother, Mary, by whom he had a legal claim to the throne, he was also descended from David by virtue of his adoption by Joseph, who was in a different but royal line of descent. In other words, Jesus was descended from David by both his natural mother and adopted father, thereby exhausting both lines, so that, if he is not the Messiah, there is at any rate no other.[1] All this could have been investigated by the Sanhedrin just as it later was by Matthew, who gives Joseph's genealogy, and by Luke, who gives the genealogy of Mary.

4. *The appearance of the Messiah was to be preceded by a forerunner, who was to be like Elijah.* This was spoken of in the last two chapters of the Old Testament. "See, I will send my messenger, who will prepare the way before me. Then suddenly the Lord you are seeking will come to his temple; the messenger of the covenant, whom you desire, will come" (Mal. 3:1). "See, I will send you the prophet Elijah before that great and dreadful day of the LORD comes" (Mal. 4:5). John the Baptist was this forerunner. Jesus himself so identified him (Matt. 17:12–13), and this was John's own testimony when an official delegation was sent to him by members of this very Sanhedrin (John 1:19–24).

5. *The Messiah was to do many great works and miracles, and Jesus had performed the prophesied miracles and more.* Isaiah had written, "The Spirit of the Sovereign LORD is on me, because the LORD has anointed me to preach good news

to the poor. He has sent me to bind up the brokenhearted, to proclaim freedom for the captives and release from darkness for the prisoners, to proclaim the year of the LORD's favor" (61:1–2). "Then will the eyes of the blind be opened and the ears of the deaf unstopped. Then will the lame leap like a deer, and the mute tongue shout for joy" (35:5–6). Jesus referred to these texts himself in regard to his own ministry and clearly regarded them as sufficient proof of his messianic claims (Luke 4:16–21; Matt. 11:1–6).

We know that the leaders of the Sanhedrin accepted the factualness of these miracles; for, although they had attempted to deny them at first, it was actually their fear that all would follow Jesus because of his miracles that caused them to arrest, try, and condemn him (John 11:47–50).

6. *It was prophesied that the Messiah would make a public entry into Jerusalem riding on a donkey, and this Jesus had done.* No one could deny this fact. It had happened in full view of the residents of Jerusalem just three days before. The prophecy was in Zechariah: "Rejoice greatly, O Daughter of Zion! Shout, Daughter of Jerusalem! See your king comes to you, righteous and having salvation, gentle and riding on a donkey, on a colt, the foal of a donkey" (Zech. 9:9).

7. *It was prophesied that the Messiah should be betrayed by a close friend for thirty pieces of silver.* "Even my close friend, who I trusted, he who shared my bread, has lifted up his heel against me" (Ps. 41:9). "So they paid me thirty pieces of silver" (Zech. 11:12). In an ironical twist, the leaders of the Sanhedrin were in the process of fulfilling this prophecy themselves that very night by using Judas as an informant (Matt. 26:14–15; 27:3–8).

8. *The Messiah was to be a man of poverty and suffering in his first advent and was to be despised and rejected by the leaders of Israel, as Jesus was.* Isaiah had foretold it, "He grew up before him like a tender shoot, and like a root out of dry ground. He had no beauty or majesty to attract us to him, nothing in his appearance that we should desire him. He was despised and rejected by men, a man of sorrows, and familiar with suffering. Like one from whom men hide their faces he was despised, and we esteemed him not" (53:2–3). The Sanhedrin was fulfilling this prophecy even at the moment of the trial. They were despising Christ. They were rejecting him. Yet so far were they from any impartial presentation of the evidence or any desire to hear his defense that this strange irony escaped them.

God's Son

There was another part to the accusation on the basis of which Jesus was executed. This is his claim to be the unique Son of God. How could this be defended? We remember as we ask this question that as Jesus used the phrase he was not using the words "Son of God" in some general sense in which all men or at least all religious men might be supposed to share. He was using it in an exclusive way, meaning that he was of the same essence as God, whom he termed Father, and that he therefore possessed the same attributes and exercised the same authority as Jehovah. This was a most shocking claim to those steeped in the Judaism of Christ's day, of course. It ran against everything they believed concerning the unity and transcendence of God. It seemed blasphemous and abhorrent. But the claim, abhorrent as it may have been, was not so inconceivable that they could not have asked in all fairness whether anything of this nature could possibly be suggested by the Scriptures of Israel. Again, this does not mean that they would necessarily have accepted Christ's claims, even if the Old Testament suggested their possibility. But it does mean that he should not have been condemned out of hand without the benefit of this defense and inquiry.

Walter Chandler, from whom I have borrowed much of this material, writes, "What the judges of the Sanhedrin should have done in examining the merits of the defense of Jesus was: 1) to consider whether, in the light of Hebrew scripture and tradition, a god of flesh and bone, representing the second person of a Duality or a Trinity of gods, was possible; 2) to weigh thoroughly the claims of Jesus, in the light of testimony properly adduced at the trial, that he was this second person of a Duality or Trinity of gods."[2]

In defense of this claim we may make the following three points:

1. *There are references in the Old Testament to precisely the kind of unique Son of God that Jesus claimed to be.* A clear reference is Isaiah 9:6, where one who was to be born into the human family is called "The Mighty God." "For to us a child is born, to us a son is given, and the government will be on his shoulders. And he will be called Wonderful, Counselor, Mighty God, Everlasting Father, Prince of Peace." Similarly, Psalm 2, which is to be understood as a messianic prophecy, declares of the coming Messiah, "He said to me, 'You are my Son; today I have become your Father'" (v. 7). What could possibly be clearer than the statement of this psalm that the Messiah was to be a person uniquely begotten of God the Father? What could more clearly suggest a human being who was at the same time God than Isaiah's prophecy that the coming Messiah was to be called "The Mighty God, The Everlasting Father"? We may readily admit that this is hard to understand. We may not see how an individual can be both God and man at the same time. But the point is not whether or not we understand it but whether the Scriptures, which the Jewish leaders and Christ both fully accepted, teach it. If they do, then the claim of Jesus to be God's unique Son cannot be rejected outright.

2. *The Old Testament also speaks of an incarnation,* that is, God becoming flesh. This is what Isaiah speaks of in the verse cited earlier: "The virgin will be with child and will give birth to a son, and will call him Immanuel" (7:14). Immanuel means "God with us." So the prophecy is that God should become man by means of a virgin birth. Again, we may have great difficulty in understanding this, even in believing it. But the point is that, whether we believe it or not, this is at least what the Old Testament teaches and is what Jesus claimed.

3. *There are significant passages in the Old Testament in which Jehovah (or the Son of Jehovah) is portrayed as having appeared on earth among men.* One exam-

ple is the appearance of an individual called "the angel of the LORD" to Hagar. The passage reads, "The angel added, 'I will so increase your descendents that they will be too munerous to count.' The angel of the LORD also said to her, 'You are now with child and you will have a son. You shall name him Ishmael, for the LORD has heard your misery.' . . . She gave this name to the LORD who spoke to her: 'You are the God who sees me,' for she said, 'I have now seen the one who sees me'" (Gen. 16:10–11, 13). We should not infer that the phrase "angel of the LORD" in the Old Testament always refers to God himself, but that is certainly the meaning here. For the one who appeared to Hagar as an angel spoke as God, and Hagar addressed him in this way, saying, "I have now seen the one who sees me"

Again, there are appearances of a similar figure or figures to Abraham, the father of the Jewish nation. On one occasion, we are told, "The LORD appeared to Abraham near the great trees of Mamre while he was sitting at the entrance to his tent in the heat of the day. Abraham looked up and saw three men standing nearby. When he saw them, he hurried from the entrance of his tent to meet them and bowed low to the ground. He said, 'If I have found favor in your eyes, my lord . . .'" (Gen. 18:1–3). In the account that follows, these figures sometimes appear as three, sometimes as one; always they speak as if they were themselves God: "Then the LORD said to Abraham, 'Why did Sarah laugh?'" (v. 13), "Then the LORD said, 'Shall I hide from Abraham what I am about to do?'" (v. 17), "The LORD said, 'If I find fifty righteous people in the city of Sodom, I will spare the whole place for their sake'" (v. 26). The language of this story indicates that Abraham firmly believed that Jehovah had appeared to him and become a guest in his tent. The question may be asked, as Chandler does, "If Abraham could not recognize Jehovah, who could or can?"[3]

The point of these passages is that the Old Testament contains references to the appearances of God on earth in human form, that the appearance of the Second Person of the Godhead was prophesied, and that Jesus amply met every reasonable test that might be raised to determine whether or not he was this one. This defense might not have convinced the Jewish rulers of Christ's innocence, even if it had been presented. But it was a reasonable and adequate defense, reasonable in that it was based on the clear teaching of the Old Testament Scriptures and adequate in that it was sufficient to create "reasonable doubt" of Christ's guilt, if not, in fact, ample evidence that he was indeed who he declared himself to be.

Who Is He?

If it is true that the Sanhedrin was guilty for its refusal to hear the defense of Jesus, how much more guilty are people who refuse to consider his claims and defense today. More guilty? Yes, more guilty even than the Sanhedrin. For although it is true that these men willfully refused to consider even a shred of evidence in Jesus' defense, they nevertheless did not have before them that greatest of all evidences for his divinity that we have today: his miraculous resurrection from the dead. Nor did they have available the full teaching of the New Testament and the works of the many doctors and theologians of the Christian church who have, since their time, clearly presented who Jesus is, why he came to die, the meaning of his resurrection, and the need for the response of faith that people are called on to make to him.

That evidence is available to you, whoever you may be. If you reject it or, worse yet, refuse even to consider it, your guilt is greater than the guilt of the Jewish Sanhedrin. But if, on the other hand, you will consider it and accept it, it is sufficient by the power of the Holy Spirit to lead you to saving faith in Jesus. Who is Jesus? He is the Messiah, the Son of God. He is your Savior.

230

Before the Cock Crows

John 18:15–18, 25–27

Simon Peter and another disciple were following Jesus. Because this disciple was known to the high priest, he went with Jesus into the high priest's courtyard, but Peter had to wait outside at the door. The other disciple, who was known to the high priest, came back, spoke to the girl on duty there and brought Peter in.

"You are not one of his disciples, are you?" the girl at the door asked Peter.

He replied, "I am not."

It was cold, and the servants and officials stood around a fire they had made to keep warm. Peter also was standing with them, warming himself. . . .

As Simon Peter stood warming himself, he was asked, "You are not one of his disciples, are you?"

He denied it, saying, "I am not."

One of the high priest's servants, a relative of the man whose ear Peter had cut off, challenged him, "Didn't I see you with him in the olive grove?" Again Peter denied it, and at that moment a rooster began to crow.

I seldom come to this story of the denial of the Lord Jesus Christ by Peter that I do not think of two passages from other books in the Bible. They are unrelated technically. Yet they are related,

1411

for they indicate in advance the two most important lessons to be learned from Peter's temptation. One is from the first psalm. It is the verse that describes the folly of the man who "walks" in the counsel of the ungodly and "stands" in the way of sinners and "sits" in the seat of the mockers (v. 1). This describes Peter. The psalm describes him as well when it goes on to add that the man who lives like this is "like the chaff which the wind blows away" (v. 4). Peter, like chaff, was certainly blown about by the temptation that came to him while he warmed himself at the fire in the high priest's house.

It was a bad place to be, and Peter certainly paid the price of being there. As Spurgeon writes, "Peter was on dangerous ground. When his Master was being buffeted, he was trying to make himself comfortable. We read of the high priest's servants that they warmed themselves, and Peter stood with them, and warmed himself. He stood with them, and they were rough servants of ill masters. He was in bad company, and he was a man who could not afford to be in bad company; for he was so impulsive, and so easily provoked to rash actions."[1]

On the other hand, whenever I think of Peter's denial, I also think of that prophecy of Christ's concerning Peter that is recorded in Luke's Gospel. There Jesus says, "Simon, Simon, Satan has asked to sift you as wheat. But I have prayed for you, Simon, that your faith may not fail. And when you have turned back, strengthen your brothers" (22:31–32). This teaches us that although Peter, like the ungodly man of Psalm 1, would be blown about like chaff at threshing time, nevertheless Jesus had prayed for Peter with the result that Peter would come forth stronger from the experience. That is, the chaff in Peter would be blown away. But the Peter whom God had re-created by means of the new birth would be strengthened.

We should be strengthened too. We shall be if we can learn from Peter's mistakes. Do you think that you do not need to learn? If that is the case, then you of all people need to, for John has undoubtedly intertwined the story of Peter's fall with the story of the Jewish and Roman trials to show that even the followers of Christ are not free from guilt in their relationships to him. True, they do not hate him, like Caiaphas. They are not indifferent to him, like Pilate. Yet they deny him many times, as Peter did.

Why is this? No doubt because we are too fond of the world and too enamored of its company. Matthew Henry once wrote, "Those that warm themselves with evil doers grow cold towards good people and good things, and those that are fond of the devil's fire-side are in danger of the devil's fire."[2]

In Defense of Peter

In order to understand fully the importance of Peter's fall for ourselves, we need to see that it was *Peter,* the leader of the disciples, and not another who denied Jesus. If this had been Nicodemus, we should not be surprised. Nicodemus is the one who came to Jesus by night, no doubt for fear of what others might think; there is no indication in Scripture that Nicodemus ever entirely came out for him. Likewise, we would not have been surpised had this been the rich young ruler. He loved riches more than he loved Jesus and thus "went away sorrowful." We might also have expected a denial from those who watched Jesus at a distance, as many did, who never confessed him at all. A denial from any of these would have been no surprise at all. Yet this was not Nicodemus or the rich young ruler or these others. This was Peter—the bold, the courageous, the one who had told Jesus, "Even if all fall away on account of you, I never will" (Matt. 26:33).

The point is that if Peter fell, then anyone can fall—the strongest as well as the weakest. In fact, it may even be the strongest who are in the greatest danger.

But let us not just talk about this generally. Let us talk about specifics in the case of Peter. What can be said in Peter's defense? One thing that can be said about Peter is that *he at least followed Jesus* when all others (except possibly John) had abandoned him. True, in the Garden at the moment of the arrest they had all scattered into the enveloping darkness. But most of them undoubtedly continued their flight on up the Mount of Olives and down the other side to Bethany, where they had been staying on each of the previous nights and where they imagined themselves to be safe. Peter, on the other hand, quickly stopped his flight and then, joining forces with the unnamed disciple (v. 15), followed the arresting party back to Jerusalem and eventually made his way into the high priest's house. This was not the decision of a coward. As Barclay says, "The tremendous thing about Peter was that his failure was a failure that could only have happened to a man of superlative courage. True, Peter failed; but he failed in a situation which none of the other disciples even dared to face. He failed, not because he was a coward, but because he was a brave man."[3]

A second commendable characteristic follows from this one, namely, that *Peter loved Jesus.* It was for this reason alone that he followed him. I am sure that when we think of those who loved Jesus and who were in Jerusalem at this time, we think preeminently of Mary Magdalene who for love's sake alone lingered around the garden tomb after the resurrection to try to find and care for the Lord's body. We are right to think of her, for Mary truly did love him. She loved him even when her faith and hope in him had failed. But no less a motivation drew Peter to Jerusalem when all common sense dictated the safety of a nocturnal flight to Bethany. Why else did Peter follow the arresting party? Why else did he seek entry into the high priest's home? Because he loved Jesus! He wanted to know what would become of him. Thus, he failed in a situation into which he would not even have come had he not loved Jesus much.

Third, *Peter had tried to defend Jesus.* In the Garden he had drawn a sword and attacked the head of the arresting column, a man named Malchus, and had cut off his ear. This was an act of the flesh, of course. It was contrary to the spirit and will of Christ and was, in fact, rebuked by him. But it was a strong act nevertheless, done out of a passionate (though misguided) concern for his master.

Finally, to go back even farther into the history of Peter's experience, we recall that on an earlier occasion *it was Peter who confessed Jesus* as "the Christ, the Son of the living God," when the other disciples were silent (Matt. 16:16; cf. John 6:68). This is no miserable specimen chosen from among the ranks of Christ's worst followers. This is the best. Yet it is precisely this one who falls, not only dreadfully but speedily and with such slight provocation.

It was a maid who asked the first question. Moreover, she even begins her remarks with a negative (this is quite apparent in the Greek), as if to say, "Surely you are not one of his disciples, are you?" It was not a formal accusation. It was not even a very strenuous challenge. Yet Peter, overcome by the uncertainty and terror of the moment, replies, "I am not" (v. 17). From this point on, having denied his Lord once, he finds it easy to do so again, once to an unspecified group (v. 25) and a third time to the kinsman of the man whose ear he had cut off (vv. 26–27).

Steps of His Fall

Why did Peter fall? If Peter was as strong as we say and yet fell, it is important to know the steps of his fall so that we may avoid them. There are several.[4]

First, Peter was *overconfident*. Earlier Jesus had warned his disciples that they were going to abandon him. But Peter said in effect, "Lord, I do not know about these others; as I look around at these other disciples, I sense that they are not the kind of people that I, Peter, would have chosen. It may very well be that they will deny you—but not I, not Peter." Jesus reiterated his warning. But Peter replied, "Even if I have to die with you, I will never disown you" (Mark 14:31). We can hardly miss the conclusion that if we indulge ourselves in such overconfidence, if we think that we are invulnerable because we are strong, have certain obvious talents, are wise or can analyze the tendencies and dangers of our culture, then we are well on our way to falling. Jesus has said, "Apart from me you can do nothing" (John 15:5). Nothing means *nothing!* Whenever we forget that, we are in trouble.

Second, Peter *failed to pray*. The Lord did not fail to pray. This seems a strange reversal. If we were to pick someone who, in our opinion, did not need to pray, it would obviously be the Lord. If we were to pick someone who needed prayer, it would be Peter. Yet Peter is sleeping in the Garden while the Lord is pouring out his soul before his heavenly Father. Peter had been warned. He had been admonished to watch and pray. Unfortunately, the church and many Christians are asleep today with no less warning. Paul said, "Pray continually" (1 Thess. 5:17). Yet it is often the case that we do not pray because we do not think it necessary.

Third, Peter *"followed at a distance"* (Luke 22:54). A moment ago we pointed out that Peter had at least followed when the others had apparently fled.

That is true. But although Peter followed, he followed at a great distance; and that was not entirely commendable.

It is true of many in our time, as can be easily observed. Many legitimately, truly, honestly do follow Jesus. But they follow at a distance, because they do not want to become too "fanatical" or "lose touch" with the world that surrounds them. Moreover, they think they are safe at a distance, though they are actually in greater danger. When Jesus calls a person to follow him, he calls him to follow in his footsteps, which means "right behind me." But these hold back, thinking that the closer they are to Jesus the greater their danger will be. Actually, although their exposure is greater, the danger is less. For Christ is the victor. He has guaranteed victory. The place to be really safe, though in the midst of battle, is next to him.

"With Them . . . with Him"

The fourth step in Peter's fall is the step emphasized by John. It is found in the contrast between a phrase in verse 18 and a phrase in verse 26. In verse 18, it says of Peter as he stood around the fire, "Peter also was standing *with them*." Then in verse 26, after several had begun to challenge him, the kinsman of the man whose ear Peter had cut off asked, "Didn't I see you *with him?*" Peter, who had been with him (that is, with Jesus), is now in the courtyard of the high priest with those who are Christ's enemies.

Is this true of us, that we are more with those of the culture in which we live than with Jesus? This does not mean that we are to go out of this world. We are not called to detach ourselves to some kind of spiritual ghetto. We are to be in the world. But—this is the point—we are not to be of it. We are to be with Christ in the midst of the culture, not with them whose culture it is.

I would like to ask this question of you, the question that was asked of Peter: "Didn't I see you with him?" I would like to ask it forcefully. Have you been with Jesus? Have you been with him in fellowship? Have you been with him in Bible study? Have you been with him in prayer? If your answer is yes, as I trust it will be, I then want to follow up that question in this way. First, if you have been with him, then *you have been seen with him.* You may think that you have not been seen. You may think that you are a secret believer. You may think that your family is so non-Christian that you cannot possibly let your family know what has happened, so you do not confess Christ openly. But if you are really Christ's, the difference will be seen in you so clearly that whether you want to or not you will have been observed to have been with Jesus. Your immediate family will notice it right away. Those with whom you work will notice it shortly. If you come to fellowship with other Christians in a good church, as you should, you will be noticed by many additional people as well.

Next I want to ask: If you really have been with him and have been seen with him, is it not true that *certain things will be expected of you* because you have been with him? Again, you may not want those things to be expected of you. You may have noticed that there is even a sense in which those who are unsaved demand too much of us who profess Christ. They demand something approaching perfection, and we are not perfect. If we get the notion that we are perfect, we are in trouble indeed. Yet there is a sense in which the world is right to expect certain things, and our Christian brothers and sisters are right to expect them also.

For example, they should expect certain things in regard to our profession. We say we are Christ's, that he is our Savior and Lord. We are seen in his company. Therefore, we should profess what he professes. If we do not profess that, if we do not receive his teaching personally, then he is not our Lord, no matter what we may say. If we follow him, his doctrine should be our doctrine.

Again, if we follow Jesus, his priorities should be our priorities, his values should be our values. This means that we are not at liberty to borrow our culture from the world. We are not at liberty to assume the world's values and adopt the world's theology. Our theology and values must be his.

Again, the marks of the church that Jesus talked about in the seventeenth chapter of John, just one chapter before this, should characterize us as well. We should be filled with joy. We should be characterized by holiness. We must stand with him in his truth. We should be engaged in the mission to which he commissions us. There should be an observable unity among Christian people. All we do should be characterized by love. If we have been with Christ, if (like Peter) we have been associated with him in his ministry, then the world has a right to expect certain patterns of behavior and character from us.

Commitment and Cleansing

If you have been with Christ, there is a call in this text to commitment. So much of our discipleship today is halfhearted. We say we will follow Jesus, but we follow afar off, as Peter did. This is not the kind of discipleship that Jesus lays before us.

Spurgeon once had an opportunity to talk to a girl who was halfhearted. She was trying to live in the world and at the same time follow Christ. He said to her, "There are three things you can do, and those three things I will set before you by an illustration. When you get outside the Tabernacle, there will be a tramcar. Now, go up to the car, and put one foot on the car, and keep the other foot on the ground, and if you do not come down with a smash I am very much mistaken. Yet many people try to keep in with the world and keep in with Christ, and they will never do it; but will make a terrible fall of it before long. Now, the second thing that you can do, is that you can keep standing in the world in the mud, and not get into the car at all. You can stop there, and let the tramcar go by: that is all fair and straight. If you want to live in the world, and be of the world, well, live in the world, and take what pleasure it can give you, and reap the fruit of it at last. But there is a third thing you can do, namely, get right off the road into the car, and let the car take you right away where it is going. Now, it is this third thing that I commend to you. Get right into Christ, and let the Lord Jesus, by the power of his Holy Spirit, carry you right away from the unclean place where you now stand, bearing you in safety along the tramlines of holiness till he brings you to the terminus of glory at his own right hand."[5]

You may be saying, as some do, "I understand clearly what you are teaching. I know this is the kind of discipleship Christ calls for. But in my case it is too late. I am like Peter. I know I should have followed Christ wholeheartedly. I know I should have been near to him. But I have followed at a distance. I have denied him. I have compromised my faith hundreds of times and more. I can never be Christ's disciple."

If you are thinking along these lines, let me assure you that it is not too late. With God it is never too late. It is true that sin brings consequences and that some sins bring consequences so terrible that they remain with us for life. But in this matter of discipleship God always begins with you where you are right now. You may have denied Jesus once. You may have denied him a hundred times. It makes no difference. Jesus comes to you now with the call of discipleship. He says, "Follow me now." Then he sets a new way before you.

We have an illustration of this in the case of Peter. On the one hand, we have Peter described in the eighteenth chapter of John, warming himself by the fire of Christ's enemies. He is cold, lonely, left out. He gets such warmth as he can from those who are determined to do away with his Master. It is a sad picture. Yet a little later, in the twenty-first chapter, there is another Peter and another fire. This fire is kindled by the Lord, the fire on which he prepared breakfast for the disciples. And the same Lord whom Peter had denied in chapter 18 appears in chapter 21 to recommission him to service.

May I carry this concept a step further? This fire reminds us of that described by Isaiah in Isaiah 6, after he had seen the Lord in his glory. He had seen Christ in his holiness, and he had been impressed with his own sin. He said, "I am a man of unclean lips, and I live among a people of unclean lips" (v. 5). But what happened? God sent an angel with a coal from off this altar to purge away the sin, and after that, when Isaiah heard the question, "Whom shall I send? And who will go for us?"—Isaiah, the man who was conscious of his sin, said, "Here am I. Send me" (v. 8). Peter heard that question and responded in the same way, for when Jesus came to him after his resurrection and asked, "Simon, son of John, do you truly love me more than these?" Peter answered, "Yes, Lord, you know that I love you" (John 21:15). The Lord said, "Feed my lambs."

So it has been with all who have ever served the Lord Jesus Christ faithfully. Those who serve—who are really used in God's service, who are a blessing to other people, who take the gospel of eternal life to those who need to hear it, who keep on in the midst of difficulty—these are not those who have never denied Christ. They have! They have denied him many times and in many ways. But they have found the grace of the Lord Jesus Christ even in the midst of their denials and have been purged from their sin. Then with a sense of their own weakness, but an even greater awareness of Christ's strength, they have gone on to live for him.

231

The Roman Trial

John 18:28–32

Then the Jews led Jesus from Caiaphas to the palace of the Roman governor. By now it was early morning, and to avoid ceremonial uncleanness the Jews did not enter the palace; they wanted to be able to eat the Passover. So Pilate came out to them and asked, "What charges are you bringing against this man?"

"If he were not a criminal," they replied, "we would not have handed him over to you."

Pilate said, "Take him yourselves and judge him by your own law."

"But we have no right to execute anyone," the Jews objected. This happened so that the words Jesus had spoken indicating the kind of death he was going to die would be fulfilled.

Τhe trial of Jesus of Nazareth, as a result of which he was crucified, is in reality two separate trials, one Jewish and one Roman. The trials are separate as far as the jurisdictions, charges, and judges are concerned. The only common elements are the accusers and the accused. The reason for the two trials is that the Jewish court had lost the power to administer the death penalty by the first Christian century; thus, since the leaders of Israel were determined to have Christ executed, they were forced to secure a Roman verdict along with their own.

This makes for a unique and fascinating situation, for it means that in this one instance a man was tried, on the one hand, by a court of heaven seeking to apply the revealed law of God and, on the other hand, by a court of man seeking to apply what is generally thought to be the most highly developed form of law we know.

Jewish law was probably the most humane system of law ever devised. So great was Jewish respect for human life, that it was practically impossible to execute a person under the jurisdiction of a Hebrew court. Roman law was excellent as measured by the comprehensiveness of its coverage, systematization of formal statutes, elaboration of court procedures, and the affixing of penalties. It has been said of the ancient world that Judea gave religion, Greece gave letters, and Rome gave law. The laws of Rome have been passed on to the Western world as the basis of its judicial systems. The Germans were never defeated by the legions of Rome and, in fact, were eventually the people who overthrew the declining Roman Empire. Yet they unquestioningly adopted the Roman laws and edicts. Even today the *Corpus Juris Civilis* of Justinian is carefully studied in the great universities of the world.

Walter Chandler summarizes the issue thus: "Jesus was arraigned in one day, in one city, before the sovereign courts of the universe; before the Sanhedrin, the supreme tribunal of a divinely commissioned race; before the court of the Roman Empire that determined the legal and political rights of men throughout the known world. The Nazarene stood charged with blasphemy and with treason against the enthroned monarchs represented by these courts; blasphemy against Jehovah who, from the lightning-lit summit of Sinai, proclaimed his laws to mankind; treason against Caesar, enthroned and uttering his will to the world amidst the pomp and splendor of Rome. History records no other instance of a trial conducted before the courts of both Heaven and earth; the court of God and the court of man; under the law of Israel and the law of Rome; before Caiaphas and Pilate, as the representatives of these courts and administrators of these laws."[1]

Considering the nature of Roman law, with its careful attention to procedure, we might think that the trial before Pilate would be much easier to understand than the trial before the Jewish Sanhedrin. Yet this is not the case. On the contrary, although the Hebrew trial has its puzzling elements (we might, for example, ask how Jesus could possibly be rejected by the leaders of his own people, those who should have known who he was on the basis of the Old Testament prophecies), the rejection is nevertheless understandable. He was rejected because he was hated, and he was hated because he had revealed the leaders' sin. None of this makes sense where the trial before Pilate is concerned. Pilate did not hate Jesus. If anything, he seems to have respected him. He even acquitted him, pronouncing him innocent on three separate occasions. Yet he eventually turned Jesus over to be crucified.

Frank Morison has rightly said, "We do not get rid of the mystery of Christ when we bring Him to the Roman bar; we increase it tenfold."[2]

The Roman Procurator

Perhaps the greatest mystery in the case of the Roman trial is the marked contrast between what we know of Pilate's character (as revealed in the secular sources) and his conduct at the trial of Jesus (as revealed in the Gospel narratives).

Pilate was not a noble character. In fact, if it were not for his influential connections through marriage, he would never have come even to the relatively insignificant post he held as procurator of Judea. He came from Spain, being a native of Seville. He had joined the legions of Germanicus in the *Pilate history* wars on the Rhine. After peace had been secured, he went to Rome to make his fortune. There he met and married Claudia Proculla, the youngest daughter of Julia who was the daughter of the emperor Augustus. From the perspective of Pilate's future this was a wise move. Claudia had connections with the highest levels of Roman government. But morally it was a disgrace; for Julia, who thereby became Pilate's mother-in-law, was a woman of such depraved and coarse habits that even in decadent Rome she was notorious. Augustus, her father, avoided her presence and eventually banished her. It is reported that afterward, whenever someone would mention the name of his daughter to him, Augustus would exclaim, "Would I were wifeless or had childless died!" Unlike Pilate, a man of nobler instincts would not have married into such a family.

Nevertheless, through his new connections Pilate applied for and was awarded the procuratorship of Judea, which post he assumed in A.D. 26. He was the sixth procurator. Those before him were: Sabinus, Caponius, Ambivus, Rufus, and Gratus.

These earlier rulers had exercised great care in their respect for the religious prejudices of the Jews and had governed the people wisely. In particular, they had carefully avoided exhibiting any emblems, flags, or standards that, because they bore the images of the emperor, were offensive to the Jewish population. Even Vitellius, the legate of Syria, when he was marching against the Arabian king Aretas, ordered his troups to march around Jewish territory rather than carry their battle standards through it. Yet Pilate, in obstinate folly and in defiance of the established policy of the earlier procurators, provoked a confrontation on this and other matters. *w/ the Jews.*

Three incidents stand out. First, when Pilate arrived in Judea, he sent soldiers to Jerusalem by night carrying ensigns blazoned with the images of Tiberius. That he did this by night indicates his awareness that there might be trouble, but that he did it at all indicates his insensitivity to the feelings of those whose land he was to govern. Nor did subsequent developments prove him wiser. When their city was thus defiled, great numbers of the Jews of Jerusalem flocked down to Caesarea, where Pilate was staying, to demand that the standards be removed. Pilate refused, and the stalemate went on for five days. At last the procurator grew angry, summoned the people to the stadium, surrounded them with soldiers and gave notice that they would be killed if they did not immediately and quietly disperse. To his surprise they threw themselves to the ground, bared their necks, and declared that they would rather die than see their holy city contaminated. When he saw that he could get his way only by wholesale slaughter Pilate reluctantly backed off and had the ensigns lowered.

Pilate's actions were not typical of Roman administrators. In fact, thanks to Josephus, we have a nearly parallel story with an entirely different result. It involved a Roman officer named Petronius. Petronius had a much greater incentive to enforce his will than Pilate had to enforce his, for he had been specifically commanded by the emperor to place the imperial image in the Jewish temple. But Petronius sensed the problem, tried negotiations, and when those failed bravely reported his decision not to enforce the decree and the reasons for his decision to Caius. Petronius was an example of Roman courage and diplomacy at their best. Pilate's conduct reveals the opposite characteristics.

A second incident reveals the same flaws in Pilate's character. He had determined to build an aqueduct to bring water from the Pools of Solomon into Jerusalem. In itself this was commendable and would have been favored by the citizens of the city. But Pilate startled and enraged them by the foolish act of raiding the sacred "Corban" treasury in order to fund the work. The Jews considered this money set aside to God to be used only in his work. To plunder it was sacrilege. Yet Pilate went ahead. Later, when he learned that the people would be sending citizens to beg for the restoration of the temple monies, he sent soldiers into the crowd disguised as common people who, on a prearranged signal, drew hidden clubs and daggers and attacked the demonstrators. In this episode Pilate had his way, but he intensified the hatred of the people of Roman rule.

Josephus and Philo also tell of a third episode in which Pilate, despite his previous experiences, insisted that votive shields dedicated to Tiberius be placed in the palace of Herod. Again the Jews objected, and Pilate refused to have the shields removed. At this point a petition signed by the leading men of the nation, including the names of four of the sons of Herod, was sent to the emperor, asking for the removal of the offensive objects. Significantly, Tiberius granted the request, and the shields were taken out of Herod's palace and hung in the temple of Augustus at Caesarea instead.

We might add to these examples an incident recorded by Luke, in which the "blood" of certain Galileans was "mixed with their sacrifices" (Luke 13:1). We know nothing about this incident. But the reference suggests that Pilate attacked these people in the moment of their worship. If so, it is another example of his cruel and reckless dealings with the Jews.

In each of these incidents and from each of the writers through whom we learn of them we receive an amazingly consistent picture. It is a picture of one who obviously did not have the sensitivity or strength of character to rule well. He was stubborn, proud, corrupt, violent, and cruel.

Pilate

The Gospel Picture

Yet the mystery comes in at this point, for as soon as we turn to the Gospel accounts, we find a portrait not of one who is cruel and insensitive but rather of one who seems to be sensitive to the cause of justice through his apparent desire to have Jesus of Nazareth acquitted. The Gospel writers would have no cause to enhance Pilate's character. He was the one who actually carried out the crucifixion of their Lord. We may assume, therefore, that the accounts of his actions that they give are correct. But this does not seem to agree with what we know of Pilate elsewhere. The true Pilate is arrogant, overbearing, and unyielding. This Pilate is attempting every stratagem and compromise he knows to have Jesus acquitted.

First, he reopens the case to the obvious surprise and consternation of the Jewish leaders. This is the essential point of the verses with which John begins his account of the trial. The Jewish leaders must have arranged with Pilate to have a hasty morning confirmation of the verdict that they were to reach the night before. But instead of the quick ruling they expected, Pilate began a formal hearing. What had happened to Pilate in the preceding eight or nine hours? Why had he changed his mind?

As the trial goes on we see Pilate's concern demonstrated in other ways. Three times over he declares that Christ is innocent (John 18:38; 19:4, 6). Again, when the leaders are adamant in opposition to his verdict, he tries a series of subterfuges. He sends Christ to Herod, hoping that Herod will take the matter out of his hands (Luke 23:6–12). He offers a choice between Jesus or Barabbas, wishing that Jesus might be set free (Matt. 27:15–26; Mark 15:6–15; John 18:39–40). Finally, he scourges Jesus, thinking that the sight of the bleeding, broken man might move his accusers to pity (John 19:1–5).

Behind Every Man

What accounts for this unnatural change in Pilate's character? Why is he trying to release the Lord? There have been three possible explanations: the first of which is clearly not right (though we should consider it), the second of which probably has some truth (but only some), the third of which alone seems to be the truly adequate reason.

The first explanation is that Pilate was more noble than the secular historians give him credit for being. This is an obvious possibility. But it is clearly not right; for it is the secular historians and not the biblical writers who have the best motivations for placing the Roman ruler in a good light. They have no reason to slander him. Hence, we must believe that he really was the kind of man they picture. Conversely, the biblical writers have no reason to place him in a good light at all. If they do, it is clearly because (on this occasion at least and for whatever reason) he acted precisely as they portray him.

The second explanation probably contains some truth. It is that Pilate was impressed by the person of Jesus. We can imagine this to be true because of what we believe concerning the presence and overriding dignity of Christ. But we have to admit that there is very little in the narratives to suggest this as Pilate's real motivation. We sense that Pilate may have been impressed, but if he had put it into words he would probably have dismissed Christ as "a harmless religious fanatic" and little more. Certainly this was no overriding reason to spare him.

The third explanation, which I suspect is the real one, is outlined in detail by Frank Morison, in the work referred to already. He reminds us that on the morning of the trial Pilate, according to Matthew's account, received an urgent warning from his wife, Claudia, who was in the city with him over this particular weekend, saying that he should have nothing to do with Jesus and giving as her reason that she had dreamt about him. Matthew reports this: "When Pilate was sitting on the judge's seat, his wife sent him this message: 'Don't have anything to do with that innocent man, for I have suffered a great deal today in a dream because of him" (27:19). To those who live in the twentieth century this may seem almost inconsequential. But the Romans were particularly superstitious where dreams were concerned and seldom undertook any grand enterprise without some inquiry as to what the gods or fate deemed favorable. To Pilate his wife's warning would therefore have been quite serious, and he might well have determined to extricate himself at whatever cost from his earlier agreement to consent to Jesus' death.

Moreover, this generally overlooked factor in the events of the Roman trial makes sense of several other elements, as Morison indicates. He suggests:

1. That Pilate and Claudia were probably spending the night together on the evening Jesus was arrested.

2. That Claudia would therefore have known of the visit of Caiaphas (or whoever made up the Jewish delegation) and would have learned of its purpose, either through being present or through asking Pilate about it afterward.

3. That she went to bed with thoughts of Jesus in her mind and then, quite understandably, dreamed of him with forebodings.

4. That she awoke in the morning to find that Pilate had already risen and left the palace and therefore knew at once the business on which he was embarked and her own need for haste.

5. That she quickly wrote the message Matthew records and forwarded it to her husband, saying that he was not to condemn "that *righteous* man."

Morison concludes, "It was she who stiffened the Roman instinct for justice in Pilate, at a moment when he was tempted, from personal considerations, to humor the prejudices of the Jewish camarilla, and commit Jesus on their recommendation alone. It was she who was the author of that resplendent phase when the tyrant was seen for a few hours in the guise of a patient administrator anxious to weigh the truth to the last ounce. . . . While the stimulus lasted his handling of this difficult and perplexing case was well-nigh perfect. No more just hearing than this could any man have asked or obtained in any court of that far-off day. The restraining influence of one who clearly believed that Jesus was innocent is obviously upon it. It was only as the stimulus faded against the grinding and growing opposition of the Jewish party that the threat of Caesar's intervention became paramount, and he ended as he intended to begin, by delivering the Prisoner into their hands."[3]

Life's Crises

With that we confront the second great mystery of the Roman trial. The first is that Pilate acted out of character in his obvious desire to have Christ acquitted. We have analyzed that and studied the reason. The second mystery is that, in spite of this great desire and in spite of his power to see that his will was carried out, in the end Pilate consented to Christ's execution.

One lesson in this is the impossibility of a neutral stance where Christ is concerned. Pilate clearly wanted to release him. But he was not a believer in Christ. He was not a follower of Christ. He merely wanted to be innocent of Christ's condemnation; and, of course, he failed miserably. He could not be neutral, and neither can we be. We must either be for the Lord Jesus Christ or against him. Either we are for him, in which case he will strengthen us and enable us to live for him even in the midst of great trials. Or we are against him, no matter how humane, noble, or understanding we may consider ourselves to be.

The second lesson concerns the need to be prepared for life's crises. When Pilate arose that morning, he certainly did not expect to be confronted by the greatest decision of his career. That morning, all he thought he was going to do was consent to a routine condemnation that was basically not much of his affair. Yet suddenly the crisis was on him. Jesus was there, and Jesus was either innocent or guilty. What was Pilate to do? How would he act? We know the outcome. He failed. It would be wise to conclude, therefore, on the basis of his experience as well as our own, that we should never count on either a sense of nobility (which Pilate undoubtedly thought to be true in his case), insight (which is always expected of judges), or the warning of friends (as was the case in the urgent communication from his wife) to be adequate to lead us to do the right thing in a crisis situation.

What will? The only thing that is adequate is the life of the Lord Jesus Christ within and a close relationship with him out of which he can speak to us and lead us to do right in spite of our natural inclinations.

232

Jesus before Pilate

John 18:33–38

Pilate then went back inside the palace, summoned Jesus and asked him, "Are you the king of the Jews?"

"Is that your own idea," Jesus asked, "or did others talk to you about me?"

"Am I a Jew?" Pilate replied. "It was your people and your chief priests who handed you over to me. What is it you have done?"

Jesus said, "My kingdom is not of this world. If it were, my servants would fight to prevent my arrest by the Jews. But now my kingdom is from another place."

"You are a king, then!" said Pilate.

Jesus answered, "You are right in saying I am a king. In fact, for this reason I was born, and for this I came into the world, to testify to the truth. Everyone on the side of truth listens to me."

"What is truth?" Pilate asked. With this he went out again to the Jews and said, "I find no basis for a charge against him."

The previous study dealt with two puzzling aspects of the Roman trial: one, the contrast between what we know from secular sources regarding Pilate's character—insensitive, impetuous, rude—and the way the four Gospels indicate he actually conducted the trial; the second, that Pilate pronounced Christ innocent and yet condemned him to be crucified. These elements make a study of the Roman trial quite difficult and suggest levels of mystery that are possibly unfathomable.

There is one aspect of the Roman trial that is not the least bit mysterious, however. It is the tendency of human nature meticulously to go through all the external forms required by a situation while at the same time denying the very reality the forms stand for. There are two examples of this in the second segment of Christ's trial. On the one hand, there is the example of the Jewish rulers who, we are told, "to avoid ceremonial uncleanness the Jews did not enter the palace; they wanted to be able to eat the Passover" (John 18:28). Here were men engaged in a most vile act, the judicial murder of Jesus; yet they were concerned about being ceremonially defiled. They had convicted an innocent man of crimes worthy of death, breaking scores of their own laws in the process. They were about to seek a parallel conviction from Pilate by illegally and unconscionably changing the nature of the accusation made against their prisoner. Yet they were concerned about a ritual purification.

The other example of this human tendency is Pilate, who made a great show of justice while actually allowing mob action to force his acquiescence in the death of a man whom he knew was innocent.

The Formal Indictment

Some students of the Roman trial of Jesus have insisted that the real trial was before the Jewish Sanhedrin and that this was merely an informal hearing. But their argument overlooks the actual stages of the trial as they are recorded for us by the New Testament authors. A Roman trial had four essential elements: the indictment, the examination, the defense, and the verdict. Each of these is present in Christ's trial. The official nature of the proceedings is indicated by Pilate's opening words: "What charges are you bringing against this man?" (v. 29). As Chandler observes, "This question is very keenly indicative of the presence of the judge and of the beginning of a solemn judicial proceeding. Every word rings with Roman authority and strongly suggests administrative action."[1]

Pilate's question seems to have caught the Jewish leaders by surprise, however. For instead of replying with a formal indictment, as they should have been prepared to do, they attempted to evade the question by answering: "If he were not a criminal, we would not have handed him over to you" (v. 30).

At the very least, the reply of the leaders suggests that the priests and scribes regarded their own trial as sufficient and were coming to Pilate merely to secure a formal signature to effect the execution. They were saying, "You should accept the judgment that he is worthy of death merely because we say so." On the other hand, there may be more to it than this, as was argued in our earlier treatment of the Jewish trial. As we saw in that study, we can hardly suppose that the Jewish Sanhedrin launched into the trial of Jesus at this relatively late hour in Passover week without some understanding with Pilate that he would hear the case and concur in their verdict early on this particular morning. It is clear that the Jews expected a perfunctory endorsement of the verdict already arrived at by their own court. When Pilate surprised them by apparently intending to open the case anew and conduct a formal hearing, they were temporarily caught off guard and replied with this evasion.

Pilate said that if they were unwilling to make a formal accusation, they obviously did not need him and therefore should prosecute the case according to their own laws and inflict whatever penalties they were legally entitled to impose. It is possible that at this point Pilate did not understand that the Jews were seeking the death penalty in Jesus' case, but it is far more likely that he understood this all too well and was speaking as he did merely to remind the priests that they were under the rule of Rome and would have to conform to Rome's rules if they wished to have Christ executed. In a later incident involving the apostle Paul, the same principle was stated: "It is not the Roman custom to hand over any man before he has faced his accusers and has had an opportunity to defend himself against their charges" (Acts 25:16).

The unanticipated stubbornness of Pilate clearly thwarted the Jews in their designs. But they were resourceful and, therefore, produced an accusation on the spur of the moment. John does not record it; he passes instead to the heart of the accusation and Pilate's examination of Jesus on this point. But Luke gives the accusation in full. It has three parts. "We have found this man subverting our nation. He opposes payment of taxes to Caesar and claims to be the Christ" (Luke 23:2).

This is not the crime of which Jesus had been convicted in their own court. Chandler writes, "In the passage from the Sanhedrin to the Praetorium, the indictment had completely changed. Jesus had not been condemned on any of the charges recorded in this sentence of St. Luke. He had been convicted on the charge of blasphemy. But before Pilate he is now charged with high treason.... Why? Because blasphemy was not an offense against Roman law, and Roman judges would generally assume cognizance of no such charges.

"The Jews understood perfectly well at the trial before Pilate the principle of Roman procedure so admirably expressed a few years later by Gallio, proconsul of Achaia, and brother of Seneca: 'If it were a matter of wrong or wicked lewdness, O ye Jews, reason would that I should bear with you: but if it be a question of words and names, and of your law, look ye to it; for I will be no judge of such matters.' This attitude of Roman governors toward offenses of a religious nature perfectly explains the Jewish change of front in the matter of the accusation against Jesus. They merely wanted to get themselves into a Roman court on charges that a Roman judge would consent to try. In the threefold accusation recorded by the third Evangelist, they fully accomplished this result."[2]

The first charge was that Christ was "perverting the nation." This was indefinite. Had Pilate taken it seriously, it would have had to have been supported by specific examples of sedition. Still, it was a real offense. It was, in fact, the precise charge that the Jewish court had tried to prove against Jesus in reference to his claim to be able to tear down the temple and rebuild it in three days. The Jews had been unable to prove this in their court because of the contradictory testimony of their witnesses.

The second charge was also serious. In fact, it was more serious than the first in that it was a specific treasonable act under Roman law governing a captive state. The only problem with this charge is that it was clearly false. On an earlier occasion the nation's leaders had attempted to trap Jesus on this very issue, but he had acquitted himself admirably. They had come to him with a trick question, asking, "What is your opinion? Is it right to pay taxes to Caesar or not?" (Matt. 22:17). They reasoned that if he said yes, they could denounce him to the people, saying, "What kind of Messiah is this who counsels abject subservience to Rome?" On the other hand, if he replied no, they could denounce him to Rome, saying "You have an insurrectionist on your hands." But what did Christ answer? He asked for a coin and demanded of his questioners, "Whose portrait is this? And whose inscription?" (v. 20). When they replied, "Caesar's," he gave that ruling that has become the classical biblical statement of the separation of church and state, involving the proper responsibilities of and to each. He said, "Give to Caesar what is Caesar's, and to God what is God's" (v. 21). In this charge the leaders were therefore guilty of the most flagrant and malicious of lies.

The third charge was the greatest and most serious of the three, that Jesus had claimed to be "Christ, a king." It was serious because it was true. It was also serious because it was the claim about which Rome was most sensitive and against which she was most on her guard. When Pilate heard this charge he gathered his robes about him, motioned for Jesus to follow him, made his way back into the palace (which John alone records) and began the examination, the second part of every Roman trial. Not content with receiving the formal accusation alone, Pilate now sought to determine whether the charges preferred against Jesus were true.

The Examination

Each of the Gospel writers records the question with which Pilate began his interrogation. It is simply, "Are you the King of the Jews?" (Matt. 27:11; Mark 15:2; Luke 23:3; John 18:33). With this question Pilate, it would appear, impatiently brushed aside the two lesser charges as unworthy of serious consideration and proceeded at once to examine Jesus on that charge which, if true, would unmistakably brand him Caesar's enemy.

John records Christ's full reply. As we read it, it seems like an evasion—"Is that your own idea or did others talk to you about me?" (v. 34)—but actually Jesus' reply is much to the point. For having heard the charge first from the lips of the Jews and now from Pilate himself, Jesus wishes to know first of all in what sense the question is being put to him. What was the nature of the charge? If the question were being asked from a Roman point of view, one answer would be given; for Christ was not a king from Rome's perspective. On the other hand, if the question were being asked from a Jewish perspective, quite another answer would be given; for Jesus was the Jews' Messiah.

Pilate's reply, while abrupt, is nevertheless also directly to the point at this stage in the examination. He asks, "Am I a Jew? It was your people and your chief priests who handed you over to me. What is it you have done?" (v. 35). This means, "I am no Jew. I ask my question as a Roman administrator and, as such, purely religious questions have no interest for me. What I want to know is: What have you done that might affect the sovereignty of Caesar?"

The Defense

At this point, although the interrogation continues, Jesus begins his defense by introducing what in modern law would be called a plea of confession and avoidance. This is a plea which admits, either in words or in effect, the truth of the accusation but which nevertheless introduces some new matter to avoid the guilt which normally would follow. For example, we may imagine a case in which a man is on trial for murder. The judge asks, "Did you shoot and kill John Smith on the date in question?" The defendant might answer, "Yes, I did, Your Honor; but you should know that I discovered him in my dining room near an open window trying to steal my silver chest and that when I discovered him he came at me with a knife. My plea is justified homicide and self-defense." Here the defendant admits to the killing but pleads extenuating circumstances. In the same way, the Lord now admits to the charge of having claimed to be a king but describes his kingship in such a way that it is seen to be no threat to the legitimate claims of Caesar.

Jesus first explains the nature of his kingdom negatively: "My kingdom is not of this world. If it were, my servants would fight to prevent my arrest by the Jews. But now my kingdom is from another place" (v. 36).

We do not know whether Pilate understood what Jesus was saying in this reply, but one phrase immediately caught his attention, the phrase "my kingdom." Jesus seemed to be saying that this was not an earthly kingdom, but Pilate could take no chances on this crucial issue. He therefore picked up on this phrase and (probably) advanced on Christ threateningly to demand sternly, "You are a king, then!" (v. 37).

This time Jesus replies to the question with a positive affirmation: "You are right in saying that I am a king. In fact, for this reason I was born, and for this I came into the world, to testify to the truth. Everyone on the side of truth listens to me" (v. 37).

Jesus' defense has two parts. One is a negative definition of his kingdom. It is "not of this world." The proof is that his disciples did not fight to prevent his arrest by the Jewish authorities. The other is a positive definition of the kingdom. It is of "the truth." That is, it is a kingdom ruling over people's minds and aspirations. Chandler writes, "His was not an empire of matter, but a realm of truth. His kingdom differed widely from that of Caesar. Caesar's empire was over the bodies of men; Christ's over their souls. The strength of Caesar's kingdom was in citadels, armies, navies, the towering Alps, the all-engirding seas. The strength of the kingdom of Christ was and is and will ever be in sentiments, principles, ideas, and the saving power of a divine word."[3]

Pilate could not fully appreciate this instruction. "Truth?" he asked. "What is truth?" Then he turned away, convinced at last that whatever Jesus' peculiar ideas, he was certainly no worse than any other religious fanatic and was, at least from Rome's point of view, perfectly innocent of any capital offenses.

The Verdict

The last phase of the Roman trial followed immediately upon Pilate's examination of Jesus and Jesus' defense. John tells us that, having concluded this examination, "he went out again to the Jews, and said, 'I find no basis for a charge against him'" (v. 38). *Absolvo! Non fecisse videtur!* Standing alone these phrases indicate the close of the trial and mark it as being an official court proceeding.

Pilate had tried and acquitted Jesus. Why then did he not release him or, if need be, place him in protective custody as a later Roman ruler did with the apostle Paul when his life was threatened (Acts 21:31–33; 23:12–24)? This is the question that the human race has asked of Pontius Pilate for nearly two thousand years. Pilate was guilty of nothing at all up to this point. In fact, he had conducted the trial with precision, wisdom, and dispatch. He had reached the right verdict. But now, in spite of his calling as a Roman governor and judge, the high example of many thousands of Roman administrators before him, and the power of the legions in Palestine, he failed to do the right thing by immediately setting Christ free. The mood of the crowd forestalled him. Then he settled down into a series of irregular and illegal proceedings that eventually ended in the prisoner's execution. Pilate was a coward. This is the only proper analysis of his character and the ultimate explanation of why he failed to do right in this situation.

What does this mean? It means that in the true, eternal issues of the case it is Pilate who was judged by the Lord and found wanting. I have titled this chapter "Jesus before Pilate," but we must never forget that in another and far more important sense it is also "Pilate before Jesus." In the former Jesus was tried and found innocent. Rightly so. In the latter Pilate was tried and found guilty.

So are all who stand before Christ. He is the only perfect person who ever lived. His standard for us is perfection. We all fall short, each one. For "there is no one righteous, not even one; there is no one who understands, no one who seeks God. All have turned away, they have together become worthless; there is no one who does good, not even one" (Rom. 3:10–12). We stand condemned. But it is for such condemned men and women that Christ died. He died to bear the punishment for their sin and thereby free them from God's righteous judgment and curse.

Has he done that for you? He has if you are a subject of his kingdom, which you have entered (if you have entered it) by a believing response to his truth and person. That response entails the belief that Jesus is who he says he is (the Son of God) and did what he said he would do (die for your sin), coupled with a personal commitment to follow him as your Savior and Lord.

233

Christ's Kingdom Not of This World

John 18:36–37

Jesus said, "My kingdom is not of this world. If it were, my servants would fight to prevent my arrest by the Jews. But now my kingdom is from another place."

"You are a king, then!" said Pilate.

Jesus answered, "You are right in saying I am a king. In fact, for this reason I was born, and for this I came into the world, to testify to the truth. Everyone on the side of truth listens to me."

I n the first of his two great letters to Timothy, the apostle Paul tells us that Jesus Christ "while testifying before Pontius Pilate made the good confession" (1 Tim. 6:13). That good confession is not found in the synoptic Gospels—Matthew, Mark, or Luke—for they contain only a five-word response from Jesus. When Jesus was asked if he were the king of the Jews, they report him as answering, "It is as you say" (Matt. 27:11; Mark 15:2; Luke 23:3), after which he said nothing. It is only in John that the good confession of Jesus before Pilate is reported to us fully.

We can be glad that John recorded it. For one thing, it teaches us what a "good confession" is. This confession is good as to the manner in which it is

given. It was not rude or brusque or condescending or veiled in mysteries,
as our confessions often are. It was simple, kind, direct, and helpful. Though
Christ was soon to be condemned by Pilate, he did not despise him but rather
treated him with the respect due him because of his office. Again, the confession of our Lord was good as to its matter, for here, before one who was
rightly concerned with earthly sovereignty, Christ spoke of divine versus
human affairs and of God's sovereignty. This teaches us how we should speak
of spiritual things and what we should say.

A second reason why we should be glad that John has included these words
is that they contain a definition of the nature of Christ's kingdom in the very
words of Jesus and at a most important moment.

Those who have studied the meaning of the kingdom of God in the Old
and New Testaments know that this is a very complex subject, the reason
being that the phrase is used in so many different ways. Sometimes it seems
to refer in an abstract way to the reign or rule of God. At other times it refers
to a coming future rule of Christ or God upon earth. In one key text (Luke
17:21, and parallels) the kingdom of God is said to be "among" or "in the
midst" of this world, presumably in the person of Christ and his disciples.
In a fourth series of passages the kingdom is something into which men
and women enter. This is confusing, and it is compounded by the fact that,
according to one writer at least, "Jesus nowhere defined what he meant by
the phrase."[1]

Well, it may be true that Jesus nowhere gives a careful theological definition of "the kingdom of God." There are not many terms he did do this with.
But still these verses in John's Gospel may be brought forward as something
very closely approaching it.

Christ, a King

The jumping-off point for Christ's definition of his kingdom is with the confession that he is indeed a king, whatever the appearances may be to the contrary. He did not look like a king. He was bound and beaten (Luke 22:63–65).
He was to be beaten further still. Yet no king, seated upon a throne at the pin-
nacle of world power, was more entitled to be called a king than he.

This fact is important, for what is true of the king is no less true of his
kingdom. Charles Haddon Spurgeon wrote of this more than a hundred
years ago: "To this day, pure Christianity, in its outward appearances, is an
equally unattractive object, and wears upon its surface few royal tokens. It is
without form or comeliness, and when men see it, there is no beauty that
they should desire it. True, there is a nominal Christianity which is accepted
and approved of men, but the pure gospel is still despised and rejected. The
real Christ of today, among men, is unknown and unrecognized as much as
he was among his own nation eighteen hundred years ago. . . . Christ chanted
in cathedrals, Christ personified in lordly prelates, Christ surrounded by
such as are in kings' houses, *he* is well enough; but Christ honestly obeyed,

followed, and worshiped in simplicity, without pomp or form, they will not allow to reign over them. . . .

"We are satisfied that Christ is the king still where he was wont to be king, and that is not among the great ones of the earth, nor among the mighty and the learned, but amongst the base things of the world and the things which are not, which shall bring to nought the things that are, for these hath God from the beginning chosen to be his own."[2]

A Spiritual Kingdom

Jesus says his kingdom is "not of this world." That says a great deal in it-self and also by implication.

So far as the statement itself is concerned, it is a denial of the importance for Christ of those things that usually concern earthly monarchs. One concern is for geography. Kings rule a certain carefully defined territory. They protect that territory from others. When they fight, it is usually over this or other territory they wish to annex. But this is not Christ's concern, His kingdom is not of this world. Another concern of this world's rulers is with taxes. There has never been a kingdom without taxes. Taxes pay for the government, army, public works, and of course for the army of bureaucrats who collect the taxes and do a host of other things. But Christ's concern is not with taxes, His kingdom is not of this world. This world's princes are concerned with pomp and ceremony, prestige and privileges, acclaim. Not so Christ. It is of his kingdom as the hymn states:

> For not with swords' loud clashing,
> Nor roll of stirring drums—
> With deeds of love and mercy
> The heav'nly kingdom comes.

It is not only in a negative way that this definition of the kingdom of God speaks to us, however. It also speaks by implication. Christ has said that his kingdom is not of this world. But if that is true, from whence does it come? If his kingship is not of this world, it is either from hell or from heaven.

There is a kingdom which is the kingdom of hell. We do not mean by this that somewhere in the universe there is a geographic territory known as hell over which Satan presides, along the lines John Milton painted in *Paradise Lost*. There is a geographical hell, just as there is a geographical heaven. But Satan does not rule there. God rules hell. That is what makes hell so horrible. On the other hand, this does not mean that there is not a satanic, hellish kingdom. On the contrary, there is; and it is this we are speaking about. It is of this kingdom that Jesus spoke when he referred to a kingdom being divided against itself and therefore being unable to stand (Mark 3:23–26). It is a "spiritual" kingdom founded on hate, pride, jealousy, anger, and cunning. It is the opposite of Christ's kingdom at every point. Is this Christ's source? Is this the source of his kingdom? We recall that the Pharisees thought so. Just before Christ's words about Satan's kingdom being divided against itself, they had said, "He is possessed by Beelzebub! By the prince of demons he is driving out demons" (Mark 3:22).

This is one logical explanation of the authority and kingship Christ so obviously possessed and demonstrated. But is it an adequate explanation? Can it explain the nature of Christ and the qualities of his rule? If it cannot—and who can seriously maintain that Christ's character and ministry were demonic—then the source must be heaven and Christ must be the Son of God. Sheer logic forces any honest person to that position.

The same logic applies to Christ's person. After you have disposed of the one truly impossible explanation of who Jesus is (that he is "a good man"), there are only three things that can be said of him. One, he is God, as he claimed. Two, he was crazy, for he mistakenly claimed to be God when he was not. Or three, he was a deceiver, for he knew he was not God, yet claimed to be God in order to gain a following through such deception. There are no other possibilities. The one who would face Christ honestly must decide among them. Is the Christ who has been proclaimed by so many throughout so many thousands of years of human history insane, a deceiver, or God? He cannot be put off with any nonsense about being a good teacher or a good man.

This was the dilemma Jesus put before everyone when in the Roman hall of judgment he said, "My kingdom is not of this world." Rule out this world, where deception is all too universal and obvious, and there are only two possibilities left: hell or heaven. If you cannot say, "He is from hell," then he is from heaven, and his kingdom is too. And whatever your opinion of it may be or whatever your wishes may be, you are his subject, and you are obliged to fall before him and confess him to be your Lord and your God.

When Jesus says, "My kingdom is not of this world," many utter a sigh of relief and say, "Well, thank God that Jesus' kingdom has nothing to do with us. It is a spiritual kingdom. Hallelujah! We can keep on as we have been and do as we please." Nothing is farther from the truth, for when we say that Christ's kingdom is not of this world, what we are really saying is that Christ's kingdom is of heaven and therefore has an even greater claim over us than do the earthly kingdoms we know so well. There is real sovereignty in an earthly kingdom. There is genuine authority which we may not flout. But over these is Christ, and we flout his kingship not merely at the peril of our fortune and lives but at the peril of our eternal souls.

Why risk such loss? Why not come to this king and confess his lordship? He has promised to rule in justice and with mercy, and he has assured us that his yoke is easy and his burden is light.

Two Kingdoms

There is a third area where Christ's words about his kingdom apply, and that is in their relationship to earthly powers, of which Pilate and the Roman Empire were examples. In modern American history there has been a tendency so to stress the legitimate principle of the separation of church and state that we have almost come to the point of saying that the church and state are not related to each other at all. This is wrong. Jesus deals with it not only in these verses, which speak of the nature of his kingdom, but also in the continuation of the discourse in chapter 19, in which the responsibility of Pilate over against the heavenly kingdom is stressed. In these later verses Pilate had begun to quiz Jesus again, and Jesus gave him no answer.

Pilate said, "Do you refuse to speak to me? Don't you realize I have power either to free you or to crucify you?"

Jesus replied, "You would have no power over me if it were not given to you from above. Therefore the one who handed me over to you is guilty of a greater sin" (19:10–11).

This reply speaks directly to the church/state problem. While it is true that the church and state each have their legitimate spheres of authority, and while it is also true that the church and state should have separate organizations, neither possessing the right to appoint officers or authorities in the other—nevertheless, it is not true that they are totally unrelated, for in many areas they have the same concerns, and both are responsible to the same divine sovereign.

Some have said, for example, that the Christian community should be so separated from the secular sphere that Christians should not go into politics, that believers in general should not vote in elections, that we should withdraw from the culture as much as possible, live in distinct communities, have Christians as friends exclusively, work for Christian companies, and so on. But Jesus refutes this when he says that his kingdom is not "of" the world. The key word is "of." If he had said "in," we would separate. But he said "of" and therefore means that we are to be actively "in" the world though not "of" it in terms of its values and goals. To turn to the other side, some have said that the state has nothing to do with the concerns of Christian people; that it is not in business to "regulate morality," for example. But again this is wrong; for when Jesus reminded Pilate that his authority came from God, he was also reminding him that it was to be exercised in accord with the character of that one whose authority it is.

When the state develops and enforces laws against homicide, what is that but the legislation of morality? It is the state's way of saying, "We agree that life is precious and that it is wrong to take it away. In this we support the sixth of God's Ten Commandments." Again, when the state makes laws against larceny and burglary, what is it doing but enforcing the eighth commandment? The same is true of its requirement of legal marriages, contracts, labor negotiations, and similar formalities in a hundred different areas. In

each of these areas the state is dealing with morality. Jesus emphasized in
his words to Pilate that the state is responsible for this before God, just as
the church is responsible.

This is the significance of Christ's mention of sin: "Therefore, the one
who handed me over to you is guilty of a greater sin." Sin is a transgression
of the law of God and is therefore punishable by God and will be punished
by him. So Jesus was telling Pilate, "Your sin may not be as great as those who
have hated me and turned me over to you. But their sin does not excuse
your sin. You are still a sinner, and you will be judged for it."

Entering Christ's Kingdom

The final point Jesus made about his kingdom is that it is not entered into
by secular means. The heavenly kingdom and the earthly kingdom overlap
at some points, but not here. The same person may be in both; the emperor
can also be a Christian. In some areas they have corresponding concerns.
But they are nevertheless different kingdoms and are entered differently.

Jesus spelled this out in two ways. In one of the beatitudes of the Sermon
on the Mount he indicated the manner in which we must enter, saying,
"Blessed are the poor in spirit, for theirs is the kingdom of heaven" (Matt.
5:3). This does not mean, "Blessed are the poor-spirited" or "Blessed are failures." To be poor in spirit is the opposite of being rich in pride. It means to
be humble. So Christ's first requirement for entering his kingdom is to humble yourself and take up the position of a suppliant before him. It is to pray
with the publican, "God be merciful to me, a sinner."

Second, in his words before Pilate Jesus shows that this also has a positive
dimension in the area of our response to his truth. Humility is a prerequisite, but it does not produce salvation in and of itself. Rather, we must also
respond to that truth that Jesus came to earth to communicate. It consists
in this: that Jesus is God, that he died on our behalf, and that those who have
nothing to present to God in terms of their own merit nevertheless can come
boldly to God on the merit of Jesus.

234

What Is Truth?

John 18:37–38

"You are a king, then!" said Pilate.

Jesus answered, "You are right in saying I am a king. In fact, for this reason I was born, and for this I came into the world, to testify to the truth. Everyone on the side of truth listens to me."

"What is truth?" Pilate asked. With this he went out again to the Jews and said, "I find no basis for a charge against him."

There are two ways to define something, and both are necessary. One way is by telling what the object in question is. The other way is by telling what it is not. Both are important because if you cannot say what it is not, then the object may very well be everything and consequently nothing. Some persons' definitions of God are like that; he is everything and therefore nothing at all. On the other hand, it is also necessary to say what the object is, because the negatives at best merely narrow down the possibilities.

This basic principle is important in the matter of the examination of Jesus by Pilate, for the crucial issue was the claim of the Lord to be a king and consequently to possess a kingdom. Was this kingship and kingdom to be thought of as in opposition to that of Caesar, whose interests Pilate was obliged to represent? Was it an earthly kingdom? Or was it something else, something that did not threaten Caesar's legitimate interests and that, therefore, neither he nor Pilate should fear? These were valid questions. So, in his conversation with Pilate, Jesus was careful to define the nature of his kingdom accurately. He defined it negatively by affirming that it is "not of this world." Now he defines it positively, showing that it is of "the truth" and that it was for the very purpose of bearing witness to the truth that he came into the world. In developing this he says, "For this reason I was born, and for this I came into the world, to testify to the truth. Everyone on the side of truth listens to me" (John 18:37).

Pilate's Question

The interesting thing about this definition of Jesus' kingdom is that Pilate's response was not in the nature of a further pursuit of the matter or even a recognition of the importance of what Jesus said. Rather, it was a cynical response based on what was to Pilate the seeming impossibility of ever knowing what truth is. "What is truth?" he said, and then walked out.

When Sir Francis Bacon came to write his famous eassay "On Truth," he suggested that Pilate's famous words were facetious. Bacon began, "What is truth? said jesting Pilate; and would not stay for an answer." Whatever these words were they were far from facetious, however. Pilate had just looked into the eyes of the Son of God and had heard him exclaim, "For this reason I was born, and for this I came into the world, to testify to the truth." No one who has had that experience could be joking. Moreover, it was far from a laughing matter. The situation was grave, and the question that welled up from Pilate's deep cynicism was the disillusioned and despairing cry of his age.

It is this that makes Pilate the preeminently modern man. We readily admit that there are elements of this trial that we can identify with only with difficulty. Obviously Pilate's concern for Caesar's rights is foreign to us. Even more so are the petty rivalries among the Jewish leaders and between these men and Pilate. But our inability to identify does not hold true at this point. On the contrary, here we detect the disillusioned voice of our own culture and recognize the current widespread view, not only that truth in the ultimate sense may be unknowable but that it may in fact not even exist as an object of our inquiries.

In Pilate's day disillusionment with truth was disillusionment with Greek philosophy. Pilate may have been no philosopher, but he was aware, as were all Romans, that the Greeks had excelled in precisely this field and yet had failed to solve the ultimate philosophical questions. The man who had tried hardest was Plato. Plato understood that the basic problem in acquiring knowledge of what is true is that there must be knowledge of more than particulars if there is to be meaning. In the language of philosophy the word "particulars" means "things," those things that we see in the world. We are surrounded by thousands of them at any given moment, and we know by experience and projection that there are many thousands, indeed millions, more. In a sense we know these particulars because we observe them. But real knowledge is something that goes beyond these individualized things to that general concept or form that gives them meaning.

For example, when we talk about chairs we can easily list many styles and types of chairs, some of them quite different from others. There are rocking chairs, spindle-back chairs, desk chairs, stuffed chairs—the list seems endless. Yet when we speak of a chair we obviously have some general idea of a chair into which these particulars fit. Plato said that what is so obviously true on this level must be true in every other area as well.

But where do these ideals come from? On the level of chairs we may argue that they come from the human mind, and thus we may localize the ultimate meaning of the universe there. But if we do that, we immediately want to ask: But where does the idea of the mind or of man himself come from? And where do we find absolutes in those areas about which men apparently disagree—morals, the proper structuring of human society, religion, and so on? Popular Greek thought answered: From the gods. But then, where does the idea of the gods come from? Plato recognized that in pursuing this necessary kind of argument one must move backward and upward to one great universal from which every meaning comes. But here is the problem. Although Plato and the other Greeks understood the necessity of finding such a grand, overriding universal, they nevertheless never found a place from which the universal could come nor a way in which it could be known surely. It was out of the despair of this search that Plato is reported to have said wistfully, "It may be that some day there will come forth from God a Word who will reveal all mysteries and make everything plain."

After Plato there were other attempts to solve this same great problem, but these were no more successful. Consequently, Greek philosophy gradually descended into a growing cynicism expressed in the "grin-and-bear-it" philosophy of the Stoics, the "if-it-feels-good-do-it" philosophy of the Epicureans, or the "leap-of-faith" philosophy of the various mystery religions. Pilate knew all this. So he asked (quite correctly from the perspective of the philosophical thought before him), "What is truth?" meaning that speculations in this area had proved both impractical and meaningless.

The Situation Today

One proposed solution to the problem of truth (though it is actually a denial of a solution) is the relativism that has grown out of the philosophy of Wilhelm Friedrich Hegel (1770–1831). Hegel was a German professor who, in a series of brilliant books, advanced the proposition that truth is not an absolute but rather is something that is always evolving through the flow of world history. In Hegel's view it is the result of a synthesis which comes about in this fashion. Every fact, theory or "truth" may be called a thesis, which by its very existence produces an antithesis. At first these appear as opposites, but in time they come together to form a synthesis. This synthesis in turn becomes a new thesis producing its own antithesis, and so on. According to this system truth is relative. It depends upon whom you are asking and of what period you are asking. What is true now may not have been true ten or twenty years ago, and it may not be true ten or twenty years from now. Or again, it may be true for me but not for you. This is Hegel's heritage for the modern world.

Most people today speak of what is true or false purely on a subjective basis. That is, they determine whether a thing is true or not on the basis of how it makes them feel.

In the winter of 1976–77, the Public Broadcasting System aired a six-part film series entitled *Scenes From a Marriage.* It was by Ingmar Bergman and was originally for Swedish viewers. On the surface it is merely a perceptive analysis of the breakup of what appears to be an ideal marriage. But it is actually more than that. It is an analysis of our culture, as most Bergman films are, and it is filled with personal and political implications. In the first of these six scenes there is a speech by Johan, the husband, which unintentionally reveals the weaknesses both of Johan and Marianne, his wife, and of their marriage. They are being interviewed for a national magazine. They are sitting on a sofa. The interviewer asks, "Are you afraid of the future?"

Johan replies, "If I stopped to think, I'd be petrified with fear. Or so I imagine. So I don't think. I'm fond of this cozy old sofa and that oil lamp. They give me an illusion of security which is so fragile that it's almost comic. I like Bach's *St. Matthew Passion* though I'm not religious, because it gives me feelings of piety and belonging. Our families see a lot of each other and I depend very much on this contact, as it reminds me of my childhood when I felt I was protected. I like what Marianne said about fellow-feeling. It's good for a conscience which worries on quite the wrong occasions. I think you must have a kind of technique to be able to live and be content with your life. In fact, you have to practice quite hard not caring about anything. The people I admire most are those who can take life as a joke. I can't. I have too little sense of humor for a feat like that. You won't print this, will you?"

The speech is devastating. There is a denial of security but a wish for security feelings. There is denial of religious values but a desire for religious feelings. In fact, feelings are all there are. Therefore it is no surprise that the solution to living that Johan puts forward is *technique*—"You must have a kind of technique to be able to live and be content with your life." What happens when the technique fails? The answer is that the marriage breaks up, as this one does. Thus does Bergman dramatize what is happening to our society.

Today as never before, on thousands of campuses and in millions of homes, the question of truth is not even asked. Instead people are asking, "Does it work?" "Is it practical?" "How does it make you feel?" Obviously our own lack of meaning is linked to the failure of this quest, and the declining moral tone of our culture—expressed in presidential scandals, industrial pay-offs, legalized immorality, shoplifting, and many other things—flows from it.

Word to Modern Man

Here we turn to the answer to the modern dilemma, for if Pilate's question is preeminently the modern question, then the statement of Christ which provoked it is preeminently a word to our own disillusioned culture. This is not the first time Jesus had spoken of truth and its nature. Earlier he had spoken of himself as "the truth" (John 14:6). He had called the Holy Spirit the "spirit of truth" (John 14:17; 15:26; 16:13). He referred to the Bible as "truth" (John 17:17). He even spoke of the need to "worship . . . in truth" (John 4:23–24) and to "do" the truth (John 3:21). All these references are totally understandable in view of the Old Testament conception of what truth is and how it functions. But here before Pilate, in the very last references to truth in the entire Gospel, Jesus refers to it in a way which even a Gentile like Pilate could fathom: "For this I came into the world, to testify to the truth. Everyone on the side of the truth listend to me." This says several important things that Pilate and our own culture need to know.

First, it says that there *is* such a thing as truth and that *truth is an entity*. That is, truth is singular. It is not in fragments that would require us to speak of "truths" in the sense of unrelated facts or items. Truth holds together. Therefore, there is no phase of truth that is not related to every other phase of truth. The nature of God is related to the structure of the atom. The inspiration and inerrancy of the Bible are related to the multiplication table. All things that are true are part of the truth and stand in a proper and inescapable relationship to God, who is himself the truth.

Second, the Lord indicates by his statement that truth is not only an entity, it is *objective*. That is, it is there to be observed and discussed, and we can observe it and discuss it without prejudice. This is involved in Christ's statement that he has come to bear witness to the truth, as one might to any fact submitted in a court of law.

This has implications in two areas. On the one hand, it says something about the way the Christian should approach scientific truth. He may approach it dispassionately and analytically. On the other hand, this also says something about the nature of religious truth. For if truth is an entity and truth is objective, then religious truth is not something beyond the range of analysis and verification. It is not something to be reached by a great "leap of faith." Rather, it is something that may be studied and that will therefore inevitably throw light upon our natures and the nature of the universe. Just as the biologist might look through a microscope to study the nature of the microscopic world, so we look through the microscope of the Word to see our true condition. In that Book we find that God has done what needs to be done by sending his Son as our Savior. Jesus died for us. He rose for us. He reigns for us. That is objective truth. Therefore, it may be studied and applied to our lives as any other truth can.

Third, the words of the Lord to Pilate indicate that *truth must come from above,* for when Jesus says that he has come to bear witness to the truth, he implies that in the ultimate sense truth is not of this world but rather must come to this world by revelation.

This is so of all truth. It is true of spiritual truth, of course; for apart from the revelation we have in God's Word, no one would even guess what is disclosed there, let alone really know it. We cannot guess what God is like nor what he has done in Jesus Christ for our salvation. It is also the case, however, with scientific truth, for although it is true that God has given us primarily a book of spiritual truth, not scientific truth, he has nevertheless given us minds capable of perceiving the revelation of himself in nature and actually leads the mind to discover what is to be found there. Sometimes scientists are unaware of this. At other times they know it. It is said that Samuel Morse, the inventor of the telegraph, was once seen bowed over the desk where he was working. "What are you doing?" he was asked.

Morse replied, "I am asking God for help. Every time I go into my laboratory I say, 'O God, I am nothing. Give me wisdom. Give me clarity of mind.'" Morse knew that truth comes from God. Consequently, we are not surprised to learn that the very first message sent over his new invention was the thankful and wondering question, "What hath God wrought?"

Fourth, the words of our Lord teach that in the ultimate sense *the truth that comes from God has been embodied in a person.* No one would ever imagine this. To us truth is abstract and may be supposed always to remain abstract. We think of truth in terms of equations and figures and propositions. But God says that truth is personal. More than that, it is a person and this person is the Lord Jesus Christ. He himself said unequivocally, "I am the way and the truth and the life" (John 14:6). This is the answer to Plato's quest. Plato had said, "It may be that some day there will come forth from God a Word who will reveal all mysteries and make everything plain." That Word has now come. The Lord is that Word. He is the One who has come to reveal all mysteries and make everything plain to those who will come to him.

235

No Fault in Him at All

John 18:38

"What is truth?" Pilate asked. With this he went out again to the Jews and said, "I find no basis for a charge against him."

In the instructions for the observance of the Passover occurring in Exodus 12 and in other parts of the Old Testament, there is a detail that has bearing on the outcome of the trial of the Lord Jesus Christ before Pilate. These passages tell us that the lamb to be killed in the observance of the Passover was to be "without blemish" (Exod. 12:5; cf. Lev. 22:17–25). In order to make sure that it was without blemish it was to be kept in the home for three days prior to the sacrifice, during which time it was to be examined carefully. Only when it was known to be flawless was it to be used in the Passover ritual.

This has bearing upon the trial of the Lord Jesus Christ before Pilate because in the plan of God he was the true Passover Lamb, who died that the angel of spiritual death might pass over all who trust in his sacrifice. He was examined to this end and found to be without blemish. We might say that at the time of his entry upon his public ministry the Lord was taken into the

1445

ouse of Israel for three years. At the beginning of that ministry he had been identified as the Lamb of God by John the Baptist, his divinely appointed forerunner. John had pointed him out, saying, "Behold the Lamb of God, who takes away the sin of the world" (John 1:29). From that point on the Lord moved in and out among the people of Israel to be examined by them— by friends and enemies alike. None could find fault with him. Now, in what is virtually the last official word pronounced on earth concerning Jesus, the Roman procurator Pilate comes forth in opposition to the determined will of the Jews and even the careless nature of his own conscience to declare Jesus innocent.

He does it three times. First, at the conclusion of the official Roman trial. In this trial Jesus had been accused of making himself to be "Christ, a king," thus an enemy of Caesar. Pilate found the charge unwarranted. After a careful examination of Jesus as to the nature of his supposed kingdom, he appeared to the crowd and declared, "I find no basis for a charge against him" (John 18:38; Luke 23:4).

The second declaration of Jesus' innocence was after Pilate had sent Jesus to Herod and had received him back uncondemned. "Look, I am bringing him out to you to let you know that I find no basis for a charge against him," Pilate said (John 19:4; cf. Luke 23:14–15).

The last occasion was after Pilate had caused Jesus to be flogged, hoping by this act to satisfy the outraged and vicious mob. Pilate declared, "I find no basis for a charge against him" (John 19:6; cf. Luke 23:22). The leaders of the people were insistent and stirred up the people to cry out repeatedly, "Crucify him! Crucify him!" So at last, Pilate, being unwilling to risk a riot and thus the loss of his own position, gave Christ over to death even though he had found him innocent. However—and this is the point we are making—it is as one uncondemned and, in fact, declared to be blameless that Christ goes to Calvary. It is as God's blameless Lamb that Jesus dies for the sin of this world.

A Universal Verdict

But it was not only by Pilate that this important verdict—"I find no basis for a charge against him"—was given. It has been given by all who have ever examined or been associated with the Lord Jesus. Think of those who had pronounced a verdict of "innocent" upon him.

There is God the Father, first of all. At the beginning of Christ's public ministry John the Baptist had identified the Lord as God's Lamb. Although John was a prophet and therefore one to be believed and trusted, we might well want to ask if John is entirely sure of this identification. After all, Israel had waited for hundreds of years for her Messiah, and the waiting of the world for the One who was to crush the head of Satan was even longer. "Is he really the one?" we might ask. "Is this really the blameless Lamb who is to die for the sin of this world?" The issue is not allowed to stand in doubt, for as soon as John has baptized Jesus, the Holy Spirit in a visible form, like a dove, is seen to light upon him; and God's voice is heard from heaven, saying, "This is my Son, whom I love; with him I am well pleased" (Matt. 3:17; Mark 1:11; Luke 3:22).

Later, on the Mount of Transfiguration, after Jesus had appeared in his glory with Moses and Elijah, the voice was heard again, declaring, "This is my Son, whom I love; with him I am well pleased. Listen to him" (Matt. 17:5; cf. Mark 9:7; Luke 9:35).

A second verdict of "innocent" was pronounced upon Christ by those who knew him best, *his disciples*. There was much about him that they did not know or understand. They did not know the purpose of his ministry, nor did they understand the necessity of his death. But one thing they knew. They had never met anyone who could match the moral excellence of his personality or teaching. John called Christ "the righteous" (1 John 2:1). Peter, in those early sermons recorded in the Book of Acts, called him the "Holy One" (Acts 2:27) and "the Righteous One" (Acts 3:14). In his first epistle he says that Jesus was "without blemish or defect" (1 Peter 1:19). Matthew confessed him as "Immanuel . . . God with us" (Matt. 1:23). Thomas confessed Christ's perfection by declaring him "My Lord and my God" (John 20:28). All these had rubbed shoulders with Jesus in the closest possible contact. They had done this for the better part of three years. They had seen him in good times and bad, facing the acclaim of the multitudes as well as enduring the insults and outrages of those who were opposed to his teaching. If anyone would have known of a weakness in Christ, these men would have known it. Yet they would unhesitatingly and enthusiastically have confessed with Pilate, "We find no basis for a charge against him."

Again, there is the testimony of *the Jewish leaders*. These men were enemies for the most part. They had no desire to think of Jesus favorably. In fact, the opposite is the case. They hated him and wished to trap him in some folly for which he could then be openly accused or in some violation of the law for which he could be officially condemned. Yet they could not succeed. And when they at last condemned him it was only because he had openly declared himself to be the unique Son of God, which statement they, without any evidence at all, judged to be blasphemy.

But perhaps we are not looking in the right place. We have spoken of the disciples of Christ, who had full opportunity to observe Jesus but who might be thought to be partial. We have spoken of the leaders, who were certainly not favorable to him but who might be said to have lacked adequate opportunity to observe him at close hand. Was there no one who was both in a position to observe Christ closely and at the same time not predisposed to judge him favorably because of friendship or some similar cause? We have no right to expect such a person, but God in his wisdom has provided such a one in *Judas*. Judas was one of the Twelve. He was with Christ throughout his ministry, thereby having full opportunity to observe him.

Yet after the betrayal Judas attempted to return the thirty pieces of silver to the chief priests and elders, saying, "I have sinned, for I have betrayed innocent blood" (Matt. 27:4). It was the equivalent of saying, "I find no fault in him at all."

Verdict of the Ages

Is that not the verdict of all who have ever associated with the Lord Jesus Christ? We have spoken of those who lived with him during his lifetime and knew him then. But what of those who have associated with him since—both friends and enemies? Is their verdict not identical?

Let us take Christ's friends first of all. These have trusted him as Savior and have been saved from their sin. But their way has not always been smooth. In the providence of God some have suffered great personal disappointment. Some have lost jobs, some families. Some have lost health. Some, like the Old Testament partiarch Job, have lost everything and have been forced to say, as he did, "May the day of my birth perish, and the night it was said, 'A boy is born!' . . . Why did I not perish at birth, and die as I came from the womb? Why were there knees to receive me and breasts that I might be nursed? For now I would be lying down in peace; I would be asleep and at rest" (Job 3:3, 11–13). Yet these have not cursed Christ. They have confessed rather that there is no fault in him at all.

Spurgeon writes of this truth, "Do you not think that out of the millions of Christians who have lived hoping in Christ some one would have told us if it is his habit to disappoint his people? Out of so many believers who dwell with Him surely some one or other of them, when they came to die, would have told us if He is not all that He professes to be. Would not some one or other have confessed, 'I trusted in Christ and he has not delivered me; it is all a delusion'? Surely, out of the many we have seen depart we should have found some one or two that would have let out the secret, and have said, 'He is a deceiver. He cannot save, he cannot help, he cannot deliver.' But never one dying believer throughout the ages has spoken ill of him, but all have said, 'We find no fault at all in him.'"[1]

This is even true in a certain sense of Christ's enemies, at least if they have taken the trouble to examine his character and teachings. They may be opposed to Christianity. They may have no desire at all to follow Jesus. Still there are few critics who have not been impressed with Christ's person and there are fewer still who would rail against him.

Do you say that there nevertheless are some? Yes, that is true in a sense. But the last word is not in yet, for one day they will be confronted with Christ in his glory and will be forced to confess, in spite of themselves, that he is who he claimed to be and that he is without fault in his conduct both to themselves and others. Paul wrote of that day, saying that "every tongue" shall confess that "Jesus Christ is Lord, to the glory of God the Father" (Phil. 2:11).

And Yet He Dies

The Lord Jesus Christ passed through every examination that could possibly be made of him and was declared to be blameless. He was weighed in every scale, measured by every standard, by friends and foes alike, and in each case he was found to be innocent. Yet now, although he is officially found to be innocent, he dies. Why is this? Death is the result of sin (Rom. 6:23; cf. 1 Cor. 15:56), but Christ was sinless. Why does the sinless One die?

We may answer the question on two levels. If we look at the question from the human point of view, the answer is that Jesus died as a result of the hatred of the Jewish leaders coupled to the moral cowardice of Pilate. This is only another way of saying that it was because of the rebellion of the human heart against God that Christ was crucified. But this is only one side of the story. The other side, the truly wonderful side, is that Jesus died because God had appointed him to be our sin-bearer.

Recently in my studies I have come across some words that present this truth so well that I quote them here at length. They are by a man who was probably the greatest evangelical preacher in Germany during the middle part of the nineteenth century, Friedrich Wilhelm Krummacher. They have been published in English under the title *The Suffering Savior*. Krummacher writes, "But tell us now, why did Jesus die? 'It is appointed unto sinners once to die, and after that the judgment'; but he was not a sinner. Even the redeemed have no other way to the heavenly world than through death, because their flesh is corrupted by sin. But in Christ's corporeality this is not the case; and yet he dies, and that in such a dreadful manner! Explain how this is. Take time to reflect. But however long and deeply you may study the subject, we tell you decidedly beforehand that you will not bring forward any rational, convincing, and satisfactory solution to this mystery.

"Hear, therefore, how we view the subject, and consider whether there is room for any other. The monstrous fact that the just and spotless Jesus, notwithstanding his holiness, was condemned to death, would compel us to the conclusion that the doctrine of a righteous God, who rules over all, is a delusion—that the will of man or chance alone govern the world—that there exists no divine retribution upon earth, and that it will not fare the worse with the impious than with the just—I say we should be necessarily compelled to inferences of this kind, if we were not permitted to assume that the immaculate Son of God suffered death in our stead. This view of the subject furnishes the only key to the mystery of the ignominious end of the just and holy Jesus.

"But if we presuppose an atonement made by Christ for sin—and we not only may do so, but are constrained to it by the clear evidence of Holy Writ—then all is plain; all is solved and deciphered, and a sublime meaning and a glorious connection pervades the whole. God threatened Adam in paradise, saying, 'In the day that thou eatest of the fruit of this tree, thou shalt surely die.' We did eat of that fruit and incurred the penalty. But the eternal Son now appears, removes the penalty from us to himself, and we live.

"On Sinai it was said, 'Cursed be everyone who continueth not in all things that are written in the book of the law to do them.' We did not continue in them, and our fate was decided. But our Surety presents himself, endures the curse for us, and we are justly delivered and absolved. God has resolved to save sinners, notwithstanding he has said, 'I will blot the name of him that sinneth out of my book.' We believe in our salvation, for he inflicted upon Christ the punishment due to us. God promised the crown of life only to the obedient; but after Christ as our representative obeyed in our name, God can bestow the crown on sinners and yet continue holy.

"Thus all becomes clear, and the most striking opposites harmoniously agree. And yet men dare to call our doctrine of the atonement made by Christ irrational, and even absurd. Look how Pilate unconsciously stands in the breach for us, by testifying to the truth that Jesus was not guilty of death. Attempt in a satisfactory and rational manner, if you can, to explain it otherwise than by the atonement made by Christ, how it was that even the holy and immaculate Son of God paid the wages of sin."[2]

No Health in Us

Yes, he is the guiltless one. But we are guilty. Of him it was said, "I find no basis for any charge against him." There was no fault to be found with Jesus. But of which of us can those words rightly be spoken? No fault in me? No fault in you? Impossible! Rather we are riddled with faults. As the ancient collect says, "We have done those things we ought not to have done; we have left undone those things we ought to have done; and there is no health in us." We have rebelled against God's righteous rule. We have broken his laws and have defaced his image in us. We deserve his just condemnation. We deserve to die. But at this point the glory of the gospel comes in. For Jesus, the Righteous One, has died for us that we might be saved from condemnation.

Has he died for you? Do you know that personally? If not, you can know it merely by committing yourself to him. You can say, "Lord Jesus Christ, I know that I am a sinner. I deserve to die for my sin, but you have died for me. I trust you as having become my Savior in your death. Receive me now as one of your followers. I promise to follow and serve you from this time forth, forever." If you will honestly pray that prayer, you are already his, for he has received you, having already done the marvelous work of regeneration in your heart.

236

Christ before Herod

John 18:38

"What is truth?" Pilate asked. With this he went out again to the Jews and said, "I find no basis for a charge against him."

The verdict of Pontius Pilate that the Lord Jesus Christ was innocent of the charges brought against him should have been followed by an immediate release of the prisoner. Or, if Pilate had reason to believe that the Jews would harm Jesus in spite of his judgment, he should have put the Lord into protective custody, as the Romans later did with the apostle Paul (Acts 21:31ff.). But when Pilate announced his verdict publicly the decision met with such opposition from the rulers and the crowds that Pilate immediately backed away from the only proper and noble course and instead attempted to bring about the release of Jesus indirectly.

He made three attempts to do this. One was to have Jesus beaten, thereby hoping to evoke pity from the bloodthirsty mob. A second was to honor the custom of releasing one prisoner at the feast which, he suggested, might be followed by releasing Jesus. A third attempt, the first Pilate tried, was to send the Lord Jesus Christ to Herod Antipas.

1451

Pilate's attempt to pass the buck was unsuccessful, as such attempts usually are. He was attempting to pass the responsibility for dealing with Christ
to Herod, but the matter simply came back to him. He could not escape it.
No more can those today escape when confronted with the person of Christ
and asked to take a stand for him.

Herod Antipas

Herod Antipas was a son of Herod the Great, who had commanded the
babes of Bethlehem to be killed in hopes of destroying the so-called "King of
the Jews" about whom he had been informed by the wise men (Matt. 2:1–18).
Old Herod was a dissolute and dangerous creature. He had had ten wives and
had murdered a number of them as well as several of his children. This had
led the emperor Augustus to say of him that it was better to be Herod's pig
than one of his sons. But however base the father was, this was even more true
of the son. Antipas was a libertine of the worst sort. Thus, although he governed adequately for a time, he lacked that ruthless tenacity of purpose that
had served his father well and so was eventually removed by the Romans.

Herod Antipas did not rule all that Herod the Great had ruled. One of the
father's wills had designated Antipas his sole successor. But there had been
various wills, and the matter was finally disposed by Augustus in the following fashion. One son, Archelaus, was given the area of Judea, Samaria, and
Idumea; that is, the southernmost region. He was termed an ethnarch. A second son, Philip, was given the area of the Decapolis; that is, the region to the
east. Herod received the title of tetrarch and was given the provinces of Galilee
and Perea; that is, the northernmost sector of the father's kingdom.

We know a few more things about Herod. For one thing, he is the ruler
who arrested and then later killed John the Baptist. John had criticized Herod
for having taken his brother's divorced wife, Herodias, while his brother was
still living, and Herod had arrested John for it. At this stage Herod seemed
to have some sensibility toward religious things, for he respected John and
even listened to him. But after he had killed John, this rapidly degenerated
to mere superstition. Thus, when told of Jesus' preaching and works, Herod
imagined that he was John the Baptist risen from the dead (Matt. 14:1–2;
Mark 6:14–16). Later, whether correct or incorrect, the rumor reached Jesus
that Herod was seeking to kill him also (Luke 13:31). Jesus replied, "Go tell
that fox, 'I will drive out demons and heal people today and tomorrow, and
on the third day I will reach my goal'" (vv. 32–33). "Fox" was an apt designation for Antipas, for he was indeed a crafty and cunning man held under
the debilitating influences of a licentious woman.

In Herod's Court

Here we must leave John's Gospel and go to Luke, for Luke alone of all
the Gospel writers tells of this incident. His account is as follows: "On hear-

ing this, Pilate asked if the man was a Galilean. When he learned that Jesus was under Herod's jurisdiction, he sent him to Herod, who was also in Jerusalem at that time. When Herod saw Jesus, he was greatly pleased, because for a long time he had been wanting to see him. From what he had heard about him, he hoped to see him perform some miracle. He plied him with many questions, but Jesus gave him no answer. The chief priests and the teachers of the law were standing there, vehemently accusing him. Then Herod and his soldiers ridiculed and mocked him. Dressing him in an elegant robe, they sent him back to Pilate. That day Herod and Pilate became friends—before this they had been enemies" (23:6–12).

This brief account tells us much about Herod. For one thing, it tells us that Herod was aware of much that was going on in his province. We know this because we are told that "from what he had heard" of Jesus "he hoped to see him perform some miracle." Second, it tells us that he had a certain curiosity about Jesus, for he was "greatly pleased" to see him. Third, however, and more seriously, it discloses more of Herod's spiritual decline, for on this occasion the reproving voice of conscience seems to be entirely absent, and we find him looking upon this solemn confrontation as simply an occasion for entertainment. When this turned out disappointingly, the curiosity with which he began soon curdled into stark contempt and cruelty.

Herod's experience should be a warning to many similarly minded persons who frequent places of Christian worship out of curiosity and are only hardened. The Lord did not reveal himself to Herod. He did not speak. God will not reveal the precious things of his Word to anyone's idle curiosity.

Curiosity Not Enough

The true measure of the tragedy which was Herod is seen, in that which in other circumstances might be thought good.

First, there is this matter of *Herod's curiosity*. God will not reveal the precious things of his Word to idle curiosity, but this does not mean that curiosity itself is all bad or that God will not on occasion use it to draw a person to him. We recall, for example, that Jesus played upon the curiosity both of Nicodemus and of the woman of Samaria in attempting to lead them to the truth about his mission. To Nicodemus he spoke cryptically of the new birth, prompting the aging leader of Israel to ask, "How can a man be born when he is old? Surely he cannot enter the second time into his mother's womb to be born!" (John 3:4). To the woman of Samaria he spoke of living water, causing her to reply, "Sir, you have nothing to draw with and the well is deep. Where can you get this living water? Are you greater than our father Jacob, who gave us the well and drank from it himself, as did also his sons and his flocks and herds?" (John 4:11–12). Curiosity itself is not bad, and this much at least can be said concerning Herod, that his curiosity had been stirred regarding Jesus.

How had it been stirred? Obviously by hearing much about him. What Jesus was doing had been the common talk of the kingdom for the space of three years, and much of this had undoubtedly come to the dissolute tetrarch's attention. He could hardly have failed to hear of Jesus' feeding of the four and five thousand, for these feedings had taken place in or near Galilee and had been accompanied by significant popular movements by those who wished to make Jesus king. Jesus had walked on the water in Galilee. He had stilled the storm. He had healed the son of a Galilean nobleman. There were other miracles. Then, in addition to these miracles, Jesus had raised Lazarus from the dead in Bethany just a week before, and the news of this great miracle had apparently spread through Jerusalem like wildfire. Herod may not have heard of all these miracles, but the main ones had undoubtedly been brought to his attention. It was undoubtedly because of this that he wished to see Jesus do some wonder.

Moreover, it was not just through idle rumor that Herod had heard of Jesus. Herod had also heard of him through John the Baptist. We have no record of what John actually said to Herod. But we can hardly imagine that John, having received an opportunity to speak to Herod, would have failed to point to Jesus. Herod may even have heard John's great text and testimony: "Behold the Lamb of God, who takes away the sin of the world" (John 1:29).

We note one other fact also. There was in Herod's household one who undoubtedly knew much about Jesus, if indeed he was not a full believer. He is none other than the husband of Joanna, one of the women who traveled about with Jesus and ministered to him out of her substance (Luke 8:3). The husband's name was Chuzas, and he is identified as Herod's steward. If Herod was interested in Jesus, as he undoubtedly was, he would have inquired about him and would undoubtedly have received information about him from his steward. Yet Herod's curiosity remained only an idle curiosity. He made no effort to see Jesus and learn from him, even when his remorse over his treatment of John the Baptist was at its zenith.

Joy and Expectation

There are two more things that might be said in Herod's favor were they not so deeply corrupted. The first is that, in consequence of his curiosity, Herod is said to have *rejoiced at seeing Jesus*. In fact, we are told that he was "greatly pleased" (Luke 6:8). Again, we are told that Herod was glad because he *"hoped to see him perform a miracle."* Are not we who follow Christ also glad in the same expectation? We too hope to see some great miracles done by him. When the gospel is preached, we hope to see those who are dead in trespasses and sins brought to spiritual life. When the teachings of Christ are put forth, we hope to see lives turned about, sin repented of, and many urged on in the straight way which Christ sets before them. Again, upon ourselves we also hope to see some miracle. We wish our eyes opened to some new and marvelous thing out of God's Word. We wish our wills changed that we might seek him with all our heart. We wish to be convicted of sin and urged on in righteousness. We wish to be made like Jesus.

Yes, we desire these things. But this godly joy and spiritual expectation were not the joy and expectation of Herod. He was "exceedingly glad," but it was a frivolous gladness, just as his curiosity was an idle curiosity. He was expectant, but it was a base expectation. He hoped only to see some wonder with which he might later entertain his guests at some low banquet and orgy. Each would have his stories. But Herod's story of a miracle done by the Galilean peasant would top them all.

A Hardened Conscience

That brings us to these points of conclusion. It is not that curiosity, joy, and expectation are bad in themselves. They are good. We might even argue that they have been given to us by God, that they, like all God's good gifts, might lead us to him. What is wrong is that in many persons they have been perverted through the hardening effect of sin.

There is no true approach to God without a painful awareness of one's own sin. This is because God is holy, and we cannot approach him in his holiness without a corresponding exposure of our own corruption. When God approached Adam and Eve in the Garden, after the fall, they hid from him because they knew they were naked (Gen. 3:10). When Isaiah saw God high and lifted up and heard the seraphim singing of his holiness, he fell back, crying, "Woe to me! I am ruined! For I am a man of unclean lips, and I live among a people of unclean lips; and my eyes have seen the King, the LORD Almighty" (Isa. 6:5). When Peter caught a glimpse of who Jesus really is on the occasion of his miracle in providing a great catch of fish in Galilee, Peter responded, "Go away from me, Lord; I am a sinful man" (Luke 5:8). Clearly Herod had undergone this kind of experience (though without profit), for the preaching of John the Baptist concerning the immorality of his life had troubled him.

In proper circumstances the conviction of sin should lead, first, to repentance, and second, to faith in Jesus Christ where alone the penalty and guilt of sin are dealt with. But where this does not take place—where conviction of sin does not lead both to repentance and faith—unconfessed sin hardens, and eventually the one who was once genuinely convicted can regard religious matters only with an idle curiosity or even antagonism.

These were the steps in Herod's fall. First, there was a genuine conviction of sin. But Herod did not welcome this conviction, being unwilling to part from his sin. He wished to be religious and keep his sin too. Therefore, second, he attempted to still the voice of conscience which, in this case, meant stilling the voice of John the Baptist. At first he tried prison. But once launched upon this course, he soon came to the position of murdering John both to satisfy Salome and also to rescue his own imagined honor. Third, having silenced the voice of conscience, which always insists upon the indispensable place of morality in true religion, Herod's religious instincts turned to superstition. He thought that Jesus was John the Baptist raised from the dead. Fourth, superstition turned to raw unbelief, for when Herod finally did have Jesus before him he looked upon him only as one who might be prevailed upon to do a trick for the amusement of himself and his court. Fifth and finally, when Jesus declined to perform for this by now rank profligate and unbeliever, Herod's interest turned to derision, and he and his men of war viciously scoffed at Jesus. Having silenced him who was the Voice, it was no marvel that Herod now failed to hear or appreciate the Word.

God Is Not Mocked

You cannot treat God lightly. You cannot mock him. If you would meet him, you must be serious about the encounter, more serious than you have ever been about anything in your life before, and you must be ready to be changed profoundly by him.

What is God anyway? An intellectual curiosity? Someone who exists to provide you with free entertainment or free blessings? Is he as idle as you? Is he as frivolous? He is the great, holy, omnipotent God of the universe who takes the business of being God seriously. "I am the LORD your God," he says. "You shall have no other gods before me" (Exod. 20:2–3). "You shall not kill. You shall not commit adultery. You shall not steal. You shall not give false testimony against your neighbor. You shall not covet" (vv. 13–17). "Be perfect, therefore, as your heavenly Father is perfect" (Matt. 5:48). "Be holy" (1 Peter 1:16; cf. Lev. 11:44). Jesus said, "If anyone would come after me, he must deny himself and take up his cross and follow me" (Matt. 16:24).

That is what God requires. If you will not do that, then your religious sensibilities will decline, as did Herod's. And the time will come when Jesus will depart from your presence, never to return. On the other hand, if you will repent of your sin and turn to him, then you will find that he has already received you and is at work to lead you in the way of righteousness. Will you come? Will you not turn your back on that sin that holds you in its grip and follow Jesus?

237

Barabbas

John 18:39–40

"But it is your custom for me to release to you one prisoner at the time of the Passover. Do you want me to release 'the king of the Jews'?"

They shouted back, "No, not him! Give us Barabbas!" Now Barabbas had taken part in a rebellion.

Christians will agree that if God is truly the sovereign God the Scriptures portray him to be, then nothing in the world is without meaning. The stars have their meaning. So do the fish of the sea, the animals, the events of history. It is true that we may not always see their meaning or understand their purposes. But they are there all the same and can teach us something.

If this is true of the Creation and the events of history in general, as it obviously is, it is certainly true of the events surrounding the arrest, trial, and crucifixion of Jesus Christ. From a secular perspective these events may be imagined to have fallen out at random as a product of the unpredictable interaction of the leaders of Israel with their particular animosities toward Jesus and the character and desires of Pilate. But this is not the case. It is true that the lead-

1457

ers of the people and Pilate did interact and that events flowed from this interaction, but what resulted was no mere accident. Rather it was that which had been specifically predetermined and even foretold prophetically by God. It was foretold that the Messiah would be betrayed by Judas (Ps. 41:9; Zech. 11:12), and be rejected and scorned by his own people (Isa. 53:3). Specific prophecies include the use of false witnesses (Ps. 35:11), Christ's silence before his accusers (Isa. 53:7), his beatings (Isa. 50:6), his being offered gall and vinegar to drink (Ps. 69:21), his being crucified with thieves (Isa. 53:12), his being pierced by a spear (Zech. 12:10), and his burial in the tomb of a rich man (Isa. 53:9). Each of these details teaches particular lessons about the work of Christ and the meaning of the Atonement.

An Important Detail

In the midst of these many predetermined and therefore meaningful details, there is a special story that is fascinating, not only for what it teaches about the death of the Lord, but also for the emphasis the Gospels give to it. It is unusual to find any given event from the life of Christ contained in all four Gospels, for the simple reason that these are not mere history but are specific portraits of Christ emphasizing one or more aspects of his life and ministry. Yet this story, the story of Barabbas, is in all four Gospels. And not only that, it occupies an important place in them (particularly in Matthew, Mark, and Luke). If we count carefully, we discover thirty-eight verses used to tell this story. This is more even than the account of the betrayal of Christ by Judas and certainly more than the accounts of those parts of the trial that only one or two of the Gospels give to us.

On the surface the story is simple enough. In fact, it is so simple that John, who recounts it in the shortest space of all, uses only three verses to do so.

The basis of the story lies in Pilate's desire to see Jesus released even though his accusers were clamoring for his death. He could have insisted on the Lord's release. But Pilate was trying to satisfy the crowds too (which is usually an impossible position to be in), so he began to search about for indirect ways to free Jesus. His first attempt had been to send him to Herod, which he was able to do because Jesus had come from Galilee and might therefore be thought to fall under the jurisdiction of the Galilean tetrarch. In a few moments he would have Christ flogged, thinking that by that act he might evoke a measure of sympathy from the mob. But before this last expedient, he hit upon another idea that at the time must have struck him as particularly fortuitous.

Pilate recalled a custom in Israel according to which—as a symbol of the mercy of God and as a reminder of their own historical deliverance out of bondage in Egypt—the people were permitted to ask at the Passover festival for the liberation of some offender who was at that moment in prison. We may suppose that as Pilate remembered this his face brightened and he moved to seize upon it as some shipwrecked sailor might seize upon a floating plank as his means of salvation. Perhaps he could use this custom to effect the release of Jesus. Pilate therefore searched through his mind to recall some criminal so notable that, were he to make the choice between this one and Jesus, the criminal would never be chosen by the people. He thought of Barabbas, who, we are told, was a robber (John 18:40), an insurrectionist, and a murderer (Mark 15:7; Luke 23:19). Matthew tells us that he was a "notorious prisoner" (Matt. 27:16). Who, Pilate thought, would ever prefer this vile rebel and murderer to the One in whom he had found no fault at all?

It may have been with pride and a certain smugness in the anticipated success of his plan that Pilate now went to the rostrum to offer the people this choice. "It is your custom," he said "for me to release to you one prisoner at the time of the Passover" (John 18:39). "Which one do you want me to release to you: Barabbas, or Jesus who is called Christ?" (Matt. 27:17).

How wise Pilate thought he was, yet how foolishly he acted! For to his immense surprise the crowd, goaded by the rulers, immediately rejected Christ and chose Barabbas. "Give us Barabbas," was their cry (John 18:40).

"What shall I do then with Jesus, who is called Christ?"

The people cried out, "Crucify him!" (Matt. 27:22–23).

It was a disaster. Here Krummacher writes, "The Savior's fate is now no longer in Pilate's hands. The majority of the multitude decides, and he is obliged to abide by its decision. Had he been bold enough to follow the dictate of his own conscience and to have said with calm discrimination, 'Justice shall be done, even though the world should perish; the guiltless Nazarene is free, and those cohorts here will know how to give effect to my decision,' his opponents inwardly rebuked, would doubtless have shrunk back thunderstruck, and the people, roused from their delusion, would have loudly applauded the energetic judge. But Pilate now stands forever as a warning example of the consequence of endeavoring to satisfy both God, who speaks within us, and the world."[1]

The World's Choice

And, of course, it was the world! And the decision of the mob was the world's decision! The world will ever choose a robber, insurrectionist, or murderer to the guiltless Christ. Why? Because Barabbas is of the world and is the world. Barabbas is one of them, and however dangerous he may be, he is at least controllable. They can handle him. But how do you handle Jesus?

Tom Skinner writes of this in *Words of Revolution*. "Barabbas is the guy who was going to destroy the system. Barabbas was going to burn them out. Barabbas was going to kill them. Why would they want Barabbas? It's very simple. If you let Barabbas go, and he starts another disturbance or another riot, you can always call out the National Guard, the federal troops or the Marines to put his thing down. All you have to do is push a few tanks into his neighborhood and you can squash whatever he's up to. You can find out where he's keeping his guns and raid his apartment. You can always stop Barabbas.

But the question is: *how do you stop Jesus?* How do you stop a Man who has no guns, no tanks, no ammunition, but still is shaking the whole Roman empire? How do you stop a Man, who—without firing a shot—is getting revolutionary results? They figured there's only one answer—get rid of him. They made the same mistake people have made down through the history of man. They thought you could get rid of the idea by getting rid of the man from whom the idea comes. So they said, 'We can get rid of Jesus. We don't want him to rule over us.'

"Barabbas would never really ask to run your life. Barabbas would exploit you, but he wouldn't ask to run your life. Jesus would ask to run your life. Jesus would ask for the right to rule over you! And that's the problem. Men would rather be enslaved to tyranny than let Jesus rule their lives. They would rather be exploited than let Christ determine their lives. So they said, 'Give us Barabbas.'"[2]

The crime of Barabbas was the same crime of which the Jewish leaders had accused Christ falsely, and their position in Israel was certainly not enhanced by Barabbas's release. Yet they chose him, so great was their opposition to Jesus.

The Sinner's Salvation

We have looked at the story of Barabbas through two sets of eyes: those of Pilate and those of the leaders of the people. Each view contains great lessons. Yet the greatest lessons are to be seen, not through the eyes of Pilate or even the eyes of the leaders, but through the eyes of Barabbas himself. From this perspective the story of Barabbas is the story of stories, for it is the story of the sinner's salvation through Jesus' death on Calvary.

We notice in the first place, as we have not noticed until now, that the name Barabbas is an Aramaic word meaning "son of a father." *Bar* means "son," and *abba* means "father." So the word itself signifies that Barabbas is a representative type of all the sons of all the fathers who have ever been born into this world. As Donald Grey Barnhouse writes in his valuable comments on this story, "We are all of Adam's race. We have been bound over for our sedition against God. We are robbers of his glory. We are murderers of our souls and the souls of others. We find ourselves bound in the darksome prison house of sin. We feel in our hearts that we merit the sentence that has been announced to us and we wait in trembling for the time of judgment. Every man loves freedom. To be put in a cell is a horrible curtailment of human liberty, and the necessity of such confinement shows what society thinks of the terrible outbreaks that endanger the smooth flow of what men call civilization."

Barnhouse continues, "The Roman soldiery had stopped the riot and had taken Barabbas. His blood-guiltiness was established. He was flung in his cell, there to wait the moment of his death. A man who is to be hanged has difficulty in keeping his hand away from his throat where the rope is soon to choke him. I have been told by a chaplain in a prison where men are executed in a gas chamber that the condemned practice long breathing, and sometimes will hold their breath until it seems that their eyes will pop from their sockets. They know that they are going to be put into a gas chamber and that they will hear a little hissing sound of incoming death, and that the breath they are now forcing into their lungs will be the last that they shall ever know. They will hold on and on, straining at the thongs that tie them to their chair, until they are forced by the inexhorable law of breathing to exhale the last breath that contained pure oxygen and take in the death that floats around them.

"Barabbas must have looked at the palms of his hands and wondered how it would feel to have the nails ripping through the flesh. He must have remembered scenes of crucifixion death, and the slow agony of the victims who suffered at times for a day or two before merciful death came to release them. He must have awakened with a start if he heard any hammering in the jail, and his mind must have anticipated the sound of the clanging hammers that would bring death near to him. And then, in his prison, he heard the vague murmuring of the crowd that roared outside like the murmur of a troubled sea. He thinks he hears his own name. He can tell that there are angry cries, and fear rises in his heart. Then he hears the sound of a key in the lock, and a jailer comes to him and releases him from the chain that is wound around him, for the Bible tells that he was bound. He must have thought that his time had come, but the jailer takes him to the door and tells him that he is free.

"In his stupefaction he moves toward the crowd. There is little welcome for him, and he senses the deep preoccupation of the people. If he meets one of his old companions in the crowd, he is greeted with but a moment's word, and then he hears the surging roar, 'Crucify him! Crucify him!' In modern language he would say to his companions, 'What's the pitch? Give me the lowdown!' And he would be briefly answered that the roar is against Jesus, and that he is to be crucified, and that the crowd had cried out for the release of Barabbas.

"Stunned, he walks nearer to the center of the scene and sees the man who is to die in his place. Finally the procession begins toward Golgatha. He follows and sees Jesus fall under the weight of the cross. He sees Simon of Cyrene pressed by the soldiers to fall in line and carry the cross, and finally they arrive at Calvary. What must have been his thoughts? He hears the echoing blows of the hammer striking the nails, and looks down at his own hands. He had thought that this would be his day. He had thought that the nails would tear his flesh. And here he is breathing the air of springtime and looking at the dark cloud that is gathering in the sky. Does he say, 'Those hammer blows were meant for me, but he is dying in my place'? He could have said it in literal truth that day.

"The cross is lifted up and he sees the silhouette against the sky. The sun grows dark and he hears voices that come to him like thunder. 'Father, forgive them, for they know not what they do.' The centurion passes near him, and seeing the look upon his face, says, 'Truly this was the Son of God.' And Barabbas, more than before, looks with wonder and amazement at the man who is dying for him. There comes a cry, 'It is finished,' and a little while later he sees the soldiers take down the body and put it in its temporary grave. He goes back to the city, and all the little things that he had expected to see no more come before his eyes with freshness of new creation. 'He took my place. Jesus took my place. They released me, Barabbas, who deserved to die, and they crucified Jesus instead of me. He took my place. He died instead of me.'"

Barnhouse concludes, "Barabbas was the only man in the world who could say that Jesus Christ took his physical place. But I can say that Jesus Christ took my spiritual place. For it was I who deserved to die. It was I who deserved that the wrath of God should be poured upon me. I deserved the eternal punishment of the lake of fire. He was delivered up for my offenses. He was handed over to judgment because of my sins. This is why we speak of the substitutionary atonement. Christ was my substitute. He was satisfying the debt of divine justice and holiness. That is why I say that Christianity can be expressed in the three phrases: I deserved Hell; Jesus took my Hell; there is nothing left for me but his Heaven."[3]

The scriptural key to the scene is found in the words of Paul in 2 Corinthians 5:21, "God made him who had no sin to be sin for us, so that in him we might become the righteousness of God." Jesus died that we might live. He was bound that we, who have all our lifetimes been subject to the bondage of sin, might be set free.

Set Free

Are you set free? Or, if I may put it this way, are you one who has chosen to remain in the dungeon to which your sins have confined you? We have imagined in the previous paragraphs how Barabbas undoubtedly received his unexpected good fortune. We have supposed that he left the prison and returned to freedom. Could we imagine it otherwise?

Suppose word had come to Barabbas that he was now free and that another prisoner, Jesus, would be dying. Suppose he replied this way: "What you are telling me cannot be true. It may apply to someone else, someone who has committed a lesser offense than I. But I am a great sinner and criminal. No, I cannot believe it. I must stay here." And suppose he had resisted when the guards attempted to remove his chains and release him? We can hardly imagine such a response. Yet this is the response of some to whom the gospel of the substitutionary atonement of the Lord Jesus Christ is preached. They think that it is for another and so do not respond to that which to them is life.

Suppose again that Barabbas had acted in this way. Suppose he had said, "I refuse to accept such a pardon, because what I have done was entirely justified. I was right to rob and murder and commit insurrection. I will not go unless the representative of Rome comes to apologize for the way I have been treated and provides me with a bill of absolvement." In that case, Barabbas would have died, for it is a principle of law that a pardon is a gift and no man can ever be compelled to accept a gift. Chief Justice Marshall ruled in the case of the condemned murderer George Wilson, who refused his pardon: "A pardon is a slip of paper. The value of the pardon is determined by the acceptance of it by the person to be pardoned. If it is refused, it is no pardon! Wilson must be hanged." We might judge such a reaction foolish, as it is. But it is a possible one, and the consequences are certain.

Again, suppose Barabbas had responded to the announcement of his liberty that he would prefer to reform himself first of all: "By this means I will prove that I have earned my freedom and truly deserve it." The magistrates would have answered that however good a man he might yet become (or not become), this nevertheless has no bearing on the crimes he has already committed and for which he was condemned to die. Future reformation cannot atone for past sin. Consequently, Barabbas's only hope was in the pardon provided through the death of the innocent Christ.

Did Barabbas reply in any one of these ways? We know he did not. In fact, it is highly unlikely that any one of them even occurred to him, so anxious was he to leave the prison and return to a free life outside.

Why then should you do differently? A pardon is offered. Jesus has died. Will you not accept his death in place of your own and quickly go forth to serve him? Charles Wesley, the brother of the famed Methodist evangelist and preacher, John Wesley, did precisely that and wrote about it in one of our greatest hymns.

> And can it be that I should gain
> An interest in the Savior's blood?
> Died He for me, who caused His pain?
> For me, who Him to death pursued?
> Amazing love! how can it be
> That Thou, my God, shouldst die for me?
>
> He left His Father's throne above,
> So free, so infinite His grace!
> Emptied Himself of all but love,
> And bled for Adam's helpless race!
> 'Tis mercy all, immense and free,
> For, O my God, it found out me.
>
> Long my imprisoned spirit lay
> Fast bound in sin and nature's night.
> Thine eye diffused a quickening ray;
> I woke, the dungeon flamed with light!
> My chains fell off, my heart was free,
> I rose, went forth, and followed Thee.

No condemnation now I dread:
Jesus, and all in Him, is mine!
Alive in Him, my living Head,
And clothed in righteousness divine,
Bold I approach the eternal throne,
And claim the crown, through Christ my own.

If you have been languishing in the gloomy dungeon of your unbelief, you may do as Wesley and so many others have done. Believe the gospel, and go forth to serve that One who out of the great measure of his love gave himself for your freedom.

238

"Behold the Man!"

John 19:1–5

Then Pilate took Jesus and had him flogged. The soldiers twisted together a crown of thorns and put it on his head. They clothed him in a purple robe and went up to him again and again, saying, "Hail, king of the Jews!" And they struck him in the face.

Once more Pilate came out and said to the Jews, "Look, I am bringing him out to you to let you know that I find no basis for a charge against him." When Jesus came out wearing the crown of thorns and the purple robe, Pilate said to them, "Here is the man!"

The eighteenth and nineteenth chapters of John's Gospel deal with the trials of Jesus of Nazareth beginning with his arrest in the Garden of Gethsemane and culminating in his crucifixion, as recorded in John 19:16–30. But strictly speaking, what we have in the first part of chapter 19 is not a trial. In fact, we have not been dealing with a trial in any strict sense since Pilate's initial verdict of acquittal recorded in verse 38 of the preceding chapter. Jesus is still in the hands of the Roman procurator; the words that were to deliver him over to be crucified have not been uttered. But the trial actually ended earlier when Pilate said, "I find no basis for any charge against him."

What occurs in the interval between the formal verdict of acquittal (John 18:38) and the execution of Jesus (John 19:16–30) is a series of attempts by Pilate to escape the people's wishes. He knew Jesus was innocent of the charges brought against him; but since the rulers wanted Jesus crucified, Pilate (1) sent Jesus to Herod hoping that Herod would solve his dilemma, (2) attempted to release Jesus instead of Barabbas in honor of Jewish custom, and (3) caused Jesus to be beaten, hoping by this means to evoke pity from the leaders and mob. None of these stratagems worked. But each, as we have already begun to see, shows much about the nature of the human heart and its sin as well as about God's plan for the redemption of the race through Jesus' crucifixion.

Each event is pregnant with meaning, for never in the entire history of the world has so much, done in so short a time, been so significant.

What Man Is This?

It was asked on an earlier occasion when Jesus had stilled the wind and waves on the Sea of Galilee, "What manner of man is this?" We may well ask the same question as we see him brought forth by Pilate after the merciless scourging by the soldiers of Rome. Here was One who, though he had been beaten unjustly, nevertheless bore himself with such dignity that the invitation of Pilate to "behold the man" is to see that which clearly overwhelms us. We hear the invitation: *"Ecce homo* (Behold the man!)" We look, and we conclude, "Never in all the history of the world has there been one like Jesus!"

Let me challenge you to behold him. Behold him first before Pilate, and ask, "Who is this one who stands before Pilate, beaten to the point of death, wearing a purple robe, crowned with thorns, ridiculed as the carnival King of the Jews?"

First of all, he is an innocent man. No crime has been proven against him. And not only has he already been pronounced innocent by Pilate, he is to be pronounced innocent several times more. It was the verdict of all who had dealings with him in these hours. First, Judas declared, "I have sinned, for I have betrayed innocent blood" (Matt. 27:4). Second, Pilate's wife sent to the Roman procurator, saying, "Don't have anything to do with that innocent man, for I have suffered a great deal today in a dream because of him" (Matt. 27:19). Third, Pilate himself declared Christ innocent: "I find no basis for a charge against him" (John 18:38). Fourth, Herod found Christ blameless, for Pilate reported of Herod's verdict, "Neither has Herod, for he sent him back to us; as you can see, he has done nothing to deserve death" (Luke 23:15). Fifth, the dying thief expostulated, "We are punished justly; for we are getting what our deeds deserve. But this man has done nothing wrong" (Luke 23:41). Sixth, the centurion in charge of the crucifixion said, "Surely this was a righteous man" (Luke 23:47). Lastly, the crowds at the cross, seeing the earthquake and the other supernatural signs accompanying his death, exclaimed, "Surely this was the Son of God" (Matt. 27:54).

This is the verdict of all who have looked at Jesus of Nazareth closely. It is the verdict of God and man, friend and foe, ancient and modern—as pointed out in a previous study.[1]

As we look at Jesus before Pilate we also notice that he is a brave man. He had been beaten mercilessly, yet there is nothing cringing or compromising about his bearing. We have never seen a scourging, so it is hard to imagine the suffering involved in it. We should remember that the victim was stripped of clothing and tied to a post in a way that fully exposed the back. Being struck with a long leather thong (into which sharp pieces of lead, bone, and rock had been inserted) literally tore the person's back into strips. Besides, the beating was so prolonged that few remained conscious throughout the ordeal and some died. Jesus bore this. Yet it was after his suffering that Pilate led him forth and called the people to "Behold the man!"

Was there wonder, even admiration in Pilate's voice as he said this? There is room to think so. I suspect that William Barclay is on the right track when he writes: "It must have been Pilate's first intention to awaken the pity of the Jews. 'Look!' he said. 'Look at this poor, bruised, bleeding creature! Look at this wretchedness! Can you possibly wish to hound a creature like this to an utterly unnecessary death?' But even as he said it, we can almost hear the tone of Pilate's voice change and see the wonder dawn in his eyes. And instead of saying it half-contemptuously, to awaken pity, he says it with a dawning wonder and an admiration that will not be repressed."[2] In wartime soldiers will frequently admire the bravery of a defeated enemy, wondering how they themselves might bear up under similar suffering were the roles reversed. Did Pilate, an old soldier, perhaps inwardly respect Christ's fortitude?

But it is not only bravery that we see in the man before Pilate. There is also majesty, and such majesty as befits the Son of God. Behold the man? Yes. But behold the King, too! And here we do not mean merely the mock king of the soldiers' devising. We mean the true King, the King of kings, whose dignity and grace shone through even in the moment of his greatest physical humiliation. This was a great man. But this was also God, as the resurrection was soon to indicate (Rom. 1:4).

Before the Crowds

Jesus appeared that day not only before Pilate. He also appeared before the crowds. Indeed, this seems to be the reason for the scourging; for with the stage presence and sense of audience psychology characteristic of a great trial lawyer, Pilate first seemed to pronounce him innocent and then suddenly produced him to have the crowd see him in his beaten and humiliated state. We know what Pilate expected—an upsurge of pity from the fickle mob. But Pilate miscalculated, for there broke forth a new round of hatred and hostility against Jesus.

Why was this? Why did the presence of Jesus incite such violent hatred? Some writers have suggested that it was an easily understood pattern of psychological reaction: the people saw mirrored in the beaten and disfigured Jesus that moral deformity that they saw, or feared to discover, in themselves. It would be similar to that distaste that so many show for the poor, the deformed, or the dead. There is fear that they will be like them. But this is not the real explanation of the crowd's increasing opposition to and hatred of Jesus. The thing that bothered them about Jesus on this occasion was what had bothered them all along. It was his sinlessness, the awareness of which was heightened by the entirely unwarranted scourging of Jesus and their culpability in that injustice. None care to admit it, but there is in the unsaved person's heart that which leads people to oppose true righteousness.

In his commentary on John, Harry Ironside tells of a meeting of the Synod of the Free Church of Scotland many years ago. One minister was invited to preach the sermon on a particular Sunday morning, and he gave a marvelous oration on the beauty of virtue. He concluded, "Oh, my friends, if virtue incarnate could only appear on earth, men would be so ravished with her beauty that they would fall down and worship her." Many went out saying, "What a magnificent oration that was!"

The same evening another man preached. He did not preach about virtue and beauty. He preached Christ and him crucified. As he closed his sermon he said, "My friends, Virtue Incarnate *has* appeared on earth, and men instead of being ravished with his beauty and falling down and worshipping him, cried out, 'Away with him! Crucify him! We will not have this man to rule over us!'"[3] The second man was right. We do not like to hear it. We resent those who tell us. But the truth is that the natural man hates God's holiness and will do anything rather than allow the light of Christ to penetrate his own deep darkness.

The Masses Today

Third, I want you to "behold the man" as he appears before the masses today. It is the same man, the same Jesus of Nazareth. But while it is true that some do hate him and openly seek to destroy his influence and even his good name, most in our day simply ignore him and thus add insult to injury, suggesting by their neglect that he is hardly worthy of attention.

Those who work on the campuses of our country think this is the case. I received an appeal letter from the head of a large Christian college organization. It said in part, "Some of these institutions and their faculty are openly hostile to the Christian faith. Their students ridicule the Bible and those who believe it. At other schools, God is simply ignored." I would like to have asked this leader how he would balance the percentages. Are most hostile? Or are most unconcerned? I believe that most are unconcerned, or at least try to be. And if this is true on the campuses, it is even more true of the nation at large. Most people will talk about anything but Christianity. And if we were to judge matters by the secular press and other media, we would be hard pressed to know that Jesus even existed, let alone discover anything accurate or significant about him.

To these we wish to say, "*Behold* the master! Do not look away. Do not be too busy. It would be tragic were you to gain the whole world and lose your soul." Yet this is precisely what many will do. They will be lost and not even know they are lost until the reality of the final judgment comes grimly upon them.

Jesus spoke of this shortly before his crucifixion. In the sermon given on the Mount of Olives in the middle of his last week in Jerusalem, Jesus used three gripping parables to teach what the final judgment would be like for such people. One parable was about ten virgins who had been invited to a wedding banquet. Five were wise and five were foolish. The five wise virgins prepared for the banquet by buying oil for their lamps. The five foolish virgins did not. As they waited in the long evening hours all the attendants fell asleep. Suddenly a cry went forth, "Behold the bridegroom is coming; go out to meet him." They rose, but the five foolish virgins had no oil for their lamps. On the advice of the wise they set out to buy some. But while they were getting their oil the bridegroom came and the wedding party followed him into the house and the door was shut. Later the five foolish virgins returned and called at the door, "Lord, Lord, open to us."

But he answered, "Truly, I do not know you."

Jesus concluded, "Therefore, keep watch, because you do not know the day or the hour" (Matt. 25:13).

The second parable was about three servants. Their master was to go on a journey. So he called the servants to him and gave each money: to the first, five talents; to the second, two talents; and to the third, one talent—each according to his ability. Then he went away, and the servants who had received five talents and two talents respectively invested the money while the third servant hid his talent in the ground. After a long time the master returned and asked for an accounting. The man who had received five talents produced those talents plus five more. The servant who had received two talents produced two talents plus two more. But the one who had been given only one talent returned only that one to the Lord, saying, "Master, I knew that you are a hard man, harvesting where you have not sown and gathering where you have not scattered seed. So I was afraid and went and hid your talent in the ground. See, here is what belongs to you" (Matt. 25:24–25). The master condemned that servant, taking away his talent and casting him forth "into the darkness" (v. 30).

Finally, the Lord told the parable of the separation of the sheep from the goats. The goats are the lost, and they are condemned because they neglected to feed the Lord when he was hungry, give him drink when he was thirsty, welcome him when he was a stranger, clothe him when he was naked, visit him when he was sick, and comfort him when he was cast in prison. They say, "But when did we see you hungry or thirsty or lonely or naked or sick?"

He replies, "I tell you the truth, whatever you did not do for one of the least of these [my brothers], you did not do for me" (v. 45). On the other hand, he welcomes those who did these things for his brethren.

Each of these parables, though quite different from the others in detail, is nevertheless one with them in its essential features. In each case, there is a sudden return of the Lord which demands an accounting. In each case, there are some who are prepared for his coming and others who are not. In each case, there are rewards and judgments. Most remarkable of all, in each case those who are lost are totally amazed at the outcome. The foolish virgins are astounded that the bridegroom will not open the door to them. The wicked and lazy servant clearly expected the master to be pleased with his zero-growth performance. The goats cannot believe that they have actually rejected Jesus. They say, "Lord, when did we see you hungry or thirsty or a stranger or needing clothes or sick or in prison, and did not help you?" (Matt. 25:44). They are overwhelmed as he sends them away unto "eternal punishment" (v. 46).

Thus it will be with our generation. We have more opportunities to learn about Christ in our day than ever before in human history. Books and magazines and radio programs and movies and television have all told about him. The call has gone forth, "Behold the man! Look to this one for salvation. He loves you, he died for you. He rose again. Turn from your sin and place your trust in him as your Savior!" But many go blithely on and will be overwhelmed in the day of God's reckoning.

Behold the King

Today is the day of God's grace. And the wisdom of the just in this day consists, as Paul expressed it, in knowing nothing among men save "Christ and him crucified" (1 Cor. 2:2). Now we see him offered to us for salvation. His death is our life. But the day is coming when this period of grace will end, and the One who was judged by the tribunals of this world will be Judge.

One author writes, "How long may it be before we hear the sound of another 'Ecce homo!'? But if we then lift up our eyes, a different form will present itself to our view than that which we saw on Gabbatha. The King of Glory will then have exchanged the robe of mockery for the starry mantle of divine Majesty, the wreath of thorns for a crown of glory, and the reed for the scepter of universal dominion."[4] What will it be in that day? Will it be judgment? Or will the rod be extended as a symbol of his gracious favor as he declares, "Come, you who are blessed by my Father; take your inheritance, the kingdom prepared for you since the creation of the world" (Matt. 25:34). The answer depends on how you behold him now and whether you will surrender to him as your Lord.

239

Who Died on Calvary?

John 19:6–7

As soon as the chief priests and their officials saw him, they shouted, "Crucify! Crucify!"

But Pilate answered, "You take him and crucify him. As for me, I find no basis for a charge against him."

The Jews insisted, "We have a law, and according to that law he must die, because he claimed to be the Son of God."

The events surrounding the crucifixion of Jesus of Nazareth are moving ahead quickly in the nineteenth chapter of John, and before long the teacher of Israel will be crucified. Who is he? Who is this One soon to give his life on Calvary? This question is important because the value of his death depends entirely upon who he was. If he was a criminal and deserved to die, his death means nothing, at least no more than the death of any one of the thousands of other criminals who have been executed down through the long centuries of human history. If he was an innocent man, his death speaks to us merely of the miscarriage of justice; his deportment, only of how a strong man can bravely bear misfortune. On the other hand, if he was God, as he claimed to be, his death has monumental significance.

The Central Issue

We see how inescapable the question is in the verses to which we come now, for although the real charge against Jesus had been veiled in the Jews' previous dealings with Pilate, it now bursts forth in a flood of sudden fury. No less than six separate charges had been brought against him. First, he had been charged with threatening to destroy the Jewish temple (Matt. 26:61). Second, he was accused of being an evildoer (John 18:30). Third, he was charged with perverting the nation (Luke 23:2). Fourth, it was said that he had forbidden Jews to pay taxes to Caesar (Luke 23:2). Fifth, he was said to have stirred up the people (Luke 23:5). Sixth, he was cited for having made himself a king (Luke 23:2). Here were six serious accusations. But these charges were not the real reason for the hatred of the Jewish leaders for Jesus or their prosecution of the case against him before Pilate. The real accusation is that he had claimed to be the unique Son of God, which they judged blasphemy. The seventh and central charge bursts forth now.

It had been there from the beginning, of course. The very first accusation against Jesus was that he had claimed he was "able to destroy the temple of God and reuild it in three days" (Matt. 26:61). On the surface this seemed to be only the irrational ravings of a madman. But Christ was not mad, and the leaders of Israel undoubtedly read into his words precisely what he intended. What he was actually saying was that he was God and that, although he would permit the leaders of the nation to kill him, he would rise again in three days. Only this explains the striking repetition of the phrase "in three days" in each of the four Gospels and the later concern of the leaders to seal and guard Christ's tomb (Matt. 27:62–64).

Why were the other charges raised then? They were raised in the Jewish court because, at first, the leaders of the Sanhedrin were unable to secure adequate evidence to convict Jesus of the charge of blasphemy. They were raised in the Roman court because the enemies of the Lord rightly believed that Pilate would never consent to convict Christ on the religious question. Before Pilate, Jesus had to be accused of being an insurrectionist and thus a threat to Caesar.

It was on the ground of insurrection that Pilate conducted the trial. Imagine his surprise then when, after having acquitted Jesus of the charge of insurrection, he suddenly hears the real charge mentioned. Pilate had said, "I find no basis for a charge against him" (John 19:6). Now his accusers reply, "We have a law, and according to that law he must die, *because he claimed to be the Son of God*" (v. 7). Up to now Pilate had been conducting the trial as if Jesus were only a man and the issues merely human issues. The crux of the matter was in Pilate's challenge to "Behold the *man!*" Now the ground is shifted entirely, and Pilate must face the entirely new question as to whether Jesus is actually the Son of God.

Was his claim to be the Son of God factual? I ask the question in this way because it is not only Pilate who is forced to face this question. You must confront it too.

The Witnesses Agree

Donald Grey Barnhouse preached a sermon in which he asked our question: "Who died at Calvary?" He pointed out in his sermon that the issue is not merely a matter of saying that the man who was killed was Jesus of Nazareth, because there is no question about that. The question is: Who was Jesus? Was he only a man? Or was he more? Was he God, as some suggested? Barnhouse called attention to this issue and then suggested that the various witnesses to this central issue be brought forward. One by one he called them to the bar and questioned them.[1]

The most important witness to any fact is *God himself.* So, although there are many witnesses to be considered, we rightly begin here. Does God Almighty bear witness to Christ's deity?

Here we forego the numerous Old Testament prophecies concerning the Messiah and the question of whether, on the basis of his words and deeds, Jesus may be declared to be that One. Instead we turn to the testimony of God rendered during the days of Christ's earthly ministry. We turn to the moment of Christ's baptism. Here we see the Holy Spirit of God descending upon the Lord Jesus Christ, like a dove from heaven. We hear God speak. He says, "This is my Son, whom I love; in him I am well pleased" (Matt. 3:17). Has such a testimony ever been rendered to another? We do not know of any. God called Abraham his friend, and David was called a man after God's own heart. But these were nevertheless still men. Here is one called God's Son. The testimony is weighty.

This was at the beginning of Jesus' ministry, before the temptation, the public acclaim, the rejection, the disappointments. What about later, after these things? Perhaps the one in whom God was "pleased" at the beginning will not be so pleasing at the end, after he has rubbed shoulders with the world. We turn to that moment toward the end of Christ's ministry when Jesus stood on the Mount of Transfiguration and was changed from his earthly into his heavenly appearance. In this moment he was clothed with light as with a garment, and in the hearing of Peter, James, and John, God Almighty spoke again from heaven, saying, "This is my Son, whom I love; in him I am well pleased. Listen to him" (Matt. 17:5).

God the Father testifies to Christ's deity.

The second witness to be summoned is *Jesus of Nazareth.* Any court should be willing to hear a man's testimony about himself. So we turn to Jesus and press our question on him: "Your name is Jesus of Nazareth?"

"Yes."

"What do you say for yourself?"

The Lord replies, "I have already given my testimony. On one occasion the leaders of Israel challenged me to give an accounting of myself, and I did this so clearly that they immediately took up stones to throw at me. I said, 'Before Abraham was born, I am' (John 8:58). On another occasion I taught the people in Solomon's porch and said to them, 'I and my Father are one' (John 10:30). Just this week in my final moments together with my disciples

I answered a question raised by Philip, saying, 'Whoever has seen me has seen the Father' (John 14:9). Last night the high priest asked me the question, 'Are you the Christ, the Son of the Blessed?' and I replied, 'I am; and you will see the Son of Man sitting on the right hand of power, and coming in the clouds of heaven' (Mark 14:61–62). It is for this claim that I am being tried and for which I will be executed."

The testimonies of God Almighty and of Jesus of Nazareth agree.

We have heard the witness of two members of the Godhead. What about the third member, *the Holy Spirit?* Before he was crucified the Lord said of the Holy Spirit, "When the Counselor comes, whom I will send to you from the Father, the Spirit of truth who goes out from the Father, he will testify about me" (John 15:26). This he has done. The entire New Testament is the Spirit's witness to Christ's deity.

Are there other supernatural witnesses from whom we should hear?

There are *angels* of heaven. What do they say? We hear their voice in the events which surround the birth of the Lord in Bethlehem. Gabriel is one of them. He appeared to Mary before the birth saying, "You will be with child and give birth to a son, and you are to give him the name Jesus. He will be great and will be called the Son of the Most High. . . . The holy one to be born will be called the Son of God" (Luke 1:31–32, 35). Later in the story the angels appear to the shepherds in the fields of Bethlehem and say to them, "Do not be afraid. I bring you good news of great joy that will be for all people. Today in the town of David a Savior has been born to you; he is Christ the Lord" (Luke 2:10–11).

What of the *demons?* They know the truth about Jesus even though they are opposed to his rule. What is their opinion of the One who now appears before Pilate? We remember that on one occasion the Lord healed a man who had been possessed by many demons. He was about to cast them out when they replied, "What do you want with us, Son of God? Have you come here to torture us before the appointed time?" (Matt. 8:29). On another occasion the demons fell down before him, saying, "You are the Son of God" (Mark 3:11).

The Human Witnesses

It is not only supernatural witnesses that attest to Christ's deity. There are also many human witnesses, among them those who knew him best. What of these? What of the writers of the Gospels? These men are the historians of Christ's life. They may rightly be supposed to have carefully investigated the things that were being told about him. Some lived with him. They were eyewitnesses of the events they describe. What do these men think of the One who stands before Pilate?

"*Matthew,* what do you think? You wrote the first of our Gospels. You are a Jew, and the Jews confess one God. You are not likely to ascribe divinity to any man without overwhelming evidence."

Matthew replies, "I believe that Jesus is the divine Savior of whom the Old Testament speaks. I have said so. I said that his birth was in fulfillment of that great prophecy of Isaiah, which says, "The virgin will be with child and will give birth to a son, and they will call him Immanuel . . . God with us" (Matt. 1:23; cf. Isa. 7:14).

"*Mark*, what about you? You traveled with Peter. You received firsthand information from him. What do you think?"

Mark answers that he introduced his Gospel with these words: "The beginning of the gospel about Jesus Christ, the Son of God" (Mark 1:1).

Luke was a physician. He was not inclined to flights of fancy or exaggeration. He has given us the most scientific of the four Gospels. Yet Luke favorably records some of the most exalted titles ever given to Jesus: "Son of the Most High" (Luke 1:32), "Son of God" (1:35), and "Christ the Lord" (2:11).

What about *John?* "John, what is your testimony?"

John tells us that he has written the most explicit words of all. His Gospel starts, "In the beginning was the Word, and the Word was with God, and the Word was God. He was with God in the beginning. Through him all things were made; without him nothing was made that has been made. In him was life, and that life was the light of men" (John 1:1–4). John's Gospel concludes, "Jesus did many other miraculous signs in the presence of his disciples, which are not recorded in this book. But these are written that you may believe that Jesus is the Christ, the Son of God, and that by believing you may have life in his name" (20:30–31).

Are there other human witnesses?

Yes, there are. *John the Baptist*, who was a first cousin of Jesus, testified, "I have seen and I testify that this is the Son of God" (John 1:34).

Martha, in whose home Jesus and his disciples often stayed, testified, "I believe that you are the Christ, the Son of God, who was to come into the world" (John 11:27).

Jesus once asked the disciples, "Who do you say that I am?" *Peter*, speaking for the rest, declared, "You are the Christ, the Son of the living God" (Matt. 16:15–16). Did Jesus recoil from that confession? If there was ever an opportunity in which he could have corrected this "mistaken" notion of who he was, it was then. He could have said, "You are wrong, Peter. I am not God's Son. I am just a man, as you are." But that is not what he said. Instead he replied, "Blessed are you, Simon, son of Jonah; for this was not revealed to you by man, but by my Father in heaven" (Matt. 16:17). The earthly witnesses and the heavenly witnesses agree.

Those at the Cross

It is said that the way in which a man dies throws much light upon who he is and how he lived. It is of interest to know how Christ died and what those who witnessed his death thought of him in his dying moments.

Two who were present were thieves who died with him. One thief was hardened and railed against Jesus, according to Luke's testimony. He said, "Aren't you the Christ? Save yourself and us!" *The other thief* replied, "Don't you fear God, since you are under the same sentence? We are punished justly; for we are getting what our deeds deserve. But this man has done nothing wrong." He then turned to Jesus and said, "Jesus, remember me when you come into your kingdom" (Luke 23:39–42).

The *centurion* was in charge of the execution party. He is a sober man. He has seen many die. What do you think, centurion? Our soldier replies, "I saw it all. I witnessed the conduct of the prisoner in his agony. No curse escaped his lips. I saw his immolation. While being nailed to the tree he even asked God to forgive those who were killing him, saying they did not know what they did. He suffered bravely, and as he died darkness covered the land, even at high noon. An earthquake came; the rocks were shaken and the graves opened. I saw these miracles. I said, 'Surely this was a righteous man. This was the Son of God'" (Luke 23:47; Matt. 27:54).

What Is Your Verdict?

At last we come to ourselves. We have not seen him in the days of his flesh, but he is proclaimed to us in Scripture and the Holy Spirit bears witness to him in countless Christian hearts. What do we say? Is he the Son of God? I give you *my testimony*. I look within my heart, and I confess that there is nothing within me to draw me to him. He is a thing apart. Left to myself I should find a lifetime of other pursuits to keep me busy. I could be as skeptical as Thomas or as hostile as the apostle Paul before his conversion. But Jesus spoke to me. He spoke through the Word of God, declaring who he is and what he has done. My heart went out to him, and I confess that he is indeed the Son of God and my Savior.

Is that *your testimony*? You know the evidence. Will you decide in favor of his claims? Or will you decide against him? The strange thing about this case is that the decision you make will not determine the destiny of the defendant. It will determine the destiny of yourself, the judge.

240

How God Views Human Government

John 19:8–11

When Pilate heard this, he was even more afraid, and he went back inside the palace. "Where do you come from?" he asked Jesus, but Jesus gave him no answer. "Do you refuse to speak to me?" Pilate said. "Don't you realize I have power either to free you or to crucify you?"

Jesus answered, "You would have no power over me if it were not given to you from above. Therefore the one who handed me over to you is guilty of a greater sin."

There are times in the history of a nation when the government disappoints or even betrays its people and it becomes natural to ask why government exists and how it should function.

In recent years we have gone through such a period in the United States. First, there was the war in Vietnam. It was never popular. But as the years of fighting dragged on and the prospects for success increasingly dimmed, opposition mounted and many began to ask whether they could really participate in the armed forces or in war-related activity. Some protested vigorously, even leaving the country to avoid the draft. On the other hand, many people resented those whom they considered "deserters" and argued that the government has a right to wage war and must be obeyed and supported

1477

when it does so. Again, there was the Watergate crisis. In this debacle, the progressive revelations of corruption, even at the highest levels of government, made many cynical and fueled an already intense disdain for government or any other form of authority.

What were Christians saying during this period? It would be nice if we were able to point to a united "Christian voice" in these crises. Unfortunately this was not the case. In regard to Vietnam, some were pacifists and some were in favor of fighting. Others were selective pacifists. That is, they were against this war but for some others. In the matter of Watergate, some were ready to pull down the system while others were hardly ready to admit that a breach of trust had occurred.

What is right? How should we view government, particularly in those times when its decisions are unpopular or when it obviously fails to conduct itself morally or do its job?

God or Caesar?

The standard answer to questions regarding a Christian's responsibility to government has always been the reply of the Lord Jesus Christ to his critics: "Give Caesar what is Caesar's, and to God what is God's" (Matt. 22:21). The background for this valuable guideline was a question about taxes: "Is it right to pay taxes to Caesar or not?" (v. 17). Christ's reply has therefore rightly been understood to give a binding, affirmative answer in that area. But what should be said beyond this? Does the Christian have duties toward the state in other areas? Are those duties independent of his Christian duties? Suppose the commands of God and the commands of the government disagree? Do we obey Caesar, arguing that God has set him over us and will therefore take care of the consequences of our act? Or do we obey God? The issues are not easy to resolve. And to go back to the matter of taxes, we see that even this is not entirely clear. The question "Should we pay taxes if we know for sure that our tax money will be used for godless or immoral ends?" shows that there are puzzling dimensions in this area also.

It is probably true that there are always going to be gray spots in connection with this subject, if for no other reason than that it is never easy to see the situation clearly. But on the other hand, we do not need to be entirely without guidelines, for the Bible provides them in a number of places. Paul's discussion of authority in Romans 13 is one example. Another is the rather extended discussion between Pilate, the representative of human government, and the Lord Jesus Christ, the representative of divine government, on the occasion of the Lord's trial leading to his crucifixion.

This issue was always at the heart of the trial before Pilate, of course, for Jesus was accused of having made himself "a king" in opposition to the legitimate rule of Caesar; the issue was whether Jesus stood in a right or wrong relationship to Caesar's government. But in another sense, the question of the legitimacy of human government did not really emerge in the earlier stages of the trial because the examination of Jesus disclosed that his was a spiritual kingdom, which Pilate assumed (perhaps too quickly) was none of his affair. Now the situation changes. Pilate begins to interrogate Jesus again, demanding, "Do you refuse to speak to me? Don't you realize I have power either to free you or to crucify you?" (John 19:10).

The Lord replies, "You would have no power over me if it were not given to you from above. Therefore the one who handed me over to you is guilty of a greater sin" (John 19:11).

This statement does not merely separate the two spheres of authority, Caesar's and God's; it brings them into relationship to one another, showing that the authority of government comes not from anything intrinsic to itself but from God. That is, it is a delegated authority. Consequently, there is always the matter of government responsibility and sin.

All Authority from God

Let us take these matters one at a time. First, there is Christ's statement that Pilate's power did not come from himself or, for that matter, even from Caesar but from God. This means that all power comes from God and is to that extent legitimated by him.

One word often translated by "power" is *dynamis,* which means "explosive power." We get our words "dynamite" and "dynamic" from it. It is used in such verses as Romans 1:16, which tells us that the gospel is the explosive "power of God unto salvation to everyone who believes." A second word frequently translated by "power" is *kratos,* which means the naked "power of rule." Though it can be legitimate, it can also be illegitimate, as in the case of the devil, whose "power of death" (Heb. 2:14) will some day be taken away by God. *Kratos* gives us the words "democracy," "plutocracy," "monocracy," and others. If Jesus had used either of these words in this sentence, he would have meant only that all power of rule comes from God, just as all life comes from him.

But Jesus did not use *dynamis* or *kratos* in his warning to Pilate. He used an even stronger word, *exousia,* which means "legitimate authority." Thus, he was saying not only that power in the sense of might comes from God but that human government is divinely authorized and therefore exercises a rule that must be recognized.

When we see this we begin to see, not merely that Jesus was acknowledging the power of Pilate as a bare fact or even pointing out that its source is to be found ultimately in God, but rather that God has legitimized human government and that it is therefore to function properly and be highly respected. He himself respected it, for he courteously answered Pilate's questions and never once suggested that Pilate did not have authority to pronounce a judgment on him.

Pilate pronounced wrongly, as we know. But he had authority to make the pronouncement even if it was wrong. His authority was from God. Jesus did not suggest that it be wrested from him because he made even so great an error as condemning the Son of God. At the very least, then, we are taught here that revolution for the sake of revolution—that is, "I would rather be king than you, so I will try to unseat you"—is unchristian. Rather we are to honor, respect, and be thankful for those who are over us, as Paul suggests in Romans (13:1–7).[1]

One other conclusion needs to be kept in mind: we are to be subject to the higher authorities. That is, Christians should be model citizens. Unfortunately, it is often the case that Christians disrespect authority—elected officials, policemen, and others—and this leads naturally to a light attitude in regard to obeying them. This ought not to be. Rather we should be scrupulous at this point. We should obey the speed limits and all other civil laws, pay our taxes honestly, and do as those who are in positions of authority instruct us. Calvin, who had a justified fear of anarchy because of the troubles of his own time and warned against it, wrote that obedience must be given even to wicked rulers: "We are not only subject to the authority of princes who perform their office toward us uprightly and faithfully as they ought, but also to the authority of all who, by whatever means, have got control of affairs, even though they perform not a whit of the princes' office."[2]

Are There No Limits?

But are there no limits? Suppose the king is a *very* wicked king, or the president a *very* wicked president? Is a command from such a king legitimate or should a Christian disobey it? The answer is that there are indeed limits. Therefore, although we must be careful to render every possible measure of obedience to those in authority (usually much more than we would wish), we must still do nothing contrary to the express commands of God in the Scriptures or to that standard of morality arising from them, even though a contrary act is commanded.

Here the second part of Christ's statement comes in, for after instructing Pilate in regard to the ultimate source of his authority, Jesus went on to speak of sin, saying, "Therefore, the one who handed me over to you is guilty of a greater sin" (John 19:11). If it were only power *(dynamis* or *kratos)* that Pilate had been given, it would be impossible to speak of sin as intrinsic in the exercise of the power, just as it is impossible to speak of sin in the case of the cat that kills the mouse or the germ that kills another germ. But since it is "authority" that Pilate has been given, this is another matter entirely. For authority, being granted by another, necessarily involves responsibility to that other one, and responsibility if it is not properly exercised involves sin against him. In other words, authority enhances human government, but it also limits it, for it is an authority bound by the moral nature of the God from whom it comes.

One limit which the Bible places on obedience to human authority concerns the *preaching of the gospel.* This is a Christian duty based upon the explicit command of Christ (Matt. 28:18–20). What should happen when authorities demand differently is illustrated in the fourth and fifth chapters of Acts. The disciples had been preaching and doing miracles, and these had created such a stir that they were called before a council of elders in Jerusalem. The authorities examined the disciples, in this case Peter and John; and then, since the miracle they had done in healing a lame man was so evident and the rulers could not deny it, these settled upon the precedent of merely commanding the disciples to keep silence. We read, "Then they called them in again and commanded them not to speak or teach at all in the name of Jesus."

Peter and John replied, "Judge for yourselves whether it is right in God's sight to obey you rather than God. For we cannot help speaking about what we have seen and heard" (Acts 4:18–20).

The apostles were threatened in connection with this command, but they went back to their preaching. When the authorities heard of it and learned that they were again back in the temple area teaching the people, they sent guards to bring them before the council (peacefully this time), and they demanded, "We gave you strict orders not to teach in this name. Yet you have filled Jerusalem with your teaching and are determined to make us guilty of this man's blood."

Peter spoke up for all the apostles, "We must obey God rather than men! The God of our fathers raised Jesus from the dead—whom you had killed by hanging him on a tree. God exalted him to his own right hand as Prince and Savior that he might give repentance and forgiveness of sins to Israel. We are witnesses of these things, and so is the Holy Spirit, whom God has given to those who obey him" (Acts 5:28–32). This enraged the Jewish rulers, and they would have killed the disciples had Gamaliel not intervened to counsel tolerance.

These stories indicate that Christians are to give precedence to the preaching of the gospel and are not to cease from it even though commanded to do so by the civil authorities. Of course, they must be willing to suffer the consequences of their persistence even though that should be imprisonment or death.

A second limit the Bible places on obedience to human authorities concerns *Christian conduct and morals*. No government has the right to command the Christian to perform an immoral or non-Christian act. We are reminded here of the Nazi era in Germany in which Christians living there were faced with a devilish state and its openly antichristian and even antihuman practices. During this period, German citizens were commanded to have no dealings with the Jews in that country. They were not to trade with them, help them, have friendships with them, or acknowledge them in any way. Such a policy was immoral. Thus, although many German Christians obeyed the government in this regard, they did not need to obey and should not have.

Some stood up against these monstrosities. One who did so was Martin Niemoeller who, for preaching the truth, was eventually thrown into prison.

We are told that another minister then visited him in prison and argued that if he would only keep silent about certain subjects and respect the government, he would be set free. "And so," he concluded, "why are you in jail?"

"Why aren't *you* in jail?" Niemoeller answered.[3]

Niemoeller's course was the right one, for by his silence the visiting minister was upholding a lie and indirectly encouraging an irresponsible and demonic regime. Similarly, in this country Christians must also speak out against racism, government and corporate corruption, discrimination, and other evils. Moreover, they must staunchly refuse to participate in them in any way even if they are commanded to do so by their government or by a business superior.

The Greater Sin

Yet we have a warning even here, for although the Lord Jesus exercised his right as the ultimate judge of the world to boldly point out Pilate's sin—it must have astonished him—he spoke at the same time of the sin of the "church" of his day and indicated that its sin was greater.

It is an interesting word: "greater." It suggests that Pilate's sin was great; he was sinning against his conscience (he knew Christ was innocent) and against his divinely given responsibility (he had pronounced Jesus innocent). It affirms that the sin of the religious leaders was greater; they were sinning out of hate-filled hearts and against their own law (which should have protected Jesus). It may imply that the sin of Judas was *greatest;* he was closest to Christ and therefore sinned against the background of the greatest knowledge. Taken together the parts of the comparison teach that the greatest danger lies, not with the state, but with those who are closest to spiritual things. Others may sin out of ignorance or neglect or cowardice. But religious people are inclined to sin out of arrogance or pride or actual hatred of God and God's truth—even when they think they are most moral.

Let us look to ourselves and to the truth of God which we profess. It is not enough to have the name of Christian. That in itself does not give us any superior insight into morality or any point of leverage from which to speak against or disobey the government which God has set up. We can only do that as we respond, painfully at times, to his own voice which comes to us in Scripture, for then we are gripped, not by a lesser authority than that of the state (that is, our own), but by a greater, even the overriding and only infallible, authority of God.

241

Christ's Fate Sealed

John 19:12

From then on, Pilate tried to set Jesus free, but the Jews kept shouting, "If you let this man go, you are no friend of Caesar. Anyone who claims to be a king opposes Caesar."

It is not always easy to know when a Christian's obligation to obey God requires disobedience to the state. If God and state were always diametrically opposed, the decision would be easy. We would obey God and disobey the state in all situations. But this is not the case. The state is often if not usually right. And what is more, it has been instituted by God and is invested with God's authority. Consequently, under normal circumstances we are to obey the government even when those who form it seem unjust. Yet what are "normal circumstances"? We are not to obey without question. How then do we decide when a particular demand by the state is wrong and requires firm Christian rebuke and opposition?

We began to deal with this question in the previous study by showing that the authority of the state is limited in at least two important areas. First, it has no right to forbid the proclamation of the gospel. If it does, we must resist,

1483

knowing that we have been given a commission to preach the gospel from Jesus himself. Second, the state has no right to command an immoral act.

But it is right here that further problems develop; for if we know our hearts, we know that it is extremely easy to consider the state hopelessly immoral, simply because it is doing something we do not like—because we are arrested for speeding, for example, or because we are taxed more than we think reasonable—and therefore resist it unjustly. Or again, we may attempt to throw off its authority, not because that authority is being exercised tyrannically or in clear opposition to the commandments of God, but simply because we do not countenance the authority of any other human being. We saw that Jesus alerted us to precisely this danger in John 19:11 by indicating that, although the sin of Pilate was great, the sin of the religious leaders was greater in that they sinned out of pride and against a greater knowledge. It seems from this comparison that the closer we are to spiritual things, the greater the danger of acting from impure motives becomes.

So what do we do? We are helped here by the unfolding of the story of Christ's appearance before Pilate, for Pilate, by contrast, shows what we should do.

Fear of Caesar

Pilate did not want to condemn Jesus; of that we are certain. That he did not want to see him executed is a bit puzzling, for he was not intrinsically strong on justice and certainly did not have any high regard for the Jews or Jewish prisoners. However, he was certainly trying to get Christ off, whatever his reasons may have been. First, he pronounced him innocent. Then, when he met with violent and almost revolutionary opposition to that decision, he tried a series of expedients: sending him to Herod, suggesting his release rather than the release of Barabbas, causing him to be beaten and then produced suddenly to evoke sympathy from the cruel mob. After these things, even after Jesus' pointed rebuke to Pilate's arrogance in verses 10 and 11, Pilate tried again to release him, for the text says, "From then on, Pilate tried to set him free, but the Jews kept shouting, 'If you let this man go, you are no friend of Caesar. Anyone who claims to be a king opposes Caesar'" (v. 12).

If Pilate was as unwilling to pass the death sentence as this verse and the other incidents show, how is it that he was eventually prevailed upon to do so? The verse gives the answer. The Jews, perceiving that Pilate could not be made to do their will save but by the strongest measures, implied that if he did not condemn one whom they considered to be a traitor, they would denounce Pilate to Caesar; and Pilate, who feared this more than anything else, complied.

Pilate is seen here in his most contemptible stance, and yet he is also most pitiable. Pilate was the governor. He spoke for Caesar and had the legions of Caesar at his call to enforce all his bidding. Yet this one who should have been above fear is riddled by it and thus made weak-kneed in the greatest moral encounter of his career. Of what was the governor afraid? He was afraid of three things. First, he was afraid of *Christ*. We see this in verse 8; for we are told that after Pilate had heard that Jesus made himself out to be the Son of God, "he was even more afraid" and determined anew to release him. This was certainly not the kind of holy reverence for Christ that a true follower of the Lord might have, but it was a true fear. Pilate thought that Jesus might actually be more than a man, perhaps one of the half-human, half-divine gods of Greek and Roman antiquity, and so move fate against him if he judged unfairly.

Second, Pilate was afraid of the *people*. He did not like them, of course. His many dealings with the Jews showed his consummate disdain and even hatred for them. Yet he knew their power and feared to have them united against him. If he had not feared the people, he would have released Jesus quickly and would have shown no concern for pacifying them.

Third, and most significant, Pilate feared *Caesar*. And with cause! The suspicious nature of Caesar Tiberius was well known, and Pilate had already had other confrontations with the Jews which had worked to his disfavor before the emperor. What if Caesar should disapprove of his handling of this matter? What if the leaders of this people should send another delegation to Caesar saying that Pilate had refused to deal forcefully with one who was guilty of high treason? If Pilate had possessed a clean record, he could perhaps have overlooked a threat based on such false charges. But his record was not clean; and it was quite possible that Pilate would lose his position and even his very life if such an accusation were made. Indeed, we know that years later Pilate was removed from office by the Proconsul of Syria and banished to France where he later died.

Pilate's failure suggests the answer to the questions raised earlier. Pilate feared man! Consequently, he was unable to do the just thing and even fell so low as to pronounce sentence on the very Son of God. We will do better only when we fear God over man and act justly regardless of the consequences.

God Is Sovereign

But we need to spell this out a bit further. What specifically does it mean to fear God more than man? And how can we personally be brought to the place where we do so? There are three requirements.

First, we must have it fixed in our minds that God is truly sovereign in human affairs. We know this because the Scriptures teach it. But in addition to knowing it, we must also have it planted in our minds so firmly that we can actually trust God when the crunch comes. Daniel was one who was able to do this. As we read his prophecy we realize that he was familiar with the concept of the sovereignty of God, for he witnessed the rise and fall of several great empires and was told in visions that it was God himself who was doing this. We think, for instance, of that great vision of the statue whose head was of gold, whose breast and arms were of silver, whose stomach and thighs were of bronze, whose legs were of iron, and whose feet were iron mixed with clay. Nebuchadnezzar had dreamed of this statue but had forgotten his dream.

He demanded that his astrologers and sorcerers tell him its meaning, but they were unable to do this since they did not even know what the dream was. At last he sent for Daniel. Daniel asked for time, and that night God revealed to him Nebuchadnezzar's dream and its interpretation. Daniel then interpreted the dream to Nebuchadnezzar, showing it to be a prophecy of four succeeding world empires, the last of which was to be overturned by the kingdom of Jesus Christ.

Daniel obviously knew God's sovereignty in the matter of the setting up and taking down of kings. But it was not only intellectually that Daniel knew this. He knew it experientially too and therefore was not afraid to stand by his convictions.

Darius, who succeeded Nebuchadnezzar's son Belshazzar, was a kind man and a friend of Daniel. But he was tricked into signing a law according to which no one was to ask a petition of any god or man for the period of thirty days, except King Darius. When Darius signed the law he was not thinking of Daniel. But soon word was brought that Daniel was continuing his practice of prayer to the God of Israel three times daily. Daniel was caught, and the king was caught too, for he had signed the order according to the law of the Medes and Persians which could not be altered. Daniel was thrown into a den of starving lions, the penalty for violating the emperor's decree.

We know that God delivered Daniel from the lions, just as he had earlier delivered his three companions from the burning fiery furnace. But the fact that God would deliver him and the others was not known to Daniel and his friends at the time the moral stances were taken. What gave these men the ability to do this, particularly when so many plausible arguments might have been raised in favor of compliance?

The answer is found in Daniel's personal knowledge of the truth of God's sovereignty. God was in control. Consequently, God was able to and certainly would accomplish what he had chosen to accomplish in these situations. Here is the way the friends of Daniel put it when called before Nebuchadnezzar on the occasion of their refusal to worship the statue on the plain of Dura. They said, "O Nebuchadnezzar, we do not need to defend ourselves before you in this matter. If we are thrown into the blazing furnace, the God we serve is able to save us from it, and he will rescue us from your hand, O king. But even if he does not, we want you to know, O king, that we will not serve your gods or worship the image of gold you have set up" (Dan. 3:16–18).

These men were able to resist the unjust demands of the powerful rulers of their day because they trusted an even more powerful ruler. Moreover, they were determined that in the ultimate analysis he (and not they) would control their lives.

Informed by Scripture

A second requirement for responsible action in the area of God and government, is that we must be thoroughly informed by Scripture. To want to do the right thing is not enough. We must know what the right thing is, and there is no way to know that apart from God's specific revelation of his standards in the Bible. We admit as we say this that even then there are areas that are ambiguous. The matter of fighting in wartime is one. Christians have been divided at this point, often with the best of intentions. Answers in the areas of abortion, artificial prolongation of life, legal defense of criminals, covert government activities, and others are not always as apparent as we might wish they were. But without the Bible there are no sure answers at all! Consequently, there is no substitute (even for the busiest of Christians) for studying the Bible and conscientiously striving to submit one's own thoughts to it.

Some would suggest that we must trust in conscience. But conscience is an unsure guide. At best, conscience tells us that we should do right when we know the right. But it does not know what is right unless the light of God's revelation shines upon it. One writer compares conscience to a sundial, which is made for the sun just as conscience is made for God's revelation. In the light of the sun a sundial may give pretty good time. But suppose it is consulted by moonlight. By moonlight it may indicate that it is ten o'clock when actually it is three in the morning. Again, by using a candle or a flashlight the sundial may be made to tell any hour one desires. It is reliable only when the light of the sun shines upon it. In the same way, the conscience is useful only when the light of God shines on the human soul from the pages of God's Book, the Bible.[1]

We need this book, and we need to grow in our understanding of it. If we do grow in our understanding, God will increasingly show his way to us, pointing out our sin and that of our society and quickening our will to do what is right before him.

Self-Surrender

One more thing is needed if we are to know what is right and actually do it, even when confronted by a contrary claim by our government or some other strong social pressure. What we need is to be willing to surrender everything. It is possible to have followed the first two steps suggested—to trust in God's sovereignty in human affairs and to study the Bible to such a degree that we know what is right—and yet fail at the crucial moment simply because the proper course is too costly.

This is what was wrong with Pilate after all. We cannot say that Pilate really believed in the sovereignty of God, but he had something like it. He believed in the power of the gods or else in some form of ultimate retribution. Otherwise he would not have been afraid when told that Jesus claimed to be God's Son. In the same way, we cannot say that he knew the moral standards of the true God as revealed in the Bible, because he had undoubtedly never read the Bible. Still he knew what was right in this situation, yet went against it. Why? If it was not from a fear of God and not from a failure to know what was right, it can have been only from the fear he would lose his position. It was this above all else that he valued. Pilate had to choose between what was right and what the world wanted. When the issue was clearly defined, he did not hesitate to choose the world and its rewards.

I think in contrast of Aleksandr Solzhenitsyn, the Russian writer who was unjustly confined in the Soviet Union's notorious prison system for eleven years and lived to tell about it in *The Gulag Archipelago*. He saw suffering such as few free people have ever seen. He saw the dehumanizing practice of the Soviet guards and the equally dehumanizing practices of some of the prisoners. He saw some break and others grow strong. He asks, "So what is the answer? How can you stand your ground when you are weak and sensitive to pain, when people you love are still alive, when you are unprepared? What do you need to make you stronger than the interrogator and the whole trap?"

Solzhenitsyn answers, "From the moment you go to prison you must put your cozy past firmly behind you. At the very threshold, you must say to yourself: 'My life is over, a little early to be sure, but there's nothing to be done about it. I shall never return to freedom. I am condemned to die—now or a little later. But later on, in truth, it will be even harder, and so the sooner the better. I no longer have any property whatsoever. For me those I love have died, and for them I have died. From today on, my body is useless and alien to me. Only my spirit and my conscience remain precious to me.'

"Confronted by such a prisoner, the interrogation will tremble.

"Only the man who has renounced everything can win that victory."[2]

Pilate failed to do the right, not because he did not know what was right—he did—but because he feared to have it suggested that he was not Caesar's friend. What irony! He wanted so much to be a friend of Caesar. But he was not Caesar's friend; he barely knew Caesar. And what is even more significant, Caesar was not *his* friend at all.

Pilate had no friends anywhere, and yet there stood before him One who, although he was God Almighty and the King of kings, nevertheless stooped to be the friend of sinners. Is he your friend? If not, may I commend him to you? He is a King! He will demand your total allegiance and faithful service, perhaps even to death. But he does not demand of you what he was unwilling to undergo himself. He died for you, and he promises that no matter what you may go through for his sake and the sake of righteousness, he will go through it with you, thereby proving himself to be "a friend who sticks closer than a brother."

242

No King but Caesar

John 19:13–15

When Pilate heard this, he brought Jesus out and sat down on the judge's seat at a place known as the Stone Pavement (which in Aramaic is Gabbatha). It was the day of Preparation of Passover Week, about the sixth hour.

"Here is your king," Pilate said to the Jews.

But they shouted, "Take him away! Take him away! Crucify him!"

"Shall I crucify your king?" Pilate asked.

"We have no king but Caesar," the chief priests answered.

There is probably no point in the entire life of the Lord where the sovereignty of God is more evident than in the final minutes of his trial before Pilate. Pilate was convinced that Jesus was innocent. He had said so (John 18:38; 19:4, 6). He wished to release Jesus and actually set about to get him released. Yet, in spite of his personal convictions, will, and efforts, Christ was crucified. Why? The answer is that God had decreed from all eternity that Pilate should sentence Christ to death, and therefore not all the powers of earth and hell combined could thwart it.

1489

This does not absolve Pilate from responsibility, as we have seen. He was to blame. Yet it does cause us to see beyond the evils of the human court to the blessed purposes of God the Father in Christ's sacrifice.

A Crucial Moment

The sovereign presence of God in this crucial moment was undoubtedly clear to John, for he has marked the point by time references, the first specific references to day and time since the start of chapter 13. Up to this point there has been much movement and uncertainty. There have been various trips by Jesus, followed by the various movements of the arresting party. There was the trial before the Jewish court (in three parts) followed by the trial before the Roman court (again in three parts). Now this comes to an end, and Pilate takes his place to render final judgment. John says, "When Pilate heard this, he brought Jesus out and sat down on the judge's seat at a place known as the Stone Pavement (which in Aramaic is Gabbatha). It was the day of Preparation of Passover Week, about the sixth hour" (John 19:13–14).

This last sentence—"It was the day of Preparation of Passover Week, about the sixth hour"—is intended to mark this historic moment by citing both the day and hour. Yet at both points it has been a puzzle for serious scholars.

The problem with the reference to the day is this. The phrase "the day of Preparation of Passover Week" most naturally designates the period immediately preceding the Passover meal, when the preparations for it (including the killing of the Passover lamb) were being made. John is saying that Jesus was crucified on the morning of the day the Passover feast began. By the most common dating of the crucifixion this would be Friday morning. By my dating, explained in detail earlier in these volumes, it would be Thursday morning after a trial beginning Wednesday night.[1] However, in either case (whether on Thursday or Friday), John's description of the crucifixion as before or at the very time of the Passover seems to conflict with Matthew, Mark, and Luke's description of the Last Supper as a Passover meal. This is a problem because Jesus clearly cannot have eaten the Passover meal on the Passover and have been crucified on that same Passover day.

What is the solution? A number of very good explanations have been offered, and it is perhaps impossible to decide finally on any one. Leon Morris, who offers a very helpful discussion of the options, feels that the apparent discrepancy is due to the existence of two different calendars at the time of Christ. In this view Jesus observed the Passover on one day in accord with one calendar, the calendar apparently followed by the sect that wrote and preserved the Dead Sea Scrolls, and was crucified prior to the official Passover observed on a different day by mainstream Judaism.[2]

My belief is that John is correct in showing that Jesus was crucified before the official beginning of the Passover, that is, at a time when the Passover lambs were being killed in preparation for it, and that the other Gospels refer to a meal with Passover characteristics but actually held one day earlier. We notice, for example, that none of the accounts mention the characteristic foods of Passover, namely, the Passover lamb and bitter herbs. Again, we note the concern of the Jewish leaders to effect the arrest, trial, and crucifixion of Jesus before the sacred days of Passover week began.

According to my understanding, the Last Supper was eaten on Wednesday night, April 5, A.D. 30, and the crucifixion took place the next morning, April 6 by our reckoning.[3]

Here we come to the second problem. John speaks of the moment at which Pilate gave his final verdict as "the sixth hour," while the Synoptics apparently fix it earlier, Mark in particular saying that it was "the third hour" when they crucified him (Mark 15:25). In ancient times hours were usually reckoned from sunrise. So John would be saying that Jesus was condemned around noon, that is, about six hours after a 6:00 A.M. sunrise; and Mark would be saying that he had been condemned and was actually on the cross by 9:00 A.M.

One attempt to solve this difficulty is to suggest that John is reckoning time by Roman rather than Jewish standards, according to which, so it is said, time was computed as we compute it, that is, from midnight. If this is so, John's reference is to 6:00 A.M. rather than noon. But does this really solve the difficulty? It is questionable, in the first place, whether the Romans actually reckoned time in this way. Morris and others believe that they did so only in legal documents.[4] But even if they did and even if John is adopting their system, there is still a difference between John and Mark of three hours. Moreover, it is then difficult to see how the many events recorded by the various Gospels could be packed into so short a time span. Assuming that the Sanhedrin began their official trial at dawn (or even slightly before dawn), it is still necessary to have time for the presentation of Jesus before Pilate, the sending of Jesus to Herod and Herod's mocking of him, the second appearance before Pilate, the discussion and choice regarding Barabbas, the scourging, and then a final interrogation by Pilate. Could this all have taken place by 6:00 A.M. or even before 9:00 A.M.? It is doubtful. Rather we shall probably be closer to the truth if we imagine the greater part of the morning to be filled with such things.

Does this mean that Mark is wrong then? Not necessarily. In the first place, we need to recognize that no one in antiquity had watches and therefore that time was always reckoned in the most general categories. Second, the day as a whole was divided, like the night, into four portions of three hours each. The nighttime periods were designated as the four watches. The daytime periods were referred to generally by the first hour of each period: the first hour, the third hour, the sixth hour, and the ninth hour. This explains why the New Testament mentions almost no hour except the third, sixth, and ninth, and why the expressions "nearly" or "about" are so frequent.[5] Bearing these facts in mind, we may say that Mark and the other synoptic Gospels indicate that Jesus was crucified during that period of the day designated as "the third hour," between the hours of 9:00 A.M. and noon, while John, who says "about the sixth hour," indicates that it was in fact getting on toward midday when the trial before Pilate was completed.

Repeating History

Having placed the moment of the official verdict to his own satisfaction, John immediately goes to the overriding issue. Jesus had been accused of having made himself a king. So Pilate now asks, "Shall I crucify your king?" The question is fraught with irony. There is irony on Pilate's side, for his question is meant to be contemptuous—who else but a beaten, itinerant preacher would be a *Jewish* king? But John, on his part, also records the words with irony, for this One actually is the King of Israel.

John then records that the chief priests answered, "We have no king but Caesar."

Nothing could be more ludicrous on the lips of the priests of Israel than this protestation. It means, "We are loyal to Caesar and to Caesar alone." But actually they hated Caesar and maintained that only God was their king. Why would they say such a thing? One would think they would have choked on it as they said it. Yet so great was their hatred of Jesus that they would rather deny their own convictions than see him escape crucifixion. Still, the leaders of Israel spoke truer than they knew. They thought that they were loyal to God and hated Caesar. But it was the Son of God, God incarnate, whom they were rejecting; so they are actually showing that indeed they do not honor God and instead choose Caesar.

Something similar had occurred early in Israel's history. The government then was a theocracy; that is, Israel was ruled by God directly through spokesmen and spokeswomen, such as Moses, the many judges, and prophetlike figures such as Samuel. This was God's design. It was good for Israel. However, the day came when, as Samuel grew old, the people looked at the nations around them and felt cheated because these had kings and they did not. They therefore came to Samuel and said, "Give us a king to lead us" (1 Sam. 8:6).

We are told that the request displeased Samuel and the Lord as well. However, when Samuel asked God what he should do the Lord replied, "Listen to all that the people are saying to you; it is not you they have rejected, but they have rejected me as their king" (v. 7).

Someone has said that human beings never learn anything from history except that they never learn anything from history. That is true in this case, for apparently nothing was learned from this earlier rejection of Jehovah's rightful and blessed rule. Earlier they had rejected Jehovah. Now they reject Jehovah's Son, in consequence of which they have since been "many days without king or prince, without sacrifice or sacred stones" (Hosea 3:4). It is a sad report, but it is a true report concerning Israel.

A Human Report

Yet it is not a Jewish report alone, for the rejection of God and Jesus is not a Jewish verdict alone. It is the verdict of the human race. What else does the fall of man mean if it is not the willful rejection of God's rule? It means, "We will not abide by his restrictions." What does the crucifixion of Jesus mean (both by Jewish and gentile hands) if it does not mean, "We will not have this man to rule over us"?

Do we doubt that this includes the Gentiles as well as the Jews? If so, we need turn only to the second psalm to see that view devastated. In that psalm the writer is viewing, not the rebellion of one man and one woman against God, not the rebellion of a few Jewish leaders and one gentile ruler against Jesus, but rather the collective rejection of the Creator by the united political kingdoms of this world. The psalmist asks, "Why do the nations conspire and the peoples plot in vain? The kings of the earth take their stand and the rulers gather together against the LORD and against his Anointed One. 'Let us break their chains,' they say, 'and throw off their fetters'" (2:1–3). The Lord is Jehovah. His anointed is Christ. So we are confronted in these verses with what R. C. Sproul calls "a massive conspiracy to overthrow the authority of God and His Anointed One."

Sproul continues by asking, "Why the hostility? Why do the kings rattle their swords in belligerence? The answer is obvious: they despise the rule of God which restricts their freedom. Again the goal is autonomy. The rule of God is regarded as ropes and chains binding them and keeping them from unbridled pursuance of their desire. So the secret weapons are unveiled, the battleships come out of dry dock, the nuclear stockpile is tapped, and the troops are mobilized as the whole world joins the cosmic-liberation movement. With the infantile resolve of the child who seeks to quench a blazing fire with a straw, the rulers set themselves against the sovereignty of God."[6]

What is God's answer? The response is not panic. It is not a flurry of preparation to resist the impending invasion of his rights. Instead we read, "The One enthrones in heaven laughs; the Lord scoffs at them. Then he rebukes them in his anger and terrifies them in his wrath" (2:4–5). The verses show that the Lord is temporarily amused by this insanity. But the laughter quickly gives way as he moves to enthrone his Son and unleash his final judgments.

A Nation under God

This brings us to the final lessons of this section. We remember in view of the references to a king and Caesar that this entire section has been dealing with the relationship between God and human rulers. We remember that God is over all and that the authority of the state, while a legitimate authority, is nonetheless subject to him. But here is a progression. In the words of the Lord we have the proper picture: God and Caesar, with God in the dominant position. In the reaction of Pilate to the threat of the Jews ("If you let this man go, you are no friend of Caesar") we have a warped position: God and Caesar, but Caesar in the dominant position. In these verses, with which the issue of God and state is closed, we have the worst stance of all. Now it is no longer God and Caesar, in whatever relationship. It is Caesar alone. God is forced out of the picture entirely. Nothing is worse than this. Tyranny is not worse, for even under the worst of tyrants, if God is in the picture, he can at least be appealed to for help and the injustices may be corrected. Without God, what is there? Nothing but the rapacious lust and cruel arrogance of human beings.

We may be more specific. Without God in the picture, there is no check on Caesar. We need a check. In America we recognize this secularly, for we have developed a system of checks and balances according to which one branch of government has control on another. Thus, the Congress makes laws that govern all citizens, but the judicial branch can declare them unconstitutional. Again, the president appoints Supreme Court judges, but Congress has the authority to impeach the president. Again, the President may initiate programs, but Congress must fund them. We recognize the need of checks and balances on the secular level because we know by experience that people in positions of power are untrustworthy. But if this is true on the merely human level, how much more true is it on the cosmic level. The united voices of the rulers of even so great a land as ours cannot be ultimate. God is ultimate. So if we forsake God, we are at the mercy of our governors.

Second, without God in the picture, we have no sure means of guiding government properly. This is not the same thing as a need for checks on our rulers. We need checks to keep government from becoming a law unto itself and therefore abusing and tyrannizing the governed. But suppose the government is not tyrannous. Suppose it operates well, as our government generally does. Even then it needs God, for it is only from God that we can receive a system of morality and a wisdom beyond our own. Only this is able to lead us upward to the fullness of those domestic blessings that God has for a people who sincerely seek his face.

There is an attempt in America today to remove every possible vestige of religion from national life. Will God be our God nationally? Or will we force him from national life? We can do either. We can have "no God but Caesar." But God help us if that happens! And God save us from it for Jesus' sake.

243

The Story of Two Thieves

John 19:16–18

Finally Pilate handed him over to them to be crucified.

So the soldiers took charge of Jesus. Carrying his own cross, he went out to the place of the Skull (which in Aramaic is called Golgotha). Here they crucified him, and with him two others—one on each side and Jesus in the middle.

T he trial of Jesus began with the arrest in Gethsemane late in the evening of what we would call April 5, A.D. 30, and ended with his crucifixion on Golgotha the next day, April 6. According to Jewish reckoning, this was all done on the fourteenth of the month of Nisan. The trial was a double trial, as we have seen in our studies of it. There was a Jewish trial and a Roman trial. In the Jewish trial, Jesus was examined on the charge of blasphemy. We have seen that if Jesus were merely a man, this charge and the condemnation that followed it were just, for Jesus had made this claim. In reality, however, the trial was unjust; for the laws of Judaism were repeatedly violated, and no defense in support of Jesus' claim was admitted. In the Roman trial, Jesus was examined on the charge of insurrection and treason, for having made himself "a king." This trial, in contrast to

the Jewish trial, was legally exact. But the result was murder, for having acquitted the prisoner of all guilt, Pilate nevertheless gave Jesus over to be crucified.

So much for human justice. Now we are to see the justice of God unfold
in his punishment of sin in Christ, so that on the basis of the death of the
innocent Christ divine love might go out to embrace and fully save the one
who trusts him.

The Crucifixion

We do not want to dwell on the crucifixion itself, for John does not do so
and neither do the other Gospel writers. We need only note that there was
no more terrible death than crucifixion.

William Barclay, late author of the popular "Daily Study Bible" series,
states the matter clearly. "Even the Romans themselves regarded it with a
shudder of horror. Cicero declared that it was 'the most cruel and horrify-
ing death.' Tacitus said that it was a 'despicable death.' Crucifixion was originally a Persian method of execution. It may have been used because, to the
Persians, the earth was sacred, and they wished to avoid defiling it with the
body of a criminal and an evildoer; so they nailed him to a cross and left him
to die there, and then left the vultures and the carrion crows to complete
the work. The Carthaginians took over crucifixion from the Persians; and
the Romans learned it from the Carthaginians. Crucifixion was never used
as a method of execution in Italy; it was only used in the provinces, and there
only in the case of slaves. It was unthinkable that a Roman citizen should die
by such a death. Cicero says: 'It is a crime for a Roman citizen to be bound;
it is a worse crime for him to be beaten; it is well nigh parricide for him to
be killed; what am I to say if he be killed on a cross? A nefarious action such
as that is incapable of description by any word, for there is none fit to describe it.' It was that death, the most dreaded death in the ancient world, the
death of slaves and criminals, that Jesus died."[1]

The method of crucifixion is detailed in the New Testament and in other
ancient documents. After sentence was passed, the victim was first subjected
to scourging, a punishment so severe that some died under it. In Jesus' case
the scourging took place before the final passing of sentence so as to evoke
pity from the mob. Next the horizontal bar of the cross was bound to the
condemned man's back. He was then led through the city to the place of
crucifixion accompanied by a centurion and four soldiers who made up the
execution party. A placard describing the crime for which he was to die was
carried before him.

Arriving at the place of crucifixion, the victim was stripped of his clothes,
which became the property of the soldiers. The crossbar was then hoisted
upward to rest upon the upright bar which had already been prepared to
receive it. The victim's hands were nailed in place. In most cases the feet
were also nailed or bound to the cross. As a result of this he could raise him-

self up from time to time, thereby alleviating the strain upon his arms and diaphragm. After hours or even days of such torture, the victim would die of shock, exposure, loss of blood, or suffocation.

Three Died on Calvary

It is interesting that as John tells the story of Christ's crucifixion he does so with great restraint, not at all emphasizing the physical aspects of the crucifixion. One reason for this is that the physical aspects were well known to his contemporaries and so needed little elaboration. But the more important reason is that John (like the other Gospel writers) has more important things to emphasize. There is the fulfillment of prophecy, for example. There are the words from the cross. One striking point, significantly mentioned in all four Gospels, is that Jesus was not the only one to die that day. He was accompanied in his death by two thieves.

Theirs is an interesting story, though John himself does not elaborate upon it. Apparently they had been guilty of robbery, which may have been part of a wider revolutionary activity on their part. The word used to describe them was also used of Barabbas (John 18:40), and it can also mean "an insurrectionist." Whatever their specific crime may have been they were caught and were now sentenced to die with Jesus. As he was nailed to the cross, they were also nailed. As he was lifted up, they were also lifted up. The pain was excruciating, and these two robbers, being filled with anguish and despair, must have cried out intensely cursing God, the Romans, the Jews, even their own fathers and the mothers who gave them birth.

But the Jews were not minding these robbers. They were thinking of Jesus, and they were adding insult upon insult to his sufferings. "You who are going to destroy the temple and build it in three days, save youself! Come down from the cross if you are the Son of God" (Matt. 27:40). "He saved others; let him save himself if he is the Christ of God, the Chosen One" (Luke 23:35). "Let this Christ, this King of Israel, come down now from the cross, that we may see and believe" (Mark 15:32). As they listened to these taunts the thieves turned their thoughts from themselves to Jesus and joined in the jeering. Matthew tells us that "the robbers who were crucified with him also heaped insults on him" (Matt. 27:44). Luke even gives the words of one: "Aren't you the Christ? Save yourself and us!" (Luke 23:39).

Suddenly something wonderful happened, a miracle. God began to work in the heart of one thief so that his cursing died down, he fell to thinking, and at last began to understand the truth about himself and Jesus. Earlier he had been cursing. Now he turned to his companion and rebuked him for the evil things he now understood him to be speaking. "Don't you fear God, since you are under the same sentence? We are punished justly, for we are getting what our deeds deserve. But this man has done nothing wrong." He then turned to Jesus and voiced his new-found faith, "Jesus, remember me when you come into your kingdom."

What did Jesus answer? Did Jesus say, "It's too late for that now; you should have thought of that when you were joining that revolutionary band"? Did he say, "I appreciate your confidence, but I don't know; if we get through this, I'll see what I can do for you"? Did he say, "We're both in the same boat, mister; we just have to grit our teeth and bear it"? We know he did not. Instead he said in quiet confidence, "I tell you the truth, today you will be with me in paradise" (Luke 23:43).

In speaking to this thief, Jesus speaks to us too. For he not only shows the way to be saved; he also gives assurance of salvation.

A Sea Captain Is Saved

Donald Grey Barnhouse was working in his study at the church one day when the janitor came to him and said, "There's a gentleman out here who wants to see you." He gave him the man's card, and Barnhouse saw that he was the British sea captain of the *Mauritania,* which was at that time the largest ocean liner crossing the Atlantic. Barnhouse took the card and went out to meet him.

The captain explained why he had come. "I'm captain of the *Mauritania,* as you can see from my card, and I go back and forth across the Atlantic about twenty-three times a year. Every other Sunday on the way down the coast of Newfoundland I get your radio broadcast out of Boston. Last Sunday, when I listened to you, I said to myself, 'I've got twenty-four hours when I land in New York. I'm going over to Philadelphia to see that preacher.' So I took the train this morning from New York and I just came down on the chance that I might see you."

Barnhouse said, "Sir, have you been born again?"

He said, "That's why I came down to see you."

By this time Barnhouse and the captain had reached the prayer-meeting room, where there was a blackboard. So Barnhouse took a piece of chalk and drew three crosses. "Let me put it very simply for you," he said. "You know that when Jesus Christ died on the cross there was a thief on either side?"

"Yes."

"And each was a sinner. He had sin *in* him." As he said this Barnhouse wrote the word "in" under both of the side crosses, representing those of the two thieves. Under the center cross he wrote, "not in!" "This man did not have sin in him. Christ was the spotless Lamb of God. Now," he continued, pointing to the first and third crosses, "in addition these men had sin *on* them." He wrote "on" over both crosses.

A puzzled expression came to the captain's face.

"Let me show you the difference between sin on you and sin in you," Barnhouse said. "Do you drive a car?"

"Yes."

"Have you ever gone through a red light?"

"Yes, I have."

"You were guilty, weren't you?"

"Yes."

"Did the police catch you?" Barnhouse asked.

"Well, no, they didn't."

"But you had that sin in you, didn't you?" Barnhouse continued. "And if the police had been there and had given you a ticket, then you would have had that sin on you as well. That's the difference between having sin in you and having sin on you. All of us have sin in us. We are all guilty. All of us also have sin on us. We are under God's judgment. This first thief had sin in him and sin on him. This second thief had sin in him and sin on him. They were exactly alike."

Barnhouse then wrote the word "on" over the cross of Christ. He said, "Christ also had sin *on* him. But he did not have sin *in* him. That sin which is on him is not his sin; it is my sin—and that of this thief." He then turned the chalk sideways and rubbed it through the word "on" over the cross of the believing thief and drew a big arrow pointing to the cross of Christ. "God justified this thief by putting all the guilt of his sin over here on Jesus Christ."

He went on to say, "Now, Christianity is simply this. Here is the perfect Christ who came and died on the cross. And here are two types of people, represented by these two thieves. Both are alike. Both have sin in them. Both have had sin on them. But in the one case, the sin that *was on* him is now *on Christ*. Sir, I am like this thief. My sin was on me, but now it is on Christ. You are either like this first thief or like this second thief. Sin is in you, in me, and it is either on yourself or it is on Christ. God says that Christ came to take away your sins. Which are you like?"

The captain was a tall, cultured man and evidently not one easily to give way to emotion. But he was greatly moved and was evidently trying to keep back tears. At last his hand moved forward, and he pointed to the cross of the repentant thief. He said, "By the grace of God, I am like this thief."

Barnhouse replied, "Your sin is on Christ. God says so."

He said, "God says so." Then he reached out and took Barnhouse's hand to say good-by. "That's all I want," he added. "I can go back now." Instead Barnhouse asked him to stay, and they spent an hour or so talking about what he should do next in the Christian life.[2]

Our Story

I tell that story at some length because the story of the believing thief, as told by Luke, and the story of the believing sea captain, as told by Barnhouse, is our story too if we have truly believed on the Lord Jesus Christ as our Savior. If it is not your story, I pray that it might be before this study is finished.

The believing thief did three things. First, he recognized his own need, and by that I mean his spiritual need and not merely his physical one. On the physical side there were many things he needed. He needed deliverance, medical attention, drugs. Failing these things, he at least needed sympathy knowing that he was about to die. But this is not what he recognized and confessed so openly. What he recognized was that he was a sinner and that he needed a Savior. At other times in his life he might have tried to explain this need away. But here he recognized it. He confessed, "Don't you fear God, since you are under the same sentence? We are punished justly, for we are getting what our deeds deserve."

Second, having recognized that he was a sinner and that he needed a Savior, he recognized that Jesus was that Savior. He may not have been able to explain the theology of justification, as I have just explained it. But he knew that Jesus was the innocent Son of God and the Savior. He showed this by saying, "This man has done nothing wrong" and by referring to the coming of Christ in his "kingdom."

Finally, having recognized his need of a Savior and that Jesus was that Savior, he committed himself to him personally. He said, "Jesus, remember *me* when you come into your kingdom." And the Lord did remember him. He remembered him on the spot, for he accepted him right then and promised that on that very day, after each had died, they would be together in paradise.

If you would be like that thief—if you would have your sin on Christ rather than on yourself and therefore be able to receive the promise of being with Christ and God the Father eternally—you need to do what he did. First, admit your sin. Second, see Jesus as your Savior. Third, commit yourself to him personally. You need to say, "Lord, I know that I cannot get to heaven on my own record, for I am a sinner, and my record condemns me. I need you as my Savior, and I ask you to accept me as one for whom you died. Receive me. Remember me in the day of your judgment." If you will pray that prayer, you can be certain that Jesus has received you just as he received the repentant thief. From a human point of view everything was against him. Yet he called upon Jesus, and Jesus, in what was his last interview upon earth, heard him, received him, and promised him an entrance into paradise.

Will you call upon him? You can never be too sinful or call so late that Jesus will not hear. He is listening for that call now.

244

This World's King

John 19:19–22

Pilate had a notice prepared and fastened to the cross. It read: JESUS OF NAZARETH, THE KING OF THE JEWS. Many of the Jews read this sign, for the place where Jesus was cru-cified was near the city, and the sign was written in Aramaic, Latin and Greek. The chief priests of the Jews protested to Pilate, "Do not write 'The King of the Jews,' but that this man claimed to be king of the Jews."

Pilate answered, "What I have written, I have written."

O f the four Gospel writers, John alone (as far as we know from Scripture) was an eyewitness of Christ's cru-cifixion, so it is not surprising that his account contains details that are miss-ing from the first three Gospels. He alone tells of how Jesus lovingly entrusted Mary to his care. He alone tells of two of Jesus' sayings from the cross: "I thirst" and "It is finished." No other but John tells us that in being crucified along with two thieves, Jesus was "in the midst." He alone tells that Christ's side was pierced by a soldier's spear and that there came forth blood and water. He alone distinctly tells us that Jesus set out for Golgotha carrying his own cross, which afterward Simon of Cyrene had to carry, as the Synoptics tell us.

things only in John

1501

These details of the events of the crucifixion vary in importance, as John himself seems to indicate by the prominence or lack of prominence he gives them. Among those that are very important is a detail concerning the title that Pilate had placed over Christ's cross.

In Three Languages

There is nothing unusual in the mere fact that John mentions the title that was placed above the cross. This title was standard procedure in cases of crucifixion, and each of the other Gospel writers likewise mentions the placard. According to Matthew, "Above his head they placed the written charge against him: THIS IS JESUS, THE KING OF THE JEWS" (Matt. 27:37). Mark writes, "The written notice of the charge against him read: THE KING OF THE JEWS" (Mark 15:26). Luke puts it this way, "There was a written notice above him, which read: THIS IS THE KING OF THE JEWS" (Luke 23:38). Each of these accounts tells us that there was a placard designating the crime for which he was crucified, and each gives us the substance of it. What John tells us and the others do not is that it was written in three languages. John says, "Pilate had a notice prepared and fastened to the cross. It read: JESUS OF NAZARETH, THE KING OF THE JEWS. Many of the Jews read this sign, for the place where Jesus was crucified was near the city, and the sign was written in Aramaic, Latin and Greek" (John 19:19–20).[1]

This is an interesting detail. For one thing, it provided us with one explanation of why the precise wording of the title in each of the Gospels differs from that in the others. The difference is not great, of course. But the suggestion has been made that it is due to the evangelists having translated different versions of the title. Pink suggests that Matthew most likely translated the Hebrew, Luke the Greek, and Mark and John the Latin.[2]

My own opinion is that this explanation, while possible, is unnecessary. It seems more likely that each writer simply gives a selected translation. The full text would have been: "This is [translated by Matthew and Luke] Jesus [given by Matthew and John], of Nazareth [added by John alone], the King of the Jews [provided by all four writers]."

John's intention in providing this detail is not, however, to explain to us how the wording of the other Gospels might have come to differ slightly. Rather it is to show that Jesus, while dying as a Jewish King, nevertheless had a relationship to the world beyond Israel. Hebrew, Greek, and Latin were the major languages of the then known world. So John is actually declaring that Jesus is a King for everyone. He is not merely a Jewish Savior, though he is that. He is the Savior of the Greeks and of the Romans as well. He is the Savior of the world.

This World's Savior

Once we have seen this we immediately think of the strong emphasis on this truth throughout John's Gospel. We think, first, of John's prologue. "The true light that gives light to every man was coming into the world. He was in the world, and though the world was made through him, the world did not recognize him. He came to that which was his own, but his own did not receive him. Yet to all who received him, to those who believed in his name, he gave the right to become children of God" (1:9–12). In these verses, from the very beginning of the Gospel, John is indicating that the provision for salvation from sin about which he is writing in the Gospel is not for the Jew only but instead is for all men and women. All have rejected Jesus. But from that vast number, composed of both Jew and Gentile, God has elected a great mixed race to be his spiritual children.

Later on in this same chapter the ministry of John the Baptist is unfolded in detail, and John's testimony to Jesus is recorded. John declared, "Look, the Lamb of God, who takes away the sin of the world" (1:29). The sacrifice of lambs, particularly at the Passover, was an exclusively Jewish institution. It would have been natural for John to have said, "Behold the Lamb of God, who takes away the sin of Israel." But this is not what John said. John recognized the universality of Christ's mission and so identified him as the world's sin-bearer.

The theme occurs again in John 3, the chapter that recounts Jesus' conversation with Nicodemus. In these verses, Jesus speaks to Nicodemus of the nature and necessity of the new birth. Then John continues: "For God so loved the world that he gave his one and only Son, that whoever believes in him shall not perish but have eternal life. For God did not send his Son into the world to condemn the world, but to save the world through him" (3:16–17). After this he repeats the idea of Jesus being the world's light (vv. 19–21).

In chapter 4 we have an example of Jesus going beyond the strict bounds of Judaism to reach a woman from Samaria and, through her, her entire town. In this account there is an interesting contrast between Jesus' open and unprejudiced attitude toward others and the suspicion and vain superiority of his own disciples toward the Samaritan woman. They were practically on her own level of understanding and certainly on the same level when they stood before God. Yet the disciples looked down on her. Jesus, who was infinitely above them all, stooped to reach her and lift her up to believe on and eventually be with him. It is significant that the story goes on to tell of the witness of the woman to her friends and fellow citizens of Samaria, at the end of which these declare forcefully, "We no longer believe just because of what you said; now we have heard for ourselves, and we know that this man really is the Savior of the world" (4:42).

In chapter 6 he is the "bread of life" given for "the life of the world" (vv. 32–35, 48–51). In chapters 8 and 9 Jesus is "the light of the world" (8:12; 9:5). In chapter 10 he is the shepherd whose task is to gather his own out of Judaism and the other folds of this world. He is to lead them into that one new fold, which is the church (10:16).

In chapter 11 John reports the unwitting prophecy of Caiaphas, the high priest, who in calculating self-interest declared, "You know nothing at all! You do not realize that it is better for you that one man die for the people than that the whole nation perish" (11:49–50). Caiaphas was not thinking of the Gentiles when he made this statement. In fact, he was not even thinking of Israel, though he claimed to be making his suggestion for the good of the Jewish people. Caiaphas was thinking of himself and of his own position and prestige. Yet, as John indicates, "He did not say this on his own, but as high priest that year he prophesied that Jesus would die for the Jewish nation, and not only for that nation but also for the scattered children of God, to bring them together and make them one" (vv. 51–52).

In the next chapter John alone of the Gospel writers tells of the Greeks who came to Jesus and to whom Christ declared, "The hour has come for the Son of Man to be glorified" (12:20–23). At the end of the chapter, he reports Jesus as saying, "I have come into the world as a light, so that no one who believes in me should stay in darkness" (v. 46). It is difficult to imagine how the universal scope of Christ's death could be more fully or more consistently presented.

Salvation for All

We should be glad that it is so presented, for it is John's way of saying that there is no respect of persons with God. Paul has written this truth theologically (cf. Rom. 2:11). But John demonstrates it practically, showing that God offers salvation to the Greek and Roman as well as to the Jew. He saves the thief on the cross as well as the centurion who commanded the execution party. He proclaims his grace to the high and low, the rich and poor, the intellectual and ignoramus, and so on for whatever categories you or I may see fit to impose on the race.

Besides, if we stop to analyze it, we can see that this is the only path open to a God of perfect justice. Barnhouse has written on this point, "There can be but one just method of salvation, and that is the method which God has devised in the infinite bounty of his being, and has brought to us by the goodness of his heart and the sacrifice that flows from his loving kindness. God says to the human race in sum: I will not look at what you have been. It makes no difference how you may have sunken in sin or how you have walked according to your standards. I will not take account of the arrogance of your pride or of the filth of your wallowing. I will not look at what you call iniquity, nor will I look at what you call goodness. I will bring you all to the gate and count you all as equal. I will ask you to admit that your gradations of human efforts and human attainments must be discarded and that you come, one and all, as bankrupts. Just admit that though you may have everything that satisfies your neighbors you have nothing that satisfies me. Then, says God, I will do everything for you and put righteousness to your account as a free gift without respect of persons."[3]

What God has done may be remembered in this fashion. We are studying the significance of the placard that Pilate caused to be erected over Christ's cross, the placard that designated his supposed crime. But we may remember that according to the Scriptures God saw another title over that cross, though the message of that invisible placard was different.

Paul tells us about it in Colossians. He writes, "When you were dead in your sins and in the uncircumcision of your sinful nature, God made you alive with Christ. He forgave us all our sins, having canceled the written code, with its regulations, that was against us and that stood opposed to us; he took it away, nailing it to the cross" (Col. 2:13–14). What is Paul getting at here? He is using the image of the placard placed over the cross of a dying criminal to say that although you and I have violated the holy law of God given at Sinai and therefore deserve to die for it, we do not need to die. For Jesus, the innocent One, took our place and died for our trespass. His cross bore the placard of our crime. In him our violation of God's just law was punished, and God can therefore reach out to justify the one who trusts him, regardless of that person's nationality, intelligence, race, or any other factor.

Have you reached out to trust him? If you are pleading your attainments or heritage, you are not trusting him. You are trusting yourself, and you cannot come. It is only when you turn from these that you find the way open. The Greek and the Roman, the Jew and the Gentile are on the same ground. "The sinner and the saintling, the powerful and the powerless, the judge and the judged, the lawyer and the lawless, the noble and the nobody, the proprietor and the pauper, the doctor and the dunce, the strong and the stripling, the glamorous and the gawky, the sophisticate and the savage, the worthy and the worthless—all may be saved from whatever their supposed class background."[4]

Lord of All

There is one more point. I have been writing about Jesus as the Savior of the world, for this is what John suggests by recording that the title placed over the cross was in the three main languages of the day. But I am sure you have noticed that the title did not actually refer to Jesus as the Savior. It actually referred to him as King—King of the Jews and of the remainder of the world as well. This suggests that his accomplishments as Savior and his identification as Lord go together. Or, to say it in other words, you cannot have Christ as Savior without having him as Lord also; he cannot be Lord unless he is Savior.

Is he your Lord? You say, "I think so, but what does that mean? What is he Lord of specifically?" I think there is an answer to that question in the significance of the languages in which the caption of the cross was written. The first language mentioned by John is Hebrew. Hebrew was the language of religion and morality. There were religions in Greece and Rome too, of course. But Hebrew was preeminently the language of religious faith, for it was in Hebrew that God had given the Old Testament, in which the only faithful representation of himself and the way of salvation was provided for the ancient world. Proclaiming Jesus King in Hebrew suggests that he is King of religion. He is himself the only true representation of God and the only sure and certain proclaimer of the way to be just before him. Jesus is Lord in this area. Consequently, if he is your Lord, he must be the One who determines what you believe concerning God and salvation. You should not say, "I think so-and-so" if Jesus is truly your King. Rather, your question must be, "What does *he* think? What is *his* teaching?"

Greek is the second language. This was the language of science, culture, and philosophy. It was the language of beauty. If Jesus is Lord in this area, then his outlook must prevail as you look out upon our culture. Is what you see what he desires? Is our culture's world-and-life-view his view? If it is not— and it is certain that it is not—then you must side with your Lord regardless of the world's opinion either of him or of you.

Finally, there is Latin, the language of law and good government. This reminds us that Jesus is the supreme lawgiver and law administrator. His laws must govern your conduct, and you must be obedient to him, even though his commands may be countermanded by the state or any other human authority.

Pilate put his inscription on the cross primarily to irritate the leaders of the Jewish people, and it did irritate them. It irritated them so much that they came back to him and requested that the wording be changed. They wanted the sign to read, "He said, 'I am King of the Jews.'" These leaders hated Jesus so much that in his death they did not want to give even the appearance of recognizing his kingship. The accusation—JESUS OF NAZARETH, THE KING OF THE JEWS—revealed their nature as it truly was. But notice that it did that for Pilate too, for in response, the cowardly recalcitrance of Pilate emerged clearly so that the one who did not have courage to acquit One whom he knew to be innocent nevertheless stupidly dug in his heels and responded, "What I have written, I have written" (John 19:22).

The cross always reveals men as they are. It reveals the soldiers' nature, the nature of the crowds, that of the faithful women and John, who was also in the city of Jerusalem at this period. It reveals our hearts as well. We cannot be hypocrites before that cross. It is too great, its scope too universal. What does the cross show you to be? Does it show you to be a sinner—without hope, under condemnation—because you have no part in the Savior? Or does it show you to be his follower? God grant that if you have not yet done so, you might find him as Savior and begin to follow him as your rightful King and Lord.

245

Scripture Fulfilled in Christ's Death

John 19:23–24

When the soldiers crucified Jesus, they took his clothes, dividing them into four shares, one for each of them, with the undergarment remaining. This garment was seamless, woven in one piece from top to bottom.

"Let's not tear it," they said to one another. "Let's decide by lot who will get it."

This happened that the scripture might be fulfilled which said,

"They divided my garments among them

and cast lots for my clothing."

So this is what the soldiers did.

At an earlier point in our study of John's Gospel I quoted some words of Martin Luther that I wish to quote again here because the point of the earlier passage and the point of this one are similar.

Luther had been preaching a sermon on John 5:39, the verse in our study of John at which I quoted him earlier; it said of the Scriptures, "And they are they that testify of me." Luther noted this and then added, "Here Christ would indicate the principle reason why the Scripture was given by God.

1507

Men are to study and search in it and to learn that He, *He,* Mary's Son, is the one who is able to give eternal life to all who come to Him and believe on Him. Therefore he who would correctly and profitably read Scripture should see to it that he finds Christ in it; then he finds life eternal without fail. On the other hand, if I do not so study and understand Moses and the prophets as to find that Christ came from Heaven for the sake of my salvation, became man, suffered, died, was buried, rose, and ascended to Heaven so that through Him I enjoy reconciliation with God, forgiveness of all my sins, grace, righteousness, and life eternal, then my reading in Scripture is of no help whatsoever to my salvation. I may, of course, become a learned man by reading and studying Scripture and may preach what I have acquired; yet all this would do me no good whatsoever. For if I do not know and do not find the Christ, neither do I find salvation and life eternal. In fact, I actually find bitter death; for our good God has decreed that no other name is given among men whereby they may be saved except the name of Jesus (Acts 4:12)."[1]

Luther's point is that the Scriptures are, both in their general outline and in specific details, God's Word to us about Jesus. It is undoubtedly this keen spiritual insight that made him the tower of strength and winsome exegete that he was. Luther believed that the Bible was God's Word and that it was about Jesus. Consequently, whenever he approached the Bible, he knew from the start who was speaking in it and what its theme was.

It would be good if all who pretend to teach the Bible in our day had a similar insight and conviction. Unfortunately, they do not. Instead of reading the Bible as the Word of God, many read it as the words of Isaiah, Matthew, John, Paul, or even "Second Isaiah," "the Deuteronomist," "Q," or some other supposed source. Instead of seeing the Bible as a book about Jesus, they see it as a collection of works with varying and sometimes even conflicting themes. As a result, the Bible does not make sense to such people, and they find it confusing. Moreover, they often also fail to believe it and in the Christ presented in its pages. Failing to believe in him, they miss salvation.

Four Prophecies

This was not the case with the apostles. Undoubtedly, there were times early in their lives and experiences of Jesus when the Bible they had (the Old Testament) was confusing. They read it and heard it taught, like most pious Jews of their day. But they did not understand it. Specifically, they did not understand its prophecies of the coming Messiah. This was even true during their three-year association with Jesus. But when he died, rose again, and came to them after those events to explain how all that had happened to him had been prophesied beforehand in the Scriptures, their confusion vanished and their outlook changed. Now they knew that the Bible was indeed about Jesus, and they saw it in a new light. In fact, they now saw prophecies of his life on many of its pages.

This was true of John, no less than the others. Much that had happened to Jesus up to this point had been in fulfillment of Scripture. One commentator has pointed out that no less than "twenty Old Testament predictions relating to events that would surround the death of Christ, words written centuries before his first advent, were fulfilled with precision within a twenty-four-hour period at the time of his crucifixion."[2] John has not drawn attention to this fulfillment of Scripture before this. Now he begins to note the events of the crucifixion which were in fulfillment of specific Old Testament prophecies, suggesting (1) that God was in charge of these events, (2) that the Scriptures do not fail, and (3) that Jesus is indeed the anointed One of God, the Messiah. There are four such prophecies:

1. The division of Christ's clothing among the soldiers of the execution party and the casting of lots for his seamless inner garment. John describes this in verses 23 and 24. It is prophesied in Psalm 22:18.

2. The giving of a vinegar solution to Jesus to drink, in fulfillment of Psalm 69:21. Jesus provoked this act by exclaiming, "I thirst." John tells of this fulfillment in verses 28 and 29.

3. The breaking of the legs of the two thieves coupled with the decision not to break Jesus' legs. John describes this in verses 31–33 and 36. It was prophesied in Psalm 34:20.

4. The piercing of Christ's side with a spear. John mentions this in verses 34–35, and 37. It is prophesied in Zechariah 12:10.

Clearly John believed, as did the other writers of the New Testament, Martin Luther and the vast host down through history who followed in their train, that the Bible is God's Word about his Son, our Savior Jesus Christ. It is where we meet him, learn of him, believe in him, and grow into the fullness of the faith. Through a study of the Word this happens. Without it, none of these things take place.

Psalm 22:18

The first of John's references to the fulfillment of Scripture in the events surrounding Christ's death is the matter of the dividing of his clothing, which John notes as a fulfillment of Psalm 22:18. It is that which we primarily want to look at in this study.

We have already seen that a condemned man was customarily taken to the place of execution by a detachment of four soldiers under the command of a centurion. It was the prerequisite of these soldiers to receive the clothes of the victim. William Barclay points out in his commentary that the Jews normally wore five articles of clothing: the shoes, turban, girdle, tunic, and outer robe. He suggests that, since there were four soldiers and five articles of apparel, each had one, and one article (the inner garment or tunic) was left over.[3] This may have been the case, or it may have been that the first four items were torn apart or otherwise divided. Regardless of that, the inner garment was without seam, being woven in one piece from top to bottom. It could not be divided. So the soldiers cast lots or gambled for it. John notes this, saying, "'Let's not tear it,' they said to one another. 'Let's decide by lot who will get it.' This happened that the scripture might be fulfilled which said, 'They divided my garments among them and cast lots for my clothing.'"

Many have read a great deal into this reference. In the early church, the mention of Christ's seamless robe suggested to Origen the wholeness of Christ's teaching. Cyprian thought that it symbolized the unity of the church. To Cyril it meant the virgin birth. In more recent times and with greater reason, it has been understood as suggesting the perfect righteousness of Christ now imparted to the sinner as the basis of his justification.[4]

There may be some truth in each of these explanations, but I doubt that John or any other of the Gospel writers had them in mind. What they are concerned to emphasize is that this specific detail of the crucifixion, like all the other details, was planned for and prophesied by God. Consequently, neither this nor any other aspect of the death of Christ was accidental.

The Suffering Savior

This is not to say that no more may be learned from this prophecy, however. On the contrary, Psalm 22 in particular seems to have been on the Lord's mind during these final hours of his earthly life. Therefore, it gives us a clue as to what he thought his suffering meant and what was to be accomplished by it.

A number of years ago in an article for *Eternity* magazine, I pointed out the significance of this psalm for understanding what occupied the anguished mind of Christ during the dark hours of Calvary. I would like to share some of those earlier conclusions here. I noted in the first place that, although there is no reason why we should know what was in Christ's mind during those three hours of darkness, between noon and three in the afternoon, when he died, there are nevertheless several clues which relate his thoughts to this psalm and thereby indicate that he was thinking of it. The first clue is that at the beginning of the period of darkness Jesus cried out with a loud voice, "My God, my God, why have you forsaken me?" (Mark 15:34), a direct quotation of Psalm 22:1. The second clue is that at the end of three hours of darkness he cried out again, saying, "It is finished" (John 19:30). This phrase is a quotation of the last verse of Psalm 22 (v. 31).

The English reader will not find this phrase in the most common English translation of Psalm 22, but it is a legitimate translation of the one Hebrew word that occurs there. The verse itself can read, "They shall come, and shall declare his righteousness unto a people that shall be born, that *it is finished.*"

This has great implications, for it means that during the hours in which the Lord hung upon the cross his mind traversed the scope of the psalm. He thought of the alienation of the One who was made sin for mankind.

He passed on to reflect on the description of suffering the psalm includes. He thought of the final section that speaks of the spread of the gospel among the Gentiles. Only after that did Jesus utter the phrase that marks the psalm's ending.

In this psalm there are three pictures of Christ that partially explain his suffering. The first verse speaks of Christ as having been *forsaken*. I have read good books suggesting that Jesus was not really forsaken by God, that he only imagined he was forsaken, that Jesus almost lost his faith in God but he recovered it later when he knew that God had sustained him. This is wrong. Christ was bearing the penalty for sin, which is death (Rom. 6:23), and death means separation from God. What is death? Certainly not physical death alone, but spiritual death! And spiritual death is the separation of the soul from the source of life, which is God. That is the penalty Christ bore for human sin—separation from God. So when he cried out in a loud voice, "My God, my God, why have you forsaken me?" it was the cry of one actually abandoned by the Father.

You and I can never pretend fully to understand this. We cannot imagine how there can be a division in the Godhead. How can God the Son be forsaken by God the Father? It is a great mystery. But it is true nevertheless. Christ was forsaken, and it was only by this means that he accomplished our salvation.

The second picture of the suffering Savior comes from Psalm 22:6: "I am a worm and not a man, scorned by men and despised by the people." Why a worm? Why this unusual image? To understand this image one must realize that the Hebrew word for worm had come to refer almost exclusively to a special kind of worm from which the people of the Near East derived a valuable crimson dye. It was much like an insect that exists in Mexico today called the *cochineal*. The worm known to the Hebrews was the *tola*. The dye was formed from its blood, released when the animal was crushed. In Hebrew the word for scarlet literally means the "splendor of the *tola*."

The *tola* is referred to several times in Scripture. It is the worm that spoiled the manna in the wilderness. The scarlet dye for the linen of the wilderness Tabernacle came from the blood of the *tola*. It is said of Saul in 2 Samuel that he dressed the women of Israel in scarlet, that is, he introduced a period of such prosperity that all their robes could be dyed.

This image throws light upon Christ's thoughts, for when Jesus thought of himself as the *tola*, he thought of himself as the worm who is *crushed* for God's people. His blood was shed for us that we might be clothed in bright raiment.

The third image refers to *execution*. The psalm says, "Rescue me from the mouth of the lions, save me from the horns of the [unicorns]" (v. 21). The animal mentioned in this verse is not really a unicorn, for a unicorn does not exist (in spite of the fact that the translators of the King James Bible probably thought so). Actually it is a type of wild ox with long pointed horns to which victims are said sometimes to have been bound for execution. As

Jesus thought about this image, he may have reflected on the forensic aspect of his death and remembered that God was putting him to death for our sin.

Christ's Soul Satisfied

Forsaken! Crushed! Executed! These ideas all help to explain Christ's crucifixion. But there is a more moving concept to come. That Jesus was, even just before his crucifixion, thinking of other people, can be seen in his words to the women when he was on the way to Golgotha ("Weep for yourselves," Luke 23:28) and in his words to Mary and John shortly after the cross was erected ("Dear woman, here is your son. . . . Here is your mother," John 19:26–27). From noon until three in the afternoon, when God shrouded the cross with darkness, his mind turned to the meaning and purpose of his suffering. His thoughts were of himself. But his mind eventually turned back again to other people as he went on to think of the fruit his work would produce in those who would later become Christians.

First, he thought of his disciples. We know this because immediately after the verse that speaks most clearly of Christ's death, the psalm goes on to say, "I will declare your name to my brothers; in the congregation I will praise you" (v. 22). Not long before his crucifixion Jesus had prayed for his disciples—in the long prayer recorded in John 17. Now, even while he is dying, he thinks of them again. Before they had been only followers. Now they are brethren, because by his death they were to become sons of God and coheirs with him of God's glory.

At the very end Jesus looked to the spread of the gospel beyond his disciples, even beyond Judaism, to the Gentiles. This is suggested by the contrast between verses 22 and 25 of this psalm. Verse 22 says, "I will declare your name . . . in the congregation." In the context of the psalm this obviously means the congregation of Israel. Verse 25 speaks about "praise in the *great* assembly." With equal clarity this speaks of the spread of the gospel beyond Israel to the Gentiles. The psalm goes on to say, "All the ends of the earth will remember and turn to the LORD, and all the families of the nations will bow down before him" (v. 27).

That verse is wonderful to me, for I am included in that number. And so are you, if you are a Gentile who believes in Jesus. He was thinking of you as he hung on the cross. He died for you. He died for you personally. If you do not believe in him, he wants you to come to him. It may help you to know that in the moment of his death he looked forward to the spread of the gospel among the Gentiles. And his soul was satisfied.[5]

246

Words from the Cross

John 19:25–27

Near the cross of Jesus stood his mother, his mother's sister, Mary the wife of Clopas, and Mary Magdalene. When Jesus saw his mother there, and the disciple whom he loved standing nearby, he said to his mother, "Dear woman, here is your son," and to the disciple, "Here is your mother." From that time on, this disciple took her into his home.

There is something particularly solemn and significant about the last words of men and women. The reason is that, in the face of death, what a person is often comes clearly to the surface and is reflected in speech. For example, Napoleon Bonaparte, the famous French general and emperor, said while waiting for his death, "I die before my time, and my body will be given back to the earth. Such is the fate of him who has been called the great Napoleon. What an abyss between my deep misery and the eternal kingdom of Christ."

Voltaire, the noted French infidel, is reported to have said to his doctor, "I am abandoned by God and man! I will give you half of what I am worth if you will give me six months' life."

Thomas Hobbes, the skeptic who corrupted the faith of some of England's great men, exclaimed, "If I had the whole world, I would give it to live

1513

one day. I shall be glad to find a hole to creep out of the world at. I am about to take a leap into the dark."

These statements and others by similarly well-known men reveal more about their true outlook on life and their true hope than anything they might have said in more fortuitous moments. They are often quite grim. Fortunately, one can hardly think of these sayings without thinking of the even more famous words of Jesus of Nazareth, the founder of the Christian faith, who in his death spoke words not of despair but of hope and thereby revealed much about his own personal faith and that of Christianity.

The Final Analysis

I have always considered it unfortunate that the seven sayings of Jesus on the cross have been termed his "last words." The implication is that Jesus did not rise again; but he did rise again, and he returned to his disciples to say many more things to them. In fact, these last teachings are actually more important than those from the cross, for they have much more to say about Christianity. On the other hand, the sayings from the cross (although wrongly termed the "last words") are nevertheless significant. They are significant because they show that (1) Jesus was in clear possession of his faculties until the very last moment, when he delivered up his spirit to the Father, (2) he understood his death was intended to provide salvation for the world, and (3) he knew his death would be effectual to that end. Moreover, the words also show his habitual concern and love for other persons, even at the moment of his most acute suffering.

The words from the cross are these:

1. "Father, forgive them, for they do not know what they are doing" (Luke 23:34). These words are a prayer for God to forgive those who were crucifying him. They show the merciful heart of the Savior.

2. "I tell you the truth, today you will be with me in paradise" (Luke 23:43). These words were spoken to the believing thief and were a confident promise of salvation.

3. "Dear woman, here is your son. . . . Here is your mother" (John 19:26–27). In these words Jesus commended his mother, Mary, to the care of the beloved disciple.

4. "My God, my God, why have you forsaken me?" (Mark 15:34; Matt. 27:46). In this saying the true nature of the atonement is made clear and the deep anguish of the Lord is revealed to us.

5. "I thirst" (John 19:28). This request shows the true humanity of the Lord. But even more important, it shows his desire that every fact of his death (as of his life) be in accord with Scripture.

6. "It is finished" (John 19:30). These are the most important words of all, for they refer not merely to his life, perfect and exemplary as it was,

but to his completed atonement for sin. Because of this we can be sure of salvation.

7. "Father, into your hands I commit my spirit" (Luke 23:46). These words show Jesus to have been in control of his life until the last and indicate that the relationship between himself and the Father, which earlier had been broken as he was made sin for us (Mark 15:34), was restored.

Two Christ Loved

Not one of the Gospels contains all seven of these statements, however. Matthew and Mark each contain one, though they allude to others. Luke and John each contain three, but their lists are different and neither one mentions the saying that Matthew and Mark contain ("My God, my God, why have you forsaken me?"). John includes the words regarding Jesus' mother and the beloved disciple, "I thirst," and the final affirmation that the work of the atonement was finished.

It is easy to understand why John includes the words of the Savior to Mary and the corresponding words to that disciple into whose care she was committed. The reason is that John was himself that disciple. Consequently, the charge was his charge and the importance of it came home to him as to no other.[1]

Let us think of these two whom Christ loved possibly more than any other two people upon earth. Let us think, first of all, of Mary and of the pain that was hers in this moment. One commentator wrote, "What sorrow it must have caused her when, because there was no room in the inn, she had to lay her newly-born Babe in the manger! What anguish must have been hers when she learned of Herod's purpose to destroy her infant's life! What trouble was given her when she was forced on his account to flee into a foreign country and sojourn for several years in the land of Egypt! What piercings of soul must have been hers when she saw her Son despised and rejected of men! What grief must have wrung her heart as she beheld him hated and persecuted by his own nation! And who can estimate what she passed through as she stood there at the cross? If Christ was the Man of Sorrows, was she not the woman of sorrows?"[2]

An anonymous poet of the Middle Ages has expressed the sorrows of Mary in these words:

> Near the cross her vigil keeping,
> Stood the Mother, worn with weeping,
>   Where He hung, the dying Lord:
> Through her soul, in anguish groaning,
> Bowed in sorrow, sighing, moaning,
>   Passed the sharp and piercing sword.
> O the weight of her affliction!
> Hers, who won God's benediction,
>   Hers, who bore God's Holy One:

O that speechless, ceaseless yearning!
O Those dim eyes never turning
From her wondrous, suffering Son!³[3]

As we think about these words and about the scene they describe, we recall the saying of the aged Simeon, spoken when the infant Jesus was presented in the temple by Joseph and Mary. God had revealed to him that he would not die until he had seen the Lord's Christ, and now, coming into the temple area at the very moment when Jesus was being presented, he took him up in his arms and blessed him. Then, after uttering that psalm of praise known as the *Nunc Dimitis,* he turned to Mary and said, "This child is destined to cause the falling and rising of many in Israel, and to be a sign that will be spoken against, so that the thoughts of many hearts will be revealed. And a sword will pierce your own soul too" (Luke 2:34–35). What strange words those were! A piercing sorrow for one highly favored by God? How unlikely it all seemed, particularly at the time Simeon spoke! Yet it all came to pass. Here at the cross we see the fulfillment of Simeon's words.

One lesson we learn from this scene is the certainty of the fulfillment of prophecy. God says, "My purpose will stand, and I will do all that I please . . . what I have said, that will I bring about" (Isa. 46:10–11).

Another lesson is that sorrow, even such acute sorrow as this, may come even to those who are greatly loved by Jesus. When it comes to us, as it may, we must not think that it is because of God's disfavor. We think of the story of the death of Lazarus and of those words to Jesus with which the account begins, "Lord, the one you love is sick" (John 11:3). Jesus loved Lazarus and his sisters. Yet Lazarus grew sick and eventually died, and the grief of the sisters was great. Love and sickness are not incompatible in God's economy. God's favor and sorrow sometimes flow along together.

But again, this is not all we can say, for although it is true that the beloved of God often suffer for God's sometimes hidden purposes, it is nevertheless true that we take comfort in his knowledge of our sorrows and his solace for us in the midst of them. In these words we notice that Jesus was aware of Mary (even in his own sorrow), cared for her, and acted to provide what was needful.

The Beloved Disciple

The other person involved in this episode is John, the beloved disciple. He is here at the cross. But the background for his appearance is the contrasting picture of the scattering disciples at the time of the Savior's arrest in Gethsemane. The Lord had warned the disciples of their approaching cowardice—"This very night you will *all* fall away on account of me, for it is written: 'I will strike the shepherd, and the sheep of the flock will be scattered'" (Matt. 26:31). They all protested. Peter said, "Even if I have to die with you, I will never disown you." The rest of the disciples agreed (v. 35).

But Jesus was right, and they were wrong. They had forsaken him, John included; Jesus was left to the scorn and cruelty of his enemies.

Yet notice, the cowardice of the disciples was only temporary. Later, after his resurrection, they would seek him at the appointed place in Galilee (Matt. 28:16) and would speak boldly on his behalf. And here, even before the resurrection, there was at least one who sought him out even while he hung on Calvary. Why? It is not difficult to discern why. That which brought John to Calvary was the same thing that brought Mary there, and the other women—Mary, the wife of Cleopas, and Mary Magdalene. It was that which later brought these and others to the tomb and which brought Mary Magdalene back even after she knew that the body of Jesus was no longer in the garden. It was love, love for Jesus. Thus, although they can do nothing at all, they still want to be as near to him as possible and linger to the end. Mary loved him. Hers was a mother's love. John loved him too; this was "the disciple whom Jesus loved" and who, quite naturally, loved him in turn.

Do you love him? I do not ask whether you have forsaken him in some moment of danger. I do not ask whether you have served him as you should have done or have failed to serve him. I do not ask whether you have denied him. I only ask, Do you love him? If you answer yes, then come to him regardless of what terrible thing you may have done in your life or regardless of what good thing you may have failed to do.

John came to him in spite of his earlier failure. What did he find? Did Jesus rebuke him? Did he look with scorn on one who could not watch with him even one short hour and then forsook him when the moment of testing came? Not at all! Jesus did not rebuke John on his return, any more than he rebuked Peter or any of the others. Instead, he gave John an unmistakable privilege. He committed his mother to his charge. If you are one who has deserted Christ, do as John did and as Arthur W. Pink admonishes in his remarks on these verses: "Cease then your wanderings and return at once to Christ, and he will greet you with a word of welcome and cheer; and who knows but what he has some honorous commission awaiting you!"[4]

"Jesus, Therefore"

We have spoken of Mary in this study and of John too. But clearly, the central figure in this moving drama is Jesus. He is the One who knows Mary's sorrows. He is the One who knows John's love. Now he speaks out of his own love to provide for each one.

The one who hangs on the cross is even at this late moment still providing for others. He is stripped of everything, yet he leaves rich legacies. To his executioners, who even now stand guard over him, he bequeaths a prayer for pardon—"Father, forgive them, for they do not know what they are doing" (Luke 23:34). To the dying but believing thief he grants the promise of salvation—"Today you will be with me in paradise" (Luke 23:43). In his words to John and Mary he grants a continuing legacy of the most tender love. By this word he gives a son to his mother and a mother to his friend.

It is customary in Catholic theology to see this word as a commending of John, and through him all Christ's disciples, to the patronage of Mary. For example, Bishop Fulton J. Sheen remarks, "When our Lord spoke of John, he did not refer to him as John for then he would have been only the son of Zebedee. Rather, in him all humanity was commended to Mary, who became the mother of men, not by metaphor, or figure of speech, but by pangs of birth."[5] Actually the opposite was the case. Jesus did not commend John to Mary, but Mary to John. The real meaning of this episode is that Jesus was caring for his mother and thus fulfilling the Old Testament commandment to "honor your father and mother" (Exod. 20:12). So must we honor that commandment. We are under a God-given obligation to honor our parents, and that obligation does not cease even though we should come of age or move far from them.

We note too that spiritual responsibilities do not remove these obligations. What could be more of a spiritual responsibility than that which the Lord himself was fulfilling? At the very moment at which he spoke these words our Lord was dying for sinners. He was offering himself as satisfaction to the outraged justice of almighty God. Yet even at this moment, he does not fail to provide for her who was his mother.

There is one thing more. When Jesus commends Mary to John, he bypasses his own unbelieving brethren and leaves her to the care of the beloved disciple instead. Is this accidental? Is it only because John happened to be near the cross at this moment? It is hard to think so. Rather, we sense that the Lord is here bringing into existence a new family based on his atonement. As Mariano Di Gangi writes, "Our Lord brings into being the brotherhood of believers. He fashions the fellowship of the household of faith. This is the new society, which is not segregated according to race or nationality. It is not predicated upon social standing or economic power. It consists of those whose faith meets at the cross, and whose experience of forgiveness flows from the cross."[6]

This is our fellowship if we are truly Christ's followers. We should conduct ourselves as those who are members of it by caring for and loving one another. Jesus said, "By this all men will know that you are my disciples, if you love one another" (John 13:35).

247

"I Thirst"

John 19:28–29

Later, knowing that all was now completed, and so that the Scripture would be fulfilled, Jesus said, "I am thirsty." A jar of wine vinegar was there, so they soaked a sponge in it, put the sponge on a stalk of the hyssop plant, and lifted it to Jesus' lips.

It is hard for those of us who have grown up in western lands to understand the horror of thirst or the importance of water to those who live in the world's desert areas. But if this is true in regard to normal circumstances, which it is, how are we to appreciate the thirst of the Lord Jesus Christ on Calvary?

In lands like ours water may be a thing of beauty or a pleasant delight. But it does not speak of life itself, which it did to those who lived in biblical lands. "Fierce thirst, and the benediction of the water which quenches it, are intensely real in the Bible," writes E. M. Blaiklock in an essay on this theme. "In Genesis the herdsmen of the patriarchs strive with the alien for the wells laboriously cut in the hot rock. In Exodus, the panic of thirst shakes and threatens Moses' leadership. Psalmists and prophets liken joy, happiness, life itself, God's grace, to the blessed stream and the fountain filled. At Sychar, and in the Temple court, the Lord likens water to

1519

eternal life; on the Mount he promises fulfillment only to those who thirst for righteousness, and the words are caught up by the closing pages of the Bible."[1]

In biblical lands thirst was a horrible reality. We cannot fully understand it. Yet we must try if we are to appreciate the second of the three words from the cross which John includes in his narrative. The Bible describes Christ's thirst by saying, "I am poured out like water, and all my bones are out of joint. My heart has turned to wax; it has melted away within me. My strength is dried up like a potsherd, and my tongue sticks to the roof of my mouth; you lay me in the dust of death" (Ps. 22:14–15). It was in the midst of suffering like this that our Lord cried out "I thirst" and was given a sponge dipped in a cheap wine like vinegar, as John indicates.

Christ's True Humanity

If it does nothing else, this incident reminds us forcefully of the Lord's true humanity, which we are sometimes in the habit of forgetting. The liberal church tends to forget Christ's deity or else denies it outright. Evangelicals do not do this; they tend to suppress the Lord's humanity, considering him so much God that he can hardly be human. But Jesus was both. He was very God of very God and very man of very man, as the creed confesses. He was not a deified man or a humanized God. He was the God-man, forever God and now forever man. In his incarnation he took our humanity to himself.

Pink writes, "While here on earth the Lord Jesus gave full proof of his deity. He spoke with divine wisdom, he acted in divine holiness. He exhibited divine power, and he displayed divine love. He read mens' minds, moved mens' hearts, and compelled mens' wills. When he was pleased to exert his power all nature was subject to his bidding. A word from him and disease fled, a storm was stilled, the devil left him, the dead were raised to life. So truly was he God manifest in the flesh, he could say, 'He that hath seen me, hath seen the Father.'

"So, too, while he tabernacled among men the Lord Jesus gave full proof of his humanity—sinless humanity. He entered this world as a babe and was 'wrapped in swaddling clothes' (Luke 2:7). As a child, we are told, he 'increased in wisdom and stature' (Luke 2:52). As a boy we find him 'asking questions' (Luke 2:46). As a man he was 'wearied' in body (John 4:6). He was 'an hungered' (Matt. 4:2). He 'slept' (Mark 4:38). He 'rejoiced' (Luke 10:21). He 'groaned' (John 11:33). And here in our text he cried, 'I thirst.' That evidenced his humanity. God does not thirst. The angels do not. We shall not in glory—'they shall hunger no more, neither thirst any more' (Rev. 7:16). But we thirst now because we are human and living in a world of sorrow. And Christ thirsted because he was man—'Wherefore, in all things it behooved him to be made like unto his brethren' (Heb. 2:17)."[2]

The Problem of Suffering

But it is not only Christ's humanity that we see in this incident. We also see answers to the problem of human pain and suffering, which is one of life's great puzzles. We know that life is filled with sorrow. How are we to deal with it? What is the biblical approach? What are the biblical answers? Not all the answers are given in this incident—it is possible that some are given nowhere—but Christ's words at least point us in the right direction.

There have been four major historical approaches to the problem of suffering apart from the biblical approach. The first is an attempt to deny that evil exists. In antiquity this view was developed in a philosophical system known as Docetism. It built upon common Greek philosophy, in which "spirit" was considered to be good and "matter" evil. It was inherent in this distinction that the spiritual world was more real than the material world. The Docetists simply went a bit beyond this to deny the ultimate reality of matter. In their view, in the ultimate analysis suffering and evil were an illusion. In our day the same approach is taken by Christian Science and by some of the Eastern religions.

What is the biblical response to this denial of evil and suffering? Quite simply, the Bible denies that answer. It acknowledges the reality of evil and the horror of suffering. The very fact that the Lord endured the suffering of the cross is disproof of that solution.

The second major approach to the problem of suffering may also be traced to Greek philosophy, to Stoicism. Stoicism was the philosophy of the "stiff upper lip." It acknowledged evil, just as it acknowledged good. But it was fatalistic. It believed that good and evil enter a person's life according to fixed mechanical laws. Nothing can be done about it. Therefore, the only possible response to evil (and good) is simply to control one's response to what happens. The proper way to live is to repress one's responses to the degree that good things do not make us joyous nor bad things make us sad. But this is not the biblical approach either. The Bible does not ask us to be stoics. Rather, it calls upon us to weep with those who weep and rejoice with those who rejoice. Jesus enjoyed himself in joyous company. Again, he was able to weep when there was suffering.

The third approach is the "pleasure first" philosophy of hedonism. In this view also evil and good are real, as in Stoicism; but the solution proposed is to fill up life with so much pleasure that suffering is simply overshadowed. We are to avoid suffering. We are to do everything in our power to have good times and good experiences. Is this biblical? Not at all. True, the Bible acknowledges good times and pleasures and encourages us to be thankful to the Lord for them. But we are not told to avoid the sufferings of life. Rather, we are to identify with those who are suffering and enter into their sufferings in order to help them by taking some of their pain to ourselves. If the Lord had followed the course of the hedonists, he would not have become a man at all.

Fourth, there is the approach that is taken by modern existentialism, particularly the variety that regards human existence as ultimately absurd. In this philosophy, life has no meaning at all. But since we are still faced with the problem of living (if we do not opt for suicide, which Albert Camus has termed the "only ultimate philosophical question"), the only way to do so is by "dialectical courage." This means to go on with a smile as if life is filled with joy and meaning, even though we know it is not.

It is this approach, perhaps more than any other, that urges Christian people to respond biblically. But in doing so we have to be very cautious. The first thing we want to say is that suffering is not meaningless, because in a universe ruled by God nothing is meaningless. Suffering is linked to sin and is therefore, in some sense, a consequence of it. There was no suffering before the fall. There is no suffering in heaven. There will be none in the redeemed earth, where there will also be no sin. But while this is true, we must nevertheless be careful not to establish a simple one-to-one relationship between a person's suffering and the same person's sin. It is true that we all suffer. It is true that we all sin. But our suffering is not necessarily for our own sin, nor in direct proportion to it. Therefore, the one who suffers most is not necessarily the greatest sinner. Nor is the one who suffers less more innocent.

Right here our Lord's pain is instructive, for although his suffering was closely linked to sin—he was suffering for sin, and it was sinful men who had caused him to suffer—his suffering was nevertheless not for his own sin, for he had none. We conclude then that although there is meaning in suffering, although it is linked to sin and is never allowed into a believer's life except for God's own, sometimes hidden purposes, it is nevertheless not always possible to tell what this meaning is. Above all, we must be cautious in explaining to someone else why he or she is suffering.

Yet there is more we can say: suffering can be redeemed. It is not the last word. We do not need to be defeated by it. R. C. Sproul writes, "That is why no true Calvinist would ever hide behind the doctrine of God's sovereignty in the face of social responsibility, in the face of the responsibilities of the agents of alleviation of suffering in this world. We know that suffering can be redeemed and that we can be used of God to bring that redemption to bear. So we are concerned about feeding the hungry, clothing the naked, healing the sick, visiting and caring for the orphan and the widow. Ultimately we know that suffering is fully redemptive in the hands of God."[3]

How is that true? It is true because Jesus entered into our suffering and finally died that we might be delivered from sin and its effects. At this point his physical thirst becomes symbolic of our spiritual thirst and his death the means of alleviating it. Horatius Bonar once wrote of that means:

> I heard the voice of Jesus say,
>   "Behold, I freely give
> The living water; thirsty one,
>   Stoop down and drink, and live."
> I came to Jesus, and I drank
>   Of that life-giving stream;

> My thirst was quenched, my soul revived,
> And now I live in Him.

If you have not come to Christ, then you need to respond to that One who died for your salvation.

Jesus and the Scriptures

This incident teaches something else also, something entirely different from these first lessons. It concerns Jesus' attitude to the Scriptures and his conscious attempts to fulfill them.

We know from the Gospels and also from study of various Old Testament passages that many significant details of the Lord's death were clearly prophesied and therefore fell out in strict conformity to the will of God. Pink writes, "Every important detail of the great Tragedy had been written down beforehand. The betrayal by a familiar friend (Ps. 41:9), the forsaking of the disciples through being offended at him (Ps. 31:11), the false accusation (Ps. 35:11), the silence before his judges (Isa. 53:7), the being proven guiltless (Isa. 53:9), the numbering of him with the transgressors (Isa. 53:12), the being crucified (Ps. 22:16), the mockery of the spectators (Ps. 109:25), the taunt of nondeliverance (Ps. 22:7, 8), the gambling for his garments (Ps. 22:18), the prayer for his enemies (Isa. 53:12), the being forsaken of God (Ps. 22:1), the thirsting (Ps. 69:21), the yielding of his spirit into the hands of the Father (Ps. 31:5), the bones not broken (Ps. 34:20), the burial in a rich man's tomb (Isa. 53:9)—all plainly foretold centuries before they came to pass. What a convincing evidence of the divine inspiration of the Scriptures!"[4]

But we notice as we study the incident of Christ's thirst, comparing it with this or any other list of fulfilled prophecies, that it has a unique quality. The Lord had nothing to do with some of these fulfillments; they fell out in simple correspondence to God's will (the false accusations, the verdicts at the trials, the crucifixion with thieves, the gambling for his garments, the fact that his bones were not broken). In others Christ played a part (in being silent before his judges, in praying for his enemies, in yielding his spirit into the hands of the Father). But here, in this unique incident of his crying out "I thirst," we are told that Jesus did so specifically in order that "the scripture might be fulfilled" (v. 28). That is, though the Scriptures certainly would be fulfilled, Jesus did not consider this a reason to do nothing, when it was within his power to bring about the fulfillment through his own action.

We know from one of our earlier studies that Jesus had been meditating upon the Scriptures during the hours of his agony. He had been thinking of Psalm 22 especially. Apparently his mind had also run over other prophecies, almost, it would seem, checking them off to assure himself that everything prophesied concerning his life had been accomplished. Was there anything in Genesis that had been left undone? No. Exodus? No. Deuteronomy? No. At last he reached Psalm 69 where it is said in verse 21, "They put gall in my food and gave me vinegar for my thirst." Already they had offered him gall to deaden his pain (Mark 15:23), but there had been no offer of vinegar for his thirst. Therefore, he calls out "I thirst" that this might be completed.

This was the last prophecy. So we are told, "When he had received the drink, Jesus said, 'It is finished.' With that, he bowed his head and gave up his spirit" (v. 30).

Fulfilling the Scriptures

The application for those who believe in the Scriptures is this. If we believe the Bible is God's Word, we believe that the prophecies it contains will come true. But do we sit back and do nothing, as some might recommend? Or do we actively seek to participate in fulfilling prophecy?

Let me give some examples. In John 17:17, Jesus prays for the sanctification of his people, saying, "Sanctify them by the truth; your word is truth." We will be sanctified. But does this mean that we are therefore to do nothing to seek to grow spiritually? Not at all. The means of our sanctification are specified in this verse. They are study of, meditation upon, and memorization of God's Word. This is our responsibility. So although ultimately we will all be made like Jesus (1 John 3:2–3), in the meantime we will be sanctified only as we use the means God has placed at our disposal.

In the same prayer Jesus prays for the unity of the church: "My prayer is not for them alone. I pray also for those who will believe in me through their message, that all of them may be one, Father, just as you are in me and I am in you. May they also be in us so that the world may believe that you have sent me" (vv. 20–21). This petition is for the present time. It is that "the world may believe." But what then? Are we free to do as we please, attack our brothers and sisters in Christ, destroy or weaken our unity? Not at all. Rather we must work at this, making "every effort to keep the unity of the Spirit through the bond of peace" (Eph. 4:3).

Again, we must work at the missionary mandate. We are told by the Lord that the "gospel of the kingdom will be preached in the whole world as a testimony to all nations; and then the end will come" (Matt. 24:14). Nothing could be clearer: The gospel *will* be preached. This is the prophecy. But the prophecy does not relieve us of the responsibility of participating in its fulfillment by becoming agents through which it comes to pass.

Is prophecy a deterrent to human action? Not at all. It is a stimulus, for none are so bold in God's service as those who know the outcome in advance and encourage themselves by claiming God's promises.

248

No Death like Jesus' Death

Nature of the Atonement

John 19:30

When he had received the drink, Jesus said, "It is finished." With that, he bowed his head and gave up his spirit.

Iff Christ is Christianity and if the final week of Christ's life is its center, then the center of that week is certainly the moment of Christ's death on Calvary. That moment is therefore the focal point of all history, and the words "It is finished" are an important expression of it.

The importance of those words, the sixth in the series of seven spoken from the cross, is that they point to Christ's death as an achievement. Elsewhere in the Gospels we are told that Jesus uttered a loud cry just before his death (Matt. 27:50; Mark 15:37; Luke 23:46); since two of the Gospels also tell us that Jesus had been given a drink just before this, it would seem that this was Christ's cry. In other words, Christ's words were not the final gasping sob of a defeated man or even the firm deliberate declaration of one who was resigned to his fate. They were a triumphant declaration that the turning point in history had been reached and that the work that Jesus had been sent into the world to do had been done.

1525

It is this that makes Christ's death unique. As an example of patient endurance of abuse and suffering, it may perhaps be matched by other deaths. As a fitting end for One who, like the prophets, bore a faithful witness to God's truth even when that truth was rejected, it may perhaps be paralleled. But Christ's death cannot be matched in its fullest sense, because Jesus (and no other) achieved our salvation by his suffering. The apostle Paul speaks of it, saying, "But when the time had fully come, God sent his Son, born of a woman, born under law, to redeem those under law, that we might receive the full rights of sons" (Gal. 4:4–5). Again he writes, "But now a righteousness from God, apart from law, has been made known, to which the Law and the Prophets testify. This righteousness from God comes through faith in Jesus Christ to all who believe. There is no difference, for all have sinned and fall short of the glory of God, and are justified freely by his grace through the redemption that came by Christ Jesus. God presented him as a sacrifice of atonement, through faith in his blood. He did this to demonstrate his justice, because in his forbearance he had left the sins committed beforehand unpunished—he did it to demonstrate his righteousness at the present time, so as to be just and the one who justifies those who have faith in Jesus" (Rom. 3:21–26).

Because Christ's atonement is so important, we need to consider it at some length. In this and the following studies we will look at the nature, necessity, perfection, and extent of the atonement.

Christ's Death a Sacrifice

When we consider the nature of the atonement we immediately find ourselves in the midst of a world of biblical ideas and imagery without which its nature cannot really be understood. Central to this world of ideas and imagery is the notion of sacrifice and the accompanying thought of substitution. Sacrifice has to do with the death of an innocent victim, usually an animal. Substitution means that this death was in place of the death of someone else.

The background of this concept lies in the truth that all who have ever lived are sinners, having broken God's law, and that the penalty for sin is death. The Bible declares, "There is no one righteous, not even one; there is no one who understands, no one who seeks God. All have turned away, they have together become worthless; there is no one who does good, not even one" (Rom. 3:10–12). Moreover the Bible declares that the penalty for sin is death. It says, "The soul that sins will die" (Ezek. 18:4). This death is not merely physical death, though it is that. It is spiritual death as well. Death is separation. Physical death is the separation of the soul and spirit from the body. Spiritual death is the separation of the soul and the spirit from God. This is what we deserve as a consequence of our sin. But Jesus took that death to himself by his sacrifice. He became our substitute by experiencing both physical and spiritual death in our place.

There is a very vivid illustration of this principle in the early chapters of Genesis. In these chapters Adam and Eve had sinned and were now in terror of the consequences. God had warned them. He had said, "You are free to eat from any tree in the garden; but you must not eat from the tree of the knowledge of food and evil, for when you eat of it you will surely die" (Gen. 2:16–17). At this point they probably did not have a very clear idea of what death was, but they knew it was serious. Consequently, when they had sinned through disobedience and then later had heard God walking toward them in the garden, they tried to hide.

They could not hide from God. No one can. So we are told that God called them out of hiding and began to deal with their transgression. What should we expect to happen as a result of this confrontation? Here is God who has told our first parents that in the day they sinned they would die. Here also are Adam and Eve who have sinned. In this situation we should expect the immediate execution of the sentence. They had sinned. So if God had put them to death in that moment, both physically and spiritually, banishing them from his presence forever, it would have been just.

But that is not what we find. Instead, we have God first rebuking the sin and then, wonder of wonders, performing a sacrifice as a result of which Adam and Eve were clothed with the skins of those animals. This was the first death that anyone had ever witnessed. It was enacted by God. As Adam and Eve looked on they must have been horrified. "So this is death," they must have said. "How horrible!" Yet even as they recoiled from the sacrifice, they must have marveled as well, for what God was showing was that although they themselves deserved to die it was possible for another, in this case two animals, to die in their place. The animals paid the price of their sin. Moreover, they were now clothed in the skins of the animals as a reminder of that fact.

This is the meaning of sacrifice: substitution. It is the death of one on behalf of another. And yet we must say, as the Bible teaches, that the death of animals could never take away the penalty of sin (Heb. 10:4). These were a symbol of how sin was to be taken away, but they were only a symbol. The real and effective sacrifice was performed by Jesus Christ. We sometimes read in theological literature that the ideas of sacrifice and substitution are alien to our culture and therefore that we cannot use these terms to speak of the meaning of Christ's death anymore, at least if we want to be understood.[1] But we must not think that it was any easier for those who lived in earlier stages of the world's history to understand them. These concepts have always been difficult; that is why God took so much time and such elaborate means to teach them.

Stilling God's Wrath

A second word for understanding the meaning of Christ's death is propitiation (Rom. 3:25). Propitiation also relates to the world of sacrifices. But unlike substitution, which refers primarily to what Jesus did in reference to us (he died in our place), propitiation describes that death in terms of its bearing upon God. The background for this term is the wrath of God which is directed against all sin. Propitiation refers to the work of the Lord Jesus Christ in which the justified wrath of God against the sinner was stilled or turned aside and the love of God was enabled to go out to save him.

An Old Testament illustration is helpful. It is the ark of the covenant and the sacrifice which involved it. The ark of the covenant was one of the pieces of furniture for Israel's wilderness tabernacle. It was a chest about a yard long, covered with gold and closed by a solid gold covering known as the mercy seat. The mercy seat had two figures of cherubim standing on either end looking inward. The cherubim had wings which stretched out over the ends of the ark and then came together over the top. The stone tables of the law of Moses were kept within this ark, and the ark itself was kept within the Holy of Holies, the most sacred part of the tabernacle.

The most significant thing about the ark of the covenant is that it was thought of symbolically as being the earthly dwelling place of God. God was thought to dwell in the space between the outstretched wings of the cherubim above the mercy seat. And of course, this is why no one but the high priest was ever to enter the Holy of Holies, and even he was to enter only once a year on the Day of Atonement. God was holy, and sinful men and women who came into his presence would be consumed.

The picture of that ark is a terrible picture, as it was meant to be. There we see God dwelling between the outstretched wings of the cherubim. There we see the law, which we have broken. As God looks down upon the affairs of men this is what he sees—the broken law. So the picture tells us that God in his holiness must judge sin and that sinners are subject to his judicial wrath.

But that is not all, for now the Day of Atonement comes, and on that day the high priest takes the blood of a sacrifice and, bearing it carefully according to all the regulations for this ceremony (for violation of these regulations entailed death), enters the Holy of Holies where it is now sprinkled upon the mercy seat between the presence of God and the law. What is symbolized now? Gloriously, the picture is now no longer of wrath directed against the violators of God's law but rather a picture of mercy in which the wrath of God against sin is satisfied and the sinner is spared. Now when God looks down from between the wings of the cherubim he sees, not the law we have broken, but the blood of the sacrifice. An innocent has died. He has borne our penalty. Thus, we can live.

In discussing sacrifice, I pointed out that the blood of animals could not actually take away sin but that these pointed forward pedagogically to the work of Christ on Calvary. That also applies here. The blood of the sacrifice sprinkled upon the mercy seat by the high priest did not remove sin, but it pointed forward to the One whose death would remove it: Jesus Christ.

When he died God's wrath against sin was literally propitiated, which God himself demonstrated by tearing the veil of the temple, separating the Holy Place from the Holy of Holies, in two from top to bottom. Thus did God show that the way into his presence was now open for all who should believe in Jesus.

An interesting sidelight on this meaning of God's death is the speed with which blood sacrifices disappeared in the ancient world once the gospel of Christ was proclaimed. At the time of Christ's death sacrifices were performed everywhere—in the Roman and barbarian worlds as well as within Judaism. But, as Adolf Harnack once pointed out in a striking passage, "Wherever the Christian message . . . penetrated, the sacrificial altars were deserted and dealers in sacrificial beasts found no more purchasers. . . . The death of Christ put an end to all blood-sacrifices." Why did this happen? Harnack explains, "His death [Christ's] had the value of an expiatory sacrifice, for otherwise it would not have had strength to penetrate into that inner world in which the blood-sacrifices originated."[2] Sacrifices ceased because the death of Christ alone met the need they were supposed to satisfy.

Reconciliation

A third word used for describing the effects of Christ's death is reconciliation. Second Corinthians 5:18–19 provides us with a key passage: "All this if from God, who reconciled us to himself through Christ and gave us the ministry of reconciliation: that God was reconciling the world to himself in Christ, not counting men's sins against them. And he has committed to us the message of reconciliation."

Reconciliation means "to make one," so the background for this term is the broken relationship between ourselves and God because of sin. We have already seen one example of this in Genesis, for when Adam and Eve sinned and God came to them in the Garden, our first parents hid from God. This had not been the case before their disobedience. Before there had been openness. They had talked with God joyously. Now the relationship that they had enjoyed was broken, and they showed their deep psychological awareness of this by hiding. In a sense men and women have been hiding ever since. We hide through a self-imposed ignorance of spiritual things, through our supposed sophistication or culture, or even (strange as it may seem) through religion—for many religious experiences are attempts to get away from God rather than attempts to find him.

But God comes to us; that is the glory of the gospel. Moreover, when he comes he does what is necessary to heal the broken relationship and bridge the gap. In Eden it was the inauguration of sacrifices. On Calvary it was the ultimate bridge to which the earlier sacrifices pointed. Paul writes, "For there is one God and one mediator between God and men, the man Christ Jesus" (1 Tim. 2:5). He means that it is on the basis of Christ's death that the reconciliation takes place.

Bought with a Price

The final word of those most significant for describing the death of Christ is "redemption." "Redemption" is derived from two Latin words: *re,* meaning "again," and *emere,* meaning "to buy." So redemption means "buying again" or "buying back," as in redeeming something that has been pawned or mortgaged. We use the word of material things. The Bible uses the word to signify that we are God's, but have nevertheless fallen into bondage as a result of our sin and now must be purchased out of that bondage by Christ's sacrifice.

Our bondage is to sin's penalty and power. Christ's death frees us from both. On this subject John Murray writes, "Just as sacrifice is directed to the need created by our guilt, propitiation to the need that arises from the wrath of God, and reconciliation to the need arising from our alienation from God, so redemption is directed to the bondage to which our sin has consigned us. This bondage is, of course, multiform. Consequently redemption as purchase or ransom receives a wide variety of reference and application. Redemption applies to every respect in which we are bound, and it releases us unto a liberty that is nothing less than the liberty of the glory of the children of God."[3] Paul speaks of that redemption in Romans: "justified freely by his grace through the redemption that came by Christ Jesus" (Rom. 3:24). Peter speaks of it in even more explicit terms: "For you know that it was not with perishable things such as silver or gold that you were redeemed from the empty way of life handed down to you from your forefathers, but with the precious blood of Christ, a lamb without blemish or defect" (1 Peter 1:18–19).

"It is finished," Christ's declaration from the cross, is particularly appropriate for understanding his death as redemption; for one of the meanings of the Greek word *tetelestai,* which underlies it, is "Paid in full!" The word was used in this way in secular business transactions.

Here we come back to the point with which we began. What makes the death of Christ so unique and indeed marks it out as the focal point of history is that it accomplished precisely what needed to be accomplished in regard to our salvation. We deserved to die for sin; Christ died for us. We were under the just wrath of God by reason of our transgressions; Christ bore that wrath in our place. We were alienated from God; Christ reconciled us to him. We were sold under sin; Christ bought our freedom by paying sin's price. From one perspective all this is spiritual. It has to do both with moral matters and with spiritual relationships. But from another point of view, this is as concrete and historical as the birth of Julius Caesar or the death of Socrates.

249

Why Did Jesus Die?

Necessity of Atonement

John 19:30

When he had received the drink, Jesus said, "It is finished." With that, he bowed his head and gave up his spirit.

Those who know anything at all about Christianity know that Jesus died to save us from sin, and they know that the source of the decision to save us from sin was God's love. "For God so loved the world that he gave his one and only Son, that whoever believes in him should not perish but have eternal life" (John 3:16). But why was it necessary for the love of God to achieve its end in this way? Why Jesus? And why the cross? This was the question raised by Anselm of Canterbury in his famous essay *Cur Deus Homo?* ("Why God Became Man"), in which he asked, "For what reason or necessity did God become man and, as we believe and confess, by his death restore life to the world, when he could have done this through another person (angelic or human), or even by a sheer act of will?"[1]

Was the cross necessary, or could God have saved the human race through another person or even by a sheer act of will? One writer puts it like this: "If we say that he could not, do we not impugn his power? If we say that he could

1531

but would not, do we not impugn his wisdom? Such questions are not scholastic subtleties or vain curiosities. To evade them is to miss something that is central in the interpretation of the redeeming work of Christ and to miss the vision of some of its essential glory. Why did God become man? Why, having become man, did he die? Why, having died, did he die the accursed death of the cross?"[2]

Two Necessities

In the history of Christian doctrine there have traditionally been two ways in which the necessity of the death of Jesus has been spoken of. One is what we might call *circumstantial* necessity. The other is *absolute* necessity. Let me explain.

The view that we call circumstantial necessity maintains that God, being free and infinite, always has an infinite number of possibilities open to him. Consequently, although he chose to save men and women by the death of Christ, he did not need to do so and could actually have saved them in an infinite number of other ways. If we ask at that point how we can then speak of a "necessity" in the atonement at all, the answer is that because of the circumstances under which God operated, this was the way (chosen out of many ways) that the greatest number of advantages would occur, including the greatest possible glory being given to God. God could have saved us without Christ's having died. But he could not have done so and yet have showed the greatest measure of wisdom and love in the circumstances. When we read that "without the shedding of blood there is no forgiveness" of sins (Heb. 9:22), that is indeed true. But it is true only because God has chosen to do things that way. He could have saved us without blood shedding.

The other way to talk about the necessity of Jesus' death is to see it as an absolute necessity. This means literally that, having elected to save some of Adam's fallen race, God had no other means at his disposal than the sacrifice of his beloved Son. This does not mean that God had to send Jesus. He could have elected not to save anyone. But having elected to save them, he was under the necessity of accomplishing this by the death of his Son, a necessity arising out of the perfections of his own nature.

At first glance it might be thought presumptuous for us to speak thus of something being absolutely necessary for God. "After all," someone might object, "who are we to tell God what he can or must do?" But this is not the way in which this statement is made. Obviously we cannot tell God to be or do anything. Yet he has revealed something of his nature in Scripture, and it is not impudent or improper to inquire on the basis of that revelation whether God can or cannot do a thing, particularly when it is as central to the Christian faith as the atonement. For example, is it possible for God to lie or speak falsehood? If we answer no, as we should, we are not limiting God by telling what he can or cannot do. We are simply acknowledging that deceit is impossible for one who is characterized by utter truth, as God declares himself to be. Far from dishonoring him in this, we actually honor him. Moreover, we are led to a valuable conclusion; for, on the basis of God's inability to lie, we perceive that he can always be trusted.

It is not improper or even impractical to conclude that God was under an absolute necessity in the matter of Christ's death. He may not have been. But the answer to whether he was or not is to be determined solely by the teaching of the Scripture and not by any prior conclusions as to what is required by our understanding of God's freedom.

The Divine Necessities

When we turn to the Bible we find a number of necessities pertaining to God which bear upon our subject. They are like the necessity for God to speak truth, being Truth, but they relate primarily to the matter of salvation.

The first of these necessities is the *hatred of God for sin,* which we may express by saying that God must hate sin if he is to be as he declares himself to be in Scripture. The background for this necessity is the holiness of God. In Scripture God is more often called holy than anything else. This is the epithet most often affixed to his name, for instance. We do not often read of his "loving name," "mighty name," or "eternal name." But we are often reminded of his "holy name." Moreover, this is the attribute of God which is invariably mentioned in any vision men have of him. Isaiah, in his great vision of the Lord "high and lifted up," stressed the holiness of God more than any other attribute. "Holy, holy, holy is the Lord Almighty," cry the seraphim. Isaiah's immediate reaction was to bemoan his own sinful condition: "Woe is me! I am ruined! For I am a man of unclean lips, and I dwell among a people of unclean lips, and my eyes have seen the King, the Lord Almighty" (Isa. 6:5; cf. vv. 1–6).

The holiness of God lies at the core of his being, then, and the dismay of Isaiah was the recognition that in his holiness God cannot be indifferent to anything which opposes it. Holiness involves the elements of majesty and will. When we ask, "What is that will primarily set on?" the answer is: God's majesty. Thus, God's will is inevitably directed against anything which would attempt to diminish that majesty or flaunt it. That is what sin tries to do. So God is against sin; he is wrath toward it.

Many people today do not like the idea of wrath. But like it or not, Scripture teaches that it is a necessary aspect of God's nature in relation to sin. The Old Testament alone has nearly six hundred important passages concerning God's wrath. His wrath is directed against injustice, corruption, and offenses against his own glory and majesty. The New Testament has equally important passages. Romans 1, for example, speaks of God's wrath revealed "against all the godlessness and wickedness of men who suppress the truth by their wickedness" (v. 18). Other passages speak boldly of "the wrath to come" (1 Thess. 1:10; 2:16; cf. 5:9; Rom. 2:5). The teaching of these passages is that God will not and cannot look with indifference upon the unrighteous.

A second necessity of the divine nature relating to the matter of salvation is the obligation of God to do right. This obligation is based upon God's role as ruler and judge of creation. "Will not the Judge of all the earth do right?" asked Abraham rhetorically on the occasion of God's revelation to him of the pending judgment of Sodom (Gen. 18:25). The answer was obvious: the Sovereign must do right. In fact, Abraham used this necessity to plead for the salvation of Sodom. God had told Abraham that he would destroy Sodom, and Abraham remonstrated, "Will you destroy the righteous with the wicked? Suppose there are fifty righteous within the city: will you also destroy and not spare the place for the fifty righteous that are in it? Far be it from you to do this, to slay the righteous with the wicked. Will not the Judge of all the earth do right?"

Here are two divine necessities pertaining to salvation: first, that God must hate sin, and second, that the Judge of the earth must do right. What is right where sin is concerned? The answer is judgment, as the destruction of Sodom indicates. True, we do not see the fullness of that judgment now, for God has largely withheld his judgment. Yet it must come. It must come later if not sooner; and when it comes, it must result in the eternal destruction of the sinner.

The Divine Solution

We know from the biblical record that God elected not to destroy every sinner. Out of his great love he decided to elect a great company to salvation. But the question arises: How can he do this without violating these two necessities of his very nature? How can he save those who actually deserve his just judgment? There is only one way: another must suffer the judgment in place of those who stand condemned. We hear that answer, and we are momentarily relieved. But then we ask, "Who?" and despair settles on us once again. Who is equal to such a task? Who is willing to do it? The answer is: God's own Son; the only One both able and willing to become man and to die for sinners.

Anselm, whom we mentioned earlier, put it like this: First, he said, salvation had to be achieved by God, for no one else could achieve it. Certainly men and women could not achieve it, for we are the ones who have gotten ourselves into trouble in the first place. We have done so by our rebellion against God's just law and decrees. Moreover, we have suffered from the effects of sin to such a degree that even our will is bound, and therefore we cannot even choose to please God, let alone actually please him. Our only hope is God, who alone has both the will and power to save. Second, said Anselm, apparently contradicting this first point, salvation must also be achieved by man, for man is the one who has wronged God and must therefore make the wrong right. Given this situation, salvation can be achieved only by one who is both God and man, that is, Jesus.

Anselm put the argument in these words: "It would not have been right for the restoration of human nature to be left undone, and . . . it could not have been done unless man paid what was owing to God for sin. But the debt was so great that, while man alone owed it, only God could pay it, so that the same person must be both man and God. Thus it was necessary for God to take manhood into the unity of his person, so that he who in his own nature ought to pay and could not should be in a person who could. . . . The life of this man was so sublime, so precious, that it can suffice to pay what is owing for the sins of the whole world, and infinitely more."[3]

Only thus was it possible for God to be both "just and the one who justifies those who have faith in Jesus" (Rom. 3:26). This is the ultimate necessity indicated in those well-known verses in John's Gospel. "Just as Moses lifted up the snake in the desert, so the Son of Man must be lifted up, that everyone who believes in him may have eternal life. For God so loved the world that he gave his one and only Son, that whoever believes in him shall not perish but have eternal life. For God did not send his Son into the world to condemn the world, but to save the world through him" (3:14–17). These verses say that apart from the death of Christ and faith in him, the race is lost. Given the desire of God to save us, there was just no other option.

Curse of the Cross

Yet there is still one matter. At the start of this chapter we asked, "Why was it necessary for the love of God to achieve its end in this way? Why Jesus? And why the cross?" Thus far we have answered the first half of that question; we have seen why it was necessary for the price of our salvation to be paid by Jesus. But we still have not answered why that sacrifice had to be made on Calvary. Why this death? Why this particularly horrible form of suffering?

The answer to that question is given in the Book of Galatians, in which Paul says, "Christ redeemed us from the curse of the law by becoming a curse for us; for it is written: 'Cursed is everyone who is hung on a tree'" (Gal. 3:13). What does this mean? Well, it is the Bible's answer to an objection to God's way of salvation that we might still make even after we have understood the nature and necessity of the atonement. We might understand that Jesus was the innocent Son of God and that he was therefore the only One who could take our place on Calvary, the just for the unjust. We might understand that God judged him in our place. "But that is still not right," we might argue. "Even if Jesus died willingly, it was still not right for God to punish one who was innocent of all wrongdoing." At this point Paul's answer comes in, for he points out that in the Old Testament there is a verse (Deut. 21:23) that pronounces a curse on anyone hanged on a tree as a means of execution. This may not have meant much to those who lived in that day, but it was part of the law of Israel. Thus, when the Lord Jesus Christ was taken and hanged on a tree, he thereby became a technical violator of the whole law (though through no fault of his own) and could be justly punished. In this way God remained just in his execution of Christ, and Christ remained innocent.

God's Love Commended

The conclusion to this study is that the achievement of our salvation at such cost flows from the love of God and that the love of God is thereby commended to us so that we might believe on Jesus. To save us it was necessary to pay this cost. Yet God did not hesitate to provide the sacrifice of his Son, so great was his love for us. Can we despise that love? Can we ignore it? The Bible says, "But God demonstrates his own love for us in this: While we were still sinners, Christ died for us" (Rom. 5:8).

This, of course, is the bottom line of the entire discussion, and it is this that makes it meaningful. Our discussion of the necessity of the atonement has involved us in some careful theological distinctions, and some of this is admittedly difficult for some people, for not all are theologians. Yet the bottom line is not difficult at all. Let me put it like this. The week before I first preached this material in my regular exposition of John on Sunday mornings at Tenth Presbyterian Church, I was discussing these themes at the dinner table to see how the people who were there would react to them. They did very well. But at the end a ten-year-old friend of one of my daughters asked, "What is the main point of your sermon?" It was a question her parents had been teaching her to ask so she could follow the messages better, and (I think) she wanted to get a head start. I replied that the answer was a simple one; for although the theology is difficult, the point itself is not. It is simply this:

> There was no other good enough
>   To pay the price of sin;
> He only could unlock the gate
>   Of heav'n and let us in.
> O dearly, dearly has He loved!
>   And we must love Him too,
> And trust in His redeeming blood,
>   And try His works to do.

Christ has loved us so much that he did not hold back from doing what needed to be done. Because of this we, on our part, should serve him without reservation.

250

"It Is Finished"

Perfection of Atonement

John 19:30

When he had received the drink, Jesus said, "It is finished." With that, he bowed his head and gave up his spirit.

One of the goals of Greek oratory, to which the Greek language generally lends itself, is to say much in few words—"to give a sea of matter in a drop of language." That goal is reached in the sixth of Christ's sayings from the cross: "It is finished!" In English this is only three words, in Greek just one. Yet this word sums up the greatest work that has ever been done. Spurgeon said, "It would need all the other words that ever were spoken, or ever can be spoken, to explain this one word. It is altogether immeasurable. It is high; I cannot attain to it. It is deep; I cannot fathom it."[1]

We have been trying to study it, however, and to that end we have looked at, first, the nature and, second, the necessity of the atonement. In this chapter we deal with its perfection, the aspect of Christ's death that is perhaps more directly suggested by this word than any other.

Pink writes, "This was not the despairing cry of a helpless martyr; it was not an expression of satisfaction that the termination of his sufferings was now reached; it was not the last gasp of a worn-out life. No, rather was it the declaration on the part of the Divine Redeemer that all for which he came from heaven to earth to do, was now done; that all that was needed to reveal the full character of God had now been accomplished; that all that was required by the law before sinners could be saved had now been performed; that the full price of our redemption was now paid."[2] To be sure, as Jesus spoke these words he was not yet dead. But his death was only moments away, and in any case he here speaks anticipatively of the work now done.

What did this dying utterance of the Lord mean? What was finished? How does this relate to us and our salvation?

Christ's Work Done

There are a number of things we can point to as having been finished in the moment of Christ's death. The first and most obvious one is *Christ's sufferings.* These had not taken him by surprise. Long before this the Lord had said, "I have a baptism to undergo, and how distressed I am until it is completed!" (Luke 12:50). Centuries before, Isaiah had written of him, "He is despised and rejected by men, a man of sorrows and acquainted with grief" (Isa. 53:3). Suffering marked Christ's life. He had thirsted and hungered. He had ministered for three years without even a place to lay his head. He was scorned, accused, beaten, and now subjected to the horror and indignities of the cross.

No one ever suffered as Jesus did. Yet now it is finished. No snarling enemies will spit in his face again. No soldiers will ever scourge him again. No priests will mock him. It is finished; he sits on heaven's throne, waiting until all his enemies are made his footstool. Spurgeon wrote: "Now Judas, come and betray him with a kiss! What, man, dare you not do it? Come, Pilate, and wash your hands in pretended innocency, and say now that you are guiltless of his blood! Come, ye scribes and Pharisees, and accuse him; and oh, ye Jewish mob and Gentile rabble, newly-risen from the grave, shout now, 'Away with him! Crucify him!' But see! they flee from him; they cry to the mountains and rocks, 'Fall on us, and hide us from the face of him that sitteth on the throne!' Yet that is the face that was more marred than any man's, the face of him whom they once despised and rejected."[3]

> The head that once was crowned with thorns
>   Is crowned with glory now;
> A royal diadem adorns
>   The mighty Victor's brow.
> The highest place that heav'n affords
>   Is his, is his by right,
> The King of kings, and Lord of lords,
>   And heav'n's eternal Light.

How glad we must be that none can despise him, that the sufferings of which the Savior's life were once full are finished.

The second thing we can point to as finished in the moment of our Lord's death was *his work*, that which he had been sent into the world to do. This work centered in the atonement, which we will come to in a moment, but it was more than this. It was also his entire life, undergirded by his utter obedience to the Father and filled with teachings and good works. This work was before him constantly. We are told by the author of Hebrews that on the occasion of his coming into the world he said, "Sacrifice and offering you did not desire, but a body you prepared for me; with burnt offerings and sin offerings you were not pleased. Then I said, 'Here I am—it is written about me in the scroll—I have come to do your will, O God'" (Heb. 10:5–7). In John 4:34 we read, "My food is to do the will of him who sent me and to finish his work." He spoke of the works that God had given him to do (John 5:36) and of the words that God had given him to speak (John 8:26; 14:24). He said, "The words I say to you are not just my own. Rather, it is the Father, living in me, who is doing his work" (John 14:10). Then, in his great high priestly prayer recorded in John 17, he said, "I have brought you glory on earth by completing the work you gave me to do" (v. 4).

Throughout his lifetime Jesus had this work in mind, and he devoted himself to doing it. Now it is done, and he points with satisfaction: "It is finished!" None of us can say that fully of our work, but Jesus said it of his. His work was done perfectly.

The third area to which these words apply is *the prophecies of his first coming*. We cannot say that all the prophecies concerning the Lord are finished, for some pertain to work he is yet to do—at his second coming. But those that refer to his Gospel ministry are finished. In fact, it is in direct connection with one such prophecy that these words were spoken. Psalm 69:21 speaks of vinegar being given to the dying Messiah in his thirst. So Jesus, noticing that this had not been fulfilled, said, "I thirst," and thus provoked its fulfillment as soldiers rushed to offer him a vinegar-wine solution. Immediately afterward we read, "When he had received the drink, Jesus said, 'It is finished'" (John 19:30).

It had been prophesied that the Messiah was to be born of a woman without benefit of a human father (Isa. 7:14; Gal. 4:4). This was completed. It had been foretold that he was to be the seed of Abraham and of the line of David (Gen. 22:18; 2 Sam. 7:12–13), that he should be born in Bethlehem (Micah 5:2), and he was so born. Old Testament writers had spoken of his flight into Egypt and a subsequent return to his own land (Hosea 11:1; cf. Isa. 49:3, 6). It so happened. Christ's appearance was to be preceded by that of one like Elijah (Mal. 3:1). John the Baptist filled this role. Christ's miracles were foretold—that "the eyes of the blind" should be opened, "the ears of the deaf" unstopped, "the lame man leap as an hart, and the tongue of the dumb sing" (Isa. 35:5–6). Jesus performed all these miracles. His triumphal entry into Jerusalem had been foretold (Zech. 9:9). He was to be hated (Ps. 69:4) and rejected by his own people (Isa. 8:14). A friend would betray him (Ps. 41:9). He was to be numbered with the transgressors (Isa.

53:12), pierced through hands and feet (Ps. 22:16). Soldiers were to divide his garments and cast lots for his outer cloak (Ps. 22:18). All this had been completed. There was nothing of all that had been written of him that was left undone.

Moreover, this is not just a conclusion based on our own imperfect knowledge of the Old Testament texts. This is the teaching of Scripture itself. Three times in Scripture the very word that is used in John 19:30, translated "it is finished" (*teleō*), is used of this fulfillment. Luke 18:31—"Jesus took the Twelve aside and told them, 'We are going up to Jerusalem, and everything that is written by the prophets about the Son of Man will be *fulfilled*.'" Luke 22:37—"I tell you that this must be *fulfilled* in me." Acts 13:29—"When they had *carried out* all that was written about him, they took him down from the tree and laid him in a tomb. But God raised him from the dead."

Certainly, nothing that was to be fulfilled in the life and ministry of the Messiah was left lacking in Jesus.

A Perfect Atonement

Having said all this, we must nevertheless add that the primary reference of these words is to *the atonement*. This was the acme of his sufferings, the chief of his works, and the primary focus of the prophecies. Moreover, this has major doctrinal significance; for if the work of the atonement is finished, then salvation is secured for us by God and there is nothing that we can add or hope to add to it. Indeed, we dare not attempt to add anything if we would be saved.

This is the point of the atonement that has always figured prominently in Protestant presentations of the meaning of the death of Christ, as over against Roman Catholic theology. The Roman church (and many unsound protestant churches too, for that matter) maintains that the death of Christ does not relieve the believer in Christ of making satisfaction for sins he has committed. More precisely, it distinguishes between sins committed before and after baptism, and between temporal and eternal punishment for those sins. So far as sins committed before baptism are concerned, both the temporal and eternal punishment are blotted out through the application of the benefits of Christ's death to the individual through the baptismal rite. So far as sins committed after baptism are concerned, the eternal punishments are blotted out. But the temporal punishments require the making of satisfaction by the individual himself either in this life (through a faithful use of the sacraments and by a meritorious life) or else in purgatory. While this system of salvation allows the greater part of the work to be God's and even acknowledges that the faithfulness and merit of the believer are attained only through the prevenient grace of God, it nevertheless requires the individual to contribute to his own salvation in some measure. So it is not possible to say that the work of Christ is finished. More is needed. This outlook is evident in the Mass, in which the sacrifice of Christ is reenacted constantly.

Thus, Protestant thought has always contended rightly that "the satisfaction of Christ is the only satisfaction for sin and is so perfect and final that it leaves no penal liability for any sin of the believer."[4] True, the believer often experiences chastisement for sins done in this life (though never in full measure to what he has deserved). But this is not satisfaction. It is discipline only; it is given to help us grow. Even in times of severe chastisement it is still true that "there is now no condemnation for those who are in Christ Jesus" (Rom. 8:1).

This is the burden of the Book of Hebrews, to give just one other biblical example. For, having demonstrated the uniqueness of Christ's person, office, and mission, the author of that book states, "But when this priest had offered for all time one sacrifice for sins, he sat down at the right hand of God. Since that time he waits for his enemies to be made his footstool, because by one sacrifice he has made perfect forever those who are being made holy" (Heb. 10:12–14). What can be clearer than that? What can be greater? "From whatever angle we look upon his sacrifice we find its uniqueness to be as inviolable as the uniqueness of his person, of his mission, and of his office. Who is God-man but he alone? Who is great high priest to offer such sacrifice but he alone? Who shed such vicarious blood but he alone? Who entered in once for all into the holy place, having obtained eternal redemption, but he alone?"[5] In light of those qualities and achievement it is arrogant to think that we can add anything.

> Jesus paid it all,
> All to him I owe;
> Sin had left a crimson stain;
> He washed it white as snow.

"But then, what is left for us to do?" someone asks. Nothing but to believe in God's Word and trust Jesus! Jesus himself said it. When some of the Galileans asked him on the occasion of his multiplication of the loaves and fish, "What must we do to do works of God?" Jesus replied, "The work of God is this: to believe in the one he has sent" (John 6:28–29).

Pink tells a story that may be helpful in this regard. A Christian farmer, deeply concerned over an unsaved neighbor, who was a carpenter, was trying to explain the gospel, especially the sufficiency of the finished work of Christ. But the carpenter persisted in believing that he had to do something himself. One day the farmer asked his friend to make a gate for him, and when it was finished he came for it and carried it away in his wagon. He hung it on a fence in his field and then arranged for the carpenter to stop by and see that it was hung properly. The carpenter came. But when he arrived he was surprised to see the farmer standing by with a sharp axe in his hand. "What is that for?" he asked.

"I'm going to add a few strokes to your work," was the answer.

"But there's no need to do that," the carpenter protested. "The gate is perfect as it is. I did everything that was necessary." The farmer took his axe and began to strike the gate anyway, keeping at it until in a short while it was ruined. "Look what you've done," cried the carpenter. "You've ruined my work!"

"Yes," said his friend. "And that is exactly what you are trying to do. You are trying to ruin the work of Christ by your own miserable additions to it." God used this lesson to show the carpenter his mistake, and he was led to cast himself upon what Christ had done for him.[6]

What Work for Jesus?

Yet I must not leave the impression that, having believed on Christ, there is then nothing for the Christian to do or that his conduct after he has become a believer in Christ does not matter. Let us say clearly that nothing we have done or ever will do can enter into the satisfaction that Christ made on the cross. His work is perfect; the atonement is done. But what do we say in that case? Do we say, "Well, if Christ has finished it, I will fold my hands and do nothing"? Not at all! Rather do we say, "If Jesus has finished such a great work for me, tell me quickly what work I can do for him."

Do we need a biblical example? We find one in Saul of Tarsus. When he was struck down on the road to Damascus, his first question concerned the identity of the One who was revealing himself to him. He asked, "Who are you, Lord?" But as soon as he had learned the answer—"I am Jesus, whom you persecute"—and had believed on the One who spoke, Paul's next question was: "Lord, what do you want me to do?" (Acts 9:5–6). Christ had a work for him to do. He was to be an apostle to bear the name of Christ "before the Gentiles, and kings, and the children of Israel" (v. 15).

This will not necessarily be your task. You are not an apostle, nor am I. But we each have a work to do. If we have been put in this world by Jesus and have not yet been taken home to be with him, we may be certain that we have not yet finished that work. So get on with it. Did he finish his work? Then you and I must finish our work too. Of course, there are discouragements. Of course, there is suffering and weakness and disappointment. But we must not give in to these. We must keep on until that moment when we, upon our deathbed, can say as did Paul, "I have fought the good fight, I have finished the race, I have kept the faith. Now there is in store for me the crown of righteousness, which the Lord, the righteous Judge, will award to me on that day—and not only to me, but also to all who have longed for his appearing" (2 Tim. 4:7–8).

I leave you this challenge from the pen of Spurgeon: "As long as there is breath in our bodies, let us serve Christ; as long as we can think, as long as we can speak, as long as we can work, let us serve him, let us serve him with our last gasp; and, if it be possible, let us try to set some work going that will glorify him when we are dead and gone."[7]

251

For Whom Did Christ Die?

Extent of Atonement

John 19:30

When he had received the drink, Jesus said, "It is finished." With that, he bowed his head and gave up his spirit.

For whom did Christ die? Did he die for all human beings, and thus all will be saved (the view of universalism)? Did he die for all, but, for whatever reason, not all will be saved (the view of Arminianism)? Or did he die only for certain individuals, all of whom will be saved (the view of Calvinism)? Each of these views involves problems, so that many people would rather not deal with the question. But we cannot avoid it, at least in this series of studies. It is an area of the atonement with which theology has always dealt. Besides, it is suggested by our text and by the gospel.

Our text contains Christ's sixth cry from the cross, "It is finished." But what was finished? In our last study we answered that it was, above all, the atonement. But what was the atonement? Was it the actual payment of the price for the sins of some or of all people, as the result of which they are saved? Or was it potential atonement only, that is, something that makes it possible for people to be saved but that in itself saves no one?

The Gospel of John gives us the most difficult answer, for it (perhaps more than any other Gospel) presents that view of Christ's work generally known as "limited atonement." We think of John 10, in which Jesus says, "I am the good shepherd. The good shepherd gives his life *for the sheep*" (v. 11). A few verses later he explicitly excludes certain of his hearers from that number— "You are not my sheep" (v. 26). Similarly, in John 17 the Lord explicitly prays for those *"you have given me,"* a phrase repeated six times with only slight variations. This phrase does not include everyone because those who have been given to Christ are carefully distinguished from "the world" (vv. 6, 9, 11–18).

It would be easier to skip this subject; but as in the matter of the necessity of the atonement, we would do so to our own hurt. Actually the subject is important and profitable; for what is at stake is nothing other than the nature of the atonement itself, as we will see when we study it.

"The World" and "All Men"

But first we must deal with a primary matter. This is the view that the whole discussion is wrongheaded simply because, so it is said, the Bible gives a clear answer to the question. Is it not true, one might ask, that the Bible often uses universal terms when speaking of Jesus' death? Take Isaiah 53:6. It says, "We all, like sheep, have gone astray, each of us has turned to his own way; and the LORD has laid on him the iniquity of *us all*." Does this not say that all have sinned and that it is for these, all of them, that Christ died? Again, there is Hebrews 2:9, "But we see Jesus, who was made a little lower than the angels, now crowned with glory and honor because he suffered death, so that by the grace of God he might taste death *for everyone*." Or perhaps 1 John 2:2, which seems even more unmistakable. "He is the atoning sacrifice for our sins, and not only for ours but also for the sins of *the whole world*." Do these verses not teach unambiguously that Jesus died for everyone?

Not necessarily. The reason this is not necessarily the case is that the Bible habitually uses these terms in less than an inclusivistic sense. For instance, the word "world" is sometimes used of the whole fabric of heaven and earth (Job 34:13). Sometimes it refers only to the earth (Ps. 24:1; 98:7), or only to the heavens (Ps. 90:2). There are texts in which it does mean every single human being (Rom. 3:6, 19). But again, it sometimes refers only to one large group (Matt. 18:7; John 4:42; 1 Cor. 4:9; Rev. 13:3). This last is probably the dominant meaning, just as it is in our use of the same word in English. To give an example, when the Pharisees say among themselves, "Look how the world has gone after him" (John 12:19), meaning Christ, they do not mean every person on earth or even every person in Israel. They only mean a very large group of the citizens of Jerusalem. If we insist that "world" always means "every human being," we are going to have trouble explaining how under Caesar Augustus "all the world" went to be taxed. Did everyone go—barbarians, prisoners, slaves, or others outside the Roman sphere of influence?

The point we are making is that the use of words like "all men," "the whole world," and "us all" does not in itself settle the matter. Rather, the meaning of each phrase must be determined from the context. Thus, in the case of Isaiah 53:6, it can be argued very cogently that the passage is written of God's people, all of whom certainly have gone astray (which is also true of those who are not God's people) and have been redeemed (which is not true of those who are not God's people). Similarly, in Hebrews 2:9, the reference is to the "many sons" who shall be brought to glory, as specified in the very next verse. Believers in particular redemption have usually explained 1 John 2:2 in terms of John's emphasis in writing. He is trying to show that the propitiation Christ made was not for Jews only, which might be expected, but for Gentiles as well.

The point here is not whether this particular interpretation of these verses is the correct one, though I believe it is. The point is only that they *may* be so interpreted. Consequently, the matter of limited versus unlimited atonement must be resolved on other grounds.

The Central Question

The central question in this entire discussion is not how many verses may be lined up on one side or the other or even whether or not Christ's death has sufficient value to atone for the sins of the world. The answer to the last question is obvious: Christ's death has sufficient value to atone not only for a million worlds such as ours but more besides. The question is only: Did Christ's death actually atone for the sins of anyone? Did it actually propitiate the wrath of God toward any specific group of individuals? Did it actually reconcile any single person to God? Did it redeem anyone? If it did, whom? When the question is asked in this way we can see that there are only three possible answers:

1. Christ's death was not an actual atonement but rather that which makes atonement possible. It becomes actual when the sinner repents of sin and believes on Jesus.
2. It was an actual atonement for the sins of God's elect, with the result that these are saved.
3. It was an actual atonement for the sins of all human beings, so that all are saved.

We can dismiss the third possibility immediately, for the Bible clearly teaches that not all human beings are saved and conversely that some specifically are lost. Pharaoh is an example. So is Judas. So is the rich man in Christ's parable of the rich man and Lazarus. In Revelation we have descriptions of God's final judgment on such persons. With this possibility eliminated, the choice is between numbers one and two—an actual atonement for the specific sins of the elect and an indefinite atonement for no sins in particular. What, then, is the way in which the Bible speaks of Christ's sacrifice?

The answer has already been given in our earlier studies. We talked of sacrifice and substitution, and the point was that Christ actually became a sacrifice and substitute on the basis of which those who were appointed to salvation were saved. We talked of propitiation, reconciliation, and redemption. Each of these points to a specific aspect of that which Christ accomplished. Christ did not come to make propitiation possible; he came to propitiate God's wrath against sin. He did not come to make reconciliation possible; he came to make reconciliation. He did not come to make redemption possible; his shed blood was the price of redemption.

John Murray poses the issue like this: "The very nature of Christ's mission and accomplishment is involved in this question. Did Christ come to make the salvation of all men possible, to remove obstacles that stood in the way of salvation, and merely to make provision for salvation? Or did he come to secure the salvation of all those who are ordained to eternal life? Did he come to make men redeemable? Or did he come effectually and infallibly to redeem? The doctrine of the Atonement must be radically revised if, as atonement, it applies to those who finally perish as well as to those who are the heirs of eternal life. In that event we should have to dilute the grand categories in terms of which the Scripture defines the Atonement and deprive them of their most precious import and glory. This we cannot do. The saving efficacy of expiation, propitiation, reconciliation, and redemption is too deeply embedded in these concepts, and we dare not eliminate this efficacy. We do well to ponder the words of our Lord himself: 'I have come down from heaven, not to do my own will but the will of him who sent me. And this is the will of him who sent me, that of everything which he hath given to me I should lose nothing, but should raise it up in the last day' (John 6:38–39). Security inheres in Christ's redemptive accomplishment. And this means that, in respect of the persons contemplated, design and accomplishment and final realization have all the same extent."[1]

This is called "limited atonement." But this is not a good designation, for all theologians limit it in one way or another. The Calvinist limits its scope. The Arminian limits its power. The question is rather: How does the Bible portray Christ's sacrifice? The answer is that it is portrayed as actually accomplishing that for which God ordained it. It is because it was actual that Christ looked upon "the suffering of his soul" and was "satisfied" (Isa. 53:11).

Belief and Unbelief

I can see only one possible way of avoiding this conclusion, and even that is not actually a possibility when it is once examined. It may be argued by someone that the atonement is actual and also for the sins of the whole world but that all are not saved, not because their sins are not atoned for, but because they do not believe in Christ and hence will not accept the gospel. "It is like a gift," the person might say. "It has been selected and paid for, but no one can be forced to take a gift. The world has been saved, but many persons will not be saved simply because they do not believe in Jesus."

Does that sound reasonable? It does until you ask about the nature of unbelief. Is it merely the morally neutral choice of deciding not to accept salvation? Or is it a sin? The answer is: a sin. In fact, it is the most damning of all sins. And this means simply that if Christ died for all sin and if this includes even the sin of unbelief (as it must if he truly died for *all* sin), then all are saved whether they respond to the gospel or not. Pharaoh, Judas, Muslims, Hindus, pagans will all be in heaven. John Owen, the greatest of the Puritan theologians, who did for this doctrine what Anselm did for the necessity of the atonement, wrote: "You will say, 'Because of their unbelief; they will not believe.' But this unbelief, is it a sin, or not? If not, why should they be punished for it? If it be, then Christ underwent the punishment due to it, or not. If so, then why must that hinder them more than their other sins for which he died from partaking of the fruit of his death? If he did not, then did he not die for all their sins. Let them choose which part they will."[2] If Jesus died for all the sin of the whole human race, unbelief included, then all are saved, which the Bible denies. If he died for all the sin of the race, unbelief excluded, then he did not die for all the sins of anyone and all must be condemned. The only viable position is that he died for the sin of the elect only.

And, of course, this is what the Bible teaches.

Matthew 1:21—"You are to give him the name Jesus, because he will save *his people* from their sins."

Matthew 20:28—"The Son of man did not come to be served, but to serve, and to give his life a ransom for *many*."

John 13:1—"It was just before the Passover Feast. Jesus knew that the time had come for him to leave this world and go to the Father. Having loved his own who were in the world, he now showed *them* the full extent of his love."

Galatians 3:13—"Christ redeemed *us* from the curse of the law by becoming a curse for *us*."

Ephesians 5:25—"Husbands, love your wives, just as Christ loved the *church* and gave himself up for her."

Romans 8:28–32—"And we know that in all things God works for the good of *those who love him,* who have been called according to his purpose. For those God foreknew he also predestined to be conformed to the likeness of his Son, that he might be the firstborn among many brothers. And those he predestined, he also called; those he called, he also justified; those he justified, he also glorified. What, then, shall we say in response to this? If God is for us, who can be against us? He who did not spare his own Son, but gave him up for *us* all—how will he not also, along with him, graciously give *us* all things?"

Repent and Believe the Gospel

Some will argue that if Christ did not take away the sins of all the world, then it is not possible for Christians to offer salvation to all indiscriminately. In fact, it is not possible to offer salvation to anyone, since we do not know whether the person is one for whom Christ died.

There are two answers. First, we are to offer salvation to everyone because we are told to do it and because we have ample biblical examples to that effect. We must say as Ezekiel, "As surely as I live, declares the Sovereign Lord, I take no pleasure in the death of the wicked, but rather that they turn from their ways and live. Turn! Turn from your evil ways! Why will you die, O house of Israel?" (Ezek. 33:11). Or as Isaiah, "Come, all you who are thirsty, come to the waters; and you who have no money, come, buy and eat" (Isa. 55:1). Or as Jesus, "Come to me, all you who are weary and are burdened, and I will give you rest" (Matt. 11:28). This is our great commandment and pattern.

The second answer is that, strictly speaking, the gospel is not so much an offer that people may politely accept or refuse according to their own pleasure as it is a command to turn from sin to Jesus. We have gotten into the habit of making the gospel into an offer because this is more socially acceptable in our culture, and God clearly uses our culturally conditioned efforts. But strictly speaking, the gospel is not something lying around for people to take or leave as they choose. They are called to repent. We are to call them. Only after they repent and turn to Christ can we know that they are those for whom Christ died.

Spurgeon was a great Calvinist. He believed in limited atonement. But it did not stop him from being one of the most effective evangelists of his age. He did not lie; he did not say, "Because you all are elect, Christ died for you." It was enough to say, "You are a sinner, and Jesus died for sinners just like you and me. If you would be saved, repent and believe the gospel."

God honors truth. Therefore, we will speak the truth. And what a wonderful truth this is! We proclaim not a mere possibility of salvation, but salvation itself. We preach that Jesus died for his people. He actually died in their place. He propitiated the wrath of God for them. He reconciled them to God. He redeemed them from the terrible bondage of their own guilt and wickedness. He is therefore a sufficient and suitable Savior. If he is your Savior, you will certainly come to him. Will you not come now? Do not say, "But I am not one of the elect." You do not know that. Just come to Jesus. Jesus has done everything necessary to save sinners. Are you a sinner? Then come to Jesus. He is the Savior. Come!

252

Christ's Side Pierced

John 19:31-37

Now it was the day of Preparation, and the next day was to be a special Sabbath. Because the Jews did not want the bodies left on the crosses during the Sabbath, they asked Pilate to have the legs broken and the bodies taken down. The soldiers therefore came and broke the legs of the first man who had been crucified with Jesus, and then those of the other. But when they came to Jesus and found that he was already dead, they did not break his legs. Instead, one of the soldiers pierced Jesus' side with a spear, bringing a sudden flow of blood and water. The man who saw it has given testimony, and his testimony is true. He knows that he tells the truth, and he testifies so that you also may believe. These things happened so that the scripture would be fulfilled: "Not one of his bones will be broken," and, as another scripture says, "They will look on the one they have pierced."

We have noted a strange irony in the arrest, trial, and crucifixion of Jesus: the leaders were adhering to the minutest requirements of their law while breaking its intent in hounding an innocent man to death. They would try for the open formality of two trials and an official condemnation, but they would break scores of legal safeguards and would even neglect to hear a defense for the accused. They would refuse to enter into Pilate's judgment hall lest they be defiled and be unfit to eat the Passover, but they would defile themselves with the blood of the true Passover, Jesus Christ.

"Religious scruples may live in a dead conscience," said Spurgeon.[1] Indeed they may. In fact, they may live for a long, long time. In the incident recorded in these verses, from the moments immediately following the death of Christ, we see the same principles operating.

It was the custom of the Romans, like the Carthaginians and Persians before them, to leave the body of the crucified upon the cross to rot and be devoured by birds. But in Palestine, where many things were governed by Mosaic rather than Roman law, victims were allowed to be buried. The law said, "If a man guilty of a capital offense is put to death and his body is hung on a tree, you must not leave his body on the tree overnight. Be sure to bury him that same day, because anyone who is hung on a tree is under God's curse. You must not desecrate the land the LORD your God is giving you as an inheritance" (Deut. 21:22–23). Moreover, the law said that executions were not to take place on a religious feast day, which the Passover was. In respect for these laws (though they had shown little enough respect for the Lawgiver), the religious leaders now came to Pilate, requesting that the legs of the victims be broken to hasten their deaths. When his legs were broken, the crucified man could no longer press down with his feet in order to hoist himself upward and thus relieve the pressure on his diaphragm, and he would die quickly by suffocation.

Pilate did not care for the bodies, of course. So he granted the leaders' wishes. On his order soldiers were dispatched to break the legs of the three sufferers. The legs of the thieves were broken, but when the soldiers came to Jesus they discovered that he had already died and so did not break his legs. Instead, one of them thrust a spear into his side, presumably to make sure that he really was dead, as a result of which blood and water came forth. In these verses the writer of the Gospel records these facts, indicating that they occurred in fulfillment of the Scriptures. He draws special attention to the issue of blood and water, saying that "the man who saw it has given testimony, and his testimony is true. He knows that he tells the truth, and he testifies so that you also may believe" (v. 35).

Who Is the Witness?

This verse, in which the testimony of an eyewitness is appealed to, has puzzled commentators. The difficulty is due to that fact that the witness is not specifically identified and that it is not even possible to say for certain whether one or two individuals are involved.

Three interpretations are possible. First, the writer may be referring to himself as an eyewitness of the events he describes. Second, he may be distinguishing between himself as the author and a second party who is the witness. In that case he would be saying that the testimony of the witness is authentic or genuine (*alēthinos*), and that he, the author, can confirm that it is true (*alēthēs*). The third possibility is that the author is calling God to witness, presumably because the fact that he is recording was observed by only one individual. Moffat captures this meaning in his version, for it reads, "He who saw it has borne witness (his witness is true; God knows he is telling the truth), that you may believe." Some scholars, represented by Erasmus first and by Bultmann at the present time, vary this slightly by suggesting that the second personality is Christ.

What can be said for these views? Any one of them is possible, but the balance of evidence is probably in support of the first: that the reference in both cases is to the eyewitness, who must in turn be identified as the beloved disciple and the author of the Gospel.

It is difficult to see how the identity of the witness as the beloved disciple would have been denied at all were scholars not at one time looking for arguments to show that the apostle John was not the author of the Gospel that bears his name. To begin with, the beloved disciple has just been mentioned as being present at the cross, for it was into the keeping of this one that Jesus entrusted his mother (vv. 26–27). Again, John is the only disciple of the Twelve who is mentioned as being at the cross; he is referred to on several occasions throughout the narrative of these last hours (13:23; 19:26; 20:2; 21:7, 20) and is likely the unnamed disciple who secured Peter's admission to the court of the high priest. The two appear together again in John 20 and 21. So far as 19:35 is concerned, it is significant that the way of referring to the witness here is directly parallel to the last verses of the Gospel in which the "disciple whom Jesus loved" is identified as "the disciple who testifies to these things" (21:24). There is no reason to reject the further conclusion that this same disciple is also the apostle John; for on two occasions at least the beloved disciple must be identified as one of the Twelve (in the account of the Last Supper and in the closing event of chapter 21), and his close association with Peter as well as the fact that the apostle John is unmentioned by name anywhere else in the Gospel more than suggests the identification.

Some have thought it strange that, having introduced himself into the narrative in this way, the author should then add "and he knows that he tells the truth." But it is not really strange. The author (if he is John, Zebedee's son) has already been presented as a historical figure present at the crucifixion: thus, there is now every reason for him to draw attention to himself in this capacity. If this is his concern, it is possible that the solemnity with which he writes may be due, not primarily to any supposed mystical or sacramental significance of the blood and water, though it may include it, but to the fact that he can produce only one witness. He knows that normally it is on the testimony of two or three witnesses that a truth is established (Num. 35:30; Deut. 17:6; 19:15; cf. John 8:13–18).[2]

Blood and Water

But why should this particular incident receive the attention it does? Indeed, why should it be emphasized at all? The death of Jesus, the central point of the Gospel, has been recorded in just one verse entirely without editorial comment on John's part. Now a seemingly minor matter, the fact that the legs of Jesus were not broken and that blood and water flowed from his side when pierced, receives "disproportionate" attention. We can be sure that the emphasis is for some good reason, even though we may not know what it is. Moreover, we can be sure that it is profitable for us to examine these verses and search the meaning out.

Let me suggest three interpretations of the blood and water that I do not consider to be the right emphases and then suggest four important meanings from which we can learn.

One wrong meaning, which is nevertheless quite popular today, is that the issue of blood and water from Christ's side signifies the two sacraments. No less weighty a scholar than Oscar Cullmann has forcefully argued this.[3] But it is not convincing. In addition to the fact that John does not really use the words "blood" and "water" in this way (though Cullmann thinks he does), it is a rather fatal defect in this interpretation that the early church did not use "water" to mean "baptism" or "blood" to signify "the Lord's Supper." This is an interpretation that arises from the perfectly understandable concerns of sacramentalists, but it is not really suggested by the Gospel.

A second wrongheaded approach is that which sees the incident mystically. That is, as Eve issued from the side of Adam, so the church issues from the side of Christ, the second Adam. That may have homiletical or devotional value, but that is not what John meant.

A third approach, which has had much popularity among certain groups of evangelicals but which I still believe to be mistaken, is medical. Over a hundred years ago a doctor in England by the name of William Stroud published a book entitled *A Treatise on the Physical Cause of the Death of Christ*. He argued that Jesus' death was due to a ruptured or broken heart. Such a condition may be caused by great mental agony, he argued. He said that it "is usually attended with immediate death, and with an effusion into the pericardium (the capsule containing the heart) of the blood previously circulating through that organ; which when thus extravasated, although scarcely in any other case, separates into its constituent parts, so as to present the appearance commonly termed blood and water."[4] The trouble with this is not the validity of the explanation of how "blood and water" actually issued from Christ, though other doctors have questioned Stroud's thesis, but that the event has no meaning as Stroud explains it. The appeal of the explanation is the suggestion that Jesus died of a "broken heart." But that is not how Jesus died, according to the Gospel accounts. He died triumphantly, having dismissed his spirit. Moreover, even if the dismissal of his spirit might be assumed to have been effected by what we call a coronary thrombosis, this medical fact would be unknown to John and is therefore obviously not the reason why he has recorded it so solemnly in his narrative.

The Essential Points

Why did John record this incident? I would suggest that it was for any or all of the following reasons, each of which is suggested by the text itself or by other important New Testament passages.

1. The entire unfolding of events (which, we must remember, involved the failure of the soldiers to break the legs of Jesus as well as the piercing of his side by a spear) testified beyond any doubt that *Jesus was really dead*. The breaking of the legs was to hasten death, as John indicates. The only reason Jesus' legs were not broken was that he was already dead. But lest there be any doubt, the spear was thrust into his side by the soldier—all carefully recorded by the witness. Why was this important? It was important in view of the later claims regarding the resurrection. Jesus had not merely swooned to revive later in the cool of the tomb and then emerge to appear to his disciples as if he had been raised from the dead. He had really died, and he was really resurrected. This was one reason why the details were important. But they were also important in view of Gnostic teachings that had begun to infiltrate the church by the time of John's writing. The Gnostics denied that Jesus was a real man and possessed a real body. This incident proves the Gnostics wrong and shows by contrast that Jesus actually tasted death for us.

We have it in our creeds. One of the earliest Christian creeds is found in 1 Corinthians: "For what I received I passed on to you as of first importance: that Christ died for our sins according to the Scriptures, that he was buried . . ." (1 Cor. 15:3–4). Similarly, the Apostles' Creed affirms that Jesus "suffered under Pontius Pilate, was crucified, dead and buried." The gospel includes a real death for sin and also a real resurrection.

2. The events John records mark *the fulfillment of Scripture*. If we look at the verses at face value, we can hardly miss seeing that it is this that John emphasizes. It was a remarkable fulfillment of Scripture too, because it was complicated and improbable. There were two prophecies involved: Psalm 34:20 ("He protects all his bones, not one of them will be broken") and Zechariah 12:10 ("They will look on me, the one whom they have pierced"). One was negative; the other was positive. The one said that the Savior's bones must not be broken; the other said that the Savior must be pierced. Moreover, it was the exact opposite of these two prophecies that the soldiers set out to fulfill. They had come to break Jesus' legs along with the legs of the two thieves, and they had no intention at all of piercing him with the spear. Yet they ended up fulfilling the prophecies. How can brutal men be kept from one act of violence, for which they had specific commandment, and be led to enact another for which they had no commandment? There is only one answer. By overruling circumstances, the God who inspired the prophecies made sure that they were fulfilled.

Will he not do so with all the prophecies of his Word, including those that involve us for whom Christ died? Then let us trust God's Word. Spurgeon wrote, "That our Lord's bones should remain unbroken, and yet that he should be pierced, seemed a very unlikely thing; but it was carried out. When next you meet with an unlikely promise, believe it firmly. When next you see things working contrary to the truth of God, believe God, and believe nothing else. Let God be true and every man a liar. Though men and devils should give God the lie, hold you on to what God has spoken; for heaven and earth shall pass away, but not one jot or tittle of his word shall fall to the ground."[5]

3. The fact that Jesus' bones were not broken also points to him as *the Passover Lamb* slain for the sins of his people. A moment ago we quoted Psalm 34:20, which tells us, "He protects all his bones, not one of them will be broken." This is the verse John refers to; there is no other quite like it in the entire Old Testament. But if we are candid, we must admit that a careful reading of this psalm does not at once suggest that this verse should be applied to the Messiah. It refers rather to the righteous man about whom David is writing. What is wrong then? Is this a case of invention on John's part? Not at all. It is true that he is referring to this psalm, but he is thinking of something greater. He is remembering that in the institution of the Passover it was explicitly indicated that not a bone of the Passover lamb should be broken. Exodus 12:46 declares, "It must be eaten inside one house; take none of the meat outside the house. Do not break any of the bones." Again, Numbers 9:12 says, "They must not leave any of it till morning or break any of its bones." This seemingly pointless detail in the Passover ritual and this seemingly pointless detail in the death of Jesus combine in God's providence to identify Jesus as the Passover Lamb through whom we have a spiritual deliverance.

John has seen this all along, of course, and he has described the events of the crucifixion in such a way that the timing of Christ's death at the very time the Passover lambs were being killed is kept in view. In fact, at the very beginning of this section John indicates that these things were done because it was "the day of preparation" of the Passover.

Every Jew knew the significance of the Passover. This was the event in which God delivered the people from their slavery in Egypt. God had said that on this night he would bring the last of his ten great judgments upon Egypt, a judgment in which the firstborn of every household would be killed. God would send his angel to slay the firstborn throughout the whole land. The Jewish homes would be spared only if they followed these instructions. They were to take a lamb, which was to have been kept in the home for three days and was to be without blemish or spot, and were to kill it. Then they were to take the blood of the lamb and spread it upon the doorposts and lintel of the house. The angel of death would come, but wherever he would see the blood he would "pass over," and the inhabitants of that house would be spared. This was the great national event and festival that the Jews were beginning to remember the day that Jesus of Nazareth was killed. What John is indicating (and God who speaks through him) is that Jesus is the perfect fulfillment of that important Old Testament figure. We are sinners. We deserve to die. The angel of God's judgment is coming. But Jesus has died in our place. His blood has purged our sin; now, because of his death, the angel of judgment will pass by all who trust in him.

4. This leads to the fourth reason John wrote these verses, particularly the verses that mention the water and blood. John calls attention to this incident as fulfilling the prophecy in Zechariah 12:10. Many students have stopped with that verse. But the meaning of what John is saying is to be found just five verses farther in the passage, namely Zechariah 13:1, which really belongs with the preceding section. That verse speaks of a day when "a fountain will be opened to the house of David and the inhabitants of Jerusalem, to cleanse them from sin and impurity." Certainly John knew this verse. Moreover, he knew from the Old Testament how important "blood" was for cleansing from sin (e.g., Lev. 17:11) and how important "water" was for purification from uncleanness. Therefore, when he saw these two elements issue from the pierced side of Christ and recalled this prophecy, he recognized it as teaching that all *deliverance and cleansing from sin and its defilement* are to be found in Jesus' death.

Someone else recognized it. William Cowper, the English poet, wrote the great hymn "There Is a Fountain Filled with Blood" in commemoration of this incident.

> There is a fountain filled with blood
>   Drawn from Immanuel's veins;
> And sinners plunged beneath that flood
>   Lose all their guilty stains.
>
> The dying thief rejoiced to see
>   That fountain in his day,
> And there may I, as vile as he,
>   Wash all my sins away.
>
> E'er since by faith I saw the stream
>   Thy flowing wounds supply,
> Redeeming love has been my theme
>   And shall be till I die.
>
> Dear dying Lamb, Thy precious blood
>   Shall never lose its power,
> Till all the ransomed church of God
>   Be saved to sin no more.

John the apostle, William Cowper, and countless others have seen these truths and have rejoiced in Christ's death as that through which we have salvation. In one sense, every believer has rejoiced in these truths, even though he or she may not have understood these particular verses as I have interpreted them. Are you one of that number? Are you one who by faith has spread the blood of the perfect Passover upon your doorpost? Have you believed in Jesus? If not, may the spear that pierced Christ's side prick your heart also. May *your* heart be broken as you look at him. This was John's purpose in recording these verses: that you might look to Jesus and trust him. There is salvation in such a believing look. Look to Jesus. There is life in this moment for all who believe on him.

253

With the Rich in His Death

John 19:38–42

Later, Joseph of Arimathea asked Pilate for the body of Jesus. Now Joseph was a disciple of Jesus, but secretly because he feared the Jews. With Pilate's permission, he came and took the body away. He was accompanied by Nicodemus, the man who earlier had visited Jesus at night. Nicodemus brought a mixture of myrrh and aloes, about seventy-five pounds. Taking Jesus' body, the two of them wrapped it, with the spices, in strips of linen. This was in accordance with Jewish burial customs. At the place where Jesus was crucified, there was a garden, and in the garden a new tomb, in which no one had ever been laid. Because it was the Jewish day of Preparation and since the tomb was nearby, they laid Jesus there.

The verses that conclude the nineteenth chapter of John are not the first in which we meet with secret discipleship, but they give the saddest and most striking example of that condition. Secret discipleship is discussed first in John 12, where the author, after having summarized the rejection of Jesus by his own people in accordance with Isaiah's prophecy, adds, "Yet at the same time many even among the leaders believed in him. But because of the Pharisees they would not confess their faith for fear they would be put out of the synagogue; for they loved praise from men more than praise from God" (vv. 42–43). The verses in John 12 do not name these secret believers—they were *secret* believers, after all. But we find two examples in John 19:38–42—Joseph of Arimathaea and Nicodemus.

We do not know a great deal about either of these men, but what we do know is significant. We know that they were each rich and prominent. Both were members of the Sanhedrin. They believed in Jesus, at least to some degree, though whether or not they were born again we cannot tell. Nicodemus had confessed at the beginning of Jesus' ministry that he was at least "a teacher from God" (John 3:2). But the fear which had kept him from coming to Jesus openly on that occasion—he came by night, a fact that John reiterates each time he mentions him—also kept him from Jesus during his earthly ministry and kept him silent while Jesus was being condemned and crucified. Joseph of Arimathaea is described as "a disciple" (John 19:38; cf. Matt. 27:57), "a prominent member of the Council, who was himself waiting for the kingdom of God" (Mark 15:43), "a good and upright man" (Luke 23:50). We are told that he "had not consented" to the decision of those who had condemned Jesus (Luke 23:51). Yet Joseph's protests were apparently silent ones, and we cannot really say that he was converted either. He may have been; the description is a bit more hopeful in his case than in that of Nicodemus. But we cannot be sure. Neither is mentioned again in the New Testament or in other early Christian documents.

Do you say, "But these were at least in Jerusalem caring for the body of the Lord when his more open, vocal disciples had fled"? That is true, but it says more about the failure of the Twelve than it does about the discipleship of Joseph and Nicodemus. Many memorials have been built, many stained-glass windows installed, many chairs of theology endowed by those who have come no closer to the possession of eternal life than to have a guilty conscience. Are you one who is like Nicodemus or this counselor from Arimathaea? If so, I hope to disturb you by showing how close you are to those millions who adhere to Christianity but have no saving faith at all. I hope to move you to become something more in Christ's church than a funeral director. I should like you to become a witness to the living God.

How will I do this? In two ways. I want to show first the cause of secret discipleship, and also how unnecessary and dangerous this is. Then I want to show the sad results of a failure to confess Christ openly.

Fear of the Jews

There is no mystery as to what kept Joseph of Arimathaea and Nicodemus from confessing Jesus. It was fear, "fear of the Jews," as John tells us. When I read this explanation in John 19, I cannot help contrasting it with the slightly different explanation John 12 gives of the same failure to confess Jesus openly. There it was said that many did not confess him because "they loved the praise of men more than the praise of God" (v. 43). That leads me to think that fear of ridicule lives on as a deterrent even after the vanity of seeking praise from others is gone.

We may suppose that in their early days Joseph and Nicodemus may have pursued the kind of life they did in order to be well thought of. Certainly many do it today. Some seek it through wealth, because the rich are generally courted by the less fortunate. Some seek it through prestigious titles and positions—by being a member of the Sanhedrin or city council or bar or civic organization. But these things fade in time, and perceptive people are eventually disillusioned by the emptiness of human honors. What then? Do they come to their senses and abandon vanity for things that are worthwhile? Sometimes, but not always or even usually. The reason most do not is that fear of what others may think or do deters them. Many who would not fail to confess Christ because of their desire for praise, nevertheless fail to confess him because they think that someone might despise them or laugh them to scorn.

Alexander Maclaren has excellent thoughts on this subject. "There is nothing in the organization of society at this day to make any man afraid of avowing the ordinary kind of Christianity which satisfies the most of us; rather it is the proper thing with the bulk of us middleclass people, to say that in some sense or other we are Christians. But when it comes to a real avowal, a real carrying out of a true discipleship, there are as many and as formidable, though very different, impediments in the way today, from those which blocked the path of these two cowards in our text. In all regions of life it is hard to work out into practice any moral conviction whatever. How many of us are there who have beliefs about social and moral questions which we are ashamed to avow in certain companies for fear of the finger of ridicule being pointed at us? . . . The political, social, and moral conflicts of this day have their 'secret disciples,' who will only come out of their holes when the battle is over, and will then shout with the loudest."[1]

Why is it that in a day when every vice of humanity is coming "out of the closet" and clamoring for recognition as a pure and natural expression of the essentially "good" human spirit, many believers (or alleged believers) fail to come out for Christ? It is fear, fear of what someone may say.

How unnecessary and dangerous this is! It is unnecessary because there is no danger in ridicule. It may be unpleasant, distasteful. We may naturally prefer a different treatment from our contemporaries and peers. But there is no danger in it. In fact, the opposite is true. When we take a stand for righteousness, we are most secure. It is when we are silent that we are most in danger, not only in this life but in regard to the life that is to come.

If you are holding back from an outright confession of Christ and a determination to stand with him whatever may come, you are probably rationalizing your failure in this fashion. You are saying, "My testimony will not do any good. What matters is that I am God's child, and I can be that in silence." Can you? Can you have confidence that you are really born again if you will not confess Christ openly? You know the Scriptures: "If anyone comes after me, let him deny himself and take up his cross daily and follow me" (Luke 9:23); "Whoever does not take up his cross and follow me cannot be my disciple" (Luke 14:27); "If you confess with your mouth, 'Jesus is Lord,' and believe in your heart that God raised him from the dead, you will be saved. For it is with your heart that you believe and are justified, and it is with your mouth that you confess and are saved" (Rom. 10:9–10); "Whoever ack-owledges me before men, I will also acknowledge him before my Father in heaven. But whoever disowns me before men, I will also disown him before my Father in heaven" (Matt. 10:32–33).

If you do not confess Christ openly and stand with him even in the face of ridicule, I do not see what right you have to consider yourself any differ-ent from Pontius Pilate, for it was fear that kept him back from righteous-ness. Do you respect Christ? So did Pilate. Do you honestly want to do the right thing? So did he. Do you say, "I find no fault in Jesus"? This was Pilate's testimony. But his fear of Caesar triumphed over his more noble instincts. Be careful that you are not following in his train.

Loss of Communion

It may be the case that you really are a believer in the Lord Jesus Christ, though for the most part secretly. If so, I want to encourage you to an early boldness by showing the sad results of failing to proclaim Christ openly.

The first result is a loss of fellowship with Christ. I think it is this that comes through most clearly in the case of Nicodemus and Joseph of Ari-mathaea. We do not know when Joseph first heard of Jesus and believed on him, but it was probably early. Nicodemus knew of Jesus from the begin-ning, for he had come to him when his teachings and miracles had first be-came known. These men might have profited from two, perhaps three years of the most intense communion and fellowship with Jesus. They could have learned from his teaching, benefited from his example, received instruc-tion from him directly as to how the advance of the kingdom of God in the world was to be carried out. We are told of Joseph that he was actually "wait-ing for the kingdom of God." Yet he missed it—because he would not con-fess Christ openly.

Again I quote Maclaren. "Any neglected duty puts a film between a man and his Savior; any conscious neglect of duty piles up a wall between you and Christ. Be sure of this, that if from cowardly or from selfish regard to posi-tion and advantages, or any other motive, we stand apart from him, and have our lips locked when we ought to speak, there will steal over our hearts a cold-ness, his face will be averted from us, and our eyes will not dare to seek, with the same confidence and joy, the light of his countenance. What you lose by unfaithful wrapping of your convictions in a napkin and burying them in the ground is the joyful use of the convictions, the deeper hold of the truth by which you live, and before which you bow, and the true fellowship with the Master whom you acknowledge and confess."[2]

Besides, it is not only communion with Christ that you lose. You also lose that blessed and valuable communion that you should and must have with other Christians. They are with Christ; if you are not with him, you are not with them either and you will suffer for it. An ember isolated from other embers soon burns out and is nothing but dead ashes. Place it near others and the flame soon grows and sets other wood burning. If you have never learned this before, put it down as a great and unalterable principle: *Christians need other Christians.* You need them. If you think you do not, you are either a fool or hopelessly proud or arrogant.

I think I can hear some objections. The first is that Christians are often a very sorry bunch. True, but is that not also the case with you, particularly if you are a secret believer? I will tell you one thing: If you refuse to identify with other believers because you think they are sorry specimens of discipleship, you are actually considering yourself superior and that is a very questionable stance for one who is supposed to have confessed his sin and turned from all self-righteousness to faith in Jesus Christ. If you really are a sinner, then you belong with those sinners for whom Christ died. If you consider yourself better than they are, what makes you think that you have actually been born into God's family?

Again, what company have you found that is superior? That of unbelievers? The world? If you are thinking along those lines, you are a great fool, for it is the world that, for all its supposed glamour and sophistication, crucified your Master. What makes you think it will treat you more kindly when once it finds that you belong to him?

I hear another objection. You say that you would like to come out for Christ but that others whom you love and respect—perhaps a husband or wife, children or parents—are holding you back. Held back by those you love? I do not see how you can say that you love them if you are unwilling to take that one stand which by the grace of God is most likely to be used by him in their conversions. More than in any other way God's grace spreads through families. If you love them, you will come out for Christ and then look to him for help in bringing them to that same belief and profession.

There are those who have done it. I think of one girl who became a Christian in Philadelphia and then went home at considerable personal loss to reach her parents for Christ. They are now believers and leaders in the Christian community in which they live. I think of another girl, a Filipino, who returned to an island village in which there was not even one single Christian. But she identified with Christ, and many have now come to know him.

Drawn by Love

I know that it is not arguments of this kind that will ultimately reach you. It is only love for Christ himself, love that will be generated at Christ's cross.

Here I may be encouraging, for it was obviously the death of Christ that brought cowardly Joseph and weak Nicodemus from their places of hiding.

It is true, much to their shame, that during the days of his ministry they had failed to profess Christ openly. But in his death—at the precise moment when even the other, bolder disciples had fled—these came forward, touched by that loving sacrifice which Jesus made for our salvation. They awoke to their cowardice—and to God's love. Again, I do not say that they were necessarily believers. Guilty consciences have done as much on many similar occasions. But the death of Christ obviously awakened something within them, and they seemed willing at last to identify themselves as his followers.

God can do that with you, if you will but look on Christ's passion. The Bible says, "God demonstrates his love for us in this: While we were still sinners, Christ died for us" (Rom. 5:8). It is in Christ's death that we see God's love. Does that not move you? True, you may have held back before, hardly knowing whether you were a true believer or not. But you *can* come forward. He died for you. He paid the price for your sin. He bore the anguish of the cross for your salvation. How can you fail to love him? If you love him, how can you fail to confess that to everyone?

I will give you one more incentive. Notice that in his burial Jesus is already taking the first step toward that exaltation at God's hand that is now his, from which he shall come forth in power at the end of the age. There was a true day of the jackal when men cursed and laughed and hated and spit upon him. There was a day of humiliation, but that day is now past. It ended with his death. Now even in his burial he is attended with love as those who have the means to care for his body and bury him honorably wait upon him. It was prophesied. Isaiah tells us that although he was to die in the company of the wicked he was to be attended by the rich in his death (Isa. 53:9). Besides, this is now followed by resurrection victory and the ascent to heaven.

The Christ you are asked to follow is not a humiliated Jewish preacher but the Lord of glory. Indeed, he does not merely ask you to come to him; he commands it. He tells you to turn from your sin and come to him openly for salvation. Will you do that? Will you come? "The Spirit and the bride say, 'Come!' And let him who hears say, 'Come!' Whoever is thirsty, let him come; and whoever wishes, let him take the free gift of the water of life" (Rev. 22:17).

254

The Not-Quite-Empty Tomb

John 20:1–10

Early on the first day of the week, while it was still dark, Mary Magdalene went to the tomb and saw that the stone had been removed from the entrance. So she came running to Simon Peter and the other disciple, the one Jesus loved, and said, "They have taken the Lord out of the tomb, and we don't know where they have put him!"

So Peter and the other disciple started for the tomb. Both were running, but the other disciple outran Peter and reached the tomb first. He bent over and looked in at the strips of linen lying there but did not go in. Then Simon Peter, who was behind him, arrived and went into the tomb. He saw the strips of linen lying there, as well as the burial cloth that had been around Jesus' head. The cloth was folded up by itself, separate from the linen. Finally the other disciple, who had reached the tomb first, also went inside. He saw and believed. (They still did not understand from Scripture that Jesus had to rise from the dead.)

Then the disciples went back to their homes.

One of the great historical evidences of Jesus' resurrection is the empty tomb. But the remarkable and startling fact is that when Peter and John arrived at the tomb on the first Easter morning, it was not quite empty. The body of Jesus was gone, but something was

1563

still there: the graveclothes. Something about them so struck John, at least, that he believed in the resurrection.

Significantly, this is the first time a disciple indicated belief in the resurrection. During the last century a well-known French critic of the Gospels, Ernest Renan, argued that Christian faith in the resurrection was the result of the rumors spread by Mary Magdalene, who had suffered a hallucination, thinking she had seen Jesus. But Mary could not have suffered a hallucination. The last thing in the world she ever expected was her Lord's resurrection. And John testifies that he believed some time before Mary returned to the tomb and met Jesus.

Events of Easter Morning

Jesus had been crucified either on Friday (as the church has generally believed) or else on Thursday (which is less widely held but which seems to fit the evidence better).[1] He lay in the tomb until the resurrection, which certainly took place before dawn on Sunday morning. At this point the women came to the tomb from Jerusalem bearing spices to anoint his body. There were at least four women and probably more. Matthew says that the group included Mary Magdalene and the other Mary, that is, Mary the mother of James. Mark adds that Salome was present. Luke says that Joanna was also along and others. These women started out while it was yet dark and arrived at the tomb in the early dawn when it was difficult to distinguish objects.

On reaching the tomb the women were astonished to find the stone removed from the entrance. We must imagine them standing about, afraid to go too close and wondering what had happened. Who moved the stone? Had the body of Jesus been stolen? Had Joseph of Arimathaea removed it to another place? What were they to do? At last they decided that the disciples must be told, and Mary Magdalene was dispatched to find them. Not one of them imagined that Jesus had been raised from the dead.

After awhile it began to grow lighter and the women grew bolder. They decided to look into the tomb. There they saw the angels. The women were afraid. But an angel said, "Do not be afraid, for I know that you are looking for Jesus, who was crucified. He is not here; he has risen, just as he said. Come and see the place where he lay. Then go quickly and tell his disciples" (Matt. 28:5–7).

Mary meanwhile found the two chief disciples, Peter and John, presumably in John's house where the beloved disciple had taken Jesus' mother on the day of the crucifixion (John 19:27).

The two disciples started for the tomb, running and leaving Mary far behind. Outrunning Peter, John arrived at the tomb first, stooped to look through the narrow opening, and saw the graveclothes. Then Peter arrived, out of breath and in a hurry; he brushed John aside and plunged into the tomb. When John saw the graveclothes, he saw them only in a cursory manner and from outside the tomb. The Greek uses the most common word for seeing *(blepō)*; it suggests nothing more than sight. But when Peter arrived he scrutinized the graveclothes carefully. The Scripture uses a special word *(theoreo)* for what Peter did (from it we get our words "theory" and "theorize"). Moreover, it tells what Peter saw. The Bible says that Peter "went into the tomb. He saw the strips of linen lying there, as well as the burial cloth that had been around Jesus' head. The cloth was folded up by itself, separate from the linen" (John 20:6–7). At this point John entered, saw what Peter had seen (this time the word is *oraō*, meaning "to see with understanding"), and believed in Jesus' resurrection (v. 8).

After this the appearances of the Lord began. Jesus appeared first to Mary Magdalene who arrived back at the tomb after John and Peter had returned to the city. Next he appeared to the women, then to Peter alone, then to the Emmaus disciples, finally, later that night, to all the disciples as they were gathered together in the upper room. All the disciples who saw the risen Lord believed. But John believed first, and he did so before he actually saw Jesus. What made him believe? What did he see that convinced him of Jesus' resurrection?

Jewish Burial

It is helpful at this point to know something about the modes of Jewish burial. Every society has its distinct modes of burial. In Egypt, bodies were embalmed. In Rome and Greece they were often cremated. In Palestine they were neither embalmed nor cremated. They were wrapped in linen bands that enclosed dry spices and placed face up without a coffin in tombs, generally cut from the rock in the Judean and Galilean hills. Many of these tombs exist today and can be seen by any visitor to Palestine.

Another factor of Jewish burial in ancient times is also of special interest for understanding John's account of Jesus' resurrection. In *The Risen Master*, published in 1901, Henry Latham calls attention to a unique feature of Eastern burials that he noticed when in Constantinople during the last century. He says that funerals he witnessed often varied in many respects, depending upon whether the funeral was for a person who had been poor or for one who had been rich. But in one respect all the arrangements were identical. Latham noticed that the bodies were wrapped in linen cloths in such a manner as to leave the face, neck, and upper part of the shoulders bare. The upper part of the head was covered by a cloth that had been twirled about it like a turban. Latham concluded that since burial styles change slowly, particularly in the East, this mode of burial may well have been practiced in Jesus' time. He argued that this is all the more probable since the practice in 1900 meshes nicely with what is told of the graveclothes in John's Gospel.

There is additional evidence for this thesis. Luke tells us that when Jesus was approaching the village of Nain earlier in his ministry, he met a funeral procession leaving the city. The only son of a widow had died. Luke says that when Jesus raised him from death two things happened. First, the young man sat up; that is, he was lying upon his back on the bier without a coffin. Second, he began to speak. Hence, the graveclothes did not cover his face. Separate coverings for the head and body were also used in the burial of Lazarus (John 11:44).

We have every reason to believe that Joseph of Arimathaea and Nicodemus buried Jesus Christ in a similar manner. The body of Jesus was removed from the cross before the beginning of the Jewish Sabbath, washed and wrapped in linen bands. Seventy-five pounds of spices were carefully inserted into the folds of the linen. Aloe was a powdered wood like fine sawdust with an aromatic fragrance; myrrh was a fragrant gum that would be carefully mixed with the powder. Jesus' body was encased in these. His head, neck, and upper shoulders were left bare and a linen cloth was wrapped about the upper part of his head like a turban. The body of Jesus was then lovingly placed within the sepulcher where it lay until sometime on Saturday night or early Sunday morning.

The Resurrection

What would we have seen had we been there at the moment at which Jesus was raised from the dead? Would we have seen Jesus stir, open his eyes, sit up, and begin to struggle out of the bandages? That would have been a resuscitation, not a resurrection. It would have been as if he had recovered from a swoon or had merely been raised from death as he had raized Lazarus. He would have been raised in a natural body rather than a spiritual body; that was not the case at all.

If we had been present in the tomb at the moment of the resurrection, we would have noticed either that the body of Jesus would have seemed to have disappeared or else that it was changed into a resurrection body and passed through the graveclothes and out of the sealed tomb just as it was later to pass through closed doors. John Stott says that the body was "vaporized, being transmuted into something new and different and wonderful."[2] Latham says that the body would have been "exhaled," passing "into a phase of being like that of Moses and Elias on the Mount."[3]

What would have happened then? The linen cloths would have subsided once the body was removed because of the weight of the spices that were in them, and they would have been lying undisturbed where the body of Jesus had been. The cloth which surrounded the head, without the weight of spices, might well have retained its concave shape and have lain by itself separated from the body cloths by the space where the Lord's neck and shoulders had been.

This is exactly what John says he and Peter saw when they entered the sepulcher. John was first at the tomb, and as he reached the open sepulcher in the murky light of early dawn he saw the graveclothes lying. There was something about them that attracted John's attention. First, it was significant that they were there at all. John stresses the point, using the word for "lying" at an emphatic position in the sentence. We might translate, "He saw, lying there, the graveclothes" (v. 5). Furthermore, the clothes were undisturbed. The word that John uses *(keimena)* occurs in the Greek papyrii of things that have been carefully placed in order. One document speaks of legal documents, saying, "I have not yet obtained the documents, but they are lying collated." Another speaks of clothes that are "lying (in order) until you send me word." Certainly John noticed that there had been no disturbance at the tomb.

At this point Peter arrived and went into the sepulcher. Peter saw what John had seen, but in addition he was struck by something else. The cloth that had been around the head was not with the other clothes. It was lying in a place by itself (v. 7). What was even more striking, it had retained a circular shape. John says that it was "wrapped together." We might say that it was "twirled about itself." There was a space between it and the cloths that had enveloped the body. When John saw this he believed.

What did John believe? I imagine that he might have explained it to Peter like this. "Don't you see, Peter, that no one has moved the body or disturbed the graveclothes? They are lying exactly as Nicodemus and Joseph of Arimathaea left them on the eve of the Sabbath. Yet the body is gone. It has not been stolen. It has not been moved. Clearly it must have passed through the cloths, leaving them as we see them now. Jesus must be risen." Stott says, "A glance at these grave clothes proved the reality, and indicated the nature, of the resurrection."[4]

How foolish in the light of such evidence are non-Christian explanations of the events of Easter morning. Some have taught that the body of Jesus was stolen, but in that case the presence of the graveclothes is inexplicable. They would have been removed along with the body. Others have taught that Jesus revived in the tomb and escaped after having unwound the linen bands. In that case the linen would have been displaced. Even if we can imagine that Jesus replaced the clothes where they had been and somehow moved the stone, there is still a problem with the spices, for these would have been scattered about the tomb. Of this there is not the slightest suggestion in the Gospel. None of these explanations will do. The disciples saw everything in order, but the body was gone. Jesus had indeed been raised, and in a resurrection body.

What John Believed

There are a few lessons that arise out of this narrative. The first is that God has provided perfectly adequate evidence of the resurrection of Jesus Christ from the dead. The evidence consists of the claims of those who saw Jesus between the day of his resurrection and the day of his ascension into heaven, the empty tomb, the changed character of the disciples, the authenticity of the records, and the evidence of the undisturbed burial garments. The evidence is there, and the evidence of the graveclothes alone was sufficient to quicken faith in John. We conclude that if men fail to believe, it is because they will not believe, not because the evidence is lacking.

Second, the experiences of Peter and John at the tomb indicate that the body of the Lord was glorified. It was sown a natural body and was raised a spiritual body. In this body Jesus lives, seated at the right hand of God where he intercedes for his own until the moment when he will return again in judgment. Today we need not think of Jesus as the vulnerable Jesus of history. Jesus died, but he died once for all. He was buffeted and spat upon and cursed, but that will not be repeated. We pray today to a powerful Lord, to an exalted Lord. This Lord will return one day to take his own to be with him in glory.

Finally, the transformation of the body of Jesus Christ points to a new mode of life for all believers. He is the first fruit. We, the harvest, shall be like him in our bodies as well as in his traits of character. Our resurrection bodies will be better than our old physical bodies. They will not be our physical bodies resuscitated. Our bodies hamper us. They tie us to earth, to habits, even to traits of character that we have inherited from our parents through their genes. They slow our thought processes. When we are sufficiently tired they carry us away in sleep. Eventually they die. But we are to gain by death. The resurrection body will not hamper us. The body of the risen Christ is the forerunner of our bodies, and it was and is wholly subservient to his wishes. It did not hamper him. It freed him. In that body he knew no pain, no suffering, no want. For us there will also be freedom. There will be no want. There will be unlimited awakefulness and unlimited opportunities for service.

In one of his great sermons on the resurrection D. L. Moody tells the story of a bright young girl about fifteen years of age who was suddenly cast upon a bed of suffering, completely paralyzed on one side and nearly blind. She could hardly see, but she could hear. As she lay in bed one day she heard the family doctor say to her parents as they stood by the bedside, "She has seen her best days, poor child." Fortunately the girl was a believer, and she quickly replied, "No, doctor, my best days are yet to come, when I shall see the King in his beauty." Her hope, like ours, lay in the resurrection.

255

The Day Faith Died

John 20:11–16

But Mary stood outside the tomb crying. As she wept, she bent over to look into the tomb and saw two angels in white, seated where Jesus' body had been, one at the head and the other at the foot.

They asked her, "Woman, why are you crying?"

"They have taken my Lord away," she said, "and I don't know where they have put him." At this, she turned around and saw Jesus standing there, but she did not realize that it was Jesus.

"Woman," he said, "why are you crying? Who is it you are looking for?"

Thinking he was the gardener, she said, "Sir, if you have carried him away, tell me where you have put him, and I will get him."

Jesus said to her, "Mary."

She turned toward him and cried out in Aramaic, "Rabboni!" (which means Teacher).

If there is any story in all literature more poignant than the story of Mary Magdalene's meeting with Jesus in the garden on the first Lord's day, I do not know what it is. But to understand it we have to put ourselves in the frame of mind of the disciples between the afternoon of Jesus' crucifixion and the morning of his resurrection, and that is not easy to do. Our experience of Easter is one of faith and joy. But in the days that elapsed between Christ's death and resurrection, those who were closest to him were filled with the deepest disillusionment and gloom. They had been told of Christ's resurrection, but they had not understood it. Therefore, when Jesus died, there is a sense in which they died also.

For three years this mixed body of men and women had followed Jesus in his itinerant preaching ministry. They did not understand much of what he said. But they tried to, and what they did understand they believed. When Jesus died, their faith died, and they began to demonstrate the death of faith by scattering back to where they had been before Jesus had called them to discipleship. The women went home. Cleopas and Mary returned to their village. The others would have returned to Galilee eventually, for they did this anyway even after they had been convinced of Christ's resurrection. In earlier days they had given good testimonies—"You are the Christ, the Son of the living God" (Matt. 16:16), "We believe and are sure that you are the Christ, the Son of the living God" (John 6:69)—but in the period between the crucifixion and the resurrection this had become past tense. They had believed once, but it was over.

I Will Not Believe

No one better illustrates the death of faith than Thomas. We are not told much about him, only that he was inclined to a very sober estimate of things. We call him "doubting Thomas," but to speak accurately, he was no doubter at this point. He was an outright unbeliever. Alexander Maclaren has written, "Flat, frank, dogged disbelief, and not hesitation or doubt, was his attitude. The very form in which he puts his requirement shows how he was hugging his unbelief, and how he had no idea that what he asked would ever be granted. 'Unless I have so-and-so I will not,' indicates an altogether [different] spiritual attitude from what 'If I have so-and-so, I will,' would have indicated. The one is the language of willingness to be persuaded, the other is a token of a determination to be obstinate."[1]

It was not a very commendable attitude, but thus it was. And thus it was with all the disciples—before the resurrection.

We Had Hoped

Moreover, it was not only faith that had died in these disciples; hope had died also. They had possessed such great hopes. Yet all these had been dashed into pieces by Christ's crucifixion.

The great example of the death of hope is the statement of the Emmaus disciples recorded in Luke 24:21, though it was, of course, true of them all. Like the others, these two disciples had looked for the dawning of Messiah's reign upon earth. They thought that Jesus was that Messiah; so they had followed him, looking for a place in his kingdom. But now the inconceivable had happened. Jesus had died, and their hopes had died with him. So clouded were their minds by this disappointment that they did not even recognize the Lord when he drew near them on the Emmaus way. He asked what they had been talking about and why they were sad. They answered, "Are you only a visitor to Jerusalem and do not know the things that have happened there in these days?"

"What things?"

They answered, "About Jesus of Nazareth. He was a prophet, powerful in word and deed before God and all the people. The chief priests and our rulers handed him over to be sentenced to death, and they crucified him; but we had *hoped* that he was the one who was going to redeem Israel" (Luke 24:17–21). Isn't it interesting that they used the word "redeem," because, of course, that is precisely what the Lord was doing—redeeming Israel, and all who should thereafter believe on him as Savior from sin. But that is not what they were thinking. They were thinking of the national, temporal, messianic redemption upon which their hopes had been set throughout the three years of his ministry. They had hoped for that, but when Jesus died they knew at last that it was not coming.

Love Lives

Faith had died and hope had died. But there was one thing that had not died—love. For in spite of their cruel disillusionment and virtual despair, the disciples all still loved their Master and could not cease thinking of him and grieving over him. The great example is Mary.

We do not know a great deal about Mary of Magdalene. But we must be careful to distinguish what we do know from those spurious details that have been added to the account by years of tradition. The Bible tells us that Mary had been the object of Christ's special grace, and that he had sent seven demons out of her (Luke 8:2). For no sound reason at all, church tradition identified her with the unnamed sinner of Luke 7, who anointed the feet of Jesus in the house of a wealthy Pharisee—probably because Mary of Bethany later did the same thing in the house of Lazarus, and there was a confusion of these two accounts and the two Marys. After this she was assumed to have been a prostitute before Christ saved her, and by the seventeenth century "Magdalene" was being used as a word to describe a reformed prostitute. We do not know whether this was her case or not. But Christ had saved her from something terrible, and she had learned to love him. Jesus said that the one who has been forgiven much, loves much (Luke 7:47). This was true of Mary. Thus, earlier in Jesus' ministry we learn that she ministered to him out of her substance (Luke 8:3), and we find that at the end she is still trying to do this by anointing his body.

We will never understand the account of Christ's appearance to Mary at the tomb unless we recognize that it was love, and only love, that brought her here. She had possessed faith once, as had the others. She had hoped. But now faith and hope were gone. Only love caused her to seek the body and held her close to the tomb.

Mary was one of the group of women who had been in Jerusalem at the time of the crucifixion and who had therefore witnessed the Lord's agonies. We read on three separate occasions that she was among those women who saw the crucifixion (Matt. 27:55–56; Mark 15:40; John 19:25). No doubt she witnessed the other events as well—the roar of the crowd as, goaded by the priests, they shouted, "Take him away! Crucify him! Crucify him!"; the judgment of Pilate; the procession to Calvary, during which time Christ fell under the weight of the cross and had to be relieved of it by Simon of Cyrene in order that the death march might proceed; the driving of the nails; the terrible cries ("I thirst"; "My God, my God, why have you forsaken me?"); the darkness; the earthquake; at last death. Mary witnessed all this. It would have been a severe strain on even the strongest of men. Who could stomach such things? Yet, through it all, there is Mary. What keeps her there? Not curiosity, certainly. Not faith. Not hope in a miracle. Mary is there only because she loves Jesus and consequently will not leave until the end.

And even then her love lived on, for though Jesus was gone, Mary still wished to do something for him. She determined to buy spices, and the others agreed. They did this just before the shops closed for the Passover Sabbath. The Sabbaths went by, first the Passover Sabbath (which, in that year, probably fell on a Friday) and then the regular Saturday Sabbath. Thus, it was on the following Sunday morning that Mary and the other women made their way to the tomb to perform their last services. They knew that the stone had been placed over the entrance to the burial cave, for they were asking, "Who will roll away the stone for us from the door of the tomb?" If we ask, "But then how did they expect to anoint the body?" the answer is that they did not know. They hoped that someone might be there to move the stone, but they were not really thinking clearly at that point.

Upon reaching the graveyard they noticed that the stone had been moved. It suited their purpose, but it was not what they had been expecting. So they stopped and asked themselves what they should do. At last they decided that the disciples, Peter and John, should be told. So Mary was either dispatched or else volunteered to tell them. While she was gone (and, therefore, unknown to her), the remaining women went forward, saw and heard the angels, and then rushed off in amazement to convey the angels' message: "He is not here. He is risen, just as he said" (Matt. 28:6). Shortly after they had gone, Peter and John arrived, having received Mary's message and then raced to the tomb.

Where was Mary? She had been left behind by Peter and John, gentlemen that they were! But that did not disturb her, for her mind was on Jesus. Quite naturally she set out for the tomb once more.

I wonder if you can identify with the strain this woman was under. She had seen the person she loved most in all the world taken from her and brutally executed. She had planned to perform some last rites on the body, but this had been frustrated, at least temporarily. She had been going back and forth from the city to the tomb in the dark or semidark for what must have seemed hours. Now she arrives back at the tomb to find Peter and John and the other women gone. She is alone, totally deserted, and it is beyond her emotional capacity. She bursts out weeping. Undoubtedly she had wept before, at the crucifixion. The days of the Sabbaths had been filled with weeping. How she could find more tears is almost beyond understanding. But there were some. It is therefore with tear-filled eyes that she looks into the sepulcher and sees the angels.

"Woman, why are you crying?" they ask her.

She answers, "They have taken my Lord away, and I don't know where they have put him." Mary is not startled by the angels, as the women who preceded her were. Perhaps she did not even recognize that they were angels. We read, therefore, that "at this, she turned around and saw Jesus standing there" (John 20:14).

Rabboni

Mary did not recognize Jesus, even after he had spoken to her. It is foolish to ask why she didn't recognize him. Later when he presented himself to the Emmaus disciples, they did not recognize him either; so perhaps his appearance was changed. Besides, Mary was not seeing clearly, and she certainly did not expect the resurrection. "Woman, why are you crying? Who is it you are looking for?" It was the voice of Jesus, but Mary did not recognize it. She imagined that the One speaking to her was the gardener.

Mary answered in what is surely one of the most touching sentences in all human literature. "Sir, if you have carried him away, tell me where you have put him, and I will get him."

Barnhouse writes of this poignant offer, "She was still thinking in terms of a dead body. She had been weeping for three days and three nights and her heart was empty even though she still had a few tears left. She had passed through unutterable anguish and had been for many hours without sleep. She had been three times out to the tomb and twice back to the town. [Now] she offered to carry away the full weight of the body of a man, plus the hundred pound weight of myrrh and aloes. The Bible tells us that the body had been anointed with one hundred pounds of spices which Nicodemus had wrapped in the linen which enshrouded the body (John 19:39). Even if Jesus were slight of weight, Mary was offering, without thinking, to carry away a weight of body and linen cloth and ointments which would go beyond the strength of many a strong man. But she did not think of this for she loved the Lord Jesus Christ, and though her faith and hope were dead, her love was strong. Here is one of the greatest character portrayals in all of literature, human or divine. Here is the heart of a good woman. Here is love, offering to do the impossible as love always does."[2]

At this point Mary must have turned her back on Christ once again; for later, after he had called her name, we read that she turned back to him. She was not interested in the gardener. She had made her request of him in her grief and confusion. But her heart was still true to the Lord, and she turned back to the tomb where she had seen his body last.

"Mary!"

"Rabboni (Master)!"

As Mary responded to his pronunciation of her name, she turned back to Christ again. When she had supposed him to be only the gardener, she had no interest in him or anything he might say. But now she had heard her name from Jesus' lips; and as sheep know the voice of their shepherd when he calls them by name, so she recognized him and responded joyfully, "Master!" In that moment Mary experienced her own resurrection, for she was reborn. Faith had died, but now it came leaping from its tomb. Hope had evaporated, but now it gathered again around the person of the Lord.

The Greatest of These

You may be one who has never known any of these three responses to Jesus Christ—neither faith nor hope nor love. You say that you cannot believe, that you have no grounds for hope, that you do not see how you can love him. If this is your case, may I suggest that you begin with love. Begin with the knowledge that he loves you. That love is shown by his death for you. He commends his love to you by this fact. The Book of Romans says, "But God demonstrates his love for us in this: While we were still sinners, Christ died for us" (Rom. 5:8). Can you not focus on his death on your behalf and love him for that? I am convinced that if you do focus on his death, you will hear him call your name and, when he does, you will recognize him and respond gladly.

"John! Mary! Peter! Alice! James! (Whatever your name is!)"

"Master!" In that moment faith will be born in you and hope will triumph. You will be his forever.

Faith, hope, and love! Three great virtues! "But the greatest of these is love" (1 Cor. 13:13).

256

New Relationships for a New Age

John 20:17

Jesus said, "Do not hold on to me, for I have not yet returned to the Father. Go instead to my brothers and tell them, 'I am returning to my Father and your Father, to my God and your God.'"

$$I$$n the last century the well-known German historian Adolf Harnack made popular a phrase that in his judgment summed up the whole of Christianity: "the fatherhood of God and the brotherhood of man." This, said Harnack, is the teaching of the Scriptures. We all have one father, and we are all brothers and sisters in the one family of God, which is the human race.

Harnack should have known better than that, for in defining the message of the Bible in this way he made two fundamental errors. First, the use of the word "Father" for God and the words "brother" and "sister" for men and women occurs only in reference to believers. God is not said to be the Father of all men, nor are all men and women said to be brothers and sisters. In fact, as in the case of Christ's conversation with the rulers of his day (found in John 8), some persons are said to be children of their "father the devil" (John 8:44). We are all God's offspring, as Paul indicated in speaking to the

Athenians (Acts 17:28). We are his creatures. But only those who believe on Christ are said to be *children* of their heavenly Father.

Second, Harnack erred in failing to see that the relationships of which the Bible speaks are not things intrinsic to humanity but rather something new that has been established by the death, burial, and resurrection of Jesus Christ.

This latter truth is particularly evident in the verses to which we come now, because in these verses, for the first time and therefore significantly following his death and resurrection, Jesus begins to introduce these themes into his teaching. He had spoken of God as Father before, but not in this way. Before this he had not referred to the disciples as brothers at all. Now because of the new age of the church that he had ushered in, he also ushers in a new set of relationships.

It is interesting to contrast what Jesus did as he entered into his kingdom with what another king, mentioned in literature, did as he entered into his. The king is Henry V, whose character is carefully analyzed by Shakespeare in the three plays *Henry IV, Part 1, Henry IV, Part 2,* and *Henry V.* In his youth the young prince Hal had friends who were not a credit to him. They were low types, the kind who spent their time drinking, gambling, and running around with loose women. The best known of these lowly companions was John Falstaff about whom other plays were written. In these days Henry did not live like a king. But the time came when he ascended the throne and, although his friends thought that now they would be ushered into the palace and be able to carry on their dissolute life under the king's protection, the new king turned his back on them and began to conduct himself as worthy of his new position.

In a similar way our Lord had what we might call "low" companions during the days of his earthly ministry, though of course he did not defile himself through his association with them. But by contrast, when he entered into glory through his death, resurrection, and ascension, he did not turn his back on his companions but rather ushered them into relationships that before this were uniquely his own. Now God becomes their Father as well as his, and they are given family privileges.

A Problem Text

There are three new relationships in this verse: a new relationship to Christ, a new relationship to the Father, and a new relationship to one another. But this is a problem verse, and it is only when we understand the importance of the first of these new relationships, the new relationship to Christ, that we can begin to sort out the difficulties.

The main difficulty is that the Lord tells Mary Magdalene, "Do not hold on to me, for I have not yet returned to the Father." Yet we know from a parallel incident in Matthew that he apparently allowed the other women who had been to the tomb to touch him just a few minutes later on the same day (Matt. 28:9). Again, we might ask, "Why shouldn't Mary touch him?" This would have been the most natural thing in the world, and it seems harsh to our way of thinking to have Jesus rebuke her or stop her obvious act of love and adoration in midcourse.

We must acknowledge that there is no general agreement by commentators on how to interpret this verse. Nor can we even say that there is a conservative view versus a liberal one. Students of the Gospel are simply undecided. The three general categories of interpretation are, however, well suggested by the footnote at the bottom of page 1156 in the New Scofield edition of the Bible. It suggests, "(1) That Jesus spoke to Mary, acting, as it were, as the High Priest fulfilling the Day of Atonement (Lev. 16). Having accomplished the sacrifice, He was on His way to present the sacred blood in heaven; and, between the meeting with Mary in the garden and the meeting of Mt. 28:9, He had so ascended and returned—a view in harmony with types. (2) That Mary was gently rebuked by Christ in the command, 'Touch me not' (lit., 'Stop clinging to me'). The Lord taught Mary that now she must not seek to hold Him to the earth but, rather, become His messenger of new joy. And (3) that He merely meant: 'Do not detain me now; I am not yet ascended; you will see me again; run rather to my brethren,' etc."[1]

One thing we can say of this difficulty: it does suggest the basic reliability of the narratives, as do all apparent contradictions or difficulties. If the writers of the four Gospels were making their stories up in collusion with each other, they would certainly not have allowed such problems to stand. Matthew and John would not have allowed the contradiction between one person being forbidden to touch Jesus and others being permitted to touch him, or at least they would have provided some explanation. They would have settled on how many angels there were at the tomb and who saw them. They would either have explained why Jesus was not always recognized or else have eliminated this obvious embarrassment to their claims concerning the resurrection. The reason why these difficulties are allowed to stand is that, whatever the explanation of them may be and whether or not the disciples themselves knew the explanation, this is simply the way things happened. Consequently, they record them accurately as witnesses. The alleged discrepancies have the ring of truth about them.

Yet that does not help us determine how this verse should be taken. I would suggest that whatever the particular tone of the words may be and whether or not Christ actually ascended to the Father many times between his resurrection and final ascension from the Mount of Olives forty days later (I believe he did, though not for the reasons suggested by the first of the Scofield notes), the main sense of the passage is that Mary's relationship to Jesus (and also that of the other disciples) is now different. They are to know him in a different way than they did during the days of his earthly ministry.

Here a verse from Paul's second letter to the Corinthians is illuminating. Paul says in the context of arguing that all things have become new for those who are in Christ, "So from now on we regard no one from a worldly point of view. Though we once regarded Christ in this way, we do so no longer"

(5:16). To know Christ after the flesh is obviously to know him as the disciples did during the days of his earthly ministry—as a man whom they could hear and see and handle (cf. 1 John 1:1–3). To know him as we do today is to know him spiritually, that is, by the internal testimony of the Holy Spirit who reveals the Lord Jesus Christ to us as the Son of God and Savior. We notice, for example, that this is the emphasis with which this chapter of John ends, for John summarizes his account of Christ's works by saying, "Jesus did many other miraculous signs in the presence of his disciples, which are not recorded in this book. But these are written that you may believe that Jesus is the Christ, the Son of God, and that by believing you may have life in his name" (20:30–31).

This means that Mary was now to know Christ as her Savior, and we are to know him as the Son of God and our Savior too. Do you thus know him? The Holy Spirit is given to lead you to that knowledge. Come to him. Believe on him. If you do not know him as the Son of God and your Savior, you do not really know him at all. If you do, then the other relationships follow.

God Our Father

The first new relationship which follows upon our new relationship to Christ is a vertical one. It is our relationship to God the Father. But we must notice that while it is analogous to Jesus' relationship to the Father, it is nevertheless not identical to his. It has been pointed out many times by those who have studied this verse that when our Lord said that he was ascending to the Father he did not say, "I am returning to *our* Father and *our* God." He said rather, "I am returning to my Father and your Father, to my God and your God." If he had said the former, he would have been putting himself on the same level as the disciples—as a man only. Instead, he indicates that while it is true that God has now become our Father in a way that was not true previously, this is nevertheless not the same as his relationship. He is the Son of God in a unique sense, for he is God (cf. John 1:1–2; 10:30). We enter into an analogous relationship only because of what he has done for us through his atonement.

What is involved here is our adoption into the family of God. We are not naturally born into God's family. We are alienated from God and are born outside it as heirs of sin and death. But God is gracious; therefore, by the death of Christ and by the application of that death to us by the Holy Spirit, God brings us back into fellowship with himself and grants us family privileges.

Could anything be more utterly unexpected or overwhelming than the new relationship with God that is bestowed on his children? It is hard to think so. Justification is overwhelming enough, for it is all of grace. God did not need to justify us. Having justified us he could still have left us on a much inferior level of status and privilege. But he has gone far beyond what we could ever conceive of or expect by taking us into his own family where our status and privilege are that of daughters and sons. So great is God's condescension in this act of adoption that we would be inclined to dismiss this relationship, thinking it presumption, were it not that God has made a special effort to seal these truths to our hearts. As Paul has written, "No eye has seen, no ear has heard, no mind has conceived what God has prepared for those who love him—but God has revealed it to us by his Spirit" (1 Cor. 2:9–10).

What are these privileges? One is prayer, for access to God is based on our adoption. It is only because of our adoption that we can approach God as "Father," and it is only through the Spirit of adoption that we can be assured that he is indeed our Father and that our prayers are heard by him. This is what Paul is speaking of when he says, "For you did not receive a spirit that makes you a slave again to fear, but you received the Spirit of sonship. And by him we cry, 'Abba, Father'" (Rom. 8:15).

A second and related privilege of our new relationship to God is that we can have confidence before him. We are his children, and we can know that nothing can ever destroy that relationship. If God is our Father, he will help us in the days of our spiritual infancy, teaching us to walk spiritually and lifting us up when we fall down. If he is our Father, he will care for us throughout the days of our earthly pilgrimage and will abundantly bless us. As our Father, he will guide us in the way we should go and eventually bring us home to heaven to be with him forever.

Brothers and Sisters

It is not only that Christians have a new relationship to God as a result of his act of adoption. They also have a new relationship to one another. Before, they were outside the family of God, each going his or her own way in opposition to and sometimes in only thinly veiled hostility toward each other. Now they belong to a new family and must love each other and work together as brothers and sisters. "Consequently, you are no longer foreigners and aliens, but fellow citizens with God's people and members of God's household" (Eph. 2:19).

This is suggested by the word "brethren" in our text. It is a powerful and unexpected word, for it has not been used in this sense before in John's Gospel. The word occurs four times in chapters 2 and 7. But on each occasion it refers to those who were Christ's brethren according to the flesh, that is, to the children of Mary by Jesus' adoptive father, Joseph. In chapter 20, for the first time (and once more in 21:23), it refers to those who have believed on Christ and have therefore entered into God's family.

The attitudes that should flow from these new relationships do not always follow naturally or easily. But that is all the more reason to grasp this concept forcefully and work at the relationships. John White has put the task in these terms, "You were cleansed by the same blood, regenerated by the same Spirit. You are a citizen of the same city, a slave of the same master, a reader of the same Scriptures, a worshiper of the same God. The same presence dwells silently in you as in them. Therefore you are committed to them and

they to you. They are your brothers, sisters, your fathers, mothers and children in God. Whether you like or dislike them, you belong to them. You
have responsibilities toward them that must be discharged in love. As long
as you live on this earth, you are in their debt. Whether they have done much
or little for you, Christ has done all. He demands that your indebtedness to
him be transferred to your new family."[2]

Membership in God's family does not mean that we will be insensitive to
faults on the human level. Indeed, we must be sensitive to them if we are to
have any hope of reducing them and improving the quality of our family fellowship. But it does mean that we will not be overly sensitive to the faults of
our brothers and sisters in Christ and even less that we will be critical. Instead, we will be intensely committed to each other with a proper family loyalty and will work to help each other live the Christian life.

257

The Best News Ever Heard

John 20:18

Mary Magdalene went to the disciples with the news: "I have seen the Lord!" And she told them that he had said these things to her.

The story of Christ's appearance to Mary Magdalene and his commissioning her to tell the disciples of his resurrection concludes with the statement that she did what he told her to do. This is deceptively simple because it is actually a record of the first announcement of the best news this world has ever heard. It was an announcement of the Lord's resurrection.

When World War II ended, the joyful news was flashed around the globe, and at once people everywhere were ecstatic. I was just a lad at the time. My father had been in the service for some years, and the family was then stationed at a large military base in the southern United States. We were far from the action. But even now I can recall the yelling and shouting that occurred when news came of the war's end. The ending of World War II was great news. Yet, great as that news was, it did not compare with the truly stupendous news of the resurrection of Jesus Christ. This message was better then, and it is even better today.

Unshakable Evidence

Let me ask a very simple question and then give a few plain answers. Why is the resurrection of Jesus Christ the best news the world has ever heard? The answers are: because it is true, because it came after an apparent defeat, because of all that it proves, and finally because it demands a lifesaving response from each of us.

First, Jesus' resurrection is good news *because it is true.* It is always possible to have reports of events that sound like good news but later prove to be disappointments because the facts of the reports are wrong or the events did not actually happen. Referring again to World War II, this very thing occurred several times before the war really ended. False reports of the war's end spread; they were eventually proved false and so were terribly disappointing. The same was true of reports of a near end to the war in Vietnam. This was not the case with news of Jesus' resurrection.

We do not have space in one message to go into the evidences for the resurrection of Jesus Christ at length, but we can suggest a few of them. The first great evidence for the resurrection of Jesus Christ is the evidence of the narratives themselves. These stand up to the most stringent of critical scrutinies. To begin with, they are apparently four independent accounts. They were obviously not made up in collusion; for if they were, they would not possess the number of apparent contradictions they contain: the number of angels at the tomb, the number of women who went to the garden, the time of their arrival, and other things. These accounts can be harmonized, but the point is this: had the writers gotten together to make up a story, the apparent discrepancies would have been eliminated. On the other hand, it is also apparent that they did not make up the stories separately, for if they had done this, there would never have been the large measure of agreement they possess. The setting and the characters are the same, and the sequence of events makes sense. What does this mean? Just this: If the accounts were not made up in collusion and if they were not made up separately, the only remaining possibility is that they were not made up at all. That is, they are four true, independent accounts by those who knew the facts they wrote.

Next there is the evidence of the empty tomb, coupled with the evidence of the moved stone and the undisturbed graveclothes. How are we to account for these things? Some have imagined that either the Roman or Jewish authorities moved the body. But they had no reason to do this, especially since it would have involved violating the officially sealed tomb; and, had this occurred, it is inconceivable that the true circumstances would not have been revealed later after the disciples had appeared in Jerusalem, proclaiming their belief in Jesus' resurrection. It would have been easy for Jesus' enemies to produce a body had there been one. On the other hand, the friends of Christ did not steal the body of Jesus, for they would hardly have been willing to die (as most of them later did) for a deception.

It is possible to add the changed character of these men as an evidence, for whatever happened turned them from disillusioned cowards into mighty proclaimers of the Christian message.

Then, too, we must add the fact that Jesus appeared, not just to one or two women in a garden under somewhat eerie circumstances, but to a wide variety of people in numerous circumstances. Paul lists many such appearances, noting that one time Jesus appeared to a group of five hundred believers (1 Cor. 15:6).

Again, one of the great evidences of the resurrection is the unexpected and unnatural change of the day of worship from Saturday, the Jewish day of worship, to Sunday in Christian services. Nothing but the resurrection of Jesus on Sunday explains it.

What are we to say of these evidences? Matthew Arnold, not overstating the case, once said, "The resurrection of Jesus Christ is the best attested fact in history." Lawyers in particular have seen this truth. Some of the best books on the resurrection have been written by lawyers, some of whom originally set out to disprove it. I am thinking of men like Frank Morison, Gilbert West, J. N. D. Anderson, and others. Sir Edward Clark, another English jurist, once wrote, "As a lawyer I have made a prolonged study of the evidences for the first Easter day. To me the evidence is conclusive, and over and over again in the High Court I have secured the verdict on evidence not nearly so compelling. . . . As a lawyer I accept it unreservedly as the testimony of men to facts that they were able to substantiate."[1]

This is the first reason why the resurrection of Jesus Christ is good news. It is good news, not merely because it is a nice story which gives us an opportunity for a holiday once a year, but because it is true. As truth it is one of the most stupendous and important facts of history.

Wellington Defeated

Second, the resurrection of Jesus Christ is good news *because it came after an apparent defeat*. A victory is always good news, but news of victory after news that a battle has apparently been lost is even better.

Let me illustrate this by the way in which news of the Battle of Waterloo first came to England. There were no telegrams or radio sets in those days, but everyone knew that a great battle was pending and they were anxious to hear what would happen when Wellington, the British general, faced Napoleon. A signalman was placed on the top of Winchester Cathedral with instructions to keep his eye on the sea. When he received a message, he was to pass the message on to another man on a hill. That man was to pass it to another. And so it was to go until news of the battle was finally relayed to London and then across England. At length a ship was sighted through thick fog on the English Channel. The signalman on board sent the first word—"Wellington." The next word was "defeated." Then fog prevented the ship from being seen. "Wellington defeated!" The message was sent across England, and gloom descended over the countryside. After two or three hours the fog lifted, and the signal came again: "Wellington defeated the enemy!" Then England rejoiced.

In the same way, Jesus' death plunged his friends into sadness. It was an apparent defeat. But on the third day he rose again in victory. When Jesus died men might have cried, "Christ is defeated, wrong has triumphed, sin has won." But after three days the fog lifted and the full message came through to the world: "Jesus is risen; he has defeated the enemy."

Essential Doctrines

Third, the resurrection is good news *because of all that it proves*. What does it prove? The answer is: It proves all that needs to be proved. It proves the essential doctrines of Christianity.

In the first place, it proves that there is a God and that the God of the Bible is the true God. Reuben A. Torrey, who often spoke and wrote well on these themes, put it this way: "Every effect must have an adequate cause . . . and the only cause adequate to account for the resurrection of Christ is God, the God of the Bible. While here on earth, as everyone who has carefully read the story of his life knows, our Lord Jesus went up and down the land proclaiming God, the God of the Bible, 'the God of Abraham, Isaac and Jacob' as he loved to call him, the God of the Old Testament as well as the New. He said that men would put him to death, that they would put him to death by crucifixion, and he gave many details as to what the manner of his death would be. He further said that after his body had been in the grave three days and three nights, God, the God of Abraham, the God of Isaac and the God of Jacob, the God of the Bible, the God of the Old Testament as well as the God of the New Testament, would raise him from the dead. This was a great claim to make. It was an apparently impossible claim. For centuries men had come and men had gone, men had lived and men had died, and so far as human knowledge founded upon definite observation and experience was concerned, that was the end of them. But this man Jesus does not hesitate to claim that his experience will be directly contrary to the uniform experience of long, long centuries. . . .

"That was certainly an acid test of the existence of the God he preached, and his God stood the test. He did exactly the apparently impossible thing that our Lord Jesus said he would do. . . . The fact that Jesus was thus miraculously and marvelously raised makes it certain that the God who did it really exists and that the God he preached is the true God."[2]

Second, the resurrection proves Jesus' deity. When Jesus lived on earth, he claimed to be equal to God and that God, this God, would raise him from the dead three days after his execution by the Roman authorities. If he was wrong in this, his claim was either the raving of a deranged man or blasphemy. If he was right, the resurrection would be God's way of substantiating the claim. Did he substantiate it? Did Jesus rise from the dead? Yes, he did! So the resurrection is God's seal on Christ's claim to divinity. This is why Paul, who knew that Jesus had been raised, writes that Jesus was "declared with power to be the Son of God by his resurrection from the dead" (Rom. 1:4). This is good news! If Jesus is God, then God is like Jesus. It means that God is not distant, arbitrary, or unreal. He is a God who loves us and who came to earth to give himself a ransom for our sins.

Then, too, the resurrection proves that all who believe in Jesus Christ are justified before God. Paul teaches this in Romans also, for he states that Jesus "was delivered over to death for our sins and was raised to life for our justification" (Rom. 4:25). How does this happen? Jesus had claimed that his death would atone for man's sin. He said that he had come "to give his life as a ransom for many" (Matt. 20:28). He died as he said. But the question still remained: Can it be true that the death of this one man is acceptable to God on behalf of others? Suppose he had sinned? In that case, he would have been dying for his own sin rather than the sins of others. Did he sin? Or was his atonement accepted? Three days pass. Christ rises. Thus, his claim is established. God has shown by the resurrection that Christ was sinless and that he has accepted his atonement.

Torrey said this: "When Jesus died, he died as my representative, and I died in him; when he arose, he rose as my representative, and I arose in him; when he ascended up on high and took his place at the right hand of the Father in the glory, he ascended as my representative and I ascended in him, and today I am seated in Christ with God in the heavenlies. I look at the cross of Christ, and I know that atonement has been made for my sins; I look at the open sepulcher and the risen and ascended Lord, and I know the atonement has been accepted. There no longer remains a single sin on me, no matter how many or how great my sins may have been."[3]

The resurrection of Jesus Christ also proves that the believer in Christ can have a supernatural victory over sin in this life, for Jesus lives to provide supernatural power to do it. This is an argument developed in the sixth chapter of Romans. In the opening verses of that chapter Paul writes, "We were therefore buried with him through baptism into death in order that, just as Christ was raised from the dead through the glory of the Father, we too may live a new life" (Rom. 6:4). This means that by faith all who believe in Christ are united to Christ so that his power becomes available to them. We may be weak and utterly helpless, unable to resist temptation for a single minute. But he is strong, and he lives to give help and deliverance. Victory is never a question of our strength, but of his power. His power is what we need.

Torrey, whom I have just quoted, tells a story that illustrates this point. He tells of four men who were once climbing the most difficult face of the Matterhorn. There was a guide, a tourist, a second guide, and a second tourist, all roped together. As they went over a particularly difficult place, the lower tourist lost his footing and went over the side. The sudden pull on the rope carried the lower guide with him, and he carried the other tourist along also. Three men were dangling over the cliff. But the guide who was in the lead, feeling the first pull upon the rope, drove his ax into the ice, braced his feet, and held fast. The first tourist then regained his footing, the guide regained his, and the lower tourist followed. They then went on and up in safety.

So it is in this life. As the human race ascended the icy cliffs of life, the first Adam lost his footing and tumbled headlong over the abyss. He pulled the next man after him, and the next and the next until the whole race hung in deadly peril. But the second Adam, the Lord Jesus Christ, kept his footing. He stood fast. Thus, all who are united to him by a living faith are secure and can regain the path.[4]

Finally, Jesus' resurrection is evidence for our own resurrection and of a life with Jesus in glory beyond the grave. Jesus said when he was here on earth, "I am going . . . to prepare a place for you. And if I go and prepare a place for you, I will come back and take you to be with me that you also may be where I am" (John 14:2–3). He is preparing that place now. Can we trust him? Was he telling the truth? The resurrection vindicates these claims.

Come and Learn

I have given three good reasons why the resurrection of Jesus Christ is the best news this world has ever heard: (1) because it is true, (2) because it came after an apparent defeat, and (3) because of what it proves. But there is a fourth reason also. Jesus' resurrection is good news *because it demands a life-saving response in faith from each of us.* Have you responded in faith to this One who died for you and rose again on that far-off first Easter morning?

This is worth asking, because we recall that according to Mark's Gospel those to whom Mary first gave this report did not respond positively. They did not believe her: "When they heard that Jesus was alive and that she had seen him, they did not believe it" (16:11). It was only after Christ's further appearances and a further proclamation of the message that they came to him.

There is some news that is restricted by its very nature. It applies to one or two individuals but not to everyone. A promotion is good news to the man who receives it but not to the two or three others who failed to get the job. The results of an election are good news to the winning party but not to the losing party. Even so generally applicable a report as a reduction of federal taxes is good only to those who pay taxes or who live in the country where the reduction is to take place. Almost all human news is so restricted. But the news of the resurrection is for all. What is your relationship to the risen Lord? Have you heard the good news? Have you believed it? Have you trusted in him? This is the heart of Christianity. It is not to be found in the liturgies of the churches, nor in the specific formulations of Christian theology, important as they may be. Christianity is Christ, the risen Christ. He died and rose again for you. Won't you come to him?

258

The Real Last Words of Christ

John 20:19–20

On the evening of that first day of the week, when the disciples were together, with the doors locked for fear of the Jews, Jesus came and stood among them and said, "Peace be with you!" After he said this, he showed them his hands and side. The disciples were over-joyed when they saw the Lord.

I do not know who it was who first conceived the idea of preaching on the so-called "seven last words of Christ," but whoever he was, he certainly struck upon a popular note. From my early days I remember sermons preached on this theme, generally on Good Friday or during the weeks preceding Easter. No doubt you remember many such sermon series also. It has always struck me as a bit incongruous, however, that in speaking of the seven last words of Christ the choice has always been made of those words spoken by Jesus in the hours immediately preceding his death by crucifixion—"Father, forgive them; for they do not know what they are doing" (Luke 23:34); "Woman, here is your son" (John 19:26); "Today you will be with me in paradise" (Luke 23:43); "I am thirsty" (John 19:28); "My God, my God, why have you forsaken me?" (Mark 15:34; Matt. 27:46); "Father, into your hands I commit my spirit" (Luke 23:46); "It is fin-

1587

ished" (John 19:30)—when actually these were not the last words Christ spoke upon earth nor, for that matter, even the most significant.

To say that these sentences were the *last* words of Christ is to imply that with the speaking of them the words of Christ ceased. It is to say that there was no resurrection. Since this is wrong, I am going to suggest that in the closing chapters of John's Gospel we actually have a series of "last" words, spoken after the resurrection, which may be more important and may have a greater claim to our attention than the sayings more commonly thought of.

What are these words? They are: "Peace be with you" (20:19–21); "As the Father has sent me, so I am sending you" (20:21); "Receive the Holy Spirit" (20:22); "Stop doubting and believe" (20:27); "Blessed are those who have not seen, and yet have believed" (20:29); "Feed my sheep" (21:16–17; cf. v. 15); and "Follow me" (21:19; cf. v. 22). These seven sayings may be described as: a great bequest, a great commission, a great consolation, a great challenge, a great benediction, a great responsibility, and a great invitation. We are going to look at the first of these—a great bequest—in this study.

Shalom

John introduces this first great word of the Lord Jesus Christ by writing, "On the evening of that first day of the week, when the disciples were together, with the doors locked for fear of the Jews, Jesus came and stood among them and said, *'Peace be with you!'* After he said this, he showed them his hands and side. The disciples were overjoyed when they saw the Lord" (20:19–20).

I know that when Jesus greeted his disciples by speaking of peace in the upper room on the evening of the day in which he rose from the dead, he used a very common greeting. The word was *Shalom*. It was often used the way we use the word "Hello." Still, there is more to it than that. For one thing, it was never used in a flippant manner. It did not mean "Hi." It was a serious greeting. For another, it was always related in some measure to the thought of peace being God's gift, and is therefore much more closely paralleled in English by the wish, "God bless you."

Moreover, in the New Testament the thought of God's giving peace to men is always connected with what Jesus accomplished by his death and resurrection. Thus, in the Book of Romans Paul writes of peace as one of the results of our justification: "Therefore, since we have been justified through faith, we have peace with God through our Lord Jesus Christ" (Rom. 5:1). It is certainly in this sense that Jesus uses the word in his greeting to the assembled group of disciples. He had gone to the cross. He had been raised from the dead. Now, as the result of what he had accomplished, he was dispensing real peace to those who believed on him.

What is peace? One definition applies the word to a relationship between countries, calling it "an agreement to end hostilities." Another calls it "public order." A third definition calls peace "harmony in personal relations."

None of these definitions, good as they are, does justice to what Jesus really meant when he offered peace to men.

When Jesus spoke of peace to his disciples he was speaking, first of all, of peace *with* God. This is the peace bought by his suffering on the cross, and it is significant because of the fact that people are not at peace with God naturally. According to the Bible men are at war with God. They are opposed to him. Consequently, it was up to God to make peace through Christ's cross.

It follows from this that the peace must be on God's terms. Aboard the battleship USS *Missouri* in Tokyo Bay, off the coast of Japan, General Douglas MacArthur, commander of the armed forces of the United States in the Far East, received the symbols of surrender of the Japanese people. Japan had been decisively defeated as a result of the war in the Pacific, and she surrendered on this occasion on America's terms. What would we think of a case in which the Japanese arrived at the peace table prepared to bargain on terms of a settlement? We would say, "How ridiculous! The time for bargaining is past." At this point, MacArthur was to dictate terms of peace, and the people of Japan were to receive them.

"Well," says God, "if you recognize this truth on the human level, recognize it spiritually. This is the way it must be between myself and rebellious, sinful men and women. People come to me to present their terms. They say, 'If you do so-and-so for me, then I'll serve you and we can get along together.' But there is no room for bargaining. If you want peace, you must receive it in the way I provide it. Jesus died to make peace. If you are going to enter into my peace, it must be by faith in him and what he has done."

The wonderful thing is that when we come to God on such terms we find that he is not hostile. He is no longer looking toward us in wrath. There are no frowns. Instead, he receives us with smiles and makes us his daughters and sons.

The Peace of God

When Christ offers us peace he does so in another sense also. It is true that he offers us peace *with* God. This is what is mentioned in the verse I quoted from Romans: "Therefore, since we have been justified through faith, we have peace with God through our Lord Jesus Christ" (5:1). But it is also true—gloriously true—that he offers us the peace *of* God also. It is God's own peace offered to us. The Bible speaks of this peace when it says, "Do not be anxious about anything, but in everything, by prayer and petition, with thanksgiving, present your requests to God. And the peace of God, which transcends all understanding, will guard your hearts and your minds in Christ Jesus" (Phil. 4:6–7).

This was a wonderful word for the disciples. They had gone through the most traumatic week of their lives. For three years they had followed Jesus in and out of hundreds of villages in Palestine and had come both to know and love him. They had watched him do miracles. They had heard him teach. They knew that hostility was growing against Jesus on the part of the Jewish rulers. They had warned him not to go to Jerusalem. Still they were unprepared for what happened. Suddenly, there was an arrest by night in the Garden of Gethsemane, and they scattered in fear, presumably returning in the dark to Bethany. Jesus did not appear. When these frightened men finally got to Jerusalem several days later, after much agony, they learned that the worst had happened. Jesus had been tried and crucified. Then, almost on top of that, and before they had even adjusted to the thought of his death and burial, word came of an empty tomb and of several alleged resurrection appearances.

If ever there was an agitated and confused group, it was this small, fearful band of Christ's disciples. But then Jesus came! One minute they were alone. The next minute he was there. How glad they were to hear him calm their troubled spirits and still their hearts. "Peace! Peace be unto you!"

Do you know this peace? There is no peace in the world. Chamberlain promised the English people "peace in our time," but the words were scarcely out of his lips before Adolf Hitler was bombing Danzig for the start of World War 2. "Peace" was the cry of the students in the turbulent 60s, accompanied by their ubiquitous peace sign. But all the idealism, songs, drugs, and optimism of the decade did not create a peaceful world. We have had wars in every decade since, many of them—in South America, Africa, the Balkans, the Middle East, and other places.

This might not be so bad if it were possible for those who truly want peace to find it in the privacy of their souls. If only we could escape to a place of inner rest, away from those who hate peace and fight others for their own selfish gains. But that place does not exist, and the reason it does not exist is that we carry the seeds of turmoil in our hearts. Our basic problem is that we are not at peace with God, and deep within we know that this is the case. Moreover, this disharmony constantly breaks forth to disturb our relationships with other people and even our own personal repose. We are all agitated people. But Jesus made peace between his Father and all who trust in him by his reconciling death for sinners on the cross. Because those who know and trust Christ have heen given peace with God they can now also experience peace with others and in the innermost recesses of their souls.

Do you know this peace? There are often difficulties in life. You may be experiencing some. There are upsetting events—the death of a relative or friend, the loss of a job leaving you without a sure future, the sting of failure, the loss of friends. There are other causes of upset and agitation. Yet Jesus offers peace in the midst of them.

Many Gifts

We must not think that when Jesus spoke of peace to the disciples he was listing all the benefits of his death for them. This was only one of many gifts which are the result of his death and resurrection.

One of the additional gifts is *access* to the presence of God through prayer (Rom. 5:2). Prayer is not for everyone. There is not a line in the Bible to suggest that God listens to, much less answers, the prayer of one who is not a believer in Jesus Christ. In fact, the Bible states explicitly that the only way in which anyone can come to God in prayer is through Jesus. He said, "I am the way and the truth and the life, no one comes to the Father except through me" (John 14:6). The best man or woman in this world is unable to come into the presence of God on the basis of any merit of his own. Yet, on the ground of the death of Christ, the worst sinner who ever walked the face of this earth but who has turned from his sin and accepted Jesus Christ as his Savior can come at any time of the day or night, any day of the year, and with boldness can speak out of the longing of his heart to God and receive what he asks.

The Bible also tells us that the death of Christ gives us a sure and certain *hope*. Hope refers to the future, more particularly to what lies beyond death. Before Christ died we knew nothing of what lay beyond. He said, "I am going to prepare a place for you. And if I go and prepare a place for you, I will come back and take you to be with me, that where I am, you also may be" (John 14:2–3). He *said* these things, but we could not be certain of them. He died. Then he rose again. Now we have one who has passed through the portal of death and who has returned. It is as he said. There is a future. There is a heavenly home, and he has gone to make it ready for us.

Are these the only results of Christ's death and resurrection? No, there are more. He gives us the Holy Spirit. He gives us eternal life. We have the Bible. We have a status before God as daughters and sons. We are heirs with Christ, coheirs with him of God's glory. We have his promises, among which is his promise to meet *all* our needs "according to his glorious riches in Christ Jesus" (Phil. 4:19).

His Messengers

The final point of Christ's words to the disciples on the occasion of his first appearance to them after his resurrection was that they now had a job to do. Jesus said, "Peace be with you" (v. 21). This was for them. But if they had received God's peace through faith in his death and resurrection—as well as his many other gifts—they were nevertheless not at liberty to keep the good news to themselves. Now they were to become his messengers.

Have you believed in the Lord Jesus Christ as your Savior? Is he your Lord? If so, this commission applies to you also. How will you heed it? Will you begrudge the time it takes, giving God the bare minimum of your effort? Or will you give him your entire self to be used by him as he desires? Only the latter course assures deep personal blessing.

There is a story told in folklore of a king who commanded his subjects to bring burlap bags to the palace. It was a peculiar request, to say the least, and naturally some of the subjects were offended. No one could understand why the king had commanded them to bring bags. Those who were offended brought the smallest sacks they could. Others brought old ones or ones filled with holes. When they arrived at the palace the king did not take the sacks from them. Instead he ushered them into his storerooms and invited them to fill their sacks with gold and carry it home. Those who had come resentfully with the smallest bags received very little while those who had brought the king the largest and best bags received more.

So it is spiritually. God asks for our all, but he does not do so to make us unhappy. His way is the way of blessing. God says, "Do not come to me with thimbles. Come to me with arms and hands wide open and see if I will not fill them with every spiritual blessing. If you will be my messengers, I will make your life full and make you a blessing."

259

"So Send I You"

John 20:21

Again Jesus said, "Peace be with you! As the Father has sent me, I am sending you."

The last two chapters of John contain what I have called "the real last words of Christ." Spoken after the resurrection, as opposed to those more commonly discussed words spoken from the cross, they are words of encouragement, instruction, and promise: "Peace be with you" (20:19); "As the Father has sent me, so I am sending you" (20:21); "Receive the Holy Spirit" (20:22); "Stop doubting and believe" (20:27); "Blessed are those who have not seen, and yet have believed" (20:29); "Feed my sheep" (21:16–17: cf. v. 15); "Follow me" (21:19; cf. v. 22).

Our text contains the second of these last words, though, as we will note, it follows quite closely upon the first and leads to the third. It is John's version of the Great Commission.

The Great Commission occurs five times in the New Testament, once at the end of each of the four Gospels and once in the opening chapter of Acts. The repetition is significant. Anything God says is important; if something is repeated more than once, it is especially important. Besides, in each case the emphasis is different. Matthew emphasizes the *authority* of the Lord. Standing on a mountain, presumably looking out over numerous towns and villages, Jesus says, "All authority in heaven and in earth has been given to me. Therefore, go and make disciples of all nations" (28:18–19). In Mark the emphasis is on the *final* judgment: "Whoever believes and is baptized will be saved; but whoever does not will be condemned" (16:16). Luke presents the commission as the *fulfillment of prophecy:* "This is what is written: The Christ will suffer and rise from the dead on the third day; and repentance and forgiveness of sins will be preached in his name to all nations, beginning at Jerusalem" (24:46–47). Acts presents a *program for world evangelization:* "You will be my witnesses in Jerusalem, and in all Judaea, and in Samaria, and to the ends of the earth" (1:8).

These words are drawn from a variety of circumstances and were spoken to a variety of people. John's version is unique in that it is probably the first expression of this command and links *our* commissioning to the prior commissioning of our Lord.

Peace Be with You

John's words are linked to the first of the seven last words, which occurs just two verses before. Lest we miss this connection, John repeats it in the verse which is our text. The full text says, "Peace be with you. As my Father has sent me, so I am sending you."

This is not accidental. In fact, the reason is apparent. It is simply that we must ourselves have peace, both inwardly and outwardly, before we can effectively preach the gospel of peace to others. There are two kinds of peace involved here, as we saw in our last study. The first is peace *with* God achieved by the death of the Lord on our behalf. In ourselves we are not at peace with God. We are at war with God. But Christ has made peace by bearing the punishment due us for our sins. In bestowing this peace he provides us with forgiveness of sins and the assurance of it. The second peace is the peace *of* God. The disciples were cowering in an upper room. They were afraid, but Jesus told them to have no fear but rather to be of good courage. They were in hiding, but he told them to abandon their shelter and go out into the world as his missionaries. Christ's words seem to be the opposite of the disciples' experience. But they are reasonable because of who it is who speaks them. He is the risen Lord. He was arrested, beaten, crucified. But he rose again. It is as the One who has been triumphant over death and sin that he now speaks peace to his followers.

John Stott writes of this passage, "We learn then that the Church's very first need, before it can begin to engage in evangelism, is an experience and an assurance of Christ's peace—peace of conscience through his death that banishes sin, peace of mind through his resurrection that banishes doubt. . . . Once we are glad that we have seen the Lord, and once we have clearly recognized him as our crucified and risen Savior, then nothing and no one will be able to silence us."[1]

Into the World

The gift of peace is not the characteristic emphasis of this verse, however. Instead, as we have already indicated, the emphasis is on the connection between our commissioning and the commissioning of the Lord Jesus Christ by his Father. These words are a command to evangelize, but they are more than this; they establish a pattern for us as we evangelize. The key words are "as" and "so"—"*As* my Father has sent me, *so* I am sending you." They mean that our mission in the world is to be patterned on Christ's. He was the first missionary; our labors are to be conducted like his.

But what does that mean specifically? The first thing it means is that, as Jesus was sent "into the world," so also are we sent "into the world." This *context* is not made explicit in John 20, but it is clearly stated in that verse from Christ's high priestly prayer which is a close parallel to it. There Jesus says, "As you sent me into the world, I have sent them into the world" (John 17:18). This is the principle of incarnation, the principle of becoming one with those we would help. Think how significant it is that Jesus came "into the world." It means that he did not stay in heaven, though he certainly could have. It means that he did not shout words of salvation to us from the safety of heaven's ramparts. Having determined to come down to us, he did not even then come in the effulgence of his divine glory but rather divested himself of that glory and appeared in humble form. In fact, he did not even appear in a human disguise, which is what the Gnostics taught, but actually became a human being, just like us. He was born; he grew; he suffered; eventually he died.

That is what it means to come "into the world." Since this is the way Jesus came into the world, this is the way we are to come also. We are to become one with those to whom we are sent. If we do not, we fail in carrying out the spirit even if not the letter of the Lord's commission.

Most of us are guilty at precisely this point, and the evangelical church in particular is guilty. We have retreated from the world rather than invading the world. We have retreated to the suburbs or whatever our equivalent may be. Schools, churches, magazines, institutions, individuals—many have done this. They have retreated to where it is nice or safe or nonthreatening, and as far as one can tell from their actions, what they are actually saying is that the world can go to hell. Shame on us! We spend millions of dollars to send faithful women and men overseas to tell the Good News there. But we will not go to our cities or neighbors if to do so costs us comfort or prestige.

Here is John Stott's statement of the problem. "I personally believe that our failure to obey the implications of this command is the greatest weakness of evangelical Christians in the field of evangelism today. We do not identify. We believe so strongly (and rightly) in proclamation, that we tend to proclaim our message from a distance. We sometimes appear like people who shout advice to drowning men from the safety of the seashore. We do not dive in to rescue them. We are afraid of getting wet, and indeed of greater perils than this. But Jesus Christ did not broadcast salvation from the sky. He visited us in great humility. . . . We cannot give up preaching, for proclamation is of the essence of salvation. Yet true evangelism, evangelism that is modeled on the ministry of Jesus, is not proclamation without identification any more than it is identification without proclamation. Evangelism involves both together."

Stott continues, "Frankly, this is my own greatest dilemma and problem as a parish minister. I love to preach the Gospel—to those who will listen to it. I find no greater joy in any ministerial activity than in the exposition of God's Word, whether to believers or to unbelievers, who come to Church (or even to open-air services) to hear it. But how are we to identify with the people of the parish who will not hear? That is the problem. How can we become so one with secular men and women, as Christ became one with us, that we express and demonstrate our love for them, and win a right to share with them the good news of Christ?"[2]

Do not think that I have a simple answer to this. I do not. I am ready to confess that this is also a great problem (and failure) for me as well. But while I do not know the full answer, I do know this: We are not really fulfilling the Great Commission until we live with, befriend, love, and enter into the experiences of those to whom we are sent.

If we are going to go into the world as Christ was in the world, we are going to have to learn how to become friends with unbelievers and then work out the issues of life by their side.

To Save Sinners

The second area in which our mission is to be patterned on the mission of Jesus is its *purpose*. We are sent into the world as Christ was sent into the world—that is context. But why are we sent into the world?—that is purpose. It is seen in Paul's solemn affirmation to Timothy: "Here is a trustworthy saying that deserves full acceptance: Christ Jesus came into the world to save sinners—of whom I am the worst" (1 Tim. 1:15). Christ came into the world to save sinners. And so must we, if we would be faithful to his commission.

This can be applied profitably on two levels. First, our purpose must actually be to see others saved and not merely to fulfill our duty as witnesses by unloading a certain presentation of the gospel on them. It is true that we cannot save anyone and that our duty in one sense is simply to be Christ's witnesses. We are to share the gospel with others whether they believe or not, knowing that ultimately the drawing of the unbeliever to Christ is God's doing. But this does not mean that we have no interest in whether or not they will believe or that we should not use every means at our disposal to see that they do. Do we talk too much? Perhaps. But it can never be that we overidentify or overwork while waiting for Christ to be formed in others by God.

Jesus said, "No one can come to me, unless the Father who sent me draws him" (John 6:44). But that did not prevent him from doing everything in his power to teach others and persuade them of the truth of the gospel.

The second way in which the verse may be applied is by stressing the word "sinners." In the first case, we stressed the word "save" ("Christ Jesus came into the world to *save* sinners"). Now we must say, "Christ Jesus came into the world to save *sinners.*" Those who consider themselves theologians may be raising the objection, "But aren't all of us sinners?" Of course, that is true. But I remember as well that our Lord once said, "I have not come to call the righteous, but sinners" (Matt. 9:13). Jesus had been eating in the house of Matthew, the tax collector, and many of Matthew's low friends had come to eat with him. The Pharisees had rebuked Jesus for associating with such people. They thought that it was beneath his dignity as a distinguished rabbi. Jesus did not buy this line of reasoning. Instead, he taught that it was precisely to such persons that he was sent.

That is what I am talking about. I am saying that if we would go into the world as Christ went into the world, we must go to such people. Someone has defined a banker as a man who lends money to those who can prove they do not need it and refuses to lend money to those who do. That may be an unfair appraisal of the banking industry, but it is accurate where the philosophy of the world is concerned. The world gives to those who can give back—with interest. It expends praise, kindness, and generosity on those who do not need them. But this is not Christ's way. He went to the bankrupt. If this is his way, it must be ours also.

What would Jesus say if he were here to instruct us? He would say, "When you invite someone to dinner, invite someone who will not be able to invite you back." He would say, "Feed the hungry; give drink to the thirsty; clothe him who has nothing; visit the prisoner. None of these are in a position to return the favor."

There is one more thing that comes from Paul's statement. It is an explanation of why we do not naturally think as Christ thinks. Notice that when Paul said, "Christ Jesus came into the world to save sinners" he went on to add "of whom I am chief." Jesus came to save sinners. Paul likewise went to sinners, and the reason Paul went is that he knew he was one of them. In fact, he was the chief. That suggests why we do *not* go. We think we are better than others and are concerned to maintain our position. We feel that we would have to stoop to save sinners, and we do not want to do it. Jesus had to stoop. He laid a real glory aside in order to become man and die for our salvation (Phil. 2:5–8). We do not have to stoop. We are beggars among beggars. Our task is that of one beggar telling another where to find bread. When we get that into our heads we will actually go to those who really need us and help them as the Lord did.

Glorified in Them

Not only is our mission to be like that of the Lord in its context and purpose, it is to be like his in its *goal* as well. What is that goal? Well, in John 17, in the midst of that prayer in which the Lord intercedes for us in regard to the lives we are to live in this world, Jesus said first, "I have brought you glory on earth," and then a little later added, "All I have is yours, and all you have is mine. And glory has come to me through them" (vv. 4, 10). These verses and others teach that the ultimate goal of Jesus' coming was to glorify the Father, that is, to make his glory known. Then, because our goal is to be patterned on his, they likewise teach that we are to glorify Jesus by our thoughts, words, and actions.

This is our mission: (1) We are to go into the world, as Jesus entered into the world; (2) We are to go so that people might be saved through faith in him; (3) We are to glorify Christ, as he glorified the Father.

Some years ago Peter K. Haile, assistant headmaster of the Stony Brook School on Long Island, told a story that illustrates this point and gives a closing challenge. He had a missionary friend, a woman doctor, who went to India on rather short notice because of a pressing need in a certain hospital. She had not had time to go to language school but instead was put to work in the hospital immediately, where she spoke through an interpreter. After she had been there a while she wrote to the Hailes expressing frustration and discouragement. She had been trying to show love and gentleness to the people, but they did not seem to be responding. She asked them to pray about it. A few weeks later another letter came, this time saying that she had discovered what the problem was. It was the translator. She had been loving, but he was apparently a rude, arrogant fellow who never conveyed her concern for the patients at all. He was a barrier to her message.

We are interpreters of the Lord Jesus Christ in this world. What is the picture of Jesus that others have through our speech and actions? What picture do they have of him in me? Do they see his glory? Or do they see my lack of concern, pride, and impatience? May God make us interpreters for Christ who present him as he truly is.

260

Sins Remitted and Retained

John 20:22–23

And with that he breathed on them and said, "Receive the Holy Spirit. If you forgive anyone his sins, they are forgiven; if you do not forgive them, they are not forgiven."

One of the points at which Roman Catholic and Protestant theology part company is over the interpretation of John 20:22–23. It is not a minor matter. Consequently, since I am a Protestant and since we have now come to this text in the course of our systematic exposition of John's Gospel, it is both necessary and proper to give the Protestant view of these verses.

We begin with the acknowledgment that there is much common ground between believing Catholics and believing Protestants and that in many areas this unity is far greater than that between conservatives and liberals in either of their camps. For example, both believe in the Trinity with its corresponding assertion of the full deity of both the Lord Jesus Christ and the Holy Spirit. Both believe in the virgin birth, works of healing, Jesus' resurrection, other miracles, and the giving of the Holy Spirit to Christ's followers. We believe in Jesus' vicarious death for our sins, the inspiration and authority of Scripture,

1599

the visible return of Christ, the resurrection of the dead, the final judgment, and other doctrines. The scope of this agreement is suggested by the nearly universal use throughout Christendom of the Apostles' Creed and the Nicene Creed, which contain these teachings.

Nevertheless, there *are* differences; otherwise there would not be the various ecclesiastical and theological divisions we have. To name just a few, there are differences in the way we view church traditions, the doctrine of justification, the church, sacraments, and the role of the clergy (which is of particular interest here). On the basis of this text and some others the Roman church has built its doctrine of a special priesthood to whom has been committed the power of absolution of sin. In normal practice this authority is exercised through the confessional. Most Catholics would acknowledge that in the ultimate analysis it is God who forgives sin and that this is on the basis of Christ's death. But they would add that God does so in response to the action of the priest so that where the priest absolves, God forgives, and where the priest does not absolve, God allows the sins and judgment to remain. Protestants maintain that this is all backward. What happens is that God first forgives; then, on the basis of that forgiveness, believers (both clergy and laymen) proclaim that this is so.

The issues are the way in which forgiveness of sins comes to men and women, the role of laymen and clergy and the nature of the Great Commission with which all this is inseparably connected. It is the difference between absolution and proclamation, between the priesthood of the Roman church and the priesthood of all believers in Protestantism.

Divine Forgiveness

Why, then, does the Protestant church take these verses, the third of Christ's "last" words, as it does? Is it not simply twisting a text that in its clearest and simplest sense seems to be granting a special authority to forgive sins to a special body of chosen men and their successors? Not at all. We maintain that this is not the clear or simple meaning of the text. Nor is it the theology of the Word of God generally. There are five reasons for thinking as we do.

1. It is a teaching of Scripture, reiterated on many occasions, that there is none who can forgive sins but God only. The power of forgiving sins is his prerogative. The clearest statement of this is from an incident early in Christ's ministry. Jesus had been preaching in a certain house when friends of a paralyzed man had lowered the invalid through the roof to Christ's feet. He saw their faith and said to the paralyzed man, "Son, your sins are forgiven" (Mark 2:5). Some of the scribes immediately objected, saying (to themselves), "Why does this fellow talk like that? He's blaspheming! Who can forgive sins but God alone?" (v. 7). This was a true principle. So the Lord used it to lead them to consider his claims to divinity. He showed that in this case the healing of the body and the forgiveness of sins would be identical; consequently, when

he healed the man, as he then did, it was proof that he had power to forgive sins and was therefore God (vv. 9–10). The argument would be meaningless if human beings were able to forgive sins under any circumstances whatever.

2. There is no instance in any of the New Testament books of any apostle taking on himself the authority to absolve or pardon anyone. This is important because it relates to a fundamental rule of Scripture interpretation, namely, that every text must be interpreted within its historical and biblical context, and never in isolation. To interpret this text correctly we must ask what Jesus meant by it and what the disciples understood him to be saying.

Did the apostles understand Christ to be imparting to them the authority to forgive sins? Not at all. If they did, they would undoubtedly have claimed and exercised such powers, which we do not find. Instead, when Peter said to Cornelius, "All the prophets testify *about him* that everyone who believes *in him* receives forgiveness of sins *through his name*" (Acts 10:43), he clearly reiterated three times over that remission of sins is in Christ and by Christ. Similarly, when Paul said, "Through Jesus the forgiveness of sins is proclaimed to you" (Acts 13:38), he was pointing to Christ alone as the remitter. What the apostles did in these and other instances is preach the gospel, declaring with authority the terms on which God forgives sins, namely, on the basis of Christ's death and through faith in him alone. As John Stott says, "The Apostles understood that the authority the risen Lord had given them was the authority of a preacher and not that of a priest."[1]

3. It is a fatal defect in the Roman view of the priesthood that believers other than the apostles were present on this occasion and that the authority here given, whatever it may be, must therefore have been given to them as well as to the apostles, and therefore to Christians generally. The reason for saying this is that the group to which Jesus spoke the words recorded by John was undoubtedly the same group about which Luke writes in the last chapter of his Gospel, and we know from Luke's account that it contained at least Cleopas and the other disciple who had been with him on the road to Emmaus (cf. Luke 24:18, 33; John 19:25), and probably others who were not apostles.

Moreover, this fits the context as a whole. For the authority to "remit or retain" is preceded by (1) the gift of peace, (2) the Great Commission, and (3) the impartation of the Holy Spirit, all of which are clearly given to all Christians. If the latter gift is restricted to a special order of clergy, then peace, the Great Commission, and the gift of the Holy Spirit must be restricted to them too. If they are not restricted, as they are not, then all believers can proclaim forgiveness through faith in Christ.

4. According to the best texts, the verbs "are remitted" and "are retained" are in the perfect tense, which suggests, though it does not prove conclusively, that the forgiveness involved is something which has already been determined in heaven and is now merely proclaimed on earth. The translations which best reflect this tense would be "have been forgiven" and "have been retained." The New American Standard Bible makes this explicit by

saying, "If you forgive the sins of any, their sins have been forgiven them; if you retain the sins of any, they have been retained," and then by adding in a marginal note, "I.e., have previously been forgiven." The NASB does the same thing with Matthew 16:19 and 18:18.[2]

5. The Greek words for "whosoever" and "them" (which refers back to the first use of "whosoever") are plural. In other words, it is the sins, not of whatever person, but of whatever persons about which this verse is speaking. Leon Morris observes, "Jesus is not speaking of individuals, but of classes. He is saying that the Spirit-filled church has authority to declare which are the sins that are forgiven and which are the sins that are retained. This accords with Rabbinical teaching which spoke of certain sins as 'bound' and others as 'loosed.' This referred to classes, not to individuals, and this is surely what Jesus is saying also."[3]

We conclude that for the reasons given, John 20:23 is to be taken in precisely the way Luke records Christ's teaching given on the same occasion of which John speaks. Luke records that after Jesus had opened the disciples' understanding to know what the Bible had to say about his death for sins, he said to them, "This is what is written: The Christ will suffer and rise from the dead on the third day, and repentance and forgiveness of sins will be preached in his name to all nations, beginning at Jerusalem. You are all witnesses of these things" (Luke 24:46–48). In neither of these texts is anyone authorized to remit sins; rather all are commissioned to preach it on condition of repentance and faith.

A Few Conclusions

If this is the proper interpretation, as I believe it is, then a number of conclusions follow. First, the mission of the church in the world must contain involvement *and* proclamation.

In our earlier study of John's version of the Great Commission, verse 21, we pointed out that if we are sent into the world as Christ was sent into the world, then we must truly be *in the world* and not merely shouting the gospel to it from afar. This is the principle of incarnation. It is important. Moreover, evangelicals especially must give attention to it, for we have been far too inclined to retreat into the safety of our evangelical ghettos and merely proclaim the Word abstractly or indirectly. We do not like to get involved, and the liberal wing of the church has been superior to many of us in this area. But this is only half of the story, for if it is true that Christians must be involved *in* the world if they are to reach the world, it is no less true that they must have a message *for* the world and actually proclaim it *to* the world if they are to fulfill the Lord's commission.

There is a tendency to glorify "dialogue" today in some circles. Those advancing this approach say correctly that we must be willing to sit down beside unbelievers and learn from them. But then they add, "We must listen to them without presuming to think that we have anything to say to them.

We have nothing to teach them. We must let them teach us." In this they are wrong. Of course, we must be ready to listen to others and learn from others. The world has much to teach us, and we must learn from it if for no other reason than that we will thereby discover how to communicate the gospel better. But we cannot give up preaching. We cannot give up proclaiming the gospel of salvation that has been entrusted to us.

Second, the words of the Lord about the forgiveness and retention of sin throw emphasis upon what the Reformation theologians called the priesthood of all believers. In pre-Reformation theology the idea of the priesthood had been restricted to the clergy. These persons had special authority and prerogatives and were considered to be on a higher level than the laity. The Reformers denied that this was biblical and substituted instead a parity between clergy and laity in which there were no distinctions of privilege but only of office. In the teaching of the Reformers this meant that Christians had the same privileges before God. All had the same duties. All were to serve together within the one fellowship of the church. If a biblical distinction is to be made, it must be made between the *great* Priest, the Lord Jesus Christ, and his followers—just as it may also be made between Jesus as *the* Prophet and ourselves as lesser prophets or between Jesus as *the* King and ourselves as those who rule only because he rules.

We are not *the* priest, *the* prophet, or *the* king. But as God has sent Jesus into the world, so also does he send us into the world with the result that we are to function in each of these areas. We function as priests in offering ourselves up to God in service and in praying for and with others. We function as prophets in proclaiming what God has recorded in Scripture for our and others' benefit. We function as kings when we first rule ourselves well and then also those for whom we are responsible.

The question is, Do we who hold to the priesthood of all believers actually do these things or do we leave our responsibilities to others? Above all, do we take the gospel of God's grace in Christ to those who need to hear it and proclaim on God's own authority that those who will repent of sin and turn in faith to Christ as their Savior have had their sins forgiven and that those who will not come to Christ are not forgiven and will have to face God's judgment? Believers have many privileges. But they also have many responsibilities, chief of which is the faithful proclamation of the gospel.

Finally, there is this conclusion. We have pointed out that the privileges and duties of which Jesus speaks are for *all* believers, but we must also note that they are for all *believers.* Therefore, we warn that acquaintance with spiritual truth is not sufficient; membership in a church is not sufficient; the name of Christian is not sufficient. What is necessary is new life from God which inevitably results in a turning away from sin to faith in Jesus as the Son of God and Savior.

Here is where verse 22 comes in. It says that Jesus breathed on his disciples and said to them, "Receive the Holy Spirit." Some have imagined a contradition between John, who apparently speaks of the impartation of the Holy Spirit to the disciples on the night of the resurrection, and the author of the Book of Acts, who speaks of a special coming of the Holy Spirit at Pentecost fifty days later. But this is unnecessary. Obviously the Holy Spirit came in power in a special way on Pentecost to inaugurate the church age. But are we to suppose that there was no impartation of the Spirit or no working of the Spirit in disciples' lives before that time? Earlier in Christ's ministry, Peter had confessed that he was "the Christ, the Son of the living God," and Jesus had responded by saying that this had been revealed to Peter by God. Was this apart from the Spirit? Did Peter believe without the opening of his mind and heart by the direct action of the Holy Spirit upon him? Similarly, early on the morning of the resurrection, John had entered the empty tomb and "believed" in the resurrection. Was this insight achieved apart from the Spirit? The Holy Spirit was there all along and would be so in even greater measure at Pentecost. What Jesus is indicating in our text is that he is the source of the Spirit and that nothing can be done in the Christian life (indeed, one is not even a Christian) apart from the Spirit's activity.

Christ's breathing on, and imparting the Holy Spirit to, his disciples reminds one of the creation, in which the almighty God breathed into the first man, Adam, so that he became "a living soul" (Gen 2:7). Jesus is teaching that we must be created anew if we are truly to be his and serve him faithfully.

All Things New

Have you been made new? If so, all things are new and God's blessings are yours in full measure. Arthur Pink sees this passage as presenting all those new features of Christianity that are ours through Jesus. "1. Christ is known in a *new way*, no longer 'after the flesh,' but in spirit, on High. 'Touch me not ... ascended' (20:17). 2. Believers are given a *new title*—'brethren' (20:17). 3. Believers are told of a *new position*—Christ's position before the Father (20:17). 4. Believers occupy a *new place*—apart from the world (20:19). 5. Believers are assured of a *new blessing*—'peace' made and imparted (20:19, 21). 6. Believers are given a *new privilege*—the Lord Jesus in their midst (20:19). 7. Believers have a *new joy*—through a vision of the risen Lord (20:20). 8. Believers receive a *new commission*—sent into the world by the Son *as* He was sent by the Father (20:21). 9. Believers are a *new creation*—indicated by the 'breathing' (20:22). 10. Believers have a *new Indweller*—even the Holy Spirit (20:22). How Divinely meet that all this was on the '*first* of the week'—indication of a *new beginning*, i.e., Christianity supplanting Judaism!"[4]

Has God made these things new for you? If not, you know the way. It is through Christ, who calls you to repent of sin and turn to him in humble faith. He died for you. Believe it and come to him.

261

Faithless or Faithful?

John 20:24–28

Now Thomas (called Didymus), one of the Twelve, was not with the disciples when Jesus came. So the other disciples told him, "We have seen the Lord!"

But he said to them, "Unless I see the nail marks in his hands and put my finger where the nails were, and put my hand into his side, I will not believe it."

A week later his disciples were in the house again, and Thomas was with them. Though the doors were locked, Jesus came and stood among them and said, "Peace be with you!" Then he said to Thomas, "Put your finger here; see my hands. Reach out your hand and put it into my side. Stop doubting and believe."

Thomas said to him, "My Lord and my God!"

A number of years ago a book was published in America entitled *This Believing World*. It was a popular book because its thesis was popular—at last count it had gone through more than thirty editions. It said that everywhere and under all sorts of conditions men and women are naturally believers and are addicted to proclaiming their convictions.

The book may be right if the faith it speaks of is the kind of faith we observe generally. The world is not opposed to faith in general terms. But the book is fundamentally wrong if it is speaking of the kind of faith required in biblical Christianity. Christianity requires faith in God as he is revealed in Jesus Christ, and this means acceptance of the truth of our deep spiritual need and of the work of the divine Christ in providing the basis for our salvation from sin by his death. It involves faith in him and in the demonstration of the truth of his work and teachings by the resurrection. Is the world a "believing world" in this sense? Not at all! In fact, the opposite is the case. The world is totally disbelieving, and it remains so unless God himself brings faith out of non-faith, just as he is able to bring life out of death or the whole of creation out of nothing.

But, of course, that is precisely what God does. He not only creates and loves and dies that those whom he has made but who have fallen into sin might be redeemed, he also leads them to faith, thereby producing in them that which they could never produce in themselves.

This is the meaning of the great and moving story that is the true climax and end of John's Gospel.

Doubting Thomas

The story concerns the meeting of Jesus and Thomas one week after the resurrection. Thomas had not been with the others on that earlier Sunday when Jesus had first appeared to the disciples in the upper room. We are not told why. We are told only that Thomas was not there, had missed seeing Jesus as a result, and, when told of the appearances of the Lord, replied, "Unless I see the nail marks in his hands and put my finger where the nails were, and put my hand into his side, I will not believe it" (v. 25). In the sequel Jesus appears to Thomas to lead him to faith, and Thomas concludes the story with the highest profession of belief in Jesus recorded in the pages of any of the Gospels. He worships him, saying, "My Lord and my God" (v. 28).

This story has given us the well-known English epithet "a doubting Thomas." But we have to be careful how we use it. For one thing, we must not use it to disparage Thomas as if he only (and not the other disciples or, for that matter, even ourselves) doubted the resurrection. We remember that none of the other disciples believed either until Jesus had revealed himself to them, and neither do people today naturally believe. That is why we speak of "unconditional election" and "irresistible grace." If we do believe, it is only because God is there beforehand leading us to do it.

Again, we must not use the phrase "a doubting Thomas" to suggest even for a moment that it is just natural for some people to disbelieve and that they are therefore less guilty or are to be excused because of this disposition. We cannot fail to notice that although Jesus comes down to the level of his doubting disciple to lead him to faith, he does not at all suggest that his unbelief is excusable.

Thomas was indeed a doubter. He was not lacking in courage, loyalty, or devotion to Jesus, but he did have a gloomy disposition. He looked on the darker side of things. Therefore, when the death of the Lord was reported, he responded with the understandable declaration, "I will not believe it."

We see this characteristic in Thomas at every point at which he appears in John's Gospel. The first time he appears is in chapter 11. At this point Jesus was in a remote area of the wilderness country beyond the Jordan River where he had gone because of the danger in Jerusalem. We are told toward the end of the preceding chapter that when he had been in Jerusalem the Jews "tried to seize him, but he escaped their grasp" (10:39). Word came to him that his friend Lazarus, who lived in Bethany near Jerusalem, was sick. At first Jesus delayed for two days. But at last he announced his intention to return. Undoubtedly the disciples were frightened. They reminded him of the danger. They said, "But Rabbi, a short while ago the Jews tried to stone you, and yet you are going back there?" (11:8). Jesus was adamant. I imagine that there was a long pause as the disciples looked around at one another as if to ask if anything could be done to get him to change his mind or even if they would themselves go with him. But at last Thomas spoke up, saying, "Let us also go, that we may die with him" (v. 16). What an interesting thing to say! The words were honest, loyal, and courageous, but they were not cheerful. They were quite grim.

The second time Thomas is brought to our notice is in John 14. Here Jesus is in the midst of his final discourses to his disciples before his arrest and crucifixion. He has spoken of heaven, concluding, "I am going to prepare a place for you. And if I go and prepare a place for you, I will come back and take you to be with me, so that where I am, you may be also. You know the way to the place I am going" (vv. 2–4). These were great promises. But Thomas was unwilling to let them pass without confessing that he and presumably others also did not really know what Jesus was talking about. His gloomy reply was, "Lord, we don't know where you are going, so how can we know the way?" (v. 5).

Pink says of this incident, "He reminds us very much of John Bunyan's 'Fearing,' 'Despondency,' and 'Much Afraid,' in his *Pilgrim's Progress*—types of a large class of Christians who are [his] successors."[1]

The Other Disciples

Before we think of Christ's appearance to Thomas we must notice something else, however, for in its own way it is also very important. Even before the Lord came to Thomas, the other disciples had gone to him with the message that Jesus was risen, and it was undoubtedly because of their witness, even though it was not believed, that Thomas was with the others when Jesus appeared on that second Sunday.

Those in the Reformed, or Calvinistic, tradition sometimes give the impression that, because people are hopelessly lost in sin and only God can save them, there is little or nothing we can do. Consequently, when a person will not believe or will not even come naturally into a fellowship of Christians where the gospel is preached and Christ is likely to make himself known, we tend to give up. We say, "There is nothing we can do now. It is up to God." Well, in a sense it is up to God; it is always up to God even when results are forthcoming. But the fact that men and women are lost in unbelief and that only God can save them is no excuse for us to do nothing. On the contrary, we must do as these early disciples did. We must seek out the one who is missing. We must go to him or her and call that one to faith. We must say, "The Lord is risen. We have seen him. Come with us and believe on Jesus."

If some of us were among that first crowd of disciples, I think I know what would have happened. Jesus would have appeared and gone, and the group that had seen him would have been discussing his appearance. The name of Thomas would have come up. Someone would have said, "What shall we do about Thomas? I suppose we should seek him out and tell him."

"No," says another, "he should have been here. He is one of us. His duty was to be with us. If he had been here, he would have seen the Lord too. It's just too bad."

Again, I suppose a sense of obligation might have emerged, but the announcement might have been done in this fashion. The "faithful" might have said, "Thomas, you should have been with us on Sunday evening. The Lord appeared (and he is probably not going to appear again), but we wanted to tell you this since it is our duty as one Christian to another. Mend your ways." They could have said this. But they did not. Instead, they were so filled with joy in the knowledge that Jesus was alive that they went to tell everyone, especially those who had been with Jesus during the earthly ministry. They sought out Thomas and made sure that he was with them when they gathered together to worship on the second Sunday.

There are Christians who have a naturally gloomy temperament. These tend to go off by themselves; this is a characteristic of that temperament. Yet these are the ones who can least afford to be alone. Gloom and despair prey upon them, and such people will become more gloomy and less believing if left alone. Go to them. Find them. Bring them back into that fellowship you enjoy.

Behold My Hands

It is true, however, that in spite of their concern for Thomas, and as important as this was, the disciples could not change his mind. Nor can we change the minds of other people or convert them. God must do that. So what we read next is that Jesus appeared to lead this doubting apostle to faith.

Jesus did it by inviting Thomas to perform his empirical test, that is, by coming down to his level and engaging him in a way that would best lead him from unbelief to commitment. Thomas had asked for something he had no right to ask for. He had said, "Unless I see the nail marks in his hands and put my finger where the nails are, and put my hand into his side, I will not believe it" (v. 25). To treat the risen Lord in that fashion would be irreverent. Moreover, as he said it Thomas implied that the test was impossible; he had no intention of believing. Thomas was definitely out of line, faithless. Yet Jesus came down to his level, as he always does. He appeared to Thomas and said, "Put your finger here; see my hands. Reach out your hand and put it into my side" (v. 27).

How gracious our God is! We have no right to demand anything of him. Yet he who has created us and has died to redeem us stoops to provide what we need. Do we need evidence? If we do and if we will approach the matter honestly, we will find the proof of his deity, death for sinners, resurrection, and promised return overwhelming.

Do you say, "But I don't see it"? Then come to him. Ask for the evidence. You will find that God, who is far more anxious to reveal himself to you than you are to find him, will provide the revelation.

It is striking, however, that in this case the thing that actually convinced Thomas was not the empirical test he had demanded. He had demanded to put his finger into the holes of the nails in Christ's hands and thrust his hand into the wound in his side. But when Jesus presented himself and invited Thomas to reach out his finger and stretch forth his hand, Thomas did not actually do it. He was convinced without these assurances and fell at Christ's feet exclaiming, "My Lord and my God."

What convinced Thomas? Some have suggested that it was Christ's obvious knowledge of what Thomas had said, though Jesus had not been physically present when Thomas said it. To do that, so the argument goes, Jesus would have had to be God. But logical as this is, I do not find myself believing that this is what really got through to Thomas. What finally got through to him was the presence of Christ, identified by the wounds in his hands, feet, and side. It was the Christ of the cross who reached Thomas.

This is the greatest proof of all: the love of Christ revealed in his wounds. Charles Spurgeon once wrote of this: "In these times, when the foundations of our faith are constantly being undermined, one is sometimes driven to say to himself, 'Suppose it is not true.' As I stood, the other night, beneath the sky, and watched the stars, I felt my heart going up to the great Maker with all the love that I was capable of. I said to myself, 'What made me love God as I know I do? What made me feel an anxiety to be like him in purity? Whatever made me long to obey my God cannot be a lie.' I know that it was the love of Jesus for me that changed my heart, and made me, though once careless and indifferent to him, now to pant with strong desires to honor him. What has done this? Not a lie, surely. A truth, then, has done it. I know it by its fruits. If this Bible were to turn out untrue, and if I died and went before my Maker, could I not say to him, 'I believed great things of thee, great God; if it be not so, yet did I honor thee by the faith I had concerning thy wondrous goodness, and thy power to forgive'? and I would cast myself upon his mercy without fear. But we do not entertain such doubts; for those dear wounds continually prove the truth of the gospel, and the truth of our salvation by it. Incarnate Deity is a thought that was never invented by poet's mind, nor reasoned out by philosopher's skill. Incarnate Deity, the notion of the God that lived, and bled, and died in human form, instead of guilty man, … is itself its own best witness. The wounds are the infallible witness of the gospel of Christ."[2]

Do not misunderstand me here. If you have honest intellectual questions about Christianity, God will provide intellectual answers for them. He gave you a mind as well as a heart. He will provide what you need. But the thing that will ultimately win you is not so much the reasoned arguments, though they are often important stepping stones, but the love of Christ demonstrated by his death for you.

"My Lord and My God "

Here is some encouragement. We have been discussing Thomas, the most doubting of all Christ's apostles. But notice that when the Lord revealed himself to Thomas, Thomas moved from doubt to the greatest testimony of faith in Christ recorded by this or any other Gospel. He said, "My Lord and my God." "Lord" was sometimes used of Christ by others, often with less than its full meaning. But here it must have all the content it will bear—"Jehovah, Master, Sovereign." "God" is a new form of address; no one had previously addressed the Lord in this way. It represents a great insight of faith, perhaps even greater than that similar confession of the apostle Peter for which he was commended by Christ (Matt. 16:13–17). Then, lest all this should be thought insufficient, Thomas adds the personal pronoun, saying, "*My* Lord and *my* God." It was not enough that Jesus be both God and sovereign. He was now to be that for Thomas personally.

This is the high point of the Gospel. It is the climax. John shows here how one who began as a great doubter came by the grace of Christ to that confession with which the Gospel began: "And the Word was God" (John 1:1). It was to lead people to this conviction that the book was written (John 20:30–31).

No case is hopeless. Your case is not hopeless. God took Abraham, the pagan, and made him into a pillar of faith and the father of his people. He took Moses, the stammerer, and made him into the greatest vehicle for the communication of the word of God until Paul. He made the shepherd boy David into a king; Peter "the weak" into Peter "the rock"; John the Son of Thunder into the apostle of love; Paul, the persecuter of Christians, into a faithful ambassador and martyr. He can do that for you. Allow him to do it. Believe on Christ. Rather than being faithless, may you be one who, like Thomas, was found "faith-full."

262

A Great Benediction

John 20:29

Then Jesus told him, "Because you have seen me, you have believed; blessed are those who have not seen and yet have believed."

It is a remarkable characteristic of the Word of God that it is filled far more with blessings than with curses. There are curses, to be sure. There are warnings of judgment. But when all is put together, the blessings are far more numerous and more wonderful than any of these more somber elements.

The Bible begins with a blessing, for we are told that after each day of creation God commented upon the work, saying, "It is good." The Bible ends with a blessing, "The grace of the Lord Jesus be with God's people. Amen" (Rev. 22:21). In between are such verses as: "God blessed them and said to them, 'Be fruitful and increase in number; fill the earth and subdue it'" (Gen 1:28); "I will bless you; I will make your name great, and you will be a blessing" (Gen. 12:2); "After Jacob returned from Paddan Aram, God appeared to him again and blessed him" (Gen 35:9); "The LORD bless you and keep you; the LORD make his face shine upon you and be gracious to you; the LORD turn his face toward you and give you peace" (Num 6:24–26); "Blessed is the man who does not walk in the counsel of the wicked" (Ps. 1:1); "Blessed is the nation whose God is the LORD" (Ps. 33:12); "Blessed are they whose ways are blameless" (Ps. 119:1); "Blessed are they whose transgressions are forgiven, whose sins are covered. Blessed is the man whose sin the Lord will never count against him" (Rom. 4:7–8; cf. Ps. 32:1–2); "Blessed are the dead who die in the Lord" (Rev. 14:13). In my concordance I find 375 Old Testament passages that deal with God's blessing. I find 108 separate passages in the New Testament.

It is not surprising in view of this wonderful characteristic of our God and of his revelation to find that the Lord Jesus Christ, the incarnate God, also had many words of blessing during the days of his ministry. We think of the beatitudes of Matthew 5, an obvious example (vv. 3–11). There are blessings pronounced upon children (Mark 10:16), upon one or more of the disciples (Matt. 13:16; 16:17), upon faithful servants of God (Matt. 24:46), upon those who hear the Word of God and keep it (Luke 11:28). There is the benediction at the close of John's Gospel, which is our text: "Blessed are those who have not seen and yet have believed" (John 20:29).

This blessing, the fifth of Christ's "last" words in John's Gospel, is great for several reasons, among them that it is the last of Christ's blessings spoken while on earth. Appropriately, it is one that concerns not just a single person or a limited group of people but rather all who should believe on him as Savior.

What Does Christ Mean?

What does Jesus mean when he says, "Blessed are those who have not seen and yet have believed"? Does he mean that a subjective faith is better than an objective faith, that a faith that has no relation to evidence is better than a faith that has? Does he mean that only a faith like that is blessed? It is hard to think that this is his meaning, because he has just provided tangible evidence of his resurrection for Thomas by appearing to him and inviting him to put his finger into the holes of his hands and thrust his hand into Christ's side. Again, it is clear that John did not interpret Christ's words in this way, because immediately after this John says that he has written certain things in his Gospel in order that those who read might believe.

So we may grant that Jesus is not advocating a faith entirely without evidence. But that still does not answer the question. What does Jesus mean? I believe he is speaking, not of a subjective faith, but of a satisfied faith. He is speaking of faith that is satisfied with what God provides and is therefore not yearning for visions, miracles, esoteric experiences, or various forms of success as evidence of God's favor. More than that, he is saying that a faith without these things is not inferior to but is actually superior to a faith based upon them.

Take these things one at a time and see why this is so. Take *visions*, first of all. If you are a normal Christian, I am sure there have been times when you have been discouraged, perhaps overcome with doubt, and you have said, "Oh, if God would only reveal himself to me in some special way so that my sight, touch, or hearing could assist my faith." We remember that there were people in the Bible who had such evidence. Abraham saw visions; he spoke with the three angelic visitors; he heard the voice of God from heaven on Mount Moriah. Moses met God on the mountain; on one occasion Moses was hidden in a cleft of the rock and witnessed the fire, wind, and earthquake as Jehovah passed by. Isaiah had a vision of God high and lifted up. The disciples saw Christ in the days of his flesh. Paul was caught up to the third heaven. John himself had the magnificent visions recorded for us in the Book of Revelation. "Why can't we have something similar?" we argue. "Surely we could believe much better and be far more effective in our Christian walk and witness if we did."

But that is not true, even though we like to tell ourselves that it is. For one thing, we usually want such experiences for the wrong reason—vanity. We would have a far higher opinion of ourselves if we should be granted an experience which most do not have. For another thing, visions do not necessarily lead to greater faith. In the opening pages of *Miracles* by C. S. Lewis, the well-known Oxford professor and author tells of a friend of his who once saw a ghost. Before the vision, she disbelieved in an immortal soul. After it, she still disbelieved. Obviously, faith gives meaning to experience rather than the other way around.

Second, there are *miracles* or other special acts of God's providence. Do you pray for miracles? Do you think you could believe God better if you saw some? The opposite is the case. If you are looking for miracles (which God sometimes does provide, but seldom), you will gradually become insensitive to the thousands of normal evidences of God's mercy which you receive constantly.

Third, there are people who think they would be stronger in faith and be better able to live the Christian life were they to have *some special esoteric experience*. We read a passage like 1 Corinthians 12:9–10, where Paul speaks of God granting to some "gifts of healing by the one Spirit, to another miraculous powers, to another prophecy, to another distinguishing between spirits, to another speaking in different kinds of tongues, and to still another the interpretation of tongues," and we think that if we could only do or experience something like that, we would be stronger and happier as Christians. But that is not true either. God sometimes grants such experiences for the good of his church; the very fact that Paul lists these gifts in 1 Corinthians 12 is evidence that he does. But surely anyone who reads these chapters carefully will note that Paul does not encourage us to seek these experiences. If anything, he seems to warn against them, and he certainly does not pronounce any special blessing upon their exercise. Why? Because the blessings of the gospel are for those who live by faith and not by sight, who live by their faith in the character and benevolence of God and not in the evidence of visions, miracles, or other such experiences.

There is one other item which must not be left out, if only because it is so common in our day. It is the supposed evidence of *success,* measured by the number of people converted, church growth, income for Christian institutions and other such things. Does this mean that we are not to work to see as many people converted as possible? Does it mean that we are not to be concerned with church growth? Does it mean that we should not be concerned with the level of income necessary to run Christian schools, missions, churches, and other institutions? Not at all. But it does mean that we are not to tie our faith in God to such circumstances. We are to pray and believe and go on working even when we do not see this kind of numerical blessing.

What is faith? Faith is believing God on the basis of his Word and then acting upon it. This is true faith. It is this that God blesses. God promises a blessing upon those who have faith. We cannot repeat that enough. God blesses *faith,* and not the living out of some unusual experience.

How could it be otherwise if (1) God is to be fair in his dealings with his people and (2) the blessings of which he speaks are to be for all? Suppose it to be the other way. Suppose God's blessing were linked to the unusual. In that case, either his blessing would be for a small and select company only, or else the things we consider unusual would have to become commonplace, in which case they would cease to have the character of "special evidences." They would be like those other countless evidences of God's providence which we enjoy daily but do not regard so highly, simply because they are common. No, the blessings of God are for all; and they are based, not upon the unusual in Christian experience, but upon faith which by its very nature and definition is common to all who call upon the name of Christ as God and Savior. This is why the Gospel of John ends on this note. It ends here because John wants to encourage everyone to believe on Jesus and enjoy God's blessings.

What Blessings?

What are those blessings? There are many ways to answer that question, because faith is discussed again and again throughout the Bible. But we may answer it at this point just from John's Gospel, remembering that John's Gospel is the Gospel of faith preeminently. In John the Greek word for faith *(pistis)* always occurs in its verbal form *(pisteuō)* and is therefore translated "believe." But in that form it occurs more often in John than in any other biblical book, even Romans (which has much to say about faith) or books that are longer. We find the word 101 times in John's Gospel, compared with a combined use of "faith" and "believe" 64 times in Romans and only 22 times in Mark. So John is obviously concerned with faith and considers it of prime importance. What does he say of the blessings that flow from it? The following ten items are prominent.

1. It is by faith that we become *children of God* and thus enter into the privileges of being in God's spiritual family. John indicates this at several points but especially in the first chapter, where he says, "Yet to all who received him, to those who believed in his name, he gave the right to become children of God" (1:12). Certainly this is a great blessing and the source of many others that follow.

2. It is through faith that we have *eternal life.* This is the teaching of the best-known verse in the Gospel, John 3:16. "For God so loved the world that he gave his one and only Son, that whoever believes in him shall not perish but have eternal life." Death is an "enemy" (1 Cor. 15:26). But death shall be conquered by faith, which unites us to Christ who conquered it.

3. By faith we are *delivered from judgment.* John quotes Jesus as saying, "I tell you the truth, whoever hears my word and believes him who sent me has eternal life and will not be condemned; he has crossed over from death to life" (5:24).

4. John 6:35 teaches that faith ushers us into the blessings of *spiritual satisfaction* now: "I am the bread of life. He who comes to me will never go hungry, and he who believes in me will never be thirsty." To come to Christ is to believe on Christ; that is what the parallelism suggests. So belief in Christ is set forth as the key to having all spiritual longings fulfilled.

5. Jesus also calls faith the means for entering into the final *resurrection:* "I am the resurrection and the life. He who believes in me will live, even though he dies; and whoever lives and believes in me will never die" (11:25–26). The blessings of the resurrection are for those who believe on Jesus.

6. Faith in Jesus is also said to be the way in which we become *blessings to others,* as the Holy Spirit who communicates all God's blessings works through us. This is taught in John 7:38–39: "'Whoever believes in me, as the Scripture has said, streams of living water will flow from within him.' By this he meant the Spirit, whom those who believed in him were later to receive." The image is of a broad river flowing through a desert land, giving life and joy to all who come upon it.

7. Through faith we see *the glory of God.* "Then Jesus said, 'Did I not tell you that if you believed, you would see the glory of God?'" (11:40). Without faith we will be like the heathen, who are surrounded by the glory of God in nature, yet either do not see it or else attribute it to that which is not God by a worship of idols. It is only as we look to God that our eyes are increasingly opened to see what he is doing.

8. Faith is the secret of *a holy life.* Jesus said, "I have come into the world as a light, so that no one who believes in me should stay in darkness" (12:46). In biblical language, darkness is the darkness of sin (cf. 1 John 1:5–10). So walking in the light means walking in holiness by means of the spiritual and moral life which God gives.

9. The blessing of *a fruitful and effective life* comes by faith. Jesus said, "I tell you the truth, anyone who has faith in me will do what I have been doing. He will do even greater things than these, because I am going to the Father" (14:12). This does not necessarily refer to what we would call miracles, though taken together the disciples may well have performed more miracles than Jesus did. It refers rather to the many works of witnessing, preaching, and Christlike service performed by Christian people. They are performed by those who take God at his word and go out boldly to do his bidding.

10. Finally, it is through faith that we receive the benefits of *Jesus' prayers on our behalf.* He said, "My prayer is not for them alone. I pray also for those who will believe in me through their message" (17:20). If, as we are told in James, "the prayer of a righteous man is powerful and effective" (5:16), how much more shall the prayers of the Lord Jesus Christ avail for us! If we lacked all other promises of blessing through faith, this alone should be enough.

Only Believe

What I have written here applies most directly to those who are Christians, to those who have believed on Jesus and to whom these blessings are therefore given. But it applies to non-Christians too in that you are challenged to believe on the Lord Jesus Christ as your Savior.

Do not say, as many do, "I think I could believe in Jesus if he would just appear to me in some special way. I could believe if I had some miraculous vision." That is not true, though you may think so. Pharaoh did not believe though he witnessed the greatest collection of signs and wonders ever granted to one man at one period of history. Those things are of no use to you. The problem is not miracles or the lack of them. The problem is sin. You are a sinner, and Jesus is the answer to your sin. He died for you, bearing your punishment. Now you must come to him in simple faith. You cannot see him. But you can find him if you seek him with your whole heart.

263

Why This Book Was Written

John 20:30–31

Jesus did many other miraculous signs in the presence of his disciples, which are not recorded in this book. But these are written that you may believe that Jesus is the Christ, the Son of God, and that by believing you may have life in his name.

Have you ever read a book and wondered afterward why anyone would write it? I have read quite a few books like that, and I have thought of a number of reasons why they were written. Sometimes people write because their jobs depend on it. This is particularly true of professors in some colleges and universities. They must "publish or perish." If they don't, they do. Some people write because they think it is good for them to write. President Kennedy once gave Richard Nixon some advice along this line. He said it was good for a public figure to write a book, because it disciplined him to think and work in a certain way. Still other persons write as an ego trip. They want their names to be known.

These reasons for writing are largely unworthy, of course. But next to books that evoke answers like these are others so clear in their point and so helpful in developing it that their worth is immediately apparent. Such are

1617

the classics. Such is the Bible. So too is that one part of the Bible, the Gospel of John, which we have been studying.

Why was the Gospel of John written? The author tells us why in the verses that close chapter 20 and that therefore properly close the book (since chapter 21 is in the nature of an epilogue). John says, "Jesus did many other miraculous signs in the presence of his disciples, which are not recorded in this book. But these are written that you may believe that Jesus is the Christ, the Son of God, and that by believing you may have life in his name" (vv. 30–31). John is saying that there were many other things about which he could have written but that the things he did write were chosen rigorously on the basis of a two-part goal. That goal centers in a person, the Lord Jesus Christ. The first part, the chief, is that those learning about Jesus might believe that he is the Christ, the Son of God. The second part, a consequence of the first, is that the one believing might have eternal life through Christ's name.

Other Books, Other Authors

This is what sets John (and also the Bible as a whole) apart from most other books, including some very good ones. Many are written to glorify the writer. I think of a book entitled *Dear Me*. It was about the author. Other books are memoirs of famous people. John is not like this, however, and neither is the Bible as a whole. The inspired writers freely identify themselves. But then they lose themselves in their theme and never glorify either themselves or their achievements. On the contrary, if they speak of themselves at all, it is to tell of their own shameful failures that we might glorify God the more.

There is no example more striking in this regard than the apostle John. He was alert and sensitive. He was a member of the small band of disciples and had therefore traveled with Jesus during the days of his ministry. He was even a member of what we might call "the inner circle," composed of Peter, James, and John. John must have known more about Jesus by way of actual fact, sympathy, and direct experience than anyone. Yet so far was he from calling attention to himself or his own superior knowledge that he does not even mention himself by name while composing the Gospel.

Spurgeon, in one of his excellent sermons, points to the amazing reserve the apostle John exercised in refusing to use personal reminiscences and details to embellish his Gospel. "He omits, as if of set purpose, those places of the history in which he would have shone. He and James and Peter were frequently selected by the Master to be with him when others were excluded, but of these occasions he says nothing. At the resurrection of the daughter of Jairus it is said of the disciples, as well as of the relatives and the multitude, that the Lord put them all out, and only suffered the three to be with him. This was a singular honor, but John does not say a word about the raising of the daughter of Jairus. . . . Even more striking is the fact that the Master when he took with him the eleven to the garden, left the major part of them at the gate, but he led the three further into the garden, and bade them wait at about a stone's-cast distance, where some of them heard his prayers, and observed the bloody sweat. John, who was one of them, says nothing about it. He leaves out that which would have brought John into the front, in order that he may fill up the whole foreground of his canvas with the portrait of his Lord. Everything is subordinated to the one grand end 'that ye should believe that Jesus is the Christ.'"[1]

The purpose that John had and reveals so clearly should be the goal of every Christian. When John the Baptist was approached about the astonishing success of Jesus in gathering disciples to himself, he replied, "He must increase, but I must decrease" (John 3:30). So Jesus must. We must be certain that even in our witnessing we do not detract from him.

Another reason why many books are written is to satisfy curiosity. These books generally sell well because people have great curiosity about certain things. Over the years there have been scores of books by people who have worked for those who are famous and who pretend to let us in on their secrets. People buy these books because they want to know details about the lives of the people involved. But John, though he deals with the most famous person who ever lived, does not write in that fashion.

We would have. Had I been writing about Jesus, I would have recorded a physical description. I would have told how tall he was, how much he weighed, the color of his eyes and hair, and other items of that nature. I would have told of his childhood, his first friends, what people thought of him before he began his earthly ministry. I would have told what finally happened to Nicodemus (did he actually become a believer or not?), the reaction of the leaders of Israel to news of Christ's resurrection, and other such things. Our love for Christ tends to ennoble everything he did and would have caused us to be as faithful as Samuel Johnson's Boswell in recording it. But the Holy Spirit did not so lead the Gospel writers. As John indicates, he wrote only that which would lead us to faith in Jesus as the Christ and Son of God, not to satisfy our understandable but useless curiosity.

Chain of Witnesses

Here is how John's concluding words must be taken. It is as though he is saying, "Look, you have been reading and studying my Gospel for some time now, and you have come to the end. Have you grasped my purpose? Can it be that you have missed it after all this time? In case you have missed it, let me spell it out, Jesus did many, many things, but I have not recorded all of them. I have recorded only a part. But I have recorded that part so that you, *you* might believe that Jesus is the Christ, the Son of God, and that believing you might have life through his name."

Have you ever thought of the Gospel of John in that light? Have you noticed that for all its deep theology the Gospel is really nothing more than a series of testimonies to Christ?

Let us consider them in sequence. In the opening pages of the Gospel, after John's own introduction, we have the first testimony—that of *John the*

Baptist. As John tells it, the leaders of Jerusalem came to the Baptist to ask who he was, and after denying that he was Elijah, "that prophet," or the Christ, John described himself as one who had come simply to announce the Messiah and point to him. The next day he had his chance. Jesus passed by, and John pointed him out to two of his own disciples, saying, "Look, the Lamb of God, who takes away the sin of the world" (1:29). Later he formalized his witness saying, "I would not have known him, except that the one who sent me to baptize with water told me, 'The man on whom you see the Spirit come down and remain is he who will baptize with the Holy Spirit.' I have seen and I testify that this is the Son of God" (vv. 33–34).

The same chapter contains three further testimonies to Jesus. When John had pointed Jesus out to his disciples, they left John and followed Jesus. They then spent the rest of the day with Jesus and were so impressed that one of them, *Andrew,* immediately set off to find his brother Peter and said to him, "We have found the Messiah (that is, the Christ)" (v. 41). In the next verses Jesus finds *Philip* and calls him to discipleship, and Philip then goes to call his friend *Nathanael.* Philip's words to Nathanael are: "We have found the one Moses wrote about in the Law, and about whom the prophets also wrote—Jesus of Nazareth, the son of Joseph" (v. 45). At first Nathanael is skeptical, but after he meets Jesus and is confronted with his supernatural knowledge, he declares movingly, "Rabbi, you are the Son of God; you are the King of Israel" (v. 49).

In chapter 2 we have the first of Christ's many miracles, the changing of water into wine at a marriage feast in Cana. The climax of this story is verse 11, where we are told of the miracle's effect upon the *disciples* who alone of all the guests knew of it: "This, the first of his miraculous signs, Jesus performed at Cana in Galilee. He thus revealed his glory, and his disciples put their faith in him."

The next two chapters introduce us to three representative figures and to others who are associated with them. They give their testimonies. The first figure is *Nicodemus.* He has little understanding; it is not said that he believes. But the account of his conversation with Jesus leads into John's own comments regarding the person and work of the Savior. He is described as "God's one and only Son" (3:18), whom God gave so that the world might not perish (v. 16).

The *woman of Samaria* dominates chapter 4. Unlike Nicodemus, who was a person of repute and privilege, she was an immoral representative of a despised race. She was also a woman. But Jesus revealed himself to her and led her to faith. Her testimony is in the form of a question that she asked the men of the city after she had conversed with Jesus. She said, "Come, see a man who told me everything I ever did. Could this be the Christ?" (v. 29). As a result of her witness many of the *citizens of Sychar* came out to meet Jesus and later said to the woman, "We no longer believe just because of what you said; now we have heard for ourselves, and we know that this man really is the Savior of the world" (v. 42).

At the end of chapter 4 we have the story of the *nobleman* whose son was dying. Jesus healed the son by a word, without going to the home. The result was that the father "and all his household believed" (v. 53).

In chapter 5 Jesus himself lists the testimonies that were given to him, testimonies that God the Father provided. The first is *John the Baptist*, whose witness was that of a prophet inspired by God. The second is the witness of *Christ's works or miracles;* Jesus always attributed these to the power of the Father at work within him. The third is the direct witness of *God himself,* presumably by a voice from heaven. At last there is the testimony of the *Scriptures* that, Christ says, "are the Scriptures that testify about me" (v. 39).

In chapter 6 the *five thousand* are fed; the result is that many come to believe on Jesus. We are told, "After the people saw the miraculous sign that Jesus did, they began to say, 'Surely this is the Prophet who is to come into the world'" (v. 14). Later when Jesus refused to conform to the materialistic expectations of the crowd many of these disciples left him. But when he returned to his own small band to ask if they wanted to go away, these refused and instead gave great testimony to him. *Peter* was the spokesman. He said, "Lord, to whom shall we go? You have the words of eternal life. We believe and know that you are the Holy One of God" (vv. 68–69).

In chapter 7 "many of the crowd put their faith in him" (v. 31). Some said, "Surely this man is the Prophet" (v. 40). Others said, "He is the Christ" (v. 41).

Chapter 8 also tells us that "*many* put their faith in him" (v. 30).

Chapter 9 contains the story of the *man born blind.* This man did not seek Christ, because he could not even see to seek him out. Jesus sought him, as he seeks each of us, and he restored the man's sight both physically and spiritually. The restoration of spiritual sight is seen in the man's growing awareness of who Jesus was and of his significance for him personally. At the beginning he calls Jesus "the man" (v. 11). Later he is "a prophet" (v. 17). Still later he concludes that he must be "from God," for if he were not, "he could do nothing" (v. 33). At last, after Jesus had found him a second time and had revealed himself to be the Son of God, the man who had been born blind fell at his feet and worshiped him as "Lord" (v. 38).

Chapter 11 contains the account of the resurrection of Lazarus, and the result of this last of the miracles is that "*many* of the Jews who had come to visit Mary, and had seen what Jesus did, put their faith in him" (v. 45).

In chapter 12 Jesus enters into Jerusalem on a donkey on what we have come to call Palm Sunday. On this occasion *the people* who went out of the city to meet him cried out, "Hosanna! Blessed is he who comes in the name of the Lord! Blessed is the King of Israel!" (v. 13). Later in the same chapter we are told that "many even among *the leaders* believed in him" though they did not confess him "for fear they would be put out of the synogogue" (v. 42).

After the resurrection we have the experiences of *Peter* and *John, Mary,* the *disciples* as a whole, and eventually *Thomas.* The latter account concludes with the great confession, "My Lord and my God" (20:28). Clearly, from first to last, the Gospel is a testimony to the Lord Jesus Christ.

The ABCs

I come now to the final and most important question: If John's purpose and the purpose of the Holy Spirit who inspired his writing is to lead men and women to faith in Jesus as the Son of God and Savior, shall that purpose fail where you personally are concerned? Do you believe? You have un-doubtedly known of Christ and his work for many years. You may even have followed these studies of John's Gospel over a long period of time. What a tragedy it would be to come to the end of such a study and fail to enter into eternal life through faith in Jesus yourself. Do not allow that to happen. Be-lieve on him. Believe now.

You say, "What does that mean? What must I do?" I will make the answer as simple as I can. Think of it as the ABCs of believing. First, *A.* You must *ac-cept* the basic teachings about Jesus of Nazareth as fact. That should be easy, for they are fact. The reason many doubt them is not because the facts are uncertain—they are as well attested as any facts of history—but because they have not really investigated them. If you have difficulty at this point, begin to study the Gospels and ask yourself if these teachings and narratives ring true. Are they consistent with themselves and with what we know of human life? Is Jesus believable? Second, *B. Believe* on him personally. This is more than merely believing facts. It is believing them in relationship to yourself. It is believing that he came to die for you, that he is the way to God for you, that he is your Savior. Finally, *C. Commit* yourself to him. At this point he ac-tually becomes your Savior and your God, as he did for Thomas in the verses immediately before the text we are studying.

Will you do that? Do not put it off. People always find ways of putting off what they know they ought to do, particularly when it is good for them. Some say, "I would like more information." You have more than enough infor-mation right now. Some say, "I would like to confirm these things by some personal, emotional experience." God does not save by experiences. He does so through faith in Jesus Christ. Believe on Jesus. These things are written that you might believe in him and that believing you might have life through his name.

264

"It Is the Lord"

John 21:1-11

Afterward Jesus appeared again to his disciples by the Sea of Tiberias. It happened this way: Simon Peter, Thomas (called Didymus), Nathanael from Cana in Galilee, the sons of Zebedee, and two other disciples were together. "I'm going out to fish," Simon Peter told them, and they said, "We'll go with you." So they went out and got into the boat, but that night they caught nothing.

Early in the morning, Jesus stood on the shore, but the disciples did not realize that it was Jesus.

He called out to them, "Friends, haven't you any fish?"

"No," they answered.

He said, "Throw your net on the right side of the boat and you will find some." When they did, they were unable to haul the net in because of the large number of fish.

Then the disciple whom Jesus loved said to Peter, "It is the Lord!" As soon as Simon Peter heard him say, "It is the Lord," he wrapped his outer garment around him (for he had taken it off) and jumped into the water. The other disciples followed in the boat, towing the net full of fish, for they were not far from shore, about a hundred yards. When they landed, they saw a fire of burning coals there with fish on it, and some bread.

Jesus said to them, "Bring some of the fish you have just caught."

Simon Peter climbed aboard and dragged the net ashore. It was full of large fish, 153, but even with so many the net was not torn.

At first reading, the final chapter of John seems the strangest in the Gospel, most of all because it looks as if it has been added on. The verses that end chapter 20 seem to mark an end to the book as a whole, and the confession of Thomas which comes immediately before them is obviously the climactic point of John's narrative. What can be added after Thomas falls down and worships Jesus as "My Lord and my God"? The only thing that could possibly be added, according to our thinking, is an account of Christ's final ascension to heaven. But John 21 does not contain that incident. Instead, it deals with a miraculous catch of fish in Galilee followed by some words of Jesus to his disciples on that occasion. These difficulties, as well as others, have led some scholars to suggest that this last chapter was added to the Gospel (perhaps badly) by another writer after John had already finished it. Many have accepted this, although there is not a shred of manuscript evidence in the theory's support.

The key to understanding this chapter is to see it as a parallel to the first part of chapter 1. John 1:1–14 is a prologue, in which the *preincarnate* activity of the Lord is summarized. These verses, 21:1–25, are an epilogue. Their emphasis is upon the *postresurrection* ministry of the Lord in which he now rules his church and directs its members in their Christian growth and service. It would be proper to call this last chapter a pageant. It is history—the events and conversations really happened—but it is symbolic history by which the essential principles concerning Christ's rule over the church during this age are forcefully communicated.

We see in these verses: (1) the assembled church, (2) the possibility of serving Christ in the energy of the flesh, (3) the fruitlessness of such efforts, (4) the direction of Christian work by Jesus and the blessing that follows upon obedience to that direction, (5) Christ's temporal provision for his followers, (6) the only acceptable motive for Christian service, (7) the value of diversity within the church, (8) the importance of regular feeding upon the Word of God, and (9) the necessity for close personal discipleship for all Christians.

Christ's Own Together

The disciples had been scattering back to their accustomed haunts and homes after the crucifixion, and this had been true for some even after the resurrection. The shepherd had been smitten; the sheep were scattering. Yet here we find them in Galilee, where everyone knew them and knew that they had gone off to follow Jesus, not scattering as we might think they would, but rather holding together as if they were still a special company with a unique bond. What can account for this? Alexander Maclaren writes, "There is only one explanation . . . Jesus Christ had risen from the dead. That drew them together once more. You cannot build a church on a dead Christ; and of all the proofs of the Resurrection, I take it that there is none that it is harder for an unbeliever to account for, in harmony with his hypothesis, than the simple fact that Christ's disciples held together after he was dead, and presented a united front to the world."[1]

Moreover, it is not only significant that they were together. It is also important to note *who* were together. John says, "Simon Peter, Thomas (called Didymus), Nathanael from Cana in Galilee, the sons of Zebedee, and two other disciples were together," seven in all.

The names of Peter and Thomas, which appear in the first and second positions, are obviously significant. Thomas was the rank unbeliever to whom Jesus had appeared and whose story is told just verses before this. Peter is the denier who is to be recommissioned to service in the verses immediately following. Can we miss that the church is made up of those who were doubters, deniers, and sinners of many varieties, but who have been brought to faith by Christ and have had their sins forgiven? These are the ones who do Christian work—normal people, with all the failings we are heir to, not fictitious characters of superhuman faith and fortitude.

Again, it is not just Peter and Thomas who are mentioned. There is Nathanael, whose only other appearance in the Gospel is in chapter 1. This makes us think of chapter 1 and suspect that there may be a deliberate throwback to those opening narratives. Who took part in those narratives? Peter and Nathanael were two. We have reason to believe that John himself was another, being the unnamed disciple who, with his friend Andrew, first followed Jesus. In this last chapter John appears again as one of the sons of Zebedee. Is it not possible that the two unnamed disciples of chapter 21 are Andrew and Philip, who are mentioned in 1:40 and 43 respectively, and that John is intentionally making this parallel?

If John is making this parallel, showing that the five of chapter 1 are here at the end also, then this is a testimony to God's perseverance with those who are his own. Those whom he calls follow Christ, and these are not lost. If these are not the same disciples as in chapter 1, we at least have an indication that all kinds of disciples (including some who are not even officially named) are in Christ's fellowship.

Without Me, Nothing

The second major point of these verses is one that evangelicals in the twentieth century especially should pay attention to: the sad possibility of attempting to serve Christ in the energy of the flesh and consequently of accomplishing nothing. This is what the incident involving Peter indicates.

Peter was impatient as usual. So rather than waiting inactively for the Lord's further appearances to him and the other disciples, Peter proposed to redeem the time by fishing. The idea seemed good to the others. So the disciples set out immediately and spent the night in hard labor. The text says, "That night they caught nothing" (v. 3). Some commentaries suggest that Peter was being disobedient to the Lord in proposing this fishing trip, because, so the argument goes, he had been instructed only to return to Galilee and wait there for Jesus. I do not think it is necessary to say this. Whatever else he was doing, Peter *was* in Galilee and he *was* waiting, though obviously filling in the time by fishing. No, the point of the story is not disobedience. It is rather to teach us what happens when we try to accomplish spiritual things by our own strength and at our own direction.

We must remember that fishing symbolizes evangelism, though Peter was obviously not thinking of this at the time. At the beginning of the three-year ministry there had been a similar incident. Jesus had been teaching the multitude while sitting in Peter's boat, and after he had finished he told Peter to move out into deeper water and let down his nets. Peter replied that he had toiled all night and caught nothing. But he did what Jesus had said, with the result that his net now enclosed so many fish that it broke. Peter was impressed, and so were his partners, James and John. But Jesus said, "Don't be afraid; from now on you will catch men" (Luke 5:10). From that time on, in the vocabulary of Jesus and his disciples, "fish" obviously suggested "men and women" and "fishing" symbolized "evangelism."

In chapter 21 we find Peter fishing again with similar results. He catches nothing until Jesus comes and directs his expedition. The point is clearly that our attempts to bring forth spiritual fruit are worthless unless Jesus himself directs and blesses them.

The Lord's Intervention

There is a third element in the story. The disciples had been fishing all night. They had caught nothing. I am sure, therefore, that having toiled all night and accomplishing nothing, they were discouraged and not even thinking of the Lord. If they were thinking of anything, it was probably how tired and hungry they were; if they were looking forward to anything, it was probably getting a bite to eat and then going to bed. But it was at that moment, when they were least thinking of Jesus, that the Lord appeared. They were not seeking him, but he sought them.

We never seek Jesus of our own free will, unaided by the Holy Spirit. If we do seek him, it is only because he is there beforehand moving us to do it. One of our hymns says it nicely.

> I sought the Lord, and afterward I knew
> He moved my soul to seek Him, seeking me;
> It was not I that found, O Savior true;
>   No, I was found of Thee.
>
> Thou didst reach forth Thy hand and mine enfold;
> I walked and sank not on the storm-vexed sea;
> 'Twas not so much that I on Thee took hold,
>   As Thou, dear Lord, on me.
>
> I find, I walk, I love; but O the whole
> Of love is but my answer, Lord, to Thee!
> For Thou wert long beforehand with my soul;
>   Always Thou lovest me.

I am glad it is that way, aren't you? If spiritual blessing depended upon our seeking out the Lord, there would be no blessing. The reason there is blessing is that Jesus seeks us out, often when we least expect it.

The Lord does three things. First, he *asks a question.* The point of the question is to reveal to the disciples their own need and failure. Have you ever noticed as you have read through the Bible how God likes to ask questions? I think of Adam and Eve in the Garden of Eden after they had sinned. God asks this question, "Where are you?" And later, "Who told you that you were naked? Have you eaten from the tree that I commanded you not to eat from?" (Gen. 3:9, 11). He asked the woman, "What is this you have done?" (v. 13). Later, in the account of Cain and Abel, when Cain was displeased that his offering was rejected, God asked, "Why are you angry? Why is your face downcast? If you do what is right, will you not be accepted?" (Gen. 4:6–7). Through Nathan God asked David, "Why did you despise the word of the LORD by doing what is evil in his eyes?" (2 Sam. 12:9). God asked Isaiah, "Whom shall I send? And who will go for us?" (Isa. 6:8). The Lord asked, "Who do you say I am?" (Matt. 16:15), "You do not want to leave too, do you?" (John 6:67), "Who is it you want?" (John 18:4), "Woman, why are you crying? Who is it you are looking for?" (John 20:15). God did not ask these questions because he did not know the answers. He was not trying to figure out whether Adam was hiding behind the maple tree or the elm tree. God asks questions to get us to face the situation.

Thus it is in our story. Jesus asked, "Friends, haven't you any fish?" (v. 5). He meant, "Have you caught anything?"

They had to answer sadly, "No." They had to admit they were failures. This is what Jesus asks us when we have been trying to go it on our own. "Have you caught anything? Have you been successful? Are you satisfied?" He asks these questions so that we might recognize our hunger, need, and failure, and turn to him.

This leads to the next step in the story, for after having asked his question the Lord next *gives a command.* In this case he tells the disciples, "Throw your net on the right side of the boat and you will find some" (v. 6). Why the right side? Because that was the side they were directed to by Jesus! If he had said the left side, there would have been fish there. They would have swarmed there from every part of the lake of Galilee, so anxious would they have been to be caught. The point is not *where* the work is to be done or *how.* It is whether it is being done under Christ's direction and in obedience to him or by our own wisdom and initiative.

Perhaps this is the point at which Jesus is speaking to you as you read this chapter. You have been aware of your own emptiness and failure. You have been trying to go it on your own and have been unsuccessful, as such attempts always are. Perhaps Jesus is saying, "I have a work for you to do. I have a way for you to do it. I want you to stop what you are doing and listen to me and do what I ask you to do."

Third, the Lord *sends blessings.* First, he had asked a question; second, he had given a command. Now in response to their obedience to his command,

Jesus sends such a great catch of fish that they are unable to draw the catch to land. The fish (153 of them) symbolize men and women won for Christ. In the earlier story in Luke 5, the net was broken. Here it remains intact (v. 11), for none of those whom God has called and given to Jesus will be lost. Those whom *we* convert may well be lost; such are not true conversions. But those whom *God* calls to Christ through us will never be lost. These are given to Jesus and are held secure by both him and the Father.

A Great Discovery

There is one last point. In the middle of the story, when Jesus had first appeared on the shore and had called to the disciples, none of them recognized him. But when they obeyed his instructions and so participated in the blessing of the great catch of fish, they made the discovery that this was the Lord. John said it first: "It is the Lord!" The others undoubtedly also recognized it in that moment.

Have you made that discovery? If you have not, I can tell you how it must be made. It is made as you obey Christ's commands. He may seem distant and unreal to you. That is natural, because sin separates us from him. But if you will obey him, he will work in your life and you will find him as surely as the disciples did when they obeyed him beside the lake of Galilee. Do you ask, "But what should I do? What does he command?" If you are a Christian, you must follow his leading as I have already indicated. If you are not a Christian, you must turn from your sin and call upon him as your Savior. The Lord said, "Come to me, all you who are weary and burdened, and I will give you rest" (Matt. 11:28). John says to believers, "If we confess our sins, he is faithful and just and will forgive us our sins and purify us from all unrighteouness" (1 John 1:9).

There is no discovery greater than this. On one occasion a group of students asked the great doctor and inventor Sir James Simpson, the discoverer of chloroform, "What do you consider to be the most outstanding discovery you have ever made?" Simpson replied, "Young men, the greatest discovery I have ever made is that Jesus Christ is my Savior; that is by far the most important thing a person can ever come to know." It is true. Finding Jesus may mean a life of poverty, hardship, and even acute physical suffering. But it also means finding that One who alone is totally faithful as our Savior, Companion, and Friend.

265

"Come and Dine"

John 21:9–14

When they landed, they saw a fire of burning coals there with fish on it, and some bread.

Jesus said to them, "Bring some of the fish you have just caught."

Simon Peter climbed aboard and dragged the net ashore. It was full of large fish, 153, but even with so many the net was not torn. Jesus said to them, "Come and have breakfast." None of the disciples dared ask him, "Who are you?" They knew it was the Lord. Jesus came, took the bread and gave it to them, and did the same with the fish. This was now the third time Jesus appeared to his disciples after he was raised from the dead.

Johnohn's epilogue contains a fifth principle of Christian service, namely Christ's provision for his followers, suggested by the words "Come and have breakfast" in verse 12. I would like to consider this gracious invitation in the context of four other "comes" scattered throughout the Gospels.

Come and See

The first invitation occurs early in John's Gospel. It is "come and you will see" (John 1:39). John the Baptist had been standing by the Jordan River

1629

one day when the Lord Jesus Christ walked by. John pointed to Jesus, saying, "Look, the Lamb of God." Two of John's disciples heard this testimony and interpreted it as a command to follow Jesus. So they left John and followed him. When Jesus saw them following he stopped and asked, "What do you want?"

They answered, "Rabbi, where are you staying?"

He said, "Come and you will see."

This invitation is far more than an encouragement to these two disciples to learn where Jesus was living. It is an invitation to come to him for salvation, discovering that he is the Savior. In this context the words have the same meaning as that great invitation of Psalm 34:8 ("Taste and see that the Lord is good"). The disciples came, tasted, and saw; then they went to their relatives and friends to say, "We have found the Messiah" (John 1:41; cf. vv. 45, 49).

"Come and see." Of the five verses that we will consider, this is the only one that is directed to absolutely everyone. It is true that those who are not among the elect will not heed Christ's call and will not come. But this does not alter the fact that the invitation is to them as well as to all others. When God calls people to faith he is not mocking. He is issuing a genuine invitation, which is at the same time a command. If we do not come, it is not because we are not invited. It is because we are stubborn, sinful, and rebellious.

In his own valuable study of this verse and other invitations, Donald Grey Barnhouse notes that, in order that he might not violate human personality, Jesus graciously uses different methods to invite different people. We see it in John 1 but also throughout the book. When Andrew went to find Peter and brought him to Jesus, Jesus confronted him by making a play on his name. Peter (or Simon) meant "a little stone" or "pebble," the kind of thing that could easily be kicked about, as Peter could be. So Jesus said, "Thou art Simon, the son of Jonah; thou shalt be called Cephas [which means] . . . a stone" (v. 42 KJV). In this encounter Jesus showed his knowledge of Peter's name and character, even without being told about it. Moreover, he assumed the authority to change Peter's name, thus providing precisely the kind of leadership this vacillating disciple both needed and respected. He told him that he was going to turn Peter the jellyfish into Peter the giant.

Later in John 1, we read that Jesus calls Philip. Philip goes to get his friend Nathanael. Nathanael is skeptical and says, "Nazareth! Can anything good come from there?"

Philip invites him to "Come and see," using the same invitation Jesus had used earlier.

When Nathanael does come, Jesus approaches him by showing his supernatural knowledge of what he had been doing even before Philip called him. He said, "I saw you while you were still under the fig tree before Philip called you" (v. 48). Apparently this was what Nathanael needed, for he responded with a testimony of faith in Jesus: "Rabbi, you are the Son of God; you are the King of Israel" (v. 49).

So it is throughout the Gospel. Jesus approaches each on his or her own level. He speaks to Nicodemus on the intellectual level, discussing epistemology (how one can know). He talks to the woman of Samaria on the level of her need as a sinner and in terms of an image she could well understand: "Everyone who drinks this water will be thirsty again, but whoever drinks the water I give him will never thirst" (4:13–14). He meets the nobleman of chapter 4, the multitude of chapter 6, the man born blind of chapter 9 on the level of their physical need. At the end he reaches Mary by the utterance of her name—"Mary" (20:16)—and Thomas by the invitation to make an empirical test of the reality of his resurrection ("Put your finger here; see my hands. Reach out your hand and put it into my side," v. 27).

God is not touchy. He stoops to our level individually when he gives his call. Barnhouse writes, "I tell you, whoever you are, that God will meet you on your own ground. He will make himself so clear that if you say no to him, you will be a hypocrite when you are saying it. And forever after, you will never be able to look yourself in the eye again and call yourself an honest man."[1] If you are new in your exposure to Christian things, you should begin with this open invitation.

Come and Learn

The second invitation is one of my favorites. It is one I frequently use in opening our morning worship services at Tenth Presbyterian Church in Philadelphia. "Come to me, all you who are weary and burdened, and I will give you rest. Take my yoke upon you and learn from me, for I am gentle and humble in heart, and you will find rest for your souls" (Matt. 11:28–29). There is a lot in this verse. There is a description of our need. There is a promise of rest, and that of two kinds: a rest that is given, corresponding to justification, and a rest that is found, corresponding to sanctification. But the part of the verse I am interested in is that which speaks of learning. It is the invitation to "come and learn" of Jesus.

This is the emphasis of the passage where these verses occur. Jesus had been preaching in his own area of the country, but most of those who lived there had not believed on him. They had rejected John the Baptist, an austere prophetic figure. They had rejected Jesus, who had come eating and drinking. But some had believed, and Jesus was rejoicing in them. He prayed, "I praise you, Father, Lord of heaven and earth, beause you have hidden these things from the wise and learned, and revealed them to little children. Yes, Father, for this was your good pleasure" (Matt. 11:25–26). Now, in order to follow up on these, he issued the invitation to "come and learn" of him.

Here is a wonderful truth. No one need be an intellectual giant to understand the gospel and become wise in spiritual matters. On the contrary, although the wise are not excluded, God has actually chosen "the foolish things of the world to shame the wise" (1 Cor. 1:27). This happens when they come to Christ and learn of him.

If you will come, you will find that Jesus is a wonderful teacher. He is wise and kind. He is patient. He will teach what you most need to know. Moreover, if you will come to him and allow him to teach you, you will soon excel in that wisdom which is pleasing to God and, as Psalm 119 promises, you will have "more insight than all [your] teachers" (v. 99). I know many Christians who are like that. They have never taken formal academic degrees. Some do not even speak good English. But they are wise spiritually because they have learned from him who is wisdom itself.

Come and Rest

In Mark 6:31 we have another invitation: "Come with me by yourselves to a quiet place and get some rest" In this context the disciples had been off on a training mission, and there had been so much "coming and going that they did not even have a chance to eat." The Lord knew that they needed a vacation.

Every so often you meet some Christian worker who thinks that he has to do the whole thing by himself and who works so hard that he has a nervous breakdown. Usually a person like this has a theological reason for his behavior, for he believes that if he does not work at the pace he is working someone else might be lost. He thinks that if he does not speak to ten or twenty people each day those ten people may go to hell. He thinks that if he does not raise an extra hundred thousand (or two hundred thousand) dollars, workers will not be sent to certain fields and those who live on those fields will be lost. He carries this great burden upon his shoulders, and it is just too much for him. He breaks down under it. Where did he ever get that idea? It is not in the Bible. Salvation is of God (Jonah 2:9). We are responsible only to obey him.

I know someone will object, "But if people believe that, aren't they going to be lazy and fail to do what they should do in serving Christ?" I admit that many Christians are lazy. But it has not been my experience that these are the ones who believe what I have been teaching. On the contrary, those with the highest view of the sovereignty of God in salvation are the most active.

Why is that? It is because they know what a great privilege it is to be associated with God in the work of evangelism, and it is because they know that their labors will be blessed as he blesses. Barnhouse writes on this point: "It is a tremendous thing to come into a recognition of this fact. Then you can do your work and when you've finished you say, 'Lord, it's up to you.' When you know that, you see, you don't have to go fussing and say, 'Well, now, could I have done it better? Where could I improve?' The real question is: Were you yielded to the Lord? Did you ask the Holy Spirit to use you? Was there any part of your being that was not surrendered? If there wasn't, then you simply say, 'Lord, I am a pipe. I can carry the water. You're responsible for the pressure. You're responsible for the flow.'"[2]

Come and Eat

The fourth invitation is the one found in John 21, which we are studying. It is to "come and dine" (v. 12). The disciples had been fishing all night and were hungry. But when they came to land they found that Jesus had already prepared "a fire of burning coals there with fish on it" (v. 9). He invited them to partake of it. Then we read, "Jesus came, took the bread and gave it to them, and did the same with the fish" (v. 13). How like the Lord! Even in his resurrection glory he was not unmindful of the physical needs of his disciples, and he was active in providing for them. He continues to do so today. This truth enabled Paul to write, even while in prison, "And my God will meet all your needs according to his glorious riches in Christ Jesus" (Phil. 4:19).

This invitation involves fellowship with Jesus and not merely physical provisions. In the Bible eating always suggests fellowship. For us eating is often a hurried thing, something we do on the run to some other activity. We grab a sandwich and a glass of milk. We buy a hamburger and eat it in the car. This was not possible in Bible times. Meals required preparation, and they were more drawn out affairs. Consequently, to eat with a person was to have fellowship with him or her.

It is interesting that the Greek word *koinonia* is translated by two English words, which have the same basic meaning. One is "fellowship." The other is "communion," as in the communion service. Fellowship and communion mean the same thing. Think of that now in relation to the communion service. We invite a person to communion, or we say, "I'm going to take communion." But what this really means is that we are going to take fellowship or that we invite the other person to fellowship with us around the Lord's table. What is the church but one great fellowship? It is a fellowship of Christians with the Lord and with one another.

We sing about it in one of our communion hymns written by the great Scottish divine Horatius Bonar.

> This is the hour of banquet and of song;
> This is the heavenly table spread for me;
> Here let me feast, and, feasting, still prolong
> The brief, bright hour of fellowship with thee.

Our Lord invites us to this table that we might fellowship with him and each other, in the communion service and in the daily exercise of our life together.

Some Christians are going to heaven miserably; others are going with the joy of heaven in their hearts and on their faces. What is the difference? The difference is that the latter have learned to come and dine with Jesus and with each other. The Christian life is not a showcase for superstars. It is a shared life in which our joy is in Jesus. If you lack that joy, take time to be with him. Turn off the television. Lay aside that worthless book. Forego that useless activity. Spend time with Jesus in the Word, preferably with other

Christians, if that is possible. He will speak to you from his Word and show you the meaning of true Christian fellowship.

Come . . . Inherit

There is one more invitation. None of us has heard it yet, but we shall hear it one day if we are truly God's children. In Matthew 25, toward the end of that great sermon given on the Mount of Olives shortly before his arrest and crucifixion, Jesus had been talking of the sheep and the goats. He described their separation into two groups, the sheep on his right hand and the goats on his left. He then continues, "Then the King will say to those on his right, 'Come, you who are blessed by my Father; take your inheritance, the kingdom prepared for you since the creation of the world. For I was hungry and you gave me something to eat, I was thirsty and you gave me something to drink, I was a stranger and you invited me in, I needed clothes and you clothed me, I was sick and you looked after me, I was in prison and you came to visit me'" (vv. 34–36). To those who have known him and been changed by him the Lord says, "Come . . . take your inheritance, the kingdom prepared for you."

We do not have much of an inheritance now. Or if we do, it is destined to pass away. All we know here, save the Word of God, shall pass away. But there is an inheritance laid up for us; there is a kingdom laid up for us. And we shall surely inherit both if we are Jesus' people.

I think here of 2 Timothy 1:12, in which Paul writes of his hope of this inheritance. The words come toward the end of his life. He has labored long through many hardships. He has been beaten, stoned, imprisoned. "Yet," he says, "I am not ashamed, because I know whom I have believed, and am convinced that he is able to guard what I have entrusted to him for that day." Paul is saying that he has invested in Jesus. He has laid up treasure where "moth and rust [do not] destroy, and where thieves [do not] break in and steal" (Matt. 6:19). Now, as he comes to the end of a long life, he knows that the Lord Jesus Christ has not disappointed him.

Jesus will never disappoint anyone who trusts him.

266

Peter's Restoration

John 21:15-17

When they had finished eating, Jesus said to Simon Peter, "Simon son of John, do you truly love me more than these?"

"Yes, Lord," he said, "you know that I love you."

Jesus said, "Feed my lambs."

Again Jesus said, "Simon son of John, do you truly love me?"

He answered, "Yes, Lord, you know that I love you."

Jesus said, "Take care of my sheep."

The third time he said to him, "Simon son of John, do you love me?"

Peter was hurt because Jesus asked him the third time, "Do you love me?" He said, "Lord, you know all things; you know that I love you."

Jesus said, "Feed my sheep."

I f each of us knew how sinful we really are, we would not be so shocked or subdued by our failures. But most of us do not know the depths of our own depravity. So we *are* shocked, particularly by a fall into serious moral sin or by our surprising ability to deny Jesus Christ.

When we sin in such ways, it is a tactic of the devil to argue that, having sinned, we have forfeited our chance for a successful and happy Christian life and that we might as well go on sinning. Like most of the devil's statements this is untrue. Though we sin, we have nevertheless not forfeited our chances for a full Christian life, nor dare we go on sinning. Instead, the Christian way is that of repentance and restoration. This is the point of the story of Peter's restoration by Jesus in John 21. Peter had failed the Lord in his hour of apparent need. He had abandoned him and had compounded his cowardice by a threefold denial that he had ever known him. Yet Jesus loved Peter, and Peter knew that he loved Jesus.

Peter's Boast and Fall

To understand the story of Peter's restoration we need to understand something about Peter's fall. Its cause was self-confidence, intensified perhaps by Jesus' revelation of his weakness. It had started in the upper room when Jesus had been speaking about love. Jesus had given his new commandment—"Love one another. As I have loved you, so you must love one another" (John 13:34)—but instead of this humbling Peter, as it should have done, it actually set him thinking how much he loved Jesus. Therefore, when Jesus spoke of going away and of the fact that the disciples would not be able to follow him, Peter rightly sensed that he was speaking of his death and expostulated, wrongly, "Lord, why can't I follow you now? I will lay down my life for you" (John 13:37).

Jesus rebuked Peter by challenging his profession of loyalty: "Will you really lay down your life for me? I tell you the truth, before the rooster crows, you will disown me three times" (v. 38).

I doubt if Peter heard anything Christ said in the upper room from that point on. He certainly did not ask any more questions, though he had been prominent enough in the first half of the evening's activities. The questions are now asked by Thomas and Philip. I suspect that Peter was stunned by Christ's prophecy and was saying to himself, "He is wrong. He has no right to think so poorly of me, nor to speak that way in front of the others. I will never deny him, no matter what the others do."

I believe this because the subject came up again after the small band had left the upper room and was on its way to the Garden of Gethsemane. Significantly, it was raised by Peter, which showed that he had been mulling over Christ's words in the meantime. Jesus was speaking of the scattering of the disciples, his crucifixion, and of his intention to gather them together again after his resurrection. But Peter broke in to say, "Even if all fall away on account of you, I never will" (Matt. 26:33). Jesus repeated his prophecy of Peter's denial. But Peter answered again, "Even if I have to die with you, I will never disown you" (v. 35). According to Luke's account, Jesus told Peter that he had prayed for him that his faith should not fail. But in spite of these earnest words, Peter remained unconvinced and so went self-confidently to his downfall.

Each of the Gospels tells us that Peter denied the Lord three times. While Jesus was on trial, Peter, who waited outside in the courtyard of the high priest, was declaring, "I do not know the man. . . . I do not know what you are talking about. . . . I am not his disciple."

Restoration

This is helpful for understanding the way in which Jesus approached Peter to restore him to service. The exchange has three parts. First, Christ's question. Second, Peter's response. Third, Christ's command.

The first thing we notice about Jesus' question to Peter is the name by which he addressed him. Jesus asked, "Simon son of John, do you truly love me more than these?" (John 21:15). It was Peter's old name, the name he had possessed before he met Jesus. We read about it in chapter 1. When Peter had been brought to Jesus, Jesus had greeted him by saying, "Thou art Simon, the son of Jonah; thou shalt be called Cephas, which is by interpretation, A stone" (John 1:42 KJV). This was a play on words. The old name meant "pebble," a light, unstable thing. But Jesus said that he was going to name Peter "a rock." He was saying that he was going to turn Peter the jellyfish into a solid and courageous person. Now, in recollection of this earlier incident, Jesus goes back to the old name in order to remind Peter of his weakness.

The second thing to note about Jesus' question is the word for "love," which he uses. Again, there is a play on words, but it is lost in most English translations simply because we only have one word for love in English while the Greek has several. In the original of this paragraph there is a play on two of these Greek words. One word is *agapaō*, the great New Testament word for love; it is the word always used in relationship to God. When we read, "For God so loved the world" (John 3:16) or "God is love" (1 John 4:8), the word is *agapaō*. The other word is *phileō*, a human love expressing itself in friendship. We might say that it is the highest love of which we are capable apart from the new birth and the internal working of God's Spirit to form the character of Christ within us. We get the effect of the exchange between the Lord and Peter if we refer to the first of these loves as "one-hundred-percent love" and the second as "sixty-percent love." The exchange is as follows.

Jesus initiated the conversation by asking Peter if he loved him with the highest love possible: "Simon, son of Jonah, do you love me with a one-hundred-percent love—more than these others?" Some commentators have suggested that as Jesus said this he waved his arm about over the lake and boats and other disciples, meaning, "Do you love me more than these *things*?" But in view of Peter's earlier protestations, it is probably more specific than this. Peter had said that he loved Jesus more than the other *disciples* did and that he would prove it by dying for him if need be. He had made this profession just after Jesus had instructed the disciples to love one another with a "one-hundred-percent love." In view of this background Jesus is probably asking

Peter, "Peter, what do you have to say now? You once boasted that your love for me was one-hundred-percent and that it was greater than the love these other disciples have for me. Is it true? Do you love me that way?"

Peter, now greatly humbled by his denial of Christ, replies with the lesser word: "Yes, Lord; you know that I love you with a sixty-percent love." That is a greatly subdued Peter. He is not saying that he does not love Christ. He does love him. But he is not boasting of his love, and above all he is not saying that it is greater than someone else's love. He is simply saying that his heart is open to Christ and that Christ therefore knows that he loves him with the best love of which he, a sinful human being, is capable. Before he had declared that Christ's "knowledge" of himself and the future was mistaken. Now he appeals to that knowledge as the basis of his confidence.

The second time the Lord asks his question of Peter he uses the same word for love again, though this time he mercifully drops the comparison: "Simon, son of Jonah, do you love me with a one-hundred-percent love?" Peter replies as he did the first time, "Yes, Lord; you know that I love you with a sixty-percent love."

The third time the question is asked the Lord comes down to Peter's level and uses Peter's word: "Simon, son of Jonah, do you love me with a sixty-percent love?" This is as much as to say, "All right, Peter, I know you are incapable of the kind of love I have for you and that you are right in affirming only what you are able to do. But do you really love me even on this level? Do you really love me with a sixty-percent love?" Peter, who again has no confidence in his own ability even to see into his own heart, replies, "Lord, you know all things; you know that I love you." When Jesus then goes on to give his command it is as much as to say, "All right, Peter, I'll work with that, because I am able to bring that limited love up to the height I desire, the height at which I have ordained you to function."

The last thing we need to note about the Lord's question to Peter is its threefold repetition. Why did Jesus ask three times whether Peter loved him? The answer is obvious: because of Peter's threefold denial. Peter had denied three times. Now Jesus asks him to affirm publicly three times that he loves him. This is why "Peter was hurt"— "because Jesus asked him the third time, 'Do you love me?'"

Does it seem cruel to you that the Lord asked Peter three times in front of the others whether he loved him, in clear reference to his earlier threefold denial? It seemed to be; it was certainly painful. Yet in the ultimate analysis it was not cruel. The truly cruel thing would have been to let the matter go on festering in Peter so that throughout his entire life both he and the others would think that he was somehow inferior and unworthy of office though he had undoubtedly repented of the sin with weeping, as the Bible tells us. The kind thing was the public restoration so that Peter and the others would henceforth know that Peter's past was past and that the Lord had himself commissioned him to further service.

That is why the Bible calls for public confession of sin. God does not wish to be cruel to us, though the experience of confession is painful. It is to end the matter so that we can pick up and go on with Jesus.

Peter's Response to Jesus

Part of Peter's response to Jesus has been covered in looking at Jesus' question, the most important aspect being Peter's unwillingness to use Jesus' word for love. Peter had learned about himself from the experience. He had indeed fallen. But his faith had not failed, as Jesus said it would not (Luke 22:32). Now he was ready to strengthen his brethren.

There is another aspect of Peter's response that we have not adequately considered, however. It is Peter's repeated appeal to Christ's knowledge. In each case he answered Christ's question by affirming his love and then saying, "You know that I love you" (vv. 15–17). He might have said, "As I know my own heart, I swear that I love you." But Peter had said something like that once and had been dead wrong. Obviously there could be no confidence in his self-knowledge. What confidence there could be would have to be in Christ's knowledge of him—warts and all.

This seems illogical, of course. Peter was weak and sinful. He now knew this. Christ knew all things, as Peter had come to discover. How with that combination could Peter possibly be encouraged by an appeal to Christ's knowledge? It seems illogical, but this is actually the strength of one who has met Christ and known himself to be loved by him. Peter was a sinner. Yes! But a forgiven sinner. Therefore, though conscious of sin, Peter nevertheless knew that Jesus could look beneath the surface of his denial to see a heart that had been made new and truly loved him.

There is joy in an awareness of God's omniscience—for two reasons.

First, God knows the worst about us and loves us anyway. If God did not know all things, we might fear that someday something evil in us would spring up to startle God and turn his affection from us. He would say, "Oh, look at that horrible sin! I didn't know that was there. How terrible! That changes everything. I won't have anything to do with that person anymore." If God were not omniscient, that might well happen. But God knows all things. He knows the worst about us and loves us anyway. The Bible teaches that it was "while we were still sinners, Christ died for us" (Rom. 5:8). Second, since God knows all things he also knows the best about us, though others do not. The disciples might have been startled by Peter's defection. They might have said, "If Peter is capable of denying Jesus like that, who knows what other sins are lurking within him. He might even be a false disciple." But Jesus knew better. He knew Peter's heart and love. It is not suprising in view of this knowledge that Peter appeals to him.

Never say, "I can do it, Lord. I know I can. I know my heart." Say rather, "Lord, you know what is there. You put it there. You know what love I have for you. Take it and make it into something that will abound to your glory."

A Gracious Command

The final part of this repeated exchange between the Lord and Peter is the Lord's gracious command: "Feed my sheep." I say it is gracious because it is not what we might logically expect. Peter had been a leader and then had fallen. For Jesus to come to him mercifully and tenderly to restore him was the height of graciousness. If, having restored Peter, he had said, "All right, Peter, you can go home now and do the best you can as an active layman. You are one of mine. I do not reject you. But, of course, I can never use you in a place of leadership again"—if he had said that, who could blame Jesus? Jesus would be entirely within his rights to answer like that. But this is not what he does. Instead, he tells Peter to "feed my sheep." Earlier he had called him to evangelism ("from now on you will catch men," Luke 5:10). Now he gives him the even greater responsibility of teaching those who have been caught.

What is the prerequisite for such service? What is the only acceptable motive for leading and teaching others? It is not moral perfection in the teacher; otherwise there would be no teachers. It is not an academic degree. It is not an overwhelming urge to "bring in Christ's kingdom," not the ability to raise more money than the man before, or build a bigger cathedral than the former minister. There is only one prerequisite. It is love for Christ issuing in the desire to serve him.

"Do you truly love me?"

"Yes, Lord."

"Take care of my sheep."

This love does not get wrapped up in mystical experiences. It cares for others. John said it well in his first letter, "Dear children, let us not love with words or tongue but with actions and in truth" (1 John 3:18). If we love Christ, we will love those others for whom he also died and we will do our best to serve them in love.

267

Christ's Next-to-Last Word

John 21:17

The third time he said to him, "Simon son of John, do you love me?"

Peter was hurt because Jesus asked him the third time, "Do you love me?" He said, "Lord, you know all things; you know that I love you."

Jesus said, "Feed my sheep."

The last two chapters of John's Gospel contain the parting words of Jesus to his disciples, which I have referred to as "the real last words of Christ." In doing this, I have contrasted the words spoken after the resurrection with those seven, more commonly studied words, spoken before. These postresurrection words are: (1) "Peace be with you" (20:19, 21); (2) "As the Father has sent me, I am sending you" (20:21); (3) "Receive the Holy Spirit" (20:22); (4) "Stop doubting and believe" (20:27); (5) "Blessed are those who have not seen and yet have believed" (20:29); (6) "Feed my sheep" (21:17; cf. v. 15); and (7) "Follow me" (21:19, cf. v. 22). I have spoken of these as: a great bequest, a great commission, a great consolation, a great challenge, a great benediction, a great responsibility, and a great invitation.

As we draw to the end of chapter 21 we come to the sixth and seventh of these "last" words, and we notice something interesting about them. They are each repeated, the sixth ("Feed my sheep") three times (vv. 16, 17, and, with a slight variation, v. 15) and the seventh ("Follow me") twice (vv. 19, 22). The repetition grows out of the narrative, but it is significant in itself. When God says something once we should listen. When he says it more than once the words should command our prolonged, rapt, undivided, and obedient attention.

Christ's Sheep

We notice first that the sheep mentioned here are Christ's sheep, for he says, "Feed *my* sheep." They are his in two ways. First, by creation—he made them. Second, and even more importantly, by redemption. On an earlier occasion the Lord had said, "I am the good shepherd. The good shepherd lays down his life for the sheep" (John 10:11). In speaking to the Ephesian elders just before his final departure to Jerusalem, Paul said, "Keep watch over yourselves and all the flock of which the Holy Spirit has made you overseers. Be shepherds of the church of God, which he bought with his own blood" (Acts 20:28). If the flock were ours, we could do with it as we wished or as we thought best. But if it is Christ's, as it is, then we must do as he wishes, recognizing our responsibility to him.

Peter understood this, for years later, when he came to give instructions to the leaders of the church, he spoke of their responsibility to the chief Shepherd as a motivation for the faithful performance of their duties. "To the elders among you, I appeal as a fellow elder, a witness of Christ's sufferings and one who also will share in the glory to be revealed: Be shepherds of God's flock that is under your care, serving as overseers—not because you must, but becasue you are willing, as God wants you to be; not greedy for money, but eager to serve; not lording it over those entrusted to you, but being examples to the flock. And when the Chief Shepherd appears, you will receive the crown of glory that will never fade away" (1 Peter 5:1–4). There is nothing that will make us more diligent in Christ's service than the firm recognition that we are only undershepherds of that Chief Shepherd to whom the flock belongs and to whom we are responsible.

The Task Assigned

At this point we have a very big topic. We have "the sheep," the flock of Christ. We have the shepherd. We have ourselves as undershepherds. Even if we should restrict our attention to our own role as undershepherds, we could consider the many traits of character we must have to be effective in our assigned task or even the areas in which we must operate to fulfill it. As far as traits are concerned, we have the need for humility, hard work, self-control, temperance, gentleness, the proper management of one's own household, piety, and many other things that the New Testament mentions explicitly. Under the second category, we might consider being examples to the flock, exercising discipline and effective oversight.

But the burden of our text, while not excluding these other matters, is nevertheless more restricted. It tells us that our responsibility as under-shepherds is primarily to feed the sheep which have been entrusted to us. How? By teaching, sharing, and in any other way communicating the Word of God. There is nothing else upon which Christians can feed. So our job is to teach the Bible both by word and example.

Here we must be very practical, for the difficulty at this point is generally not one of ignorance of *what* we should do but rather of *how* the task should be done. The principles that should govern our responsibility in this area are the same as those that should govern our own personal study of God's Scriptures. There are five of them.

1. We should teach the Bible on *some regular schedule*. We recognize this need in our own study of the Word of God, for one of the things we rightly stress in this area is the need for *daily* devotions. In the Lord's Prayer we ask God to "give us this day our daily bread," and while it is true that this refers to all our daily needs, physical as well as spiritual, it certainly does not exclude the need for a daily feeding upon God's Word. For this reason a popular devotional guide is called *Daily Bread*. Another, which makes the same point, is called *Manna in the Morning*. A third is *Daily Light*. Just as we each individually need a daily period of feeding upon God's Word, so should there be a regular teaching and communicating of the Word by all who are in positions of spiritual authority.

One obvious place for this is the preaching that goes on Sunday by Sunday in a faithful, Bible-teaching church. But that is only one area. Another is some kind of a weekly Bible study or Bible class. Some exercise this responsibility in a less formal way through work with neighbors or fellow employees. The point is merely that this must be regular. An occasional testimony does not fill the bill.

2. Our teaching or otherwise communicating the truths of the Bible should also be *systematic*. That is, instead of an occasional or random comment upon the Bible or an occasional, unrelated lesson, there should be an attempt to progress in a deliberate fashion through one or more books of the Bible or even through the Bible as a whole. Many people do not really study the Bible; they do not know how. They merely read it. This is not bad. It is wonderful. But it does leave a special area of responsibility to leaders to teach those passages.

I would suggest this procedure. First, present the book as a whole, reading it carefully together four or five times. Second, divide the work into sections, just as you would divide a contemporary manuscript into chapters (not necessarily the same chapters as in our Bibles), subsections within those chapters and paragraphs. Third, relate these sections to one another, asking: Which are the main sections dealing with the main subjects? Which are introductory? Which are excursions? Applications? This study should lead to a general outline of the book. Fourth, proceed to a more detailed study of the individual sections. Ask: What is the main point of this section? To whom is it spoken? How does it apply? What are the conclusions that flow from it? Finally, study individual phrases and key words. This kind of study will not be possible in every teaching situation, but it should be done by the teacher as preparation for his or her own teaching at the very least. To feed others we must first be fed.

3. The Bible should be taught *as comprehensively as possible.* I mean by this that we are not to become specialists in prophecy or Pauline studies or the nature of the flood to such a degree that we neglect the larger picture that those we teach obviously also need to know. The Bible is balanced in its many emphases. Christianity is meant to be balanced. If we do not study and teach the Bible comprehensively, we will become unbalanced and the church will be warped.

4. We must teach the Bible *prayerfully.* One obvious lack in the American church today is good systems of effective Bible study. But having said this, it is also necessary to say that we can have good systems, even superb and highly sophisticated systems, and still miss the point of Bible study by failing to ask God to speak to us through it. The scribes were great scholars, but they became mechanical in the working out of their method and so missed the Bible's main teaching. They failed to recognize the Christ when he came.

In Psalm 119 the author gives expression to the attitude we should have when he writes, "Do good to your servant, and I will live; I will obey your word. Open my eyes that I may see wonderful things in your law" (vv. 17–18). What will happen if our study and teaching is preceded by a prayer like this? Several things. First, it will make us conscious that we are actually meeting with God in our Bible study and not merely going through a prescribed religious ritual. Second, we will be sensitive to what God is saying to us and will be able to alter our lives and behavior accordingly. Third, it will make us conscious of the needs of others so that we will be able to teach them effectively. There is nothing more exciting in our fulfillment of Christ's commission to feed his sheep than to know that God himself is actually speaking to us and through us to his people.

5. The final point is that we must study the Word of God *obediently.* When God speaks, he speaks for a purpose. He expects us to obey him. Do we obey him? If we do, our lives and the lives of those for whom we are responsible will be changed. Our churches will be changed, and so will our society.

A Word to Preachers

All this applies quite broadly, for there are very few of us who do not have some degree of responsibility for someone. We are all usually undershepherds in some way. But I want to say a special word to preachers, for the task of teaching the Word of God is particularly their own. The minister has many functions. He must administer, counsel, visit, and do scores of other things. But just as the primary responsibility of a carpenter is to build and a painter to paint, so the primary responsibility of a pastor is to teach the Word of God. Indeed, if he does not, how can he expect the other undershepherds of his flock to fulfill their share of this responsibility?

There is a decline in this area today due to a prior decline in a belief in the Bible as the authoritative and inerrant Word of God on the part of the church's theologians, seminary professors, and those ministers who are trained by them.

Inerrancy and authority go together, for it is not that those who abandon inerrancy as a premise on which to approach the Scriptures necessarily abandon a belief in their authority. On the contrary, they often speak of the authority of the Bible most loudly precisely when they are abandoning the inerrancy position. It is rather that, lacking the conviction that the Bible is without error in the whole and in its parts, these scholars and preachers inevitably approach the Bible differently from inerrantists, whatever may be said verbally. In their work the Bible is searched (to the degree that it is searched) for whatever light it may shed on the world and life as the minister sees them and not as that binding and overpowering revelation that tells us what to think about the world and life and even formulates the questions we should be asking of them.

The problem is seen in a report of a panel discussion involving a rabbi, a priest, and a protestant minister. The rabbi stood up and said, "I speak according to the law of Moses." The priest said, "I speak according to the tradition of the church." But the minister said, "It seems to me. . . . "

It is hard to miss the connection between belief in the authority and inerrancy of Scripture issuing in a commitment to expound it faithfully, on the one hand, and a loss of this belief coupled to a neglect of Scripture and an inability to give forth a certain sound, on the other.

Dr. D. Martyn Lloyd-Jones is one who makes this connection. He writes on the decline of preaching: "I would not hesitate to put in the first position [for the decline]: the loss of belief in the authority of the Scriptures, and a diminution in the belief of the Truth. I put this first because I am sure it is the main factor. If you have not got authority, you cannot speak well, you cannot preach. Great preaching always depends upon great themes. Great themes always produce great speaking in any realm, and this is particularly true, of course, in the realm of the church. While men believed in the Scriptures as the authoritative Word of God and spoke on the basis of that authority you had great preaching. But once that went, and men began to speculate, and to theorize, and to put up hypotheses and so on, the eloquence and the greatness of the spoken word inevitably declined and began to wane. You cannot really deal with speculations and conjectures in the same way as preaching had formerly dealt with the great themes of the Scriptures. But as belief in the great doctrines of the Bible began to go out, and sermons were replaced by ethical addresses and homilies, and moral uplift and socio-political talk, it is not surprising that preaching declined. I suggest that this is the first and greatest cause of this decline."[1]

So here is my word to preachers. You above all men have been given the task of feeding Christ's sheep by a careful, regular, and systematic teaching of the Bible, but you will never do this unless you are convinced of the truthfulness of every word you find there. So settle this first. Is this book the very Word of God in the whole and in its parts? Has God spoken infallibly in its pages? If not, seek another profession. If he has, then proclaim this Word with all the strength at your disposal.

"Feed My Lambs "

There is one last word based upon a slight variation in Christ's command between verse 15 and verses 16 and 17. It is a variation between "Feed my sheep" (in the second and third instances) and "Feed my lambs" (in the first).

I admit that this may be only a stylistic variation—many commentators say so. Again, it may only be a suggestion that all Christ's people are children—"lambs" as well as "sheep." But when I remember the concern of our Lord for children and the teaching of Scripture that children especially are to be brought up in the nurture and admonition of Christ, I wonder if Jesus is not saying clearly, "And when you are feeding my sheep, do not forget the children; in fact, begin with the children, for the kingdom of heaven is of such as these."

The church's best ministers have felt this and have thus spent time with children. I give two examples: Martin Luther and John Wesley. What did Luther do? He produced the Smaller Catechism which was especially for children. It was nonpolemical and presented the gospel clearly. Luther once said that he would be glad to have all his works perish except the reply to Erasmus (*The Bondage of the Will*) and this catechism. Wesley, who, like Luther, was greatly concerned for children, advised his pastors: (1) where there are ten children in a society, meet them at least an hour every week; (2) talk with them every time you see any at home; (3) pray in earnest for them; (4) diligently instruct and vehemently exhort all parents at their own houses; and (5) preach expressly on education.[2]

Such work is not glorious. It will not capture the world's attention. But it is a command of Christ, and the one who will do this will have the joy of knowing that in serving "one of the least of these" he has served Christ.

268

Roads to Glory

John 21:18–23

"I tell you the truth, when you were younger you dressed yourself and went where you wanted; but when you are old you will stretch out your hands, and someone else will dress you and lead you where you do not want to go." Jesus said this to indicate the kind of death by which Peter would glorify God. Then he said to him, "Follow me!"

Peter turned and saw that the disciple whom Jesus loved was following them. (This was the one who had leaned back against Jesus at the supper and had said, "Lord, who is going to betray you?") When Peter saw him, he asked, "Lord, what about him?"

Jesus answered, "If I want him to remain alive until I return, what is that to you? You must follow me." Because of this, the rumor spread among the brothers that this disciple would not die. But Jesus did not say that he would not die; he only said, "If I want him to remain alive until I return, what is that to you?"

As I begin this study of Christ's words about the lives and deaths of Peter and John, I am reminded of the distinction the Swiss doctor Paul Tournier makes between the world of things and the world of people and of his emphasis upon the astonishing variety in the latter. When we look at the world of things—from the smallest grain of sand or rose petal to the planets and stars—we are impressed with the infinite variety. But

1647

on further examination we see that there is a remarkable sameness. Some objects are virtually identical—the grains of sand, for instance, or manufactured objects like cars, frisbees, or boxes of detergent sitting on a supermarket shelf.

The world of persons is not like that. True, there are patterns that seem to repeat themselves. We have extroverts and introverts, active and lazy people, those who are mentally healthy (whatever that is) and those who have one or more mental disorders. But even in dealing with these general categories the thing that impresses the careful observer most is the uniqueness of the individual. People are different. A psychologist who classifies his patients too quickly is a bad psychologist. A person of whatever training who readily puts people into boxes is not wise but foolish. The reason for this seemingly infinite variety within the world of persons stems from God's purposes in creating people in his own image. Unfortunately the church, which should be most anxious to preserve and develop this variety, is often opposed to it and instead attempts to force its adherents into the same mold.

Peter and John

It is precisely this problem with which the next section of Christ's conversation with Peter is concerned. Jesus revealed something of what was in store for Peter in his service for him. "When you were younger you dressed yourself and went where you wanted; but when you are old you will stretch out your hands, and someone else will dress you and lead you where you do not want to go" (v. 18). This is a prophecy of Peter's death by martyrdom, as John points out. It is as much as to say that Peter's former boast, which he had not been able to keep ("I will lay down my life for you," John 13:37), would be granted. Peter would die for Jesus.

Peter turned around, saw John following, and in full accord with the impetuous curiosity with which he was born asked, "Lord, what about him?" (v. 21).

Jesus replied, "If I want him to remain alive until I return, what is that to you? You must follow me" (v. 22). In other words, "John's form of service will be different from yours, but that is not to be your concern." We may say on the basis of this incident that we are not to be overly concerned with, still less judge another Christian's calling, but are to get on with our own.

Youth and Age

There are several differences in these verses, either stated or implied, the first being the difference between youth and old age. Christ speaks of that in the case of Peter alone, because he contrasts his youth, in which he freely did what he wanted, with his old age, in which things would happen over which he had no control.

What are the characteristics of youth? One of them is confident preparation for action, suggested by the words "When you were younger you dressed yourself and went where you wanted." It is a period of life in which bright plans are made and first steps are taken to accomplish those plans. Another characteristic of youth is self-reliance. Alexander Maclaren writes that self-reliance "is a gift and a stewardship given (as all gifts are steward-ships) to the young. We all fancy, in our early days, that we are going to build 'towers that will reach to heaven.' Now *we* have come, and we will show people how to do it! The past generations have failed, but ours is full of brighter promise. There is something very touching, to us older men almost tragical, in the unbounded self-confidence of the young life that we see rushing to the front all around us. We know so well the disillusion that is sure to come, the disappointments that will cloud the morning sky. We would not carry one shadow from the darkened experience of middle life into the roseate tints of the morning. The 'vision splendid will fade away into the light of common day,' soon enough. But for the present this self-reliant confidence is one of the blessings of your early days."[1]

There are weaknesses of youth, as we know. There is lack of experience and therefore often foolishness. There are passions of youth which need to be disciplined and challenged. But for all the weaknesses, there are still dreams and energies without which we would all be much poorer. Therefore, when we think of God's gifts to the church we should not forget the gifts of youth, nor should we despise them. We should not attempt to put old heads on young shoulders.

The other side of this contrast is old age, and the point about age that the Lord wishes to bring out is that things will be done to us against our incli-nation. In this case Jesus is speaking of Peter's martyrdom, presumably by crucifixion. This was not something Peter would have chosen for himself, any more than we would choose the sickness, limitations of opportunity, dis-illusionments, or other problems that frequently come with advancing years. Yet these were given to Peter (as to us), and they are as necessary for the church as the dreams of youth.

I notice one very significant thing about the way John refers to the prophecy concerning Peter. He says, "Jesus said this to indicate the kind of death by which *Peter would glorify God*" (v. 19). John does not say this about the dreams of Peter's youth but about his suffering. For "it is not only by act-ing, but chiefly by suffering, that the saints glorify God."[2] When God spoke of Paul to Ananias he said, "I will show him how much he must suffer for my name" (Acts 9:16). It was in such suffering that Paul glorified God. The dif-ferences between youth, young adulthood, middle age, older middle age, and old age are God-given. We need the experiences of all and should not attempt to force the patterns of one age upon another.

Our Temperaments

The second area of differences is temperaments. In this passage there is a distinction between Peter, the impetuous disciple, and John. Every time we see Peter we see him as a man of action. He is the first to speak and the first to act—not always wisely but always first. When Jesus asked, "Who do you say that I am?" it was Peter who answered: "You are the Christ, the Son of the living God" (Matt. 16:16). When Jesus was being arrested, it was Peter who drew his sword and cut off the ear of the servant of the high priest (John 18:10). Here in John 21, after recognizing the voice of Jesus when he called from the shore, he immediately jumped into the water and made his way to Jesus. Peter is a consistent activist. John, on the other hand, is almost never the one to speak. He owns no sword. He cuts off no ears. When Jesus appeared on the shore and Peter jumped into the water to swim toward him, John remained in the boat and landed the catch that Jesus had provided. John is the thinker. Yet Jesus had a place for him just as surely as he had a place for noisy Peter. He teaches this by saying, "If I want him to remain alive until I return, what is that to you?" (v. 22).

Forms of Service

This leads to a third area of difference among Christians, namely, our callings or forms of service. These involve our spiritual gifts.

I think here of that book by the well-known Chinese evangelist Watchman Nee, the title of which is taken from this passage: *What Shall This Man Do?* Nee begins by arguing correctly that the calling of God is always a distinctive calling. That is, it is never merely general, but is always personal in the sense that it is directed to a specific individual and has a specific service in view. "When God commits to you or me a ministry, he does so not merely to occupy us in his service, but always to accomplish through each of us something definite towards the attaining of his goal. . . . He calls us to serve him in the sphere of his choice, whether to confront his people with some special aspect of the fulness of Christ, or in some other particular relation to the divine plan. To some degree at least, every ministry should be in that sense a specific ministry."[3]

Moreover, as Nee goes on to point out, because the ministries vary, so also will the gifts of those who are called by God to fill them. Nee demonstrates this point in a very interesting way. He takes Peter first of all, and he highlights his calling by the phrase "fishers of men." Peter's calling "was to bring men, urgently and in great numbers, into the kingdom."[4] That is, he was called to evangelism. It is true that all Christ's disciples are called to evangelism but not all have this gift preeminently. Peter did. Therefore we find him being used to bring three thousand persons to faith in Christ at Pentecost, and later five thousand believed as a result of his preaching.

In the same way, we have those with the gift of evangelism today. We are all to evangelize. But a man like Billy Graham obviously has this gift to an exceptional degree, and he has been used much as God used Peter. If we look to organizations, we have Campus Crusade for Christ, which is clearly strong in this area. Crusade has mobilized hundreds of thousands to tell others about Christ. It may be true, and probably is, that the Graham crusades and Campus Crusade are not particularly deep where matters of theology are concerned. But I have no sympathy with those who look down on them and say, "They don't present the gospel quite right; they don't have a proper presentation of the Calvinistic principles; the four spiritual laws are inferior to the five points." They have been used by God and many have become Christians through them. We should rejoice in these great ministries of evangelism.

Second, Nee turns to the apostle Paul and describes Paul's calling as that of a "tentmaker." He means by this the task of building up or ordering the church of God. "Whereas Peter initiated things, Paul's task was to construct. God entrusted to him in a special way the work of building his church, or in other words, the task of presenting Christ in his fulness to men, and of bringing those men as *one* into all that God had in his mind for them in Christ. Paul had glimpsed that heavenly reality in all its greatness, and his commission was to build together the gathered people of God, according to that reality."[5]

We have people who are called to this ministry in our day also. In discussing evangelism I spoke of Campus Crusade. Here we might discuss the work of InterVarsity Christian Fellowship, which is strong on teaching and building Christian character. Again, this does not mean that Crusade has no concern for discipleship; it does. This does not mean that InterVarsity is not concerned with evangelism; it is. But I say this to point to InterVarsity's unique ministry in developing Christian habits and character through small, indigenous Bible studies and grappling with current problems in a scholarly way through its publication ministry. As we look out upon the church today we see literally thousands of leaders in key positions who have been trained by InterVarsity Christian Fellowship. The same thing is true of churches. There are churches with the gift or evangelism. There are others—Tenth Presbyterian Church in Philadelphia is one of them—that have the gift of upbuilding. In Philadelphia we say that some are obstetricians; they bring the babies into the world. Others, like Tenth, are pediatricians; they nurture the child.

Finally, Nee gets to the apostle John, characterizing him as a "mender-of-nets," from that setting in which John is first seen and called by Jesus (Matt. 4:21). He means that John's specific task, exercised long after Peter and Paul had completed their work and had been taken to heaven, was to restore that which was being torn down. This may not be the best way to describe John's ministry. But it is true that he does do a work of restoration. In contemporary life I would place such study centers as the L'Abri Fellowship in Switzerland, the Ligonier Valley Study Center in Florida, and the Traci Community of New Delhi, India, in this category.

"Follow Me"

There is this brief conclusion. I have written about the advantages of the various distinctions cited—the advantages of youth and age, those who are activists and those who are thinkers, the evangelists, restorers, and builders.

But to be honest, we must also point out that each has it problems too. Those who are young tend to be foolish in their headstrong self-reliance. The old tend to become concerned with their own affairs and therefore selfish. The weakness of the activist is insensitivity to others who move at slower paces. The thinker can become lazy. The evangelist can become shallow. The builder or restorer can become critical of those whom he regards as inferior. The advantages of each age, temperament, or calling can easily be marred by sin.

But there is a solution. It is the solution Jesus told Peter (and presumably John as well): "Follow me." Why is this a solution? First, because if we are following Jesus, then our eyes will be on Jesus and he—not our own particular and imperfect form of it—will be seen as the standard of Christian service. If you have your eyes on yourself, you expect people to measure up to you and judge them to be inferior if they do not. With your eyes on Jesus, he becomes the standard for both you and them and he actually draws you together rather than allows you to be driven apart. I was walking along the street once, following another person. I turned aside much as Peter did when, looking away from Jesus, he saw what John was doing and I bumped into a telephone pole. We will bump into one pole or another if we take our eyes off Jesus.

Second, if we have our eyes on Jesus, we will see not only something about him but something about ourselves as well. What we will see about ourselves is that we are at best "unprofitable servants." There will be no room for boasting, no room for arrogant self-sufficiency. We are inadequate, unprofitable. What we need is Christ . . . in his own person, first of all, and also in one another.

269

Christ's Last Word

John 21:22

Jesus answered, "If I want him to remain alive until I return, what is that to you? You must follow me."

The last recorded words that Jesus spoke before his ascension are found at the beginning of the Book of Acts. They contain the promise of power through the Holy Spirit and the command to go into all the world with the gospel. But these are not the last words of Christ recorded in John's Gospel. It is not that John did not know of Christ's teaching on these other points. The fourth Gospel contains more instruction about the Holy Spirit than any other Gospel, and it contains its own version of the Great Commission ("As my Father has sent me, so I am sending you," 20:21). It is rather that John wished to emphasize Christ's call to discipleship as the Gospel closes. In John's Gospel the last words of Christ are: "Follow me."

Strikingly, these are also nearly the first words of Christ in this Gospel. John first quotes Christ in connection with the episode in which Andrew and the other unnamed disciple follow Jesus at the direction of John the Baptist.

1653

Jesus' first words to them are: "What do you want?" (1:38). But as soon as they reply by asking where he is spending the night, he answers by the first of his great invitations: "Come and see" (v. 39). This is an invitation to discipleship. But lest we should miss this, Christ's next utterance, an invitation to Philip, is literally "Follow me" (v. 43).

In a very real sense, then, these are the first and last words of Christ in John's Gospel. They are a reminder that Christianity is Christ, not just believing in some abstract sense, but believing in him to the point of turning our back on all else to follow him.

Self-Denial

These seventh and last words of Christ may be difficult to obey, as we will see. But they are not difficult to interpret if for no other reason than that Jesus himself supplies the interpretation in other places. The key passage is Luke 9:23–25 (and the parallel, Mark 8:34–37). Here Jesus says, "If anyone would come after me, he must deny himself and take up his cross daily and follow me. For whoever wants to save his life will lose it, but whoever loses his life for me will save it. What good is it for a man to gain the whole world, and yet lose or forfeit his very self?"

These words, like John 21:19–22, are an invitation to follow Jesus. But, unlike the verses in John, they explain what such discipleship means. Specifically, they teach that discipleship means (1) self-denial and (2) taking up one's cross in Christ's service.

The first point, self-denial, should not be difficult for any true Christian to understand, for this is where Christianity begins. To be a Christian means to have turned our back on any attempt to please God through our own human abilities and efforts and instead to have accepted by faith what God has done in Christ for our salvation. We cannot save ourselves. So becoming a Christian means dying to those old, worthless efforts to merit something from God. It means saying no to them in order that we might receive salvation as God's free gift. Christianity begins with self-denial. So in one sense the Christian life is merely continuing on in the way we have started. It is turning our back on self to follow Jesus.

This does not mean that it is easy to do, however, as I have already pointed out. We are surrounded by a world that says no to nothing. It tells us that saying yes to every desire and whim we have is not only good for us but also good for others (because we will be nicer people for them to know) and for the economy (because the world is supposed to thrive by self-indulgence). In the midst of such a culture, the word of Jesus seems unrealistic and austere, and if it does not seem austere, "we are not really letting it speak to us," as Francis Schaeffer observes in his study of *True Spirituality*.[1]

What does it mean to deny oneself in order to be Christ's disciple? The first thing it means is that we must *renounce sin*. That is, we must repent of sin and determine to go in the holy way which Christ set before us. John Stott writes of this first step, "Renunciation of sin . . . can in no circumstances be bypassed. Repentance and faith belong together. We cannot follow Christ without forsaking sin. Moreover, repentance is a definite turn from every thought, word, deed and habit which is known to be wrong. It is not sufficient to feel pangs of remorse or to make some kind of apology to God. Fundamentally, repentance is a matter neither of emotion nor of speech. It is an inward change of mind and attitude towards sin which leads to a change of behavior. There can be no compromise here. There may be sins in our lives which we do not think we ever could renounce; but we must be *willing* to let them go as we cry to God for deliverance from them."[2]

This is not a general renunciation. It is as specific as specific sins. It is a renunciation of anything that is contrary to God's revelation of himself; that is, anything contrary to the Bible. Take the Ten Commandments as one area in which renunciation of sin may be tested. The first commandment says, "You shall have no other gods before me" (Exod. 20:3). Here is an obvious negative. It tells us that we are to say no to anything that would take God's rightful place in our lives. Is it an actual idol? We must say no to the idol; we must burn it or destroy it, as many primitive people have done when they have responded to the gospel. Is it money? We must get rid of the money, for it is better to be poor and a close follower of Christ than rich and far from him. Money is not something that necessarily takes the place of God in a life. It is possible to be a devoted and deeply spiritual Christian and rich at the same time. But if money has become a god, then we must say no to it. Has another person taken the place of God? Has a business? An ambition? Your children? Fame? Achievement? Whatever it is, we must say no to it if it is keeping us from Christ.

We must test ourselves on each of the other commandments. "Thou shalt not kill." This means that we are to say no to any desire to take another's life or slander another's reputation. "Thou shalt not commit adultery." We are to say no to any desire to take another man's wife or another woman's husband. "Thou shalt not steal." We must say no to the desire to take someone else's property. If we have not said no at these points, we can hardly pretend that we are living in the newness of Christ's resurrection life. Indeed, we are not living the life of Christ at all.

The second thing self-denial involves is *renunciation of anything that is not God's will for our lives*. This is related to the previous point about sin, for sin is not God's will and must be renounced. But there are things that are not contrary to the Bible's moral code, yet because they are not God's will for us personally they must be renounced too in order that we might do his will for us. For instance, there is nothing wrong with marriage. On the contrary, marriage has been established by God and has his blessing. But marriage may not be the will of God for you; and if it is not, then you must say no to marriage consciously and deliberately. The same thing holds true for a profession. God has a plan for each life. Our business is to discover it and fulfill it. It may be that when you become a Christian you already are engaged in the work God has for you. If so, you should continue in it joyfully. On the other hand, God may want you to change professions. He may wish to call you into specific Christian work or another profession. If he does, you must be ready to obey.

Under items that may not be God's will for our lives we must give special emphasis to our possessions. This is true for two reasons. First, a love of possessions is something Jesus specifically warned about in his dealings with those who said they wished to follow him. Second, the love of possessions is a particular snare for today's affluent Christians.

On one occasion a rich young ruler came to Jesus and asked what he might do to inherit eternal life. Jesus told him to keep the commandments—not that it would ever be possible for him to keep them perfectly and receive eternal life thereby, but in order to show him his need, as the continuation of the story indicates. The young man was evidently a self-satisfied individual, because after Jesus had listed the commandments for him—"You shall not murder, You shall not steal, You shall not bear false witness, Honor your father and mother, and Love your neighbor as yourself"—the man replied ignorantly, "All these things I have done since I was a boy. What else must I do?" The Lord then put his finger on that sin which for him was greater than all others—his love of possessions. "If you want to be perfect, go and sell what you have and give it to the poor; and you will have treasure in heaven and come and follow me." The young man went away sorrowful, because he had great possessions (Matt. 19:16–26; cf. Mark 10:17–27; Luke 18:18–27).

The possession of things is in the same category as marriage or a career, in the sense that they are not wrong in themselves. Indeed, our possessions may well be the gift of God to us to be used rightly. Still, although possessions are not wrong in themselves, they are a special snare for American Christians because they so easily blind us to the needs of others, occupy our time exclusively, and make us self-satisfied and selfish. I know Christians who have immense talent. But they are useless in Christian work because they are fully occupied either managing or enjoying their possessions. Is that what God gave you your possessions for? Did he make you well-off so that you would indulge yourself while others are perishing? Did he make you rich so that you do not need to worry about anything?

Americans have more than anyone else in the world. But it has not made us more compassionate. It has made us indulgent. What would Christ say if he were here? I think he would tell many of us, "If you want to be perfect, go and sell what you have, and give it to the poor, and you will have treasure in heaven; and come and follow me."

Taking Up the Cross

Jesus' second directive to explain the meaning of following him is "take up [your] cross daily." This suggests two things. If we had lived in Jesus' day and had seen a man carrying a cross, it would have meant that the man was a condemned criminal and was on his way to a place of execution. The cross symbolized this. So when Jesus said that those who followed him were to take up their crosses he meant that they were to follow him to death, denying themselves even to the point of facing execution. In this sense the phrase "take up [your] cross" intensifies the phrase "deny [yourself]," as we have expounded it.

The second truth that this requirement suggests goes beyond the earlier statement. To deny yourself is negative. This phrase suggests the positive counterpart to self-denial. It is embracing God's will, including the denial of self, wholeheartedly.

On this point I have been helped by some of the writings of Elisabeth Elliot. She writes, "I think there is a great deal of nonsense taught about this business of bearing our cross. For example, when people shrug their shoulders and say, 'Well, I suppose that's meant to be my cross,' they suggest that the cross is some inevitable circumstance which cannot be avoided. But the cross *can* be avoided. So I think that what Jesus is getting at here is the voluntary positive acceptance of what he is asking of us, whatever it may be. It is not servility. It is not a cop-out. It is not resignation or fatalism. It is a very positive voluntary act of the will, a Yes to God. In other words, we must say No to ourselves in order to say Yes to God.

"This should be the dominant theme of our lives: 'Yes, Lord, what do you want me to do?' There are all kinds of things we cannot avoid: difficulties, blindness, a drunken husband, an intractable teenage child, a limitation of whatever sort (all of us have our particular set of limitations in which we are meant to glorify God). But we can go through life gritting our teeth, clenching our fists and even saying Yes to God in the sense of 'Well, if this is what you want, I'll take it,' without ever once in joy and voluntary obedience saying, 'Yes, Lord, I delight to do this for you.'"[3]

God's will is not grievous. The Bible calls it the way of wisdom and says, "Her ways are ways of pleasantness, and all her paths are peace" (Prov. 3:17). But sometimes it seems grievous to us, and at that point we must simply live by faith accepting the apparently "grievous" will of God gladly. Elliot concludes, "So let us carry the cross every day, not in the sense of something we hate but in the sense of something which God is asking us to do and which we therefore determine to do joyfully."[4]

"Follow Me "

We come at last to the phrase with which we started: "Follow me." I ask this question: How do we learn the kind of self-denial and taking up of the cross with which Jesus prefaces this command? The answer is: By following him and constantly keeping our eyes upon him. Does this seem like circular reasoning? It seems to be, but it is actually progressive. In order to follow Jesus we must deny ourselves and take up our crosses, but we learn these by following. So it is by degrees and by a continuous discipleship that we learn to follow and by following learn.

How could it be otherwise if Jesus is our supreme example in all things? Where else could we learn self-denial but from him who said no even to the glory of heaven in order to become man and die for our salvation (Phil. 2:5–11). The author of Hebrews captures this when, in the verses immediately following his great chapter on the heroes of the faith, he writes, "Therefore, since we also are surrounded by such a great cloud of witnesses, let us throw off everything that hinders and the sin that so easily entangles, and let us run with perseverance the race marked out for us. Let us fix our eyes on Jesus, the author and perfecter of our faith, who for the joy set before him endured the cross, scorning its shame, and sat down at the right hand of the throne of God" (Heb. 12:1–2).

He is our perfect example. It is an example of self-denial, of taking up the cross—not with a grim determination to do the "undesirable" will of God but, by contrast, to do it joyfully. It was "for the joy that was set before him" that Christ endured the cross.

He did something else too, though the disciples did not understand it at the time. He spoke of his resurrection, thereby teaching that discipleship, though it involves a true and sometimes painful death to our own desires, is nevertheless the way to the fullness of living both now and hereafter. We find this throughout the New Testament. The apostle Paul writes in Romans, "If we have been united with him like this in his death, we will certainly also be united with him in his resurrection" (Rom. 6:5). We die to self, but we do so in order that we might live to Christ. We die "that the body of sin might be done away with, that we should no longer be slaves to sin" (v. 6). We read the same thing in Galatians. "I have been crucified with Christ and I no longer live, but Christ lives in me. The life I live in the body, I live by faith in the Son of God, who loved me and gave himself for me" (Gal. 2:20). In the biblical scheme of things death is always followed by life, crucifixion by resurrection. It is this that is truly exciting and for which we thrill to follow Jesus.

When we give up trying to run our own life or when we give up that thing that seems so precious and so utterly indispensable to us, it is then (and only then) that we suddenly find the true joy of being a Christian and enter into a life so freed from the obsession that we can hardly understand how it could have had such a hold on us.

This is the primary difference between a joyless and a joyful Christian, a defeated and a victorious one. The joyless Christian may have followed Jesus in some general sense. He may have died in Christ abstractly. But he has certainly never known these truths in practice. On the other hand, the joyful Christian has found satisfaction in whatever God dispenses to him and is truly satisfied, for he has said no to anything that might keep him from the richness of God's own presence and life.

270

Things That Should Be Written

John 21:24–25

This is the disciple who testifies to these things and who wrote them down. We know that his testimony is true.

Jesus did many other things as well. If every one of them were written down, I suppose that even the whole world would not have room for the books that would be written.

In this study I come to the end of my exposition of John's Gospel. People aware of the number of years I have spent in the study and exposition of John ask, "How, after the writing of all these sermons, do you find anything new to say about John's Gospel?" In one sense I can understand this question, for I have certainly covered many subjects and explored many lines of thought while studying this book. But in another sense I cannot understand it at all. For, in studying any Scripture portion, the more one seeks to understand and expound the text, the more its truly inexhaustible nature is sensed.

My studies of John began during my years of graduate study in Switzerland, at which time I read nearly every major commentary on the Gospel and delved into hundreds of other studies of particular subjects or problems

1659

related to my study. I preached on this book on Sunday mornings at Tenth Presbyterian Church in Philadelphia for more than eight years. The result is 270 separate sermons occupying nearly 2,000 pages of printed text. There are 2,700 pages of typescript. Yet I have not covered it all; and I suspect that I could do it all over again from the beginning and learn even more than I did the first time—so infinite is God's Word.

Trying to teach John's Gospel in some depth has given me a special perspective from which to understand the last verses, and these in turn have encouraged me as I draw to an end. They are a closing attestation that identifies the Gospel writer and declares his writing trustworthy. Then comes the interesting addition: "Jesus did many other things as well. If every one of them were written down, I suppose that even the whole world would not have room for the books that would be written." Apparently the author or authors of this verse felt the immensity of what could be written about Jesus and knew that the writer had recorded only a small part.

The Book's Perfection

I sense another thing, and that is the perfection, or wholeness, of the book, expressed in a satisfying rounding off of its material. It begins with Jesus— "In the beginning was the Word, and the Word was with God" (1:1), and it ends with Jesus—"Jesus did many other things as well" (21:25). It begins with the impressive testimony of John the Baptist—"John testifies concerning him. He cries out, saying, 'This was he of whom I said, "He who comes after me has surpassed me because he was before me"'' From the fulness of his grace we have all received one blessing after another" (1:15–16). It ends with an equally impressive testimony concerning that other John, the son of Zebedee, who wrote the Gospel—"This is the disciple who testifies to these things and who wrote them down. We know that his testimony is true" (21:24).

There are a number of ways of regarding the plural "we" of verse 24. Some, perhaps the majority of conservative scholars, have taken it as merely an indirect reference by the author to himself. Others see the word as pointing to some official body of Christians who are adding their attestation to John's testimony.

The issue is not a big one, but the second view seems best. Conceivably the author of the Gospel wrote the words. Yet this is improbable. If the author composed these verses, then he is identifying himself as the beloved disciple, which he has avoided doing earlier in the Gospel. Up to this point he has been careful to remain anonymous. Moreover, the first person plural of the final phrase of verse 24 is different from John's own way of referring to himself (e.g., John 19:35). The earlier verse is like these concluding verses in that it refers to the witness of the beloved disciple and affirms that it is reliable. But there the author refers to himself as "he that saw it" and who therefore knows that his is reliable testimony. These last verses distinguish between the writer or writers and the witness: "*we* know that *his* testimony is true."

These facts suggest that the "we" of verse 24 is to be understood as representing some official body—perhaps the church or churches John served—capable of identifying the author with the beloved disciple, an eyewitness of many if not all of the events described, and of attesting his character and the inherent reliability of his testimony.[1]

A Faithful Testimony

I have said that the issue of the authorship of these last verses is not a big one, but that does not mean that there is nothing to be learned from the verses themselves considered in the light of their authorship. In fact, they have much to teach us. They teach that the doctrines of Christianity rest, not on the unstable foundation of mere wishful thinking or speculation, but on facts observed by and duly authenticated by eyewitnesses of Christ's ministry. They say three things about this foundation.

First, they affirm that the men who recorded the life and teaching of Jesus of Nazareth (in this case, John, the beloved disciple) were *eyewitnesses of the events they describe*. The first phrase of verse 24 points to this by identifying the author of the Gospel with the beloved disciple described as being present with the Lord in Galilee in the verses which immediately precede.

This is of great importance. It would be important in any attempt to establish fact, as, for example, in a criminal trial. In such trials, facts must be established by eyewitness testimony, not by hearsay. In addition to this, the issue of fact is particularly important for Christianity, more so than for virtually any other world religion. In other religions it is usually the founder's ideas that count. In Christianity it is the facts. Is Jesus who he is declared to be? Did he do what he is reported to have done? Did he teach what he is claimed to have taught? Did he actually rise from the dead? Other religions may be content to live by ideas alone. But Christians readily confess that if Jesus is not the Son of God and did not speak with the authority of God, then his ideas have no more validity than any other teacher's and are, in fact, actually worse because he claimed divinity for himself and was therefore either insanely mistaken or deliberately misleading at this point. Christians confess that "if Christ has not been raised, your faith is futile; you are still in your sins" (1 Cor 15:17). On the other hand, if Jesus is God and did rise from the dead, he deserves and indeed demands our allegiance, and it is the height of folly and even rebellion against God to neglect him. Even more, there is salvation in no one else (John 14:6; Acts 4:12).

How can these facts be established? By the eyewitness testimony of those representatives of Christ specially appointed to bear such testimony. These are the apostles, the author of the fourth Gospel being one of them.

No one knew the importance of such testimony more than John, for in his first epistle he says of the apostles' testimony, "That which was from the beginning, which we have heard, which we have seen with our eyes, which we have looked at and our hands have touched—this we proclaim concerning the Word of life. The life appeared; we have seen it and testify to it, and we proclaim to you the eternal life, which was with the Father and has appeared to us. We proclaim to you what we have seen and heard" (1 John 1:1–3).

Why was John in particular concerned with such testimony? The answer lies in the fact that John, writing in the latter years of the first Christian century, was among the last of the New Testament writers and was therefore addressing a generation unfamiliar with the eyewitnesses' testimony to Christ's life. When Paul wrote (back in the middle of that century), he could refer almost in passing to "five hundred" who had seen the resurrected Christ, "most of whom were still living" (1 Cor. 15:6). But John could not. These had died in the meantime, and John therefore found it necessary to stress this eyewitness testimony as Christianity's foundation. Besides, when John was writing, a form of Gnosticism was beginning to infiltrate the apostolic churches which denied the need for historical facts as a basis for religious belief. Indeed, it considered faith superior to the facts of history, and it spiritualized them. This threatened true faith. So John more than other writers wants to emphasize Christianity's historical foundations.

We might sum up the matter like this: "An unbelieving world required evidence for the religious claims of Jesus and his followers. And the deviation toward an esoteric religion within the Church required immediate correction by a reiteration of the historical groundings of the faith."[2] John met such demands by stressing the role of eyewitnesses in establishing the historical claims of Christianity.

Second, the writers of the concluding verses of the Gospel (whoever they may have been) affirm that *the author of the Gospel* not only was an eyewitness of the events he describes but *actually wrote these things down*. It seems a truism to say that the author of a book actually wrote the book, and it is. But it is not a foolish thing to emphasize in view of some of the criticisms of the Scriptures both in the past and now.

People who have not had the opportunity to do extensive New Testament studies can hardly be aware of the degree of reluctance in many scholarly circles to admit that the words of the New Testament go back to eyewitnesses. For many the tone of the documents and the corresponding, nonbiblical evidence compel belief in some kind of historical base for Christianity—though one senses they wish there were none. But others deny it entirely, some radically. Rudolf Bultmann of Germany is the most startling example. For Bultmann and his followers the New Testament in no sense comes from eyewitnesses. Instead, Bultmann envisions a period in which stories of Christ circulated in the church and in which they were formed and embellished (even invented) on the basis of the church's current needs and its "Spirit-led" understanding of the significance of Jesus. The New Testament is therefore the product of the church and not of the apostles, though these undoubtedly exerted an influence in the early stages. On this basis, Bultmann says we can merely affirm that Jesus existed but denies we can have any certain historical information about him.

The authors of John 21:24 did not have Bultmann in mind as they wrote, of course, but by the guidance of the Holy Spirit they did speak directly to his unbelief as well as to that of any other similarly thinking scholars. These verses say that the eyewitness actually "wrote these things." Are they right? Are they speaking truthfully? If they are—and why should the authors of these verses be lying?—then we have in this Gospel (and the others) an accurate account of what the companions of Jesus, led by the Holy Spirit, considered necessary for us to know concerning him. It follows that we can read these words with the confidence that this is the case, and that Jesus was indeed as they describe him.

These authors affirm a third thing. They have said that the author of the Gospel was an eyewitness of the events of Christ's ministry. They have added that he actually wrote the Gospel, that is, he did not merely communicate these stories verbally while allowing someone else to record them, whether accurately or not, but himself actually did the writing. This said, however, they now add that *the one who has written these things is trustworthy*. Their specific words are: "We know that his testimony is true."

Why should it be necessary to add this statement? For this reason. It is possible that a person could be an eyewitness of the life of Jesus and then sit down to write a gospel about it but for whatever reasons decide to write something other than what he had actually witnessed. He might hate Jesus and therefore invent stories to cast a shadow over his name. Again, he might admire Jesus more than is fit and therefore eliminate anything that could be thought derogatory and instead invent stories or teachings to enhance his image. Such things are possible theoretically. But the authors of these last verses declare that such was not the case. They say instead that John was a man of integrity, that his words can be trusted and that, so far as they were able to verify his teaching (whether by the testimony of other eyewitnesses or by personal interrogation) they have found it to be absolutely trustworthy.

Can we not say the same? We are in no position to verify the facts of Christ's life as they did; we live nearly two thousand years after the events. But we can note that many of these witnesses sealed their testimony by their own blood. Would they give their lives for what they knew to be a put-on? Would they suffer for a farce? To ask such questions is to answer them. Of course not! If ever there were men of integrity, it was these men. If ever a series of events of history has been ruthlessly verified, it is these events.

Do you believe them? Will you believe them? We recall that John himself said of his writing, "These [things] are written that you may believe that Jesus is the Christ, the Son of God, and that by believing you may have life in his name" (20:31).

One Thing More

There is one more thing that I must mention as I close. I note as I read the last verse of John that the authors seem to be saying that Jesus did many things, all of which are now past, and we could almost interpret that as suggesting that the life of Christ is over. Nothing could be farther from the case. On the contrary, the whole last chapter (which does not even end with an ascension) is meant to show the living Christ in fellowship with his people within the ongoing life of his church.

Due to his union with believers—"I am the vine, you are the branches . . . apart from me you can do nothing" (John 15:5)—there is a sense in which Jesus' life and works are not ended but rather continue in the church as he accomplishes his will through us. I see this in an interesting way. I note that although this Gospel ends with a reference to the "things Jesus did" (past tense), the very first verses of the very next book of the Bible speak of "all that Jesus *began* to do and teach until the day he was taken up" (Acts 1:1–2). It means, if I may put it this way, that in one sense Jesus' life, important and unique as it is, was only a beginning; it lives on in the life, deeds, words, and teachings of his redeemed community.

You are a member of that community if you have believed on Christ as your Savior. You are part of the church if you have been born again. Are you continuing Christ's works? Is his life being lived in you? While we are in this life, all that we will ever know of Jesus' earthly life has already been written. There is no more. We have it in the four Gospels and in a few scattered references in the Epistles. But his works are nevertheless going on, and it is your privilege and duty to be a channel for them.

Jesus said, "I tell you the truth, anyone who has faith in me will do what I have been doing. He will do even greater things than these, because I am going to the Father" (John 14:12).

Jesus begins that saying with the words "verily, verily" or "amen, amen." It means "truly, truly" or "what I am about to say to you is so." Jesus often began important sayings in that way. We, on our part, also say "amen." But our "amens" properly come at the end of such sayings, by which we acknowledge our acquiescence in his testimony. We have a case at the end of the Gospel. "Amen" is the way the book ends. It means "these things are true, and we who say 'amen' now stake our lives upon them." Is this the case with you?

God grant that it may be so, and to him be glory. Amen.

Notes

Chapter 222: The Final Days

1. Arthur W. Pink, *Exposition of the Gospel of John,* vol. 3 (Grand Rapids: Zondervan, 1975), 154–55. The words are quoted from M. Taylor, who is otherwise unidentified.

2. Donald Grey Barnhouse, *Tragedy or Triumph* (Philadelphia: The Bible Study Hour, 1967), 8–10.

Chapter 223: Gethsemane

1. Pink, *Gospel of John,* vol. 3, 157–58. Alfred Edersheim refers to Gethsemane in similar terms, calling it that "other Eden, in which the Second Adam, the Lord from heaven, bore the penalty of the first, and in obeying gained life" (*The Life and Times of Jesus the Messiah,* vol. 2 [London: Longmans, Green and Co., 1883], 533).

2. Donald Grey Barnhouse, *God's Grace* (Grand Rapids: Eerdmans, 1959), 14.

Chapter 224: Judas, Who Betrayed Him

1. Frank Morison, *Who Moved the Stone?* (1930; reprint, Grand Rapids: Zondervan, 1977), 30.

2. Ibid., 32.

3. A full discussion of the placing of these final events within the Passover week occurs in volume 3. It is not referred to here because the difficulty with timing exists whether or not Jesus was arrested on Thursday evening and was crucified on Friday or on Wednesday evening and was crucified on Thursday, as I maintain.

Chapter 225: The Arrest!

1. Alexander Maclaren, *Expositions of Holy Scripture,* vol. 7, "Gospel of St. John" (Grand Rapids: Eerdmans, 1959), part 3, 221.

2. Ibid., 222.

Chapter 226: The Jewish Trial

1. Walter M. Chandler, *The Trial of Jesus from a Lawyer's Standpoint* (Atlanta: Harrison Company, 1956), xvi.

2. Alfred Edersheim considers this exchange to have taken place before Caiaphas (*The Life and Times of Jesus the Messiah,* vol. 2, 548), but most modern opinion is against this interpretation. For the viewpoint expounded here see Chandler, (xvii), Leon Morris (*The Gospel according to John* [Grand Rapids: Eerdmans, 1971], 746ff.), and other commentators.

3. Mendelsohn, *The Criminal Jurisprudence of the Ancient Hebrews* (Baltimore: M. Curlander, 1891), 29. Quoted by Chandler, *Trial of Jesus,* vol. 1, 133–34.

4. Chandler, *Trial of Jesus,* vol. 1, 168–69.

Chapter 227: The Charge against the Prisoner

1. Morison, *Who Moved the Stone?,* 24.

Chapter 228: Illegalities of Christ's Trial

1. Malcolm Muggeridge, *Jesus: The Man Who Lives* (New York: Harper & Row, 1975), 170.

2. Chandler, *Trial of Jesus,* vol. 1, 229.

3. Ibid., 259.

4. Ibid., 280–81.

Chapter 229: In the Prisoner's Defense

1. I have discussed the details of Christ's genealogy at greater length in volume 1.

2. Chandler, *Trial of Jesus,* vol. 1, 334.

3. Ibid., 345.

Chapter 230: Before the Cock Crows

1. Charles Haddon Spurgeon, "In the Garden with Him," *Metropolitan Tabernacle Pulpit,* vol. 35 (London: Banner of Truth Trust, 1970), 517.

2. Matthew Henry, *Commentary on the Whole Bible,* vol. 5 (New York: Fleming H. Revell Company, n.d.), 1181.

3. William Barclay, *The Gospel of John,* vol. 2 (Philadelphia: Westminster Press, 1956), 269.

4. These are discussed in more detail in volume 4, in the chapter "Darkness before the Dawn" (John 13:36–38).

5. Spurgeon, "In the Garden with Him," 518–19.

Chapter 231: The Roman Trial

1. Chandler, *Trial of Jesus,* vol. 2, 6–7.

2. Morison, *Who Moved the Stone?,* 43.

3. Ibid., 59. Cf. 47–59.

Chapter 232: Jesus before Pilate

1. Chandler, *Trial of Jesus,* vol. 2, 149.

2. Ibid., 106–7.

3. Ibid., 114.

Chapter 233: Christ's Kingdom Not of This World

1. George Eldon Ladd, *Jesus and the Kingdom: The Eschatology of Biblical Realism* (New York: Harper & Row, 1964), 118.
2. Charles Haddon Spurgeon, "Jesus, the King of Truth," *Metropolitan Tabernacle Pulpit,* vol. 18 (Pasadena, Tex.: Pilgrim Publications, 1971), 699.

Chapter 235: No Fault in Him at All

1. Charles Haddon Spurgeon, "Our Lord's First Appearance before Pilate," *Metropolitan Tabernacle Pulpit,* vol. 28 (London: Banner of Truth Trust, 1971), 94–95.
2. F. W. Krummacher, *The Suffering Savior: Meditations on the Last Days of Christ* (Chicago: Moody, 1947), 253–54.

Chapter 237: Barabbas

1. Krummacher, *The Suffering Savior,* 260.
2. Tom Skinner, *Words of Revolution* (Brooklyn, N.Y.: Tom Skinner Associates, 1970), 74.
3. Donald Grey Barnhouse, *God's Remedy,* "Expositions of the Epistle to the Romans," vol. 3 (Grand Rapids: Eerdmans, 1954), 376–78.

Chapter 238: "Behold the Man!"

1. See Chapter 235, "No Fault in Him at All" (John 18:38).
2. Barclay, *Gospel of John,* vol. 2, 285.
3. H. A. Ironside, *Addresses on the Gospel of John* (Nepture, N.J.: Loizeaux Brothers, 1942), 821–22.
4. Krummacher, *The Suffering Savior,* 288–89.

Chapter 239: Who Died on Calvary?

1. Donald Grey Barnhouse, *Eternity* magazine (April 1962): 9–11.

Chapter 240: How God Views Human Government

1. I do not speak here of the legitimate procedure of attempting to win office through the elective process that the democratic system provides.
2. John Calvin, *Institutes of the Christian Religion,* vol. 2, ed. John T. McNeill and trans. Ford Lewis Battles (Philadelphia: Westminster Press, 1960), 1512.
3. Donald Grey Barnhouse, *God's Discipline,* "The Epistle to the Romans," vol. 9 (Grand Rapids: Eerdmans, 1958), 106–7.

Chapter 241: Christ's Fate Sealed

1. Barnhouse, *God's Discipline,* 119.
2. Aleksandr I. Solzhenitsyn, *The Gulag Archipelago, 1918–1956: An Experiment in Literary Investigation,* I-II (New York: Harper & Row, 1973), 130.

Chapter 242: No King but Caesar

1. See volume 3.
2. Leon Morris, *Gospel according to John,* 774–86. Morris's views appear on pp. 782–85.
3. The reasons for this dating are given in volume 3.
4. Morris, *Gospel according to John,* 800.
5. Frederick Godet, *Commentary on the Gospel of John,* vol. 2 (New York: Funk & Wagnalls, 1886), 379–80.
6. R. C. Sproul, *The Psychology of Atheism* (Minneapolis: Bethany Fellowship, 1974), 149–50.

Chapter 243: The Story of Two Thieves

1. Barclay, *Gospel of John,* vol. 2, 291–92.
2. This story is told by Donald Grey Barnhouse in *The Love Life* (Glendale, Calif.: Regal Books Division, G/L Publications, 1973), 270–73.

Chapter 244: This World's King

1. The Authorized Version (KJV) also has the words "in letters of Greek, and Latin, and Hebrew" in Luke's account, but these are not in the best manuscripts. This is corrected in the Revised Standard Version, the New English Bible, the New American Standard Bible, the New International Version, and other modern translations.
2. Pink, *Exposition of the Gospel of John,* vol. 3, 230–31.
3. Donald Grey Barnhouse, *God's Wrath* (Grand Rapids: Eerdmans, 1953), 61–62.
4. Ibid., 62.

Chapter 245: Scripture Fulfilled in Christ's Death

1. Martin Luther, *What Luther Says,* comp. Ewald M. Plass (St. Louis: Concordia, 1959), vol. 1, 69–70. The earlier quotation of this passage is in volume 2 of this series.
2. E. Schuyler English, *A Companion to the New Scofield Reference Bible* (New York: Oxford University Press, 1972), 26.
3. Barclay, *Gospel of John,* vol. 2, 295.
4. Cf. Morris, *Gospel according to John,* 809, n. 54; Pink, *Exposition of the Gospel of John,* vol. 3, 233; Krummacher, *The Suffering Savior,* 334–43.
5. The last two sections of this study follow the *Eternity* article, "Behind the Bronze Doors of Calvary," *Eternity* (March 1969): 13–14).

Chapter 246: Words from the Cross

1. It is not entirely certain that the beloved disciple was John, since he is nowhere unmistakably identified in the fourth Gospel, but this is a reasonable inference from the five references to him (John 13:23; 19:26f.; 20:2–10;

21:7–23; 21:24). The identification of this one will be discussed at greater length in chapter 31 ("Christ's Side Pierced," John 19:31–37).

2. Arthur W. Pink, *The Seven Sayings of the Savior on the Cross* (Grand Rapids: Baker, 1976), 48.

3. The original is a Latin poem of the thirteenth century, ascribed to Jacopone da Todi.

4. Pink, *Seven Sayings*, 57.

5. Fulton J. Sheen, *Life of Christ* (New York: McGraw-Hill, 1958), 398.

6. Mariano Di Gangi, "Words from the Cross" (Toronto: The Bible Study Hour, 1963), 21–22.

Chapter 247: "I Thirst"

1. E. M. Blaiklock, "New Light on Bible Imagery: Water," *Eternity*, (August 1966): 27.

2. Pink, *Seven Sayings*, 88–89.

3. R. C. Sproul, "The Problem of Suffering," *Tenth: An Evangelical Quarterly* (October 1977): 22.

4. Pink, *Seven Sayings*, 86.

Chapter 248: No Death like Jesus' Death

1. There has been a noticeable return to the idea of an objective atonement in some recent literature. The neoorthodox theologians Karl Barth and Emil Brunner stressed an objective atonement in their theologies (cf. Brunner's *The Mediator* and Barth's *Church Dogmatics*, vol. IV); others such as T. F. Torrance have followed them (cf. *Theology in Reconstruction*). A number of biblical theologians have also revived this emphasis: Joachim Jeremias *(The Servant of the Lord, The Eucharistic Words of Jesus, The Central Message of the New Testament)*, Otto Michel *(Roemerbrief)*, Leon Morris *(The Apostolic Preaching of the Cross, The Cross in the New Testament)*, G. C. Berkouwer *(The Work of Christ)*, Gustaf Aulen *(Christus Victor)*, and Vincent Taylor *(The Cross of Christ)*. In some of these works the substitutionary nature of Christ's death is emphasized.

2. Adolf Harnack, *What Is Christianity?*, trans. Thomas Bailey Saunders (London: Williams and Norgate, 1901), 157–58.

3. John Murray, *Redemption Accomplished and Applied* (Grand Rapids: Eerdmans, 1970), 43.

Chapter 249: Why Did Jesus Die?

1. Anselm of Canterbury, "Why God Became Man," book I, ch. 1, in *A Scholastic Miscellany: Anselm to Ockham*, ed. and trans. Eugene R. Fairweather, "The Library of Christian Classics," vol. X (Philadelphia: Westminster Press, 1956), 101.

2. Murray, *Redemption Accomplished and Applied*, 11.

3. Anselm, "Why God Became Man," 176.

Chapter 250: "It Is Finished"

1. Charles Haddon Spurgeon, "Christ's Dying Word for His Church," in *Sermons on the Gospel of John* (Grand Rapids: Zondervan, 1966), 170.
2. Pink, *Seven Sayings,* 102.
3. Spurgeon, "Christ's Dying Word," 173.
4. Murray, *Redemption Accomplished and Applied,* 51.
5. Ibid., 56.
6. Pink, *Seven Sayings,* 119–20.
7. Spurgeon, "Christ's Dying Word," 180.

Chapter 251: For Whom Did Christ Die?

1. Murray, *Redemption Accomplished and Applied,* 63–64.
2. John Owen, "The Death of Death in the Death of Christ," *The Works of John Owen,* ed. William H. Goold, vol. 10 (London: Banner of Truth Trust, 1967), 174.

Chapter 252: Christ's Side Pierced

1. Charles Haddon Spurgeon, "On the Cross after Death," *Metropolitan Tabernacle Pulpit,* vol. 33 (London: Banner of Truth Trust, 1969), 193.
2. I have discussed the authorship question, including the identity of the beloved disciple, in greater detail in *Witness and Revelation in the Gospel of John* (Grand Rapids: Zondervan, 1970), 123–30.
3. Oscar Cullmann, *Early Christian Worship,* trans. A. Stewart Todd and James B. Torrance (London: SCM Press, 1962), 114–16.
4. William Stroud, *A Treatise on the Physical Cause of the Death of Christ, and Its Relation to the Principles and Practice of Christianity* (London: Hamilton and Adams, 1847), 74–75. See the discussion of this theory in Morris, *Gospel according to John,* 819.
5. Spurgeon, "On the Cross after Death," 197.

Chapter 253: With the Rich in His Death

1. Alexander Maclaren, *Expositions on Holy Scripture,* vol. 7, "The Gospel of St. John" (Grand Rapids: Eerdmans, 1959), part 3, 287–88.
2. Ibid., 293–94.

Chapter 254: The Not-Quite-Empty Tomb

1. I have discussed the dating of these events in detail in volume 3.
2. John R. W. Stott, *Basic Christianity* (Downers Grove, Ill.: InterVarsity Press, 1959), 52.
3. Henry Latham, *The Risen Master* (Cambridge: Deighton Bell and Company, 1901), 36, 54.
4. Stott, *Basic Christianity,* 53. Parts of the preceding study have already appeared in the author's *God the Redeemer* (Downers Grove, Ill.: InterVarsity Press, 1978), 239–42.

Chapter 255: The Day Faith Died

1. Alexander Maclaren, *Expositions of Holy Scripture,* vol. 7, 321.
2. Donald Grey Barnhouse, "First Things First" (Philadelphia: The Evangelical Foundation, 1961), 57. Much of this material on Mary is based on the Barnhouse study.

Chapter 256: New Relationships for a New Age

1. *The New Scofield Reference Bible* (New York: Oxford University Press, 1967). The various views are discussed at length by most major commentators. See also David C. Fowler, "The Meaning of 'Touch Me Not' in John 20:17," *The Evangelical Quarterly* (January-March 1975): 16–25.
2. John White, *The Fight* (Downers Grove, Ill.: InterVarsity Press, 1976), 129–30.

Chapter 257: The Best News Ever Heard

1. Cited by Stott, *Basic Christianity,* 47.
2. Reuben A. Torrey, *The Uplifted Christ* (Grand Rapids: Zondervan, 1965), 70–71.
3. Reuben A. Torrey, *The Bible and Its Christ* (New York: Fleming H. Revell, 1904–1906), 107–8.
4. Ibid., 110–11.

Chapter 259: "So Send I You"

1. John R. W. Stott, "The Great Commission," in *One Race, One Gospel, One Task,* Official Reference Volumes of the World Congress on Evangelism, 1966 (Minneapolis: World Wide Publications, 1967), vol. 1, 39.
2. Ibid., 40–41.

Chapter 260: Sins Remitted and Retained

1. Stott, *One Race,* 42.
2. For a discussion of this point from the Catholic perspective as well as for references to other literature on the question, see Raymond E. Brown, *The Gospel according to John* (xiii-xxi) in "The Anchor Bible" series (Garden City, N.Y.: Doubleday, 1970), 1023–24.
3. Morris, *Gospel according to John,* 849–50.
4. Pink, *Exposition of the Gospel of John,* vol. 3, 289.

Chapter 261: Faithless or Faithful?

1. Pink, *Exposition of the Gospel of John,* vol. 3, 291.
2. Charles Haddon Spurgeon, "The Evidence of Our Lord's Wounds," *Metropolitan Tabernacle Pulpit,* vol. 34 (London: Banner of Truth Trust, 1970), 719.

Chapter 263: Why This Book Was Written

1. Charles Haddon Spurgeon, "The Main Matter," *Metropolitan Tabernacle Pulpit,* vol. 27 (London: Banner of Truth Trust, 1971), 655–56.

Chapter 264: "It Is the Lord"

1. Maclaren, *Expositions of Holy Scripture*, vol. 7, 340.

Chapter 265: "Come and Dine"

1. Donald Grey Barnhouse, *The Love Life*, 316.
2. Ibid., 321.

Chapter 267: Christ's Next-to-Last Word

1. D. Martyn Lloyd-Jones, *Preaching and Preachers* (Grand Rapids: Zondervan, 1971), 13. I have borrowed a section of this word to preachers from a chapter of my own in *The Foundation of Biblical Authority*, ed. James m. Boice, (Grand Rapids: Zondervan, 1978).
2. John Wesley, "Minutes of Several Conversations," *The Works of John Wesley* (Grand Rapids: Zondervan, n.d.), vol. 8, 316.

Chapter 268: Roads to Glory

1. Maclaren, *Expositions of Holy Scripture*, vol. 7, part 3, 384.
2. Pink, *Exposition of the Gospel of John*, part 3, 328.
3. Watchman Nee, *What Shall This Man Do?* (London: Victory Press, 1962), 9.
4. Ibid., 11.
5. Ibid., 13.

Chapter 269: Christ's Last Word

1. Francis A. Schaeffer, *True Spirituality* (Wheaton: Tyndale House, 1971), 19.
2. Stott, *Basic Christianity*, 112.
3. Elisabeth Elliot, "Denial, Discipline and Devotion," *Tenth: An Evangelical Quarterly* (July 1977): 62.
4. Ibid., 63.

Chapter 270: Things That Should Be Written

1. This does not lessen the authority or inspiration of the book in any way, for God can inspire the additions just as he can inspire the body of the work. Moreover, there are similar cases elsewhere in the Bible. For example, at the end of the Book of Deuteronomy there is an account of the death of Moses that he, presumably, did not write, though he is the author of everything that comes before. That is not a sufficient reason to consider the account uninspired. Similarly, at the end of the Book of Romans there is an addition that is apparently the work of Paul's amenuensis: "I, Tertius, who wrote this epistle, greet you in the Lord" (16:22). Though not by the authors of the bulk of the books, these additions are nevertheless part of God-breathed Scripture and are "useful for teaching, rebuking, correcting, and training in righteousness" (2 Tim. 3:16).
2. James Montgomery Boice, *Witness and Revelation in the Gospel of John*, 38.

Subject Index

Scripture Index